Upgrading & Troubleshooting Your Mac®

Mac OS X Edition

Upgrading & Troubleshooting Your Mac®

Mac OS X Edition

Discarded by MVCL

Osborne/**McGraw-Hill**

New York   Chicago   San Francisco
Lisbon   London   Madrid   Mexico City
Milan   New Delhi   San Juan
Seoul   Singapore   Sydney   Toronto

Gene Steinberg

Osborne/**McGraw-Hill**
2600 Tenth Street
Berkeley, California 94710
U.S.A.

To arrange bulk purchase discounts for sales promotions, premiums, or fund-raisers, please contact Osborne/**McGraw-Hill** at the above address. For information on translations or book distributors outside the U.S.A., please see the International Contact Information page immediately following the index of this book.

Upgrading & Troubleshooting Your Mac®: Mac OS X Edition

234567890 FGR FGR 0198765432

ISBN 0-07-219359-X

Publisher: Brandon A. Nordin
Vice President & Associate Publisher: Scott Rogers
Acquisitions Editor: Gretchen Ganser
Project Editor: Barbara Brodnitz
Acquisitions Coordinator: Emma Acker
Technical Editor: Greg Titus
Copy Editor: Eileen Dahl
Proofreader: Linda Medoff
Indexer: Valerie Robbins
Computer Designers : Lucie Ericksen and Melinda Moore Lytle
Illustrators: Michael Mueller and Lyssa Wald
Series Design: Mickey Galicia

This book was composed with Corel VENTURA™ Publisher.

Attack of the Rockoids ©2001 Gene Steinberg and Grayson Steinberg. Excerpts used with permission.
Mac® and PowerBook® are trademarks of Apple Computer, Inc., registered in the United States and other countries. iBook™ and iMac™ are trademarks of Apple Computer, Inc.
Screen reproductions in this book were created using Snapz Pro X from Ambrosia Software, Inc., and edited in Graphic Converter from Lemke Software and Adobe Photoshop from Adobe Systems, Inc.
Photos for front cover, back cover, spine, and internal design courtesy of Apple Computer, Inc., and the following: Hunter Freeman and Mark Laita.

Dedication

To my family, who made it possible for me to realize the impossible dream.

About the Author

Gene Steinberg first used a Mac in 1984 and has never looked back. He is the author of over 20 books on computers and the Internet, including *Office 2001 for Mac: The Complete Reference* and *Mac OS 9: The Complete Reference* for Osborne/McGraw-Hill, and he runs a comprehensive Mac support Web site, The Mac Night Owl (http://www.macnightowl.com). He's a contributing editor for CNET and a contributing writer for *MacHome* magazine, as well as a columnist ("Mac Reality Check") for The Arizona Republic/azcentral.com. In his spare time, he is developing a science fiction adventure series, *Attack of the Rockoids,* with his son, Grayson. You can reach Gene at gene@macnightowl.com.

About the Technical Reviewer

Greg Titus is a senior software engineer and manager with The Omni Group, where he works as both a Cocoa/WebObjects consultant and as a developer of shrink-wrap software for Mac OS X. Greg has 15 years programming experience, with the last 8 using Cocoa in NeXTSTEP and now Mac OS X. Acting as a project manager and networking/database specialist, his consulting clients have ranged from Fortune 500 companies in the areas of finance and telecommunications, to major search engine providers, to dot-coms. In the other half of his work life, he helps build OS X applications, such as OmniWeb, OmniOutliner, and OmniDictionary. You can reach Greg at greg@omnigroup.com.

Contents at a Glance

Contents

Acknowledgments

What a ride! Pouring 17 years of Macintosh experience into a book was an extraordinary undertaking, and making it seem sensible to Mac users of all levels of expertise was equally challenging.

There's no way I could have succeeded in this impossible task without the assistance of a group of very special people who provided advice, information, tips, tricks, and, in some respects, a look at Apple's future possibilities, so I could make this book as accurate and up to date as possible.

First and foremost, I should like to give special thanks to my friend and agent, Sharon Jarvis, who has always been there with sage advice to help me get over the rough spots and to make this all happen.

Certainly, Apple's corporate communications team has helped greatly in supplying information, and in some cases review hardware, for me to examine, review, and report about. Chief among these folks are Bill Evans, Keri Walker, and Nathalie Welch. I'd also like to praise Apple's Jonathan Ive and his industrial design wizards for developing the great look of Apple's newest computers, such as the iBook, the Titanium PowerBook G4, the iMac, and the Power Mac G4 series.

I'd like to single out my friend, Pieter Paulson, long-time Mac/Windows systems wizard, who provided a huge amount of information for the chapters on cross-platform issues and Mac networking.

Most of all, I must give my sincere thanks to my little nuclear family: my brilliant son (and sometimes co-author), Grayson, and my beautiful wife and business partner, Barbara, for tolerating the long hours I spent glued to my computer keyboard to finish this book on schedule.

Introduction

When Apple decided to deliver computers with two operating systems running side by side, was it a brilliant stroke or a recipe for disaster? I gave it serious thought as I pondered the best way to distill 17 years as a Mac consultant into this book.

Let me first admit that I wasn't always a Mac consultant. In fact, I trained originally as a radio broadcaster. I had a hand in writing news stories, commercials, and even a little science fiction from time to time. But things change.

When computers changed from filling large rooms to sitting on desktops, I was working for someone who had the silly idea of putting me in charge of all those strange devices. Heaven knows why. Perhaps because I had a penchant for fiddling with things and trying to fix them. I also had this annoying tendency of being somewhat of a perfectionist. (They say it's a characteristic of a Virgo, though I have never paid much attention to horoscopes and other means of predicting one's individual characteristics.)

To be perfectly honest, those first personal computers I worked on weren't Apple products. They were, in fact, PC clones, used primarily to convert documents for a typesetting system (yes, rather dull). This was in the days before PC clones actually had to be reasonably compatible with regular software, so all they could do was run that translation program and the higher-cost versions of a few popular programs the manufacturer deigned to sell.

I won't attempt to describe all the hoops and flips I had to go through whenever it was necessary to upgrade the computer's operating system software or add some extra hardware. This book isn't that long, and I would prefer to forget the late hours and sleepless nights fretting over one issue or another.

Then 1984 came. Big Brother was nowhere in sight, despite what George Orwell suggested in that famous novel, but I discovered the Apple Macintosh and a new method of personal computing. Gone were many of the hassles and headaches that afflicted computers on the other computing platform. And that graphical user interface was simply a revelation compared to the clumsy command-line instructions I had to feed that other computer to get it to do the simplest tasks.

But things weren't quite perfect in the Macintosh universe, either.

I often tell my friends that computers aren't nearly as reliable as, say, your toaster oven. For one thing, they aren't dedicated to performing a single task or a set of related tasks. They are supposed to be able to run any of thousands of software products and a large number of hardware devices, as well, with only a minimum of fuss and bother.

All those products are created by multitudes of designers and programmers, and there is plenty of room for mistakes or oversights. In fact, not 30 minutes after I first hooked up my Apple Macintosh, it froze, putting up a little rectangular screen telling me that it was sorry that a system error had occurred. There was also a Restart button that I was to click to set things right.

Now, on that first occasion, clicking on the Restart button did absolutely nothing. I discovered something called a reset switch that forced my Mac to restart.

I didn't want to go through that awful experience again without learning as much as I possibly could about that strangely shaped little computer. I first pored over the instruction manuals, then went to the local bookstore to see if there was any other information I could use. Of course, there wasn't very much available in those days. The Mac was a brave new world in terms of personal computing, and the nooks and crannies hadn't been completely explored yet.

However, I was impressed enough to tell my employers that they were using computers of the wrong platform and they had to change. Well, they listened to me. If anything, they paid just a little too much attention. They decided that I'd be responsible for ordering the new equipment and manage the systems.

Over time, they even had the crazy idea to farm me out to other companies who needed help setting up and maintaining their Mac systems. And when that company one day decided to give it all up and close their doors, I found myself working as a Mac consultant.

It's been fun discovering new things about these little computing devices, and, I have to admit it, aggravating too, especially when problems cropped up that just didn't seem amenable to the usual troubleshooting processes.

Through the years, I have made house calls to dozens and dozens of places, ranging from business users to homes owned by retirees who discovered the Internet as a neat way to keep active and stay in regular touch with family and friends.

I also became a "helper" for a Mac user group (the Arizona Macintosh Users Group, in fact). Hardly a day passes when I don't receive phone calls day and night from harried folks who wonder why their computers freeze up, why they can't surf the Internet, why they can't print a document, and so on and so forth.

Taking all those experiences, through all those years, and putting it all together in a reasonably coherent form takes me to the present day. And to this book.

Upgrading & Troubleshooting Your Mac®: Mac OS X Edition tries to make sense of Apple's two-operating system strategy. It is not just a collection of third-party instructional information on how to do things with your Mac or how to fix things up. This book is the result of a lot of reading and a lot of research, but it's also the practical result of my hands-on experience in the Mac computing universe.

Over the years, I've learned lots of new, unexpected things, things that shouldn't always work but do. I discovered how to apply all this toward solving the growing complexities and pitfalls in the Mac computing world.

Yes, someday personal computers will be just as reliable as your toaster oven. But not yet—far from it.

While most Mac users work day in and day out with few problems to hurt the workflow, problems do happen. Macs freeze more than they should; programs don't quite work as you expect; and there are hair-pulling experiences from time to time. Having to navigate through the new, Mac OS X, and the old, the so-called "Classic" Mac OS, is often fraught with unexpected consequences.

And as the computer gets, well, a little older (and that can seem to take only a few months the way products get updated these days), you may wonder whether it's time to retire it and get something new. Or perhaps there's some way to upgrade the computer to extend its working life.

This book addresses both these concerns.

How This Book Is Set Up

This book isn't intended to be an encyclopedia or a reference work. Instead, it's a hands-on manual with that focuses on both Mac OS X and Mac OS 9.1 and later.

In the first chapters, I'll show you the best ways to install new hardware and software. You'll learn about the problems you might encounter along the way, how to avoid them, and what to do if they show up anyway.

Then I'll move on to the topic of upgrading. If you'd like your Mac to run faster, or you want to add more RAM or a piece of hardware that expands its capabilities (such as high-speed networking or adding a second display), you'll learn the best way to set up the new equipment and how to set things right if something unexpected occurs. And you'll read some guidelines as to whether it's worth doing that upgrade in the first place.

Here's what you'll find in this book:

■ Lots of background information so you know why something works, and, more importantly, why things may sometimes go wrong.

■ Step-by-step descriptions of installation and troubleshooting processes covering both Mac OS X and Mac OS 9.1 and later.

■   Pointers, tricks, and guidelines to help you handle routine installations and complex setups with ease, and to diagnose both common and very obscure problems with the two operating systems.

■   Notes, tips, and cautions that give you extra bits of information and warn you when to be careful and what to avoid.

■   Case histories, which are actual stories, my own or about my clients (names omitted to protect the innocent), showing how a problem was discovered and how it was solved. Some of the problems are fairly common, ones you are apt to encounter at one time or another. Others are, well, strange, one-of-a-kind situations that were difficult to solve. Either way, I hope you'll be able to take something away from the experience in case you encounter a similar problem.

Tracking a Moving Target

When it comes to Apple Computer, predicting the future is impossible. Even as I wrote this book, Apple Computer rolled out new versions of its popular Power Mac G4 desktop computers, dubbed "QuickSilver," and was putting the finishing touches on the first major update to Mac OS X, version 10.1. Every time new products appear, the way you do things is apt to change, not to mention the fact that potential new difficulties may arise, especially when you try to mix the old and the new in your computing environment. This book includes coverage of both Mac OS X 10.1 and all the latest model Macs.

I wanted to include in this book a CD with a selection of Mac OS X system diagnostic and enhancement software, but it has become difficult—in fact, impossible—to provide current versions of the software we selected. In fact, we'd probably have to release a new CD every month to keep abreast of updates. Instead, I've created a special page at The Mac Night Owl Web site, where you'll be able to find the latest versions of some truly great software for Mac OS X (plus last-minute updates to this book). Some programs will be free, and others will be shareware, but all are worth downloading and checking for yourself. To see the lineup, just point your browser to http://www.macnightowl.com/upgrading.htm.

I hope you like the approach, and I hope it helps you have a better, more productive (even more fun-filled) Mac computing experience.

Please don't hesitate to send me your cards and letters, both compliments and brickbats. And I truly welcome your suggestions on things I might add to future editions of this book.

It's been a nice ride, and I look forward to the future of personal computing. I think some exciting things are going to be happening in the years to come, lots more exciting than any of us (even those of us who dabble in science fiction) can predict.

Gene Steinberg
Scottsdale, Arizona
Email: gene@macnightowl.com
http://www.macnightowl.com
http://www.rockoids.com

Chapter 1

Solving Mac Hookup Problems

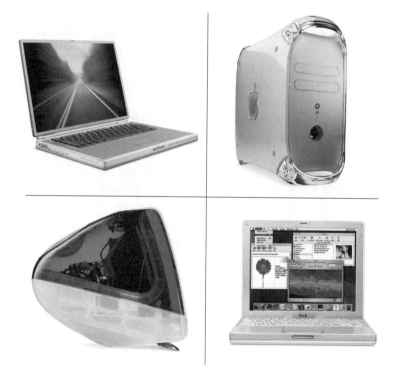

Can a fun experience turn into a nightmare? You've just brought home a brand-new Power Mac (or PowerBook, iMac, or iBook), and now you're anxious to take it out of the box and put it through its paces. If you're in a work environment, it's important from a business standpoint to get your new Mac workstation into production as soon as you can, with as little downtime as possible (and make your investment a productive one).

This chapter focuses on the basic steps to consider when deploying a new Mac, whether for home use or for your business.

Initial Installation: The First Day

If your new Mac is your first, read on. The Macintosh computing experience is quite unlike the one you encounter when you use that other platform.

For one thing, there's the great ease of setup and use. You can literally plug it in, turn it on, step through a simple setup assistant, and begin computing without further ado. This is especially true if you've bought one of Apple's consumer computers, the iMac or iBook. With those models, you don't even have to install any application software to begin, since so much of it is provided, already on your hard drive and ready to roll.

But as with any new installation, especially if the computer is meant for a large-scale setup where existing computers are already in place, you'll want to handle each step of the installation with care. While Macs are as close to true plug-and-play as a personal computer can get, there are pitfalls to consider.

The watchword for the first day is to test, test, and test some more. It's never a good idea to put a brand new computer smack into a production situation where a potential problem can mean lost time and lost money.

The next few sections of this chapter will focus on tips to help make the transition as easy as possible.

Adding a New Mac to a Home or Home Office

In this situation, it's quite likely that you are starting from scratch. This could be your first Mac or a replacement for one you've had quite a while. In either case, you'll want to consider the following guidelines for your particular situation.

Your First Macintosh

This is your first foray into the Mac operating system, so be sure to follow each step of the setup process slowly and carefully. All new Macs (iMacs, iBooks, or

PowerBooks) come with a very simple, basic set of installation instructions to refer to first. On the other hand, the instructions are so basic that you may find yourself having more questions than you'd expect even after you have it all plugged in and turned on.

If you're adding printers, scanners, extra drives, and other products, you are apt to find little help at all, unless you pour through a number of separate manuals. The arrival of Mac OS X may only complicate matters, as some hardware that works just dandy in the original or Classic Mac OS won't function in the new environment.

And that, in a nutshell, is one of the reasons why I've written this book: to guide you through the pitfalls of installing a new system and upgrading your old one. Either way, if you run into troubles of any sort, you'll want to read the relevant chapters in this book, so you can resolve the issues as quickly as possible.

As a new Mac user, it's not just a matter of turning on the computer and getting to work. Personal computers are not that simple—at least not yet. So I've assembled some tips that you'll want to consider as you set everything up:

■ **Learn your Mac fundamentals.**   This book isn't designed to be a basic how-to or tutorial. It's focused on upgrading, preventive maintenance, and troubleshooting. I'm assuming you've had some experience with your Mac. But you don't have to feel alone in the world. When you first turn on your Mac, you'll be guided through a neat set of welcome screens that will guide you through the process of registering your new purchase, making a network connection, and establishing Internet access. (The setup process might be repeated if your computer boots under Mac OS 9 and you then switch over to Mac OS X.) Well, you'll see the registration screen as long as someone else hasn't turned on the unit first to test a RAM upgrade before delivery. Once the process is finished, however, you'll find an attractive desktop and a little item on the menu bar labeled Help, where you can definitely find ways to get started. You should try it out. When you click Help, choose Mac Help (see Figure 1-1), and you'll see a window with a feature called Quick Clicks. Just click on any item to bring up an information window with instructions about how to use that feature. You'll want to pay special attention to anything related to using the Finder, as that's the core of the Mac experience. I learned how to use Macs years ago by reading everything I could, and then practicing my skills.

Initial Installation: The First Day

FIGURE 1-1 Begin the Mac OS X learning process here.

> **NOTE** *I cannot overemphasize how important it is to learn your Mac basics if you're new to the platform or computing in general. This is especially true if you are migrating from an older Mac to one of the newer models on which Mac OS X is installed. It's not unlike learning musical scales to master an instrument. You'll find your computing experience more enjoyable and more productive, and it'll be easier to cope with problems once they arise.*

■ **Test each part of your system separately.** Once you get your Mac up and running, try out all the regular functions, such as keyboard and mouse performance. Don't hesitate to take note of where things just don't seem right. You may be able to use some control panel (under the old or Classic Mac OS) or System Preferences application setting to fix the problem; but for now, just be aware that it exists.

NOTE   *One example of a setting you'd probably want to fix right away is the speed of your mouse cursor. Apple's default setting is usually too slow. Just click on the System Preferences icon in the Dock, and then click on the Mouse panel. Move the slider to the right to make it travel faster. Once you speed up the mouse, your perception of your Mac's performance is apt to rise in proportion.*

■ **You may have to shut down your Mac before adding some accessories.**   Yes, the new generation of FireWire and USB peripherals for the Mac are advertised as being "hot-pluggable," meaning you don't have to shut down your Mac to put them in and out of service. However, there are still a few peripherals out there (such as SCSI drives, still used by content creators where the highest speed is cherished), where a shut down is required before hookup. Also, when you first install a new component, no doubt there is driver software involved on an installation disk of some sort. You'll need to install the driver (software that allows the Mac to run that peripheral) before you hook up your new device. That way, it'll be ready to run as soon as it's connected. If in doubt, check the documentation that comes with the product.

■ **Don't panic if it doesn't work.**   More often than not, a little troubleshooting will fix the problem. You may have installed something incorrectly, or perhaps you're just not following the proper setup instructions. Throughout this book, you'll find chapters that cover virtually every aspect of Mac use, and you should find the answers you seek.

■ **Choose the Internet service provider (ISP) that's best for you.**   All new Macs are advertised as offering easy Internet access. The handy Setup Assistant that launches when you first boot a new Mac can help guide you through the steps of getting that new account with EarthLink, Apple's selected provider. Of course, you don't have to set up an EarthLink account. If you had an Internet account on another computer (even from the Windows platform), you should be able to set up your new Mac to work with that account in just a few minutes, if you have the proper setup information. The ISP's technical support people can probably walk you through the steps in less than 10 minutes in most cases.

Initial Installation: The First Day

NOTE *Unfortunately, some ISPs had not added Mac support to their systems when this book was written. Examples include Microsoft's MSN service and United Online, a relatively new service that combines the resources of Juno and NetZero. If these ISPs still haven't added Mac support, you can consider EarthLink, AOL, or any one of thousands of other options to get you online.*

Replacement or Additional Macintosh

If you already have a Mac that's been set up, the second one should be easy. You have already confronted the basics of setup and installation of a computing system.

Depending on whether you are planning to replace an older Mac or just add one to an existing installation, the following basic tips will help you make sure your new computer is set up properly:

■ **Use file sharing if you can.**   This is a quick way to transfer document files from your old Mac to your new one. If it's not convenient to network, consider placing them on a backup drive, but remember, your new Mac may not support the SCSI drives that worked fine on an older model.

NOTE *If your old Mac has LocalTalk and no Ethernet capability, you'll have to consider getting a hardware module, a LocalTalk-to-Ethernet adapter, to allow you to connect the two computers. I'll cover more about network issues and solutions in Chapter 17.*

■ **Don't copy the operating system software from another Mac.**   The one on your new Mac is the one designed specifically to work on that model, and that's the one that should be used. If your other Macs have a later version, it doesn't matter. Various Macs need different sets of system files, and the newer models have software ROM called, of course, Mac OS ROM in the Classic System Folder. If the Mac doesn't have the correct files, you will not be able to start it up. The system installer is designed to figure out what goes where depending on what kind of Mac you have.

NOTE *If your previous Mac was running Mac OS X, you can copy your personal User's folder, which contains all of your personal settings, including your Internet setup and stored email for Apple's Mail application.*

CAUTION

Trying to do a Finder copy of Mac OS X is not going to succeed. For one thing, many of the files used by Apple's newest operating system are marked "invisible," meaning they will not be copied. While backup programs that support Mac OS X will include these files, a fresh installation is still best, if the computer didn't come with OS X preloaded.

■ **Reinstall your applications.**   While many Mac OS X applications come as a single file or package for easy placement in the Applications folder, some—such as the version of AppleWorks for Mac OS X shipping when this book was written—may still install separate files elsewhere on your Mac. If you have a special set of preference files (which are most often installed in the Preferences folder inside the Library Folder in your personal Users directory under Mac OS X) that reflect your personal taste, and you don't want to have to recreate them from scratch, you may try to copy them over.

■ **Check for new software versions.**   If you are upgrading from an older Mac, you'll also want to inquire about updating to a Mac OS X version of your favorite software. While this will usually mean paying an upgrade fee of one sort or another, a native application will have full support for Mac OS X's robust operating system features. Many (but not all) older applications may work in the Classic environment, but with the possibility of reduced performance and reduced stability.

NOTE

If you have a large collection of fonts, you may be tempted to simply copy the contents of your older Mac's Fonts folder to the Mac OS X's repository for such files (within the Library folder) when you use file sharing. Unfortunately, you cannot copy active (in use) files this way. You'll have to make a disk copy first or duplicate the fonts in another location on your old Mac's drive and copy from there.

■ **Consider ways to share Internet access.**   If you need to access the Internet from more than a single Mac, consider looking into ways to share your connection among additional Macs. The possibilities include such programs as Vicomsoft's SurfDoubler and SurfDoubler Plus, or Sustainable Softworks' IPNetRouter (I had not seen Mac OS X versions when this book was written, but they can still be "hosted" from an older Mac). There are also Ethernet routers that serve the purpose of sharing a modem connection from such companies as Asante, Farallon, and MacSense. You may also want to explore one of the so-called "broadband" Internet

Initial Installation: The First Day

connection services, such as cable modems or DSL. Any of these setups can allow you to use a single account to deliver access to the Internet even in a home (or home office) with two or three Macs (although additional connections may require a monthly surcharge); however, these connections can be easily shared by one of those routers, too. It's also possible to use a regular Internet email program and exchange messages with each other. This may be helpful if computers are in different rooms. At least you can confine your shouting to strictly family-related matters (that is just meant as a joke, of course).

NOTE   *In addition to the options mentioned here, all of the newest Apple computers support the AirPort wireless networking system. The AirPort Base Station has its own 56K modem, which lets you share your Internet connection with any AirPort-equipped Mac; it may also distribute a broadband ISP's connections through your network. There are also wireless Internet routers available from such companies as Asante and Farallon.*

CAUTION   *Please don't forget that although AOL can give you up to seven mailboxes (screen names) per account, you can access only one of them at a time on a single account. Sharing access is, therefore, out of the question, unless you order up a second account. AOL does give you the option to transfer a screen name to a second account, if you must use them at the same time.*

Adding a New Mac to Your Office

Are you switching over to the Mac platform, installing your first computer, or just adding to an existing Mac network? Whatever the situation, you can prepare for the arrival of your new computer so that it fits into your new environment with as little fuss as possible.

Adding a New Mac to an Existing Mac Network

If your office is already using Macs, adding another to your network ought to be a fairly easy process, although there are some things you'll want to prepare for:

■   **Software licenses**   If you intend to have your new Mac serve as an extra workstation, you may need to buy an extra software license for your programs. You don't necessarily have to buy a whole new copy at the retail price; some publishers will sell you a license at a reduced price (with a larger reduction going for multiple user packs). Fonts are usually licensed on the basis of output devices (printers, imagesetters, and so on), and you generally will not have to buy another license to install fonts on an extra computer (only for extra printers).

> **NOTE** *I don't want to overemphasize this, but many programs, even basic utility packages (such as StuffIt Deluxe from Aladdin Systems), do network checks for additional users and won't launch if another copy of the program with the same serial number is found.*

- **Networking** If your new Mac is to be part of an Ethernet network, you'll want to make sure your hub or switch can accommodate the extra connection. Some Ethernet hubs or switches have an "uplink" port, which lets you daisy-chain additional hubs as needs expand. If you're using Apple's AirPort wireless networking, you'll want to make sure your new Mac is equipped with this option. As this book was written, all current Mac computers, from laptops to desktops, were equipped with slots for AirPort cards.

- **Serial printers** Mac OS X didn't ship with support for serial printers. Your only solace appears to be use of a serial to USB adapter to make that printer work with a current model. In addition, if you want to generate a reasonable volume of work and have the utmost flexibility, consider getting an inkjet printer with an Ethernet networking card or a regular network laser printer. I cover the subject of printers in Chapter 8.

- **Internet access** In the normal scheme of things, each Mac will have its own modem (in fact, all new Apple computers these days come with a built-in modem, standard issue), but in your office, that modem may not be suitable. One reason is that a modem can bypass a corporate network firewall (although in a small office this is rarely an issue). You may want to designate one or two computers to handle your Internet or email chores. If you want to set up an office email system, consider buying an office email program, such as CE Software's QuickMail. These programs work for both your interoffice and Internet email requirements.

> **NOTE** *If you have a multiplatform office, with a Windows NT or Windows 2000 server, you might want to consider Microsoft's Exchange email and collaboration system. You'll want to contact the publishers of these email systems, however, about Mac OS X compatibility issues. Another strong possibility worth considering is Mac OS X Server, which includes its own email server.*

Another option is to use a cable modem or DSL if available. You'll be able to share your Internet access across your network, since such services use an Ethernet hub. Once you've done that, any email program ought to do the trick. You can then use your favorite Internet software and enjoy both Internet and intranet (within your office) communications. Another convenient option is an Internet sharing hub. A product of this sort usually includes an Ethernet hub (or switch) as well, so you don't need a separate hub. One product I've used, the Asante 3004, also comes in a version with modem jack and print server. For a larger office, you may want to look into Netopia's line of modems and routers. Netopia's R2121 Dual Analog Router, for example, has two 56K modems built in, and you can share connections among up to 15 users.

NOTE   *If you're using AOL, you can install a copy on each of your computers (Macs or PCs), but you cannot share access to a single account at the same time, regardless of how many mailboxes (screen names) you have.*

■ **Software updates**   If your new Mac is a lot newer than the ones you've had before, you may need to look for some software updates, particularly if you are switching from the Classic Mac OS to Mac OS X. While many older programs will work just fine on the newest Macs, including iBooks, iMacs, and Power Macintosh G4s, other programs, particularly ones requiring hardware access (such as scanning software), may not function at all. This is something you'll want to check in advance before you install software on the new computer.

Adding a Replacement Mac to an Existing Mac Network

That old computer is about to be retired, and a new Mac is to replace it. If you have a spare spot on your network, you can use Apple's file-sharing feature to copy files from the old computer to the new one. But there are a few things you need to check first:

■ **Don't copy your System Folder.**   The System Folder installed on your new Mac is the one designed specifically to work on that computer. Even if you have a newer system version on the other Mac, it's best to do a normal installation from Apple's system disks to make sure that the proper files are installed. Different Macs may require different files. An example of this is the fact that new models have a software ROM (a file called Mac OS ROM in your Classic System Folder); without it, they won't boot. But such files aren't installed on older models.

NOTE

The exception to this rule is your Internet and network preferences. You'll want to copy all of the settings so they can be entered in Mac OS X's Setup Assistant. They can't be transferred directly.

CAUTION

Because Mac OS X includes a large number of files marked "invisible," a straight Finder copy just won't succeed. If you are transferring from one Mac OS X computer to another, limit system-related file transfers to the contents of your personal Users folder, unless you can take advantage of a Mac OS X–savvy backup application.

- **Consider reinstalling application software.**   True, many Mac OS X applications come as a single file or package for easy placement in the Applications folder. But some, such as the version of AppleWorks for Mac OS X shipping when this book was written, still install separate files elsewhere on your Mac. Additionally, if you have a special set of preference files (which are most often installed in the Preferences folder inside the Library Folder in your personal Users directory under Mac OS X) that reflect your personal taste, and you don't want to have to recreate them from scratch, you may try to copy them over.

NOTE

Whether you are upgrading from an older 680x0 Mac or a Power Mac that used the older or Classic Mac OS, you'll want to seriously consider contacting the publisher about a native Mac OS X version. You will probably have to pay a standard upgrade fee, but you will benefit by having an application that fully supports Mac OS X's preemptive multitasking and protected memory features for maximum stability and performance.

- **Check for updates.**   Whether you are replacing a Mac that's several years old or a more recent, less powerful model, check with the software publishers to see whether you need an update to run on a newer Mac, even from the Classic environment. There's no blanket answer to this. I have run programs several years old, ones that will never be updated, without trouble. But by the same token, other programs will crash right at launch if you attempt to run them.

Initial Installation: The First Day

What to Do If Your New Mac Doesn't Work

There's nothing worse than switching on your computer and finding out that it just doesn't work. I cannot recall a single instance in my personal experience where I've had a Mac that turned up dead on arrival, but I know it happens sometimes. One of my clients, in fact, bought a new iMac that wouldn't run until its hard drive was replaced. If the worst should happen, your best approach would be to first recheck your setup to make sure everything is plugged in properly and that the power strip, if you use one, is on.

Here are some suggestions to follow before you seek outside help:

- **Recheck all connections.** It follows that you not only have to plug it in, but also be sure that the AC outlet is operational. In a home environment particularly, some AC sockets are linked to a light switch. When you turn off the light, the power goes off, too (some architects apparently think of this as a convenience and not an annoyance). With a power strip, check for an on/off switch of some sort. Make sure all connections are tight (check this before you turn the power strip on).

- **Install driver software for peripherals.** Inkjet printers, removable drives, scanners, and so on require special software to run. While Mac OS X incorporates some of these programs as standard issue (such as Iomega's Jaz and Zip drive software) and includes drivers for a number of USB devices, many products won't work unless you run the manufacturer's installation first.

NOTE   *Much of this Mac OS X driver support isn't clearly documented, so the best thing to do is to try and see whether the product works. If not, check with the manufacturer about needed updates.*

- **Test each item, one at a time.** If you daisy-chain a set of peripherals, such as SCSI devices, the failure of one item to work can likely cause problems for the other items on the chain. You may even crash at startup. The best approach is to check your new Mac first, all by itself (with keyboard, mouse, and monitor as necessary), and when you're sure it is all right, power down and hook up the extras.

- **Swap/replace cables.** Sometimes all it takes is a bad cable, and your new computer system won't run properly. If you have a spare set (or extras used for a different product), don't hesitate to try them out to see whether the cables themselves are the source of your problems.

■ **Check the rest of this book for advice.** I have devoted separate chapters to each element of your Mac system, from RAM upgrades to the installation of new modems, drives, scanners, printers, and other peripherals. If you are adding a number of new products, you'll want to consult each of these chapters for advice on how to handle the setups to avoid potential pitfalls.

If all else fails, you should contact your dealer and insist on an immediate replacement, if possible. While most dealers will simply want to fix a product that's dead on arrival, it is usually worth arguing for another unit, even if the one you have is partly functional.

NOTE   *The Apple Store's official policy is to exchange items that arrive inoperable. Most dealers will probably adhere to the same policy without argument. If you're dealing with a mail-order or online vendor, check their posted sales policies to see how they handle such situations—consider looking for a different dealer if the one you first select doesn't have a satisfactory policy.*

If Your Dealer Doesn't Cooperate

Apple Computer has a new product warranty that entitles you to a year's free service—onsite for its professional desktop models. Laptops can actually be shipped direct to Apple for service; they'll even supply the shipping box and pay the shipping charges (but you have to arrange for service first with their customer service department).

NOTE   *While your dealer can handle repairs, you do not have to use them if you would rather have Apple arrange for service. On the other hand, if you have full confidence in your dealer, and their technicians are certified by Apple, go ahead and let them do the job. More often than not, the repair is just a matter of simply swapping one module or circuit board for another; few, if any, service people actually replace individual parts these days.*

Don't hesitate to ask Apple for assistance to resolve your problem. Apple has more stringent requirements for dealers than used to be the case, and, even if you have to go up the corporate ladder, you will usually find a sympathetic ear and a reasonable resolution to your problem.

> **NOTE**   *This is beyond the scope of this book, but Apple has, in the past, instituted extended warranty policies for some models, such as the PowerBook 190 and 5300 series, a few Performas, and some AppleVision monitors. So if you buy a used or reconditioned Mac or Apple peripheral that has developed a clear hardware problem, ask Apple customer service whether they know of such a repair or replacement program that may apply to your unit.*

Summing Up

Most new Mac installations go quickly with little fuss or bother. And where troubles crop up, more than likely you will be able to overcome any installation problem with setting up your Mac.

Mac OS X presents new possibilities for operating system software hassles, even though it's supposed to be more robust than previous Mac OS versions. In addition, maintaining the Classic environment entails even more potential hazards. Chapter 2 deals with these dicey subjects in more detail.

Chapter 2

How to Cope with System Software Hassles

It's sometimes hard enough to deal with one operating system. True, Mac OS X is the operating system that's supposed to be easier to use and maintain, and it usually is, but every time you want to use an older Mac application—one not compiled to run native in the new operating system—you must bring another operating system to life.

Indeed, every single second that you use your Mac, you are using the operating system, sometimes two operating systems. Like your car's tires, it gets more wear and tear than anything else you use on your Mac, except for the hard drive. As a result, any problem with the system software, particularly if you have booted your Mac to run the Classic OS, can easily take down your Mac for the count.

Of course, it's not terribly convenient to reinstall your system software every single day, nor should you have to. Doing it under Mac OS X, as a matter of fact, can be a royal pain, because there is no simple way to just remove the existing operating system files without a bit of juggling.

Fortunately, it shouldn't come to that. Most system problems can be dealt with simply by following some basic troubleshooting.

In this chapter, you'll learn about common problems with your Mac and what they signify. You'll also discover the best ways to reinstall your system software, both Classic and Mac OS X, should the need arise.

How to Handle System Crashes

There are going to be arguments back and forth among proponents on both sides of the computing aisle about whether Macs are as reliable as they could be. Both Mac and Windows computers can crash on occasion. There is no way to avoid this, even with an industrial-strength operating system such as Mac OS X—it just happens less often. When system crashes are no longer part and parcel of the personal computing process, the day of the true computer appliance will have arrived.

Chapter 18, which is devoted to the topic of adding system enhancements, also covers diagnosing system-related conflicts. This chapter will cover a few basics and then refer you to other chapters for more information.

■ **Frequent crashes aren't normal.** I'm not contradicting myself here. It's normal for your Classic environment to crash occasionally, but when it happens ten times a day, something is most definitely wrong. As far as Mac OS X is concerned, folks run it for weeks or months without having to restart. When troubles arise, most times it's the fault of a third-party program. I'll tell you more about how to cope with such oddities in Chapter 18.

■ **It's rarely the hardware.** Macs are very reliable. There are millions of older Macs in regular use every single day in production situations, and they keep on purring. That's true even for such compact Macs as the Mac Plus. Except for hard drives, removable devices, and similar products, which are subject to mechanical wear and tear, you should expect your Mac to last for many years, way beyond the time when you'll want to use it.

> NOTE
>
> *Reader surveys of personal computer owners published by* Consumer Reports *magazine traditionally show Macs among the top two or three most reliable product lines.*

■ **Repair or replace?** Of course, electronics aren't always perfect. Should your Mac's logic board or power supply fail, it may be time to consider whether you're really better off getting a new Mac. If you're on a budget, and if you can locate used or refurbished parts, you may actually be able to stretch the life of that old computer for quite a long time. But if the repair bills add up, the time may have arrived to visit your Apple dealer (or check a catalog or Web site) and see what's being offered.

■ **Don't forget computer viruses.** Most system oddities on Macs aren't caused by computer viruses; they are generally related to software or system conflicts. However, that doesn't mean you shouldn't check for the possibility of computer viruses. Any time you share files with another user, or even browse the Internet regularly and receive files, there is always a slight risk of infection. Please read Chapter 12 for more information on this subject.

What Those Error Messages Really Mean

Wouldn't it be nice if Apple could just put up a message that says, "Sorry, your Mac crashed because the person who programmed your word processor left out a line of code because he was late for dinner"? That and similar routine mistakes are what often cause programs to quit and your Mac to freeze.

Since programs are getting larger and larger, with millions of lines of code, the possibility of error has risen dramatically. Worse, there are so many thousands of possible combinations of Mac hardware and software that it's just too easy for conflicts to occur.

Unfortunately, it's not terribly easy to know why your Mac is behaving badly. The system error messages you see on the screen—when you see them—frequently don't give you the information you need to find out what's wrong. They seem designed more for programmers than for folks like you and me who just want to use our Macs with as little fuss as possible.

In the first edition of this book, I went to great lengths to set up a table of common system errors and their explanations. I wish I could say it helped readers, but, instead, it only made matters more confusing. I even had letters from one or two readers who disputed the definition of one system error or another. This is one of many reasons why the system error list is history.

Moreover, under Mac OS X, error messages are usually confined to a prompt that an application unexpectedly quit—and, yes, you can continue to run your Mac without having to restart.

The upshot is that a system error message, regardless of number (except for a rare few that might indicate a hardware problem), can usually be taken to mean that a program or Classic Mac OS conflict has caused your Mac to misbehave, and you need to stop using that program, get it updated, or see if there's something system related that might cause such problems.

Case History   One Line Too Many

There is no greater frustration than encountering a software conflict that the publisher of your software cannot reproduce. You begin to feel almost paranoid. You feel that perhaps you are being singled out to face a situation nobody else is facing.

This happened to me some years back when I was using a component of a now-discontinued utility program, a simple control panel that would put up a cute little menu bar icon displaying hard disk activity. Whenever I ran that program, my Mac would crash, every single time.

I dutifully contacted the publisher's technical support people and went into endless details of my particular setup, and they took me through various stages of disabling and enabling system extensions. Even with the basic set of Apple system extensions and their lone component of the program, the crashes occurred.

Technical support couldn't duplicate it.

Finally, they did the impossible (and I've never heard of a similar case), though I suppose some other publishers have done it, too. They were located in the Pacific Northwest, and I'm in the Southwest. They had one of their lead programmers pack up a PowerBook containing a copy of the program's source code (the software's heart and soul) and travel directly to my home office to see what was happening.

He arrived, set up his PowerBook, and launched his software compiling program. Before his eyes, I continued to duplicate the problem. He watched it in action, then rummaged through the long lines of arcane text that formed the source of the program that was crashing my Mac.

Finally, he stumbled upon a single line of computer code, a few words that made no sense to anyone but a software engineer. He muttered something about the code not actually doing anything in particular, but he thought that perhaps, in a rare situation, it might just create an "endless loop" that would cause a crash. How it got there, he wouldn't guess, as the original programmer (no longer connected with the company) may have put it there to access a function that was removed from the final version.

So he removed it, then recompiled the program. He copied the finished control panel to a floppy (ah, the old days when software would fit on a floppy!), and I then installed it. I restarted and crossed my fingers. The crashes stopped, for good. In days, the fixed version was ready and was incorporated into the next version of the program.

So simple, yet so complex. Imagine how difficult it is to locate an errant line of computer language in a huge word processing program that is causing a one-in-a-million system crash. My respect for the hurdles software engineers face in giving us reasonably reliable software went way up as a result of this episode.

Is It the Hardware or Software?

This is the $64 million question, and one you wonder about when your Mac crashes over and over again, and no amount of system diagnostics will set it right.

There are a few sure indications, however, of a hardware-related problem. (Other problems may seem hardware related, but are really due to other causes.) Here's a list of typical problems:

■ **Weird tones appear at startup.**   This usually indicates defective or improperly installed RAM. Try reseating or removing the RAM upgrade and see if the problem disappears (of course, you've got to leave your original RAM module where it is). If the problem doesn't vanish, contact your dealer or Apple Computer for further assistance. We'll cover the subject of RAM upgrades in more detail in Chapter 4.

■ **Screen remains dark and Mac refuses to start.**   On some of the early Power Macs, this is a symptom of a dead PRAM battery. The battery, costing from $10 to $20, is readily available from your Apple dealer. You may also find an equivalent at a specialty battery dealer or even a Radio Shack store. If your Mac has a graphic card in a PCI or AGP expansion slot, shut it down, open your Mac's case, and make sure the card is properly seated. If not, reseat the card carefully. If these two solutions don't apply, have your Mac or monitor checked for a power supply or logic board problem.

NOTE   *Before you touch anything inside your Mac, you should shut down the entire system (including monitor, external drives, and so on) and touch the power supply to ground yourself. Some manufacturers are nice enough to include wrist straps (to tap static electricity). That way you won't cause a "spike" that can fry your Mac's delicate electronics.*

■ **The picture distorts or there is a color shift.**   Restart your Mac. If the problem doesn't disappear, check your monitor adjustments. If the problem continues, contact your dealer for assistance. Some Apple Computer monitors, from the AppleVision series, are known to be troublesome. Call Apple Computer's customer service people for assistance. You'll learn more about Mac displays in Chapter 10.

■ **Date reverts to 1956 or 1904 after a cold start.**   If you power up your Mac and find the system date, network, or other settings have changed, it's time to replace the PRAM (or backup) battery. These little lithium batteries power the memory chip on your Mac that stores these settings. For more information, refer to the earlier section on why your Mac may refuse to start.

■ **PowerBook or iBook battery doesn't recharge.**   Your battery is generally good for a year or two of regular service. If you cannot get it to charge properly, you may want to recheck the AC adapter (they have been known to fail on earlier PowerBook models), or try another battery if you have one. You can buy a battery for most recent PowerBooks from your Apple dealer. If the battery still won't recharge, consult your PowerBook's documentation about resetting the Power Manager, which can impact such problems. Chapter 5 has much more information on this subject.

Extended Warranties: Are They Worth It?

As you prepare to leave the store with your new purchase, the salesperson tells you there's one more option: an extended warranty. (No, it doesn't just happen in automobile showrooms.) You can add two years (or more) to Apple's standard one-year product warranty. Is this worth it?

In practice, such policies are little different from a regular insurance policy. A third-party carrier (or Apple Computer, if it's an AppleCare policy) will cover repairs (perhaps with a small deductible for third-party policies) if your system develops a hardware problem.

The question is, do you really need this insurance? If the policy is really cheap, and you are far from a friendly neighborhood dealer or Macintosh user group, you might find this a convenient safeguard. But most electronic components will tend to fail early in their life cycle, well within your new product warranty. You should look at extended warranties with skepticism. They are a big source of profit for the dealers, and the possibility you'll actually need one is not terribly large.

NOTE   *If there is any exception to this rule, perhaps it would be an Apple laptop, be it PowerBook or iBook. These models are subject to more wear and tear than the usually stationary desktop models, and an economical policy may well be worth your consideration. The LCD display, for example, can be especially expensive to replace if it fails.*

There are occasional articles in *Consumer Reports* magazine on the subject of extended warranties, and you may want to consult them for additional insights.

The Right Way to Do a Classic System Upgrade

The vision of the one-click installation has been part and parcel of the Mac computing experience from the very first. In those days, your entire System Folder fit on a single 400K floppy disk (well, at least at the very beginning).

A Mac running Mac OS X really has two sets of system files. In this section, I'll cover the Classic version. Then I'll tell you how to perform a system upgrade with Mac OS X, a rather more convoluted process.

Today, your Classic System Folder consists of hundreds of files, and the contents can easily fill more than 400MB of storage space, even with the minimum of extras. There are so many possible combinations of Macs and required system components, there's no way to just guess what works.

The most efficient way to do a system upgrade is to run Apple's Mac OS installer. Trying to drag a completed System Folder from another Mac to yours will almost always make trouble, unless they are identical in make and model.

The Two Types of Classic System Installations

There are two types of Classic OS installations. Which you choose depends on whether you've had problems with your current system software, or whether you're upgrading to an all-new version.

- **Upgrade installation**   This is the standard option available when you double-click the Mac OS installer. The components of your System Folder will be updated with the newer versions from Apple Computer, and your System file will be updated as well. If any untouched files are damaged, they will still be present. In addition, if your System file is damaged, the update may only make matters worse.

- **Clean installation**   No, you don't have to reinstall all of your software to do a clean system installation (although you might have to consider this as a last resort to deal with serious system problems). The actual process will create a brand new System Folder. Your existing System Folder will be deactivated and renamed Previous System Folder. Nothing from your older System Folder is transferred. That means you'll have to reinstall or drag over your third-party extensions, control panels, fonts, and preferences.

NOTE *There is, technically, a third option. All recent Macs come with a set of Software Restore CDs (four of them came with my new iBook). They allow you to return the computer to shipping condition, even wipe the hard drive clean if you want. Just remember that if you take this drastic step, you should first back up all of your document files and Internet preferences, and be prepared to reinstall third-party software after the restore process is done. It is, however, a simple, if drastic, procedure.*

What's Right for You

Unless you are in a real hurry, or you're just reinstalling your system software to add or remove a component, it's best to start from scratch. And that means a clean installation.

The advantage is that no components that may be damaged from your existing System Folder are carried through, and, if you're upgrading to a new system version, you'll be assured of as reliable an upgrade as possible.

The sad side effect, however, is that you have to go through a process of merging non-Apple components from your existing System Folder. This can be confusing and perhaps time-consuming, but if you follow the suggestions in the next section, you'll be able to keep the process as painless as possible.

If you really want to try to automate the process, consider trying out Conflict Catcher (described in the section entitled "Clean System Merging: The Easy Way," later in this chapter), which does a lot of the work for you.

The Steps to a Clean Installation of Your Classic System Software

Once you're ready to proceed, first create an Apple System Profiler report of your original System Folder. You'll need it later on. Get your system CD and follow these steps:

CAUTION   *Let me remind you again that all these steps are strictly for the Classic Mac OS. The Mac OS X installation process will get its due later in this chapter.*

1. Go to the Apple menu in the Classic environment, and launch Apple System Profiler, bringing up the screen shown in Figure 2-1.

2. Choose New from the File menu to choose your report options (see Figure 2-2).

3. Since you are only concerned with the contents of your System Profile, check only the boxes at right, and uncheck the ones at left. Then click OK to begin the process, which will bring up a progress screen, as shown in Figure 2-3.

4. Once your report is generated, choose Print from the File menu to get a hard copy of the report.

NOTE   *If you don't have a printer at hand, you can simply save the profile report, but it'll take a lot more time to compare the contents back and forth when you're ready to merge System Folders.*

The Right Way to Do a Classic System Upgrade

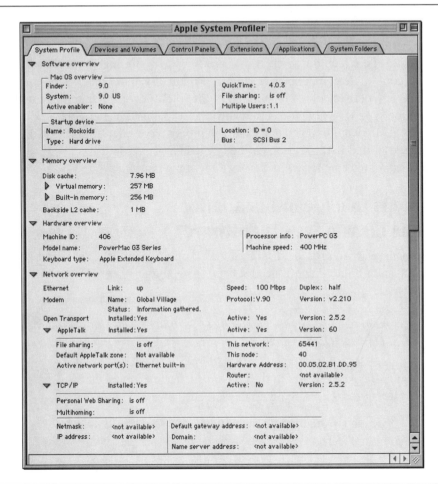

FIGURE 2-1   The Classic version of Apple System Profiler is your starting point.

5. Now you're ready for the main event. Insert the new system CD in your Mac's CD-ROM drive.

6. Restart your Mac and immediately hold down the C key, which will force your Mac to start from the system CD. Release the key when you see the Happy Mac icon.

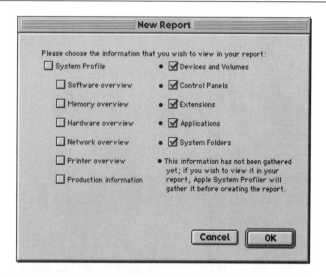

FIGURE 2-2   Configure your report options here.

NOTE   *If your Mac refuses to start from the system CD, go to the Control
Panels folder, open the Startup Disk Control Panel, and select the
CD as your startup disk. You'll just have to change it back when the
installation is through.*

7. After your Mac has started, locate and double-click on the Mac OS Install
icon, which brings up a screen similar to the one shown in Figure 2-4.
Click Continue to proceed.

FIGURE 2-3   Be patient. Lots of files have to be checked before the report is ready.

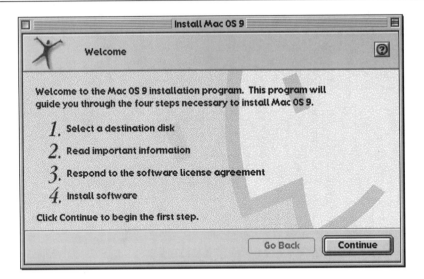

FIGURE 2-4   Here's the first part of your Classic Mac OS installation process.

8. On the next screen (see Figure 2-5), choose the Destination Disk from the pop-up menu (if your Mac has more than one drive).

9. Once you've selected the drive on which the System Folder is to be placed, click the Options button, if you're doing a clean system installation. This will bring up the screen shown in Figure 2-6.

10. Click the Perform Clean Installation check box to select that option, then click the OK button.

11. On the next screen, you'll see an Important Information message, which is actually your Mac OS Read Me file (see Figure 2-7). Go over this to make sure there aren't some last-minute steps you need to take to ensure a seamless system software upgrade. When you're finished reading the document (you can also save or print it), click Continue to move on to the next step. If you don't print the Read Me file at this point, no problem. It'll be copied to your hard drive during the normal system installation.

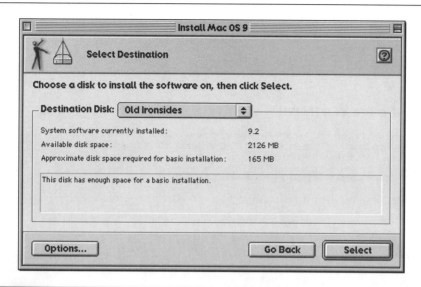

NOTE   *If you find something in the Important Information file that prevents you from doing your system installation right away, choose Quit from the File menu to end the process. You can always go back to it later.*

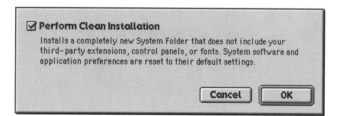

FIGURE 2-6   A clean installation can often cure system upgrade problems.

The Right Way to Do a Classic System Upgrade

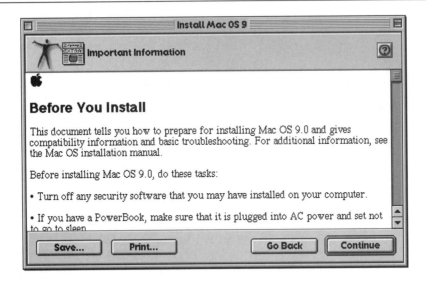

FIGURE 2-7   Don't forget the Read Me file. Don't say we didn't warn you.

12.   On the next screen, you can opt to go right on to the system installation, or you can make a few more choices. If you wish to continue with the standard installation process, click Start. You'll see a progress bar and an estimate of how long the system installation will take. Expect it to last from 5 to 25 minutes, depending on the kind of Mac you have.

NOTE   *At the very start of the installation process, the installer will check your hard drive with Disk First Aid to be sure there are no disk directory issues before the software is actually installed. If there are problems Disk First Aid cannot fix, the installation won't continue. At this point, if you have a copy, run Norton Utilities or TechTool Pro and see if they can fix the problem. I cover the subject in more detail in Chapter 13.*

13.   If you want to check or pick and choose the components of your system installation, click Customize, which brings up the screen shown in Figure 2-8.

14.   Review the Software components list. If everything is as you want, click the Start button to begin the installation. If you wish to remove or add a component, click the check box next to its name.

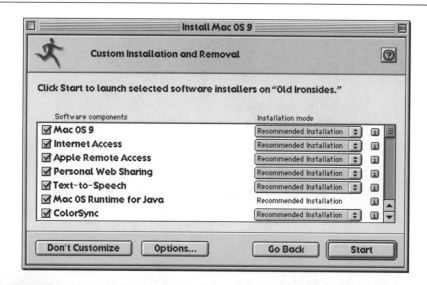

FIGURE 2-8   Do you want to add or remove some components? Make your choice here.

NOTE   *If you want to further customize the installation of software components, click the Recommended Installation pop-up menu to pick further options. Be sure you click the "i" icons for specifics on the effect of the choices you make, if you have any questions.*

15. If you have a Mac with a non-Apple hard drive, you'll want to click Options (see Figure 2-9). Then uncheck the box labeled Update Apple Hard Disk Drivers. If you don't follow this step, you'll either have to respond to a message that your drive can't be updated or, worse, confront a problem with the drive if the Apple installer tries the update anyway. Click OK to continue.

NOTE   *If your hard drive isn't formatted with Apple's Drive Setup program, you may want to contact the manufacturer of your disk formatting software to make sure it's compatible with both Mac OS 9.x and Mac OS X.*

16. Once your system installation is done, click Quit to close the installer program.

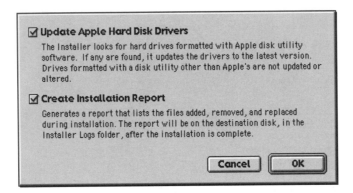

FIGURE 2-9 Avoid the warning about non-Apple drivers.

17. If you changed your Startup Disk Control Panel settings, locate the control panel on your CD (in the Control Panels folder) and select your original destination disk as the startup disk.

18. Choose Restart from the Special menu.

The first part of the system installation is finished, but you have more to do before you can get down to work with your new System Folder. Now you've got to start the merge process.

How to Merge Classic System Folders

When you complete your clean system installation, you'll have a System Folder and a Previous System Folder. The latter is simply your original System Folder, which Apple has "deblessed" (made inactive) as a consequence of your installation. Now that it's there, what do you do about it?

I have seen situations where folks have just left it there, doing nothing with it, and not taking advantage of its value. If you prefer, you can simply reinstall all your third-party control panels and extensions, redo all your program and Internet settings, and be done with it. If you can accomplish this task in a reasonably short amount of time, it may be the best choice.

But for most of us, it's better to simply merge the System Folders, moving over the non-Apple files and certain preferences files from your Previous System Folder to the new one.

This is not a trivial process, and you may expect it to take anywhere from a half hour to a couple of hours to do right. You'll also have to check the contents of each folder within your System Folder to be absolutely certain you are copying over the things you need and not the things that will replace newer system components or cause further trouble.

Here are the steps to follow:

1. Retrieve the Apple System Profiler report you made before the clean installation. Now open the Previous System Folder and the new System Folder, and place the directories side by side to compare them.

2. Choose View as List from the Finder for each folder, and make sure the name is selected (see Figure 2-10 for the result). This will make it as easy as possible to compare the two.

3. Check for any folders in your Previous System Folder that aren't duplicated in your new System Folder. Hold down the SHIFT key and select each of them.

4. Hold down the OPTION key, then drag those folders to your new System Folder. When you perform this action, a plus sign (+) will appear on the mouse cursor.

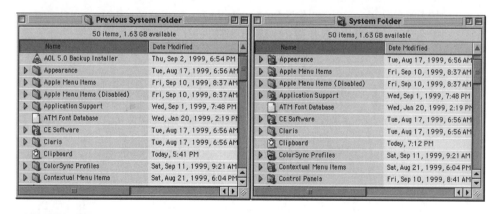

FIGURE 2-10   One from column A, one from column B (a bad joke? I agree). Compare your system components before merging.

NOTE   *You are holding down the OPTION key so that you are copying, not moving, the files to the new System Folder. That way, if something goes wrong, you can revert to your Previous System Folder.*

5. If you have any custom sounds you've added, double-click on the System file icon in your Previous System Folder to bring up the directory of keyboard layouts and sounds.

6. Select those sounds, hold down the OPTION key, then drag them to the System file in the new System Folder. It'll take a few seconds for the process to complete itself.

7. Next, open the Apple Menu Items folder in both the previous and new System Folders and compare the contents. OPTION-drag over the files not duplicated in the new System Folder.

8. The next step gets a bit more complicated. Consult your copy of the Apple System Profiler report to see which items in your System Folder are from Apple and which aren't.

9. For each folder in your two System Folders, OPTION-drag the non-Apple files from your Previous System Folder to the new System Folder, with the exceptions of the Preferences and Fonts folders.

10. Go to the Fonts folder of each System Folder. Select all the files from your old Fonts folder and OPTION-drag them to the new one. Not to worry, you won't be able to replace any fonts that are duplicated (you'll get a message they're in use).

11. After your fonts are replaced, open the Preferences folder, and OPTION-drag the non-duplicated files to the new Preferences folder.

12. What about Internet access? If you plan on going online only under Mac OS X (even with Classic applications), you can ignore the first part of this step. The second part, for your Internet software, only applies if these programs will run from the Classic environment. Should you want to go online after booting under Mac OS 9.x, OPTION-drag Apple's Internet Preferences, Modem Preferences, and the TCP/IP Preferences files to the new System Folder, and OK the message to replace the ones that are there. In addition to these basic files, you'll also want to OPTION-copy folders with the name America Online, Eudora, Explorer, or Netscape, or bearing the name of any other Internet software you use. When you copy these

additional files, stored program settings, bookmarks, downloads, email, and other files will be brought over to your new System Folder.

NOTE

If you cannot manually locate all the needed files, run Apple's search tool, Sherlock, to find a list of the files you need.

13. If everything is all right, choose Restart from the Special menu. Once your Mac has restarted, make sure it works properly. If all went well, you should be ready to enjoy your new System Folder.

NOTE

Do not delete the contents of your Previous System folder until you're sure your new installation went well. Otherwise, you'll end up having to do another clean installation.

What If the Clean Classic System Installation Goes Badly?

It doesn't happen too often (thank heavens), but sometimes reinstalling your system software only makes matters worse for your Mac. Should this happen, you can go back to using your Previous System Folder. This is why you should copy rather than move your files during the merge process.

The following process is quite drastic. You'll have to be prepared to restore all of your programs in addition to reinstalling system software. It's only recommended as a last resort.

NOTE

As I said earlier, if you have a fairly new Mac and didn't install much or any third-party software, you can use your System Restore CD (or CDs, in the most recent models) to put everything back the way it was. This is as clean an installation as you can get.

Here's what to do next:

1. Restart your Mac if it crashed. If you cannot get it to start, restart with your system CD, holding down the C key (as noted in the previous section) to get it going.

2. Go to your new System Folder on your startup drive, and remove the System file.

3. Select the folder's icon, and rename this folder "Obsolete System Folder."

> **NOTE** *Renaming an icon simply involves clicking on the name to select it, waiting for the name to highlight, then typing in the new name and pressing RETURN or ENTER to save it.*

4. Go to the Previous System Folder, select the icon, and change its name back to System Folder.

5. Open and close the folder. This has the effect of "blessing" the former Previous System Folder, so your Mac can start again.

6. Restart and verify that you're up and running again.

7. Trash the Obsolete System Folder.

8. Either continue to use your original System Folder or go ahead and try the clean system installation process again, as outlined in the earlier section entitled "The Steps to a Clean Installation of Your Classic System Software." But this time, rather than merge the Previous System Folder with the new System Folder, first verify that your Mac works properly.

9. Once you've done that, reinstall all of your third-party control panels and extensions. If you have application software that includes system components, you'll have to reinstall them as well.

> **NOTE** *Recent versions of the Classic version of Microsoft Office and the company's Internet applications are designed to run a "self-repair" routine if you launch them with missing System Folder components, so you shouldn't need to worry about them. These programs are designed to take care of themselves (though I've heard of a case or two where a complete software reinstallation was needed). These routines will even run if you access these programs under Mac OS X by way of the Classic environment.*

10. Once you've reinstalled everything, you should recheck your Mac's startup process and your programs to make sure everything works properly. Prepare to have to revisit a program's preferences and your Internet settings.

If the foregoing process doesn't work, there are some more options:

■ **Check your hard drive.** While Apple's Disk First Aid (or the First Aid component of Disk Utility) should be able to ferret out disk directory problems that may affect your Mac OS installation, don't hesitate to give it another go-around. If you have one or more of the commercial disk repair programs on hand, such as Alsoft's DiskWarrior, Symantec's Norton Utilities, or MicroMat's Drive 10 or TechTool Pro, let them do their stuff. It's always possible these programs will find a problem Apple's disk diagnostic application missed. Once you run these programs, give the system installation another try.

- **Reformat your hard drive.**   This is a drastic step, but if you have a backup (or can use a Restore disk to put everything back), this may be the best way to clear up lingering problems. It's not quite as intimidating as it sounds, as long as you can back up everything. But prepare to spend the better part of an afternoon to accomplish the task (or an entire day if you have a Mac with several big hard drives and lots and lots of files).

- **Have the Mac checked by a dealer.**   If you've tried everything possible to get your Mac to run in a stable fashion, have the hardware checked. It simply isn't normal for a Mac user to have to go through so much grief to get the computer to operate as it's supposed to.

Clean Classic System Merging: The Easy Way

The process just described is a little complex and requires lots of attention to detail. But it isn't the only way to do a clean installation of your system software.

Fortunately, there is a way to actually help you automate the process, so you don't have to get a case of blurry eyes trying to figure out what goes where and when.

The solution is a special feature of Casady & Greene's popular Conflict Catcher program (see also Chapter 18). The stock and trade of Conflict Catcher is its ability to help you diagnose possible system extension conflicts, but the program can also help you merge your disparate system elements after a clean installation. Here is how to do it:

NOTE   *For best compatibility in the Classic Mac OS environment and with Mac OS versions 9.1 and later, you'll want to use Conflict Catcher 8.0.9 or later.*

1. Do a clean system installation, as explained in the earlier section entitled "The Right Way to Do a Classic System Upgrade."

2. Install Conflict Catcher after restarting with your new System Folder. This process works best if the program is installed on both the current System Folder and the Previous System Folder.

3. Restart your Mac, and hold down the SPACEBAR, which brings up the Conflict Catcher window, shown in Figure 2-11.

4. Choose Clean-Install System Merge from the program's Special menu.

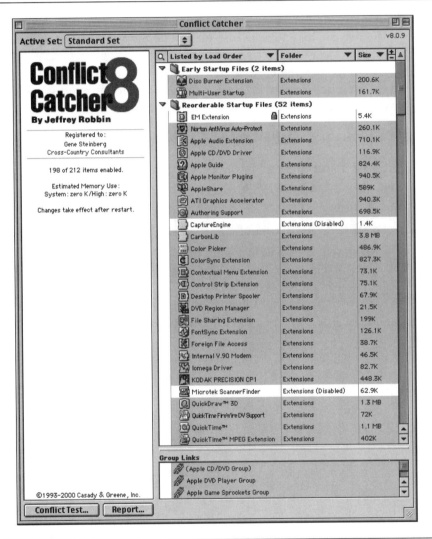

FIGURE 2-11   Conflict Catcher is still there to help, even in the world of Mac OS X and Classic.

FIGURE 2-12   Follow the prompts to run through the clean install process of your Classic system software.

5. You will then see a dialog box, shown in Figure 2-12, in which you confirm you're running the new System Folder. Click Yes to continue.

6. In the next dialog, you'll be asked to select, from the list, your present System Folder, and the one from which you want to merge. Click on your Previous System Folder (if that's what you'll be using) where requested.

7. You'll then be brought back to the prior dialog box in which you'll see the name Previous System Folder.

8. Click on the Compare Folders button. Over the next few minutes, Conflict Catcher will go to work to seek out the differences between the two Classic System Folders. As soon as its work is done, you'll see a screen containing a list of the items in your Previous System Folder that aren't duplicated in the new one.

> NOTE
>
> *As part of its scanning process, Conflict Catcher will check for corrupted files in your Previous System Folder. If you see a dialog box about it, go ahead and let Conflict Catcher attempt to fix the files.*

9. Look at the list, and select the check boxes for each item that you *don't want* to copy to your new System Folder.

> NOTE
>
> *If you're not sure about a specific system extension, don't worry. Just click the name, and Conflict Catcher will consult its reference file and let you know what the item is used for (it has a database of thousands of entries and gets it right most times).*

10. If you want to customize the merging process still further, click on the Options button. The key option is whether to Copy Items or Move Items. In the latter case, the files will just be transferred to the new System Folder. In the first case, copies will be made. You'll want to consider the first option, in case your new System Folder isn't performing as you'd like and you want to use the original ("Previous") System Folder again.

11. The next option is helpful in setting up preferences for your new System Folder. It's called Merge System File Resources, and it'll transfer the Owner Name, Computer Name and (if it applies) the password you placed in your File Sharing Control Panel, your printer selection, and your selected sounds. Once you've made the settings, click OK to begin the final leg of the journey.

12. On the next screen, click Merge Systems.

13. After the files you selected are transferred to the new System Folder, you'll return to the main Conflict Catcher screen. Here you can recheck the results of the merge process. Confirm the settings, click Continue Startup, and you're just about there.

14. If everything looks good, click Continue Startup. Your Mac's startup process will continue where it left off, with one possible exception. If the merge process added items that load before Conflict Catcher, you'll be asked to OK a restart instead.

NOTE *If you access the Internet through a regular Internet provider when your Mac has started in the Classic Mac OS, be sure that you also transfer your Internet Preferences, Modem Preferences, Remote Access folder, and TCP/IP Preferences. In addition, you'll want to locate preferences files and folders with such names as America Online, Eudora, Explorer, and Netscape (or any other Internet program you use). These files contain such critical items as program settings, bookmarks, favorites, email, downloads, and other important files. You need these settings to seamlessly connect to your provider without having to do the setups all over again; none of this is necessary if you only go online with Mac OS X software.*

The Right Way to Do a Mac OS X System Upgrade

For its new operating system, Apple reduced the number of clicks, and left the Mac user with fewer options to reinstall the system, but there are still some pitfalls. For one thing, if you've downloaded an update via the Software Update preference panel, there's always the possibility that some of the upgraded components will be overwritten if you just restarted your Mac from your Mac OS X CD and ran a simple installation.

Worse, running Software Update again may not always bring you back to where you were before you started. That's because information about the previous updates are left intact, and can't be run again.

There are two ways around this problem. One is simply to remove the receipt file, so Software Update will do its stuff again. Here's how you accomplish that task:

1. Before you reinstall Mac OS X, locate the Receipts folder within the Library folder on the top or root level of your hard drive.

2. Remove the .pkg files that identify the version of the system upgrade.

3. Drag the items to the trash and empty the trash.

4. Now restart with your Mac OS X CD, holding down the C key to boot from the disc, and proceed with a normal Mac OS X installation.

The Perilous Process of Performing a "Clean" Mac OS X Installation

Wouldn't it be nice if there was a simple "uninstall" option in the Mac OS X installer? That way you could remove what was there before running a system installation. Of course, such a feature, demanded by many Mac users, may eventually show up. But for now (at least at the time this book was written), it's not there, so you have to perform a clean installation the hard way.

If you installed Mac OS X on a separate drive partition, you could, of course, have the partition erased as part of the installation process. But you lose your previous system settings, all the applications you've previously installed under Mac OS X, and the stuff on your desktop. You could, of course, back this up, then restore it, but that entails an extra step.

Here's another method, one you might find a little easier to accomplish:

Before you attempt this method, however, you'll want to back up the contents of your Users folders and Applications folders, as a precaution, and put those backups on another drive volume.

NOTE   *If you installed any files within the Library folder on the root level of your hard drive, such as fonts or printer PPD files, back them up, as you'll have to reinstall them after the system installation.*

The Right Way to Do a Mac OS X System Upgrade

Once you've done that, you'll have to contend with a second oddity of Mac OS X, and that's the fact that many of the system-related files are marked "invisible," meaning they can't be seen, not under Mac OS X, and not under the Classic Mac OS. Obviously, if you can't see it, you can't remove it. So you'll need a program that can see and manipulate "invisible" files.

The one I suggest you consider is a shareware product, File Buddy. This handy Mac OS utility is available from either the VersionTracker.com Web site or the author's Web site at http://www.skytag.com. After you download the program, follow these steps to do your clean install of Mac OS X:

1. Launch the Startup Disk preference panel in the System Preferences application, and click on your Classic Mac OS System Folder icon (see Figure 2-13).

2. Once you've selected a new startup disk, click the Restart button.

3. After you've restarted, locate and launch File Buddy (or whatever invisible file-handling utility you acquire).

4. With the program running, go to the Cleaning menu, and chose Find Invisible Files. See Figure 2-14 for the result.

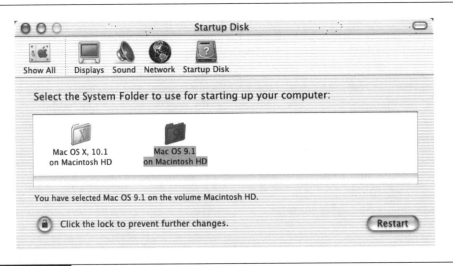

FIGURE 2-13   Select your startup volume here.

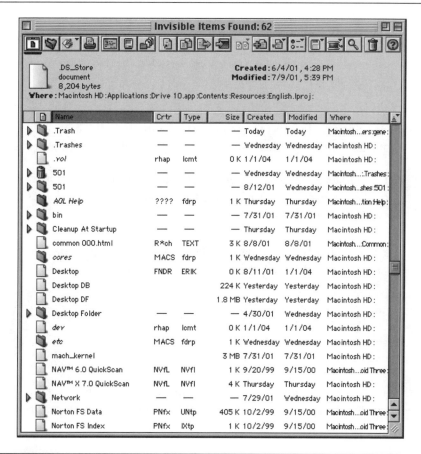

	Name	Crtr	Type	Size	Created	Modified	Where	
▶	.Trash	—	—	—	Today	Today	Macintosh...ers:gene:	
▶	.Trashes	—	—	—	Wednesday	Wednesday	Macintosh HD :	
	.vol	rhap	lcmt	0 K	1/1/04	1/1/04	Macintosh HD :	
▶	501	—	—	—	Wednesday	Wednesday	Macintosh...:Trashes:	
▶	501	—	—	—	8/12/01	Wednesday	Macintosh..shes 501 :	
	AOL Help	????	fdrp	1 K	Thursday	Thursday	Macintosh...tion:Help:	
▶	bin	—	—	—	7/31/01	7/31/01	Macintosh HD :	
▶	Cleanup At Startup	—	—	—	Thursday	Thursday	Macintosh HD :	
	common 000.html	R*ch	TEXT	3 K	8/8/01	8/8/01	Macintosh...Common:	
	cores	MACS	fdrp	1 K	Wednesday	Wednesday	Macintosh HD :	
	Desktop	FNDR	ERIK	0 K	8/11/01	1/1/04	Macintosh HD :	
	Desktop DB			224 K	Yesterday	Yesterday	Macintosh HD :	
	Desktop DF			1.8 MB	Yesterday	Yesterday	Macintosh HD :	
▶	Desktop Folder	—	—	—	4/30/01	Wednesday	Macintosh HD :	
	dev	rhap	lcmt	0 K	1/1/04	1/1/04	Macintosh HD :	
	etc	MACS	fdrp	1 K	Wednesday	Wednesday	Macintosh HD :	
	mach_kernel			3 MB	7/31/01	7/31/01	Macintosh HD :	
	NAV™ 6.0 QuickScan	NVfL	NVfl	1 K	9/20/99	9/15/00	Macintosh...oid Three:	
	NAV™ X 7.0 QuickScan	NVfL	NVfl	4 K	Thursday	Thursday	Macintosh HD :	
▶	Network	—	—	—	7/29/01	Wednesday	Macintosh HD :	
	Norton FS Data	PNfx	UNtp	405 K	10/2/99	9/15/00	Macintosh...oid Three:	
	Norton FS Index	PNfx	IXtp	1 K	10/2/99	9/15/00	Macintosh...oid Three:	

FIGURE 2-14   H.G. Wells "Invisible Man" wasn't this easy to see without his bandages.

5. Locate the following items from the list and select them:

```
.DS_Store
.hidden
.Trashies
.vol
bin
cores
dev
Developer
etc
```

```
mach_kernel
Network
private
sbin
usr
vmr
Volumes
```

6. Once selected, click the Trash button that appears in the File Buddy application window. That's it. The rest of the files can be deleted manually.

> **NOTE**
>
> *The file listing here was current as of Mac OS X 10.1. Don't be surprised if the list changes again, or if Apple finally decides to leave all files visible, so you can remove them easily.*

7. We're just about done, so hang in there. With File Buddy gone from the screen, locate, select, and trash the following items:

```
Library
mach
mach.sym
System
Users
```

> **NOTE**
>
> *if you want to retain all prior user settings and desktop files, keep the Users folder intact, or just copy it to another drive and restore its contents later on.*

8. Empty the Trash. After all files are removed, make sure your Mac OS X installation CD is in the drive and launch the Mac OS X installer application.

9. When the installer launches, click Restart and your Mac will reboot from the CD.

10. When the Mac OS X installer launches, follow the prompts and perform a normal installation of your system software.

All right, upon restarting after the system has been reinstalled, you will have to go through the process of reconfiguring your registration and Internet setups. Annoying, perhaps, but at least you'll benefit from having a clean installation, and, with the possible exception of having to restore some User settings, you won't have to endure a system merge process.

The Magic and Mystery of Preferences Files

The biggest hurdle to overcome in merging a Previous System Folder with your new, clean System Folder for your Classic environment is what to do about the preferences files.

When you want to customize your program to show a specific set of toolbar options, to use an autosave or auto-backup feature, to display fonts in WYSIWYG fashion, or a host of other options, you will look for some sort of preferences or settings feature.

Most programs store their preferences in a separate file, not in the application itself.

And it's not just the programs you install that have preferences settings. More and more of the things you customize in your Mac system software generate some sort of preferences file. At first it was just the Finder, but now there are preferences for a host of functions.

So, if you decide to do a clean system installation, you have all those Apple program preferences to worry about. You could, of course, just decide you'll redo all the settings from your Mac, but this could be time consuming, and, when it comes to the settings you use to get on the Internet, not always so easy.

The best solution is to make a backup of your Mac's Classic Preferences folder within the System Folder (when you feel you've got the settings down pat), so you can quickly restore it should the need arise for a clean system installation.

For Mac OS X, each user has his or her own preferences, but locating the file isn't all that much more complicated. Just click on the Home icon while logged in to that user's account, and you'll see a folder labeled Library. Within that folder is the Preferences folder you'll want to save.

> **NOTE**   *The most efficient way to handle all this, however, is just to leave the Users folder in place when reinstalling Mac OS X. That way, when you restart, all of your program and system settings, and the files you've put on your desktop, will be intact.*

Summing Up

As you can see, the process of handling system problems and reinstalling your system software isn't quite as intimidating a process as it seems to be. If you follow the steps in this chapter, you'll get through it most times without serious fuss.

In the next two chapters, we'll cover the highways and byways of hardware upgrades, from RAM to CPU cards. You'll also learn when to decide if the best upgrade for you is actually a brand new Mac.

Chapter 3

The Mac Upgrade Guide:
Peripheral Cards

There are so many possibilities for expanding your Mac, the mind boggles. As a result, I begin this chapter with a bit of trepidation. There's no way I can cover every conceivable installation situation specifically. Instead, I'm going to focus on general areas you need to look out for when you do one of these upgrades. More important, I'll focus primarily on upgrades for Macs that can run Mac OS X.

In this chapter, you'll learn about the kinds of products that are available and the steps to take to be sure your upgrade installation goes as easily as possible—and what to do if your upgrade doesn't work as it should.

Adding Expansion Cards

While some Macs, such as the fashionable Cube and the iMac, are designed to support RAM upgrades and not much else, most desktop Macs are set up to support peripheral cards. These cards can be used to handle a variety of features that will take your Mac to greater heights of usefulness. They include

- **FireWire cards**   The very same high-speed peripheral bus that is standard issue on new desktop Macs can be added to older models. As explained in Chapter 15, FireWire is free of many of the common ills of SCSI. You don't have to set ID numbers or worry about termination. Some very small FireWire devices even draw power from the FireWire port (and they work fine as long as you limit it to one or two), so they don't need a separate AC power supply. In addition to handling such products as hard drives, CD writers, and scanners, FireWire capability lets you capture video from a DV camcorder—all without need of a special video capture board; of course, you do need video-editing software. You'll learn more about this in Chapter 19.

- **Graphic cards**   Even if your Mac has built-in graphics hardware, you may want to look at a graphics card for a second monitor or for speedier performance. Some graphic cards offer special support for games, for example. And some of these cards also support simple video capture, so you can copy desktop video productions right to your camcorder or VCR. New Macs come with graphic cards from ATI and NVIDIA that offer perfectly capable 2D and 3D speeds. If you're in the upgrade market, you can choose from ATI and Formac (NVIDIA's GeForce 3 is provided for G4s with 4X AGP ports only). As this book was written, one company, ProMax Technology, a supplier of hardware for video editors, was also selling a selling a single card that supported two monitors.

NOTE   *Top-of-the-line Power Mac G4s are being sold with a "TwinView" version of the NVIDIA GeForce2 MX graphic card. This version has twice the video memory (64MB, compared to 32MB) and both digital (ADC) and analog outputs that can be attached simultaneously to separate displays.*

CAUTION   *Make sure that the graphic card has the connection port for your monitor. New Apple monitors use a scheme called ADC (Apple Display Connector), which combines digital video, USB, and AC power in a single connector. If you want to run one of those displays on an older Mac, you need a graphic card with, at the very least, DV (digital video) out, plus a special adapter module, such as Dr. Bott's DVIator (which costs around $150). You can also hook up a display with DV capability to a Mac with ADC courtesy of a handy ADC to DV adapter plug from Belkin.*

■ **Network card**   While all new Power Macintosh computers in Apple's line have built-in 10/100/1000Mbs Ethernet networking capability, you may want to add high-speed (or any Ethernet) capability to an older Mac with expansion slots. Such network cards (except for the gigabit variety) are relatively inexpensive, but they can help reduce network bottlenecks. If you are part of a large office network, or want to exploit the faster Ethernet capability of newer Macs, you'll also want to look into a gigabit Ethernet upgrade, which can offer greatly improved file transfer speeds (but, as you'll see in Chapter 17, they're still expensive).

■ **SCSI accelerators**   These peripheral cards can give your Mac a faster SCSI port, the ability to handle extra SCSI devices, or even a SCSI port for Macs that don't have them. If you are performing tasks that require ultra-fast hard drives, such as image editing or video production, such products are useful. Since Mac and PC SCSI accelerator cards are virtually the same, except for ROM chips (sometimes anyway) and driver software, there is a plentiful variety available.

CAUTION   *Before considering a SCSI card, make sure the manufacturer has made it compatible with Mac OS X. At the time this book was written, Adaptec, one of the largest companies offering such products, indicated it would not support some of its older products for Apple's new operating system.*

■ **Serial port cards**   Fed up with juggling modems and serial printers and dealing with software that may be flaky? You can add extra serial ports with an expansion card. This feature is also useful if you have a Mac with USB instead of the older type of serial port (though there are USB-to-serial adapters available, too).

Adding Expansion Cards

CAUTION
Once again, Mac OS X is the big question mark here. While USB isn't an issue, older serial ports are, and the version of Mac OS X shipping when this book was written didn't support the original Mac OS printer and modem ports.

- **USB adapter cards**   If you want to join in the USB revolution and add digital devices, input devices, scanners, and other USB peripherals, these cards are useful. They are also valuable if you want to move a USB device from Macs that support the feature to older models that don't.

- **Video capture boards**   New Macs have FireWire, which lets you directly input and output video from a camcorder or other video device with FireWire ports. But if you have an older video device from which you'd like to capture video, you'll need one of these cards. Some of these products are quite cheap, a couple hundred dollars or less, and are useful for a simple family function or just having a good time. Other video capture boards give you broadcast-quality video and are actually used for commercial video editing.

TIP
Have you run out of expansion ports? Although Mac OS X–compatible Power Macs come with three or four PCI expansion slots, one company, MAGMA (http://www.magma.com/), sells a line of expansion chassis that can add up to 13 extra slots (minus the one it takes up in your Power Mac).

Peripheral Card Installation Tips

Installing a peripheral card on your Mac is no more difficult than adding RAM, and sometimes it's less difficult, especially if you have one of those Macs that require complete logic board disassembly and removal for RAM and cache cards.

CAUTION
When you order a peripheral card for your Mac, make sure you get the right type. Older Macs, mostly those that came out before 1995, used an expansion bus called NuBus. Some models only had a processor direct slot (PDS) for upgrade cards. However, the only Macs that can run Mac OS X have PCI slots and (for most G4s, a single AGP slot, making them compatible with an expansion bus that is also used on PCs). Also, don't take the cross-platform issue too literally. You shouldn't buy a PC-based peripheral card and assume it'll work on a Mac. You may have to get special driver software or swap out a ROM chip to get it to run.

Once you've got the card you want to add to your Mac, here are the steps to follow:

1. First, be sure to install any software that's required for your peripheral card to run. For example, graphic cards use special drivers to provide video acceleration and custom features, such as the capability to switch resolutions with a single set of keystrokes.

2. Shut down your Mac and all attached peripherals.

3. Be sure to disconnect *all* cables, aside from the power cord, from your Mac.

4. Snap open the case. On the beige Power Macintosh G3, you'll also have to move a couple of slide switches to get at the chassis. Consult your manual or Apple's technical information database for instructions that apply to your Mac if it's not immediately obvious from the layout.

5. To drain off static electricity, touch the power supply. (It's usually a big rectangular box with drilled holes, sometimes with a label that displays its power capacity.) If you have a wrist strap, attach the other end to the power supply.

CAUTION
I happen to believe that a wrist strap is the best way to drain static electricity, but I've never run into a problem in an installation without one; I always remember to touch the power supply. Also, if you have thick, static-prone carpeting or you're in a dry climate, prepare to stay put until the installation process is complete.

6. Remove the power cord or turn off the power strip (if it's attached to one) before going to the next step.

7. Locate an empty slot for your peripheral card. Consult the manufacturer's directions about which slots to use. While it shouldn't normally matter, some companies may be specific about such things. And some setups require placing cards with similar functions in adjacent slots, such as for video capture and SCSI acceleration.

CAUTION
Newer Macs come with an AGP and several PCI slots. Never the twain shall meet. You cannot install a card for one standard in the other, so just check the box or directions before you buy a card to make sure you have the right one. Graphic cards come both ways.

Adding Expansion Cards

8. If you are installing a PCI card, you'll probably have to remove a Philips-head screw and perhaps a rear cover to install the card. Depending on the kind of Power Macintosh you have, this may not be necessary for the AGP slot.

9. Holding both sides of the peripheral card, seat it carefully in its slot, making sure you align the pins properly. If the card has an external connection jack, you'll know which direction it points to without having to check the pin layout. Press it firmly until it seems to click into place. Check visually to make sure it's seated at both ends.

10. If you need to tighten it down with a screw, make sure the leading edge of the card aligns with the screw slot (if there is a screw slot), then screw it in. This isn't always easy, as you may have to tug on the edge of the card to get it to align with the slot.

11. Repeat steps 5 through 8 if you're installing more than one peripheral card.

12. When you're finished, close everything up, and be sure the case is good and tight.

CAUTION   *Although it will work, don't try to run your Mac with the case open. Touching the wrong thing may subject you to a slight shock and the Mac to an expensive motherboard failure.*

13. Close the case and snap it shut.

14. Once everything is closed tight, reattach the mouse and keyboard and then the AC cord. Leave the peripheral jacks alone for now; you just want to make sure everything works properly.

15. Turn on your Mac and zap the PRAM. This is done by holding down the COMMAND-OPTION-P-R keys at startup and waiting for two or three startup chords to sound. If your Mac boots properly, you'll want to test a function that accesses the peripheral card's features, such as checking graphic display speed, for a graphic card.

CAUTION   *Zapping the PRAM may reset your startup settings; so, if you were normally booting under Mac OS X, don't be surprised if it starts up under your Mac OS 9.x version instead.*

16. Once you've determined that everything works properly, go ahead and shut down your Mac, and reinstall your regular peripherals.

What If It Won't Boot?

It doesn't happen terribly often, but there's always the possibility of something going wrong. If you have a problem with a peripheral card or CPU upgrade, you may see a gray screen and that's it.

If you encounter a problem of this sort, here are some steps to follow:

■ Shut down your Mac, and recheck the upgrade card. Go through the entire installation process, removing and reinserting the CPU or peripheral upgrade card.

■ Press and hold down the "cuda" switch (as described in the next section) for 30 seconds or so, which resets the logic board to accommodate the new card.

■ Close the case and try restarting, zapping the PRAM again, as described in the previous section.

■ If your Mac still won't boot, shut everything down, open your Mac, and remove the card you installed. If you need to replace it with one you removed (such as a CPU card), do that as part of this process.

■ Close your Mac and again try to boot the computer. If it works this time, you may simply have a defective or incompatible unit. Contact the dealer or manufacturer for assistance; a special ROM or software upgrade (or both) may be required for compatibility with Mac OS X.

CAUTION *Don't assume Mac OS X compatibility without checking the instructions or the manufacturer's Web site. Older peripheral cards may never be made compatible, simply because the cost of developing new software doesn't pay off. The company may, if it's still around, prefer to sell you a new card.*

Using Processor Upgrade Cards: The Good, the Bad, and the Ugly

Beginning with Apple's PCI Power Macs, a new wrinkle was added to your upgrade options: the removable CPU module.

The theory is great: you can upgrade your CPU to a faster version as easily as you could add a graphic card, SCSI card, or any other expansion card. You plug it in, and when you restart, your Mac suddenly becomes much faster. It's somewhat like getting a virtually new Macintosh for a very modest price (assuming the price

Using Processor Upgrade Cards:
The Good, the Bad, and the Ugly

you pay for your CPU upgrade is modest). Just how, though, do the theories stack up to cold, hard reality?

The fact that Mac OS X seems to favor the G4 has made many users of G3 Macs envious, and helped spur the development of such upgrades.

Here's some things to watch out for and expect when you add a new CPU card:

- ■ **You need to install the software first.** Most CPU upgrade cards use some kind of software to either turn on the card's cache feature or activate certain custom features. Some of these features may allow you to speed up the cache to provide slightly more spirited performance. Check the upgrade card's installation manual or instruction sheet for information about what software needs to be installed.

CAUTION *If you are using a CPU upgrade that requires software, you'll want to check for updates whenever you upgrade your Mac system software. The arrival of Mac OS X put the kibosh on processor upgrades from such defunct makers as Newer Technology, although the remaining contenders in the upgrade marketplace, such as Sonnet Technologies, are delivering software solutions designed to deliver compatibility for these older products.*

- ■ **Be careful about jumper switches and dials.** Some CPU upgrade cards are fitted with little jumper switches and dials. These adjustments allow you to configure the upgrade for optimum performance. They will set the speed ratio of the CPU card to the logic board bus speed or the speed of onboard cache, if any. The instructions that come with your upgrade should explain just what sort of changes are wrought by these adjustments. For the most part, it's best to stick with the standard setup. Whenever you do anything to increase the clock speed of your Mac's CPU beyond its rating, you may experience unstable performance, such as frequent crashes. If you opt to try for these changes, you should make them in small increments, checking your Mac's performance for a day or so before moving on. Other than crashes, a symptom of turning the setting too high is the inability to boot, or booting without your Mac's regular startup tone.

NOTE *In addition to possibly causing system crashes, pushing a CPU card too far may also result in premature failure. The best thing to do is just be cautious and conservative. More than likely, you'll hardly notice the slight speed boost.*

■ **You may have problems with SCSI chain devices.** This doesn't happen too often. Most accelerator card manufacturers carefully test their products, but when you upgrade to a different CPU family, such as from a G3 to a G4, you may expect some side effects. The processor upgrade manufacturers have updated their software to clear up this problem, but even if you have the latest and greatest, you should definitely test performance of all your peripheral devices after installation.

NOTE   *A few months before Apple introduced its Power Mac G4 line, they issued a firmware update for the Blue & White G3 models. Officially the update was supposed to improve performance on the PCI bus. Unofficially, it also rendered these computers incapable of using G4 upgrades. I won't get into the political issues of why it happened, except to say that the companies who produced those G4 upgrades managed to deliver their own firmware updates that were designed to eliminate the CPU upgrade block.*

■ **Don't forget the "cuda" switch.** Most Power Macs have a special CPU reset switch on the logic board called *cuda*. In order for your Mac to properly recognize the CPU upgrade, you have to press this switch and hold it down for 10 to 30 seconds. The instructions for CPU upgrade cards are sometimes clear about this subject, and sometimes not. But this little amber-colored switch is located somewhere in your Mac's logic board (where depends on the specific model, so I can only tell you that you need to look carefully for it). A side effect of pressing the cuda switch is that your Mac's date display will return to default (1956), and you'll have to change it back.

CAUTION   *Some Power Macs have two amber switches, one serving the function of the cuda switch, the other for power. The cuda switch will be the one closest to the backup battery.*

■ **New system upgrades may leave you behind.** Even if the card works just fine, there's no guarantee that Apple won't release a system version that will not support the upgrade card. A case in point is Mac OS X, which Apple claimed (long before the software was due to ship) will only support models that ship with a G3 or G4 CPU. Even if you add a G3 to a Mac with an older PowerPC chip, it may not work. That's because the computer's ROM still reports the original CPU type that shipped with the Mac, and that's what Apple's software installers check when a system installation is done. If the ROM says you don't have a G3, it doesn't matter what kind of CPU card you installed.

Using Processor Upgrade Cards:
The Good, the Bad, and the Ugly

NOTE   *Despite this limitation, it's true that the makers of processor upgrades are touting Mac OS X compatibility for many of their products, by virtue of software that will work with the Mac OS X installer. However, if you buy into this sort of upgrade, bear in mind that the upgrade company or the author of such software, and not Apple, will have to provide the technical support, because this is regarded as an unsupported installation.*

■ **A new Mac may be a better choice.**   Even if you can get a CPU upgrade for your Mac that speeds up performance by a factor of several times, the rest of the computer won't be changed. You will still have the same old CD drive and the same old hard drive. If you have an older Mac, you can bet both are relatively slow compared to what Apple offers in their recent product lines. When you consider what it may cost to upgrade those items, it begins to add up. Maybe it's time to hand off that older Mac to another member of your family (or try to sell it), and buy a new one.

NOTE   *I don't want to entirely throw cold water on getting a CPU accelerator for your Mac. If you have a lot invested in RAM and compatible peripherals, such an upgrade may extend the life of your computer, and then it makes a lot of sense to give it some serious thought.*

A Brief Look at the Types of CPU Accelerator Upgrades

The means to upgrade your Mac with a faster CPU varies from model to model. I've collected this very short list of the sort of upgrades that are available for Mac OS X–savvy models (and the previous generation, in case you want to try an unsupported installation):

■ **CPU card**   Beginning with the first-generation PCI Power Macs and some Mac OS clones, you can replace the CPU simply by removing one card and putting in another. For a while, such upgrade prospects proved expensive, but as the cost of G3 CPUs went down, you could find some real bargains in such products. Some manufacturers put so-called ZIF adapters in a CPU card, so they can standardize on a single design for CPU upgrades. See the next bullet point for an explanation about ZIF.

- **ZIF slot** Short for zero insertion force, a ZIF slot is part of the G3 and G4 Power Macintosh with PCI graphics. To install a CPU module, you simply undo a heat sink, and then lift a small latch to loosen the module. You lift it up, replace it, close the latch, reseat the heat sink, and you're done. If there's a downside, it's that all those pins beneath a ZIF module are delicate and can be easily bent, so be careful if you do this sort of upgrade.

- **Lift out processor slot** All but the first-generation Power Macintosh G4 put the processor in a convenient slot that you can remove, after popping out the heat sink. Such products as the Sonnet Technologies Encore/ST G4 Duet, which adds two processors to a single processor G4, can be installed in minutes this way. Just take the same precautions that you do for any other processor module installation.

Case History **The Case of the Recessed ZIF Slot**

For several months, I had a Blue & White Power Mac G3 hanging around, doing occasional duty. But I finally decided to install Mac OS X on it. As most folks who have tried Mac OS X can attest, performance is much more spirited when a G4 lies under the hood.

So I decided to take the plunge and got one of Sonnet Technology's Encore G4/500 ZIF modules to give the old box a new lease on life. This proved to be the beginning of an unexpected journey, one that revealed an unexpected twist and turn.

Now this isn't the first time I've run a ZIF upgrade card on that Mac. Briefly, it had one of Sonnet's 500MHz G3 upgrades, although that module has long since returned to its manufacturer (product reviewers don't get to keep the hardware they review).

To prepare for the G4 upgrade, I had to make sure the G3's boot ROM was flashed. This is the result of a peculiar property in Apple's version 1.1 firmware for the Blue & White, which I briefly referred to earlier. Although its avowed purpose was to offer "improved performance of PCI devices including built-in FireWire ports, improved support of NetBooting, and minor improvements to Open Firmware for Mac OS X Server," there was an unexpected side effect.

Apple also put in code that, in effect, disables G4 processor upgrades. I won't get into the more recent hoopla over a certain Apple firmware upgrade that made some models refuse to recognize RAM that was considered "off spec." I don't necessarily subscribe to the rampant conspiracy theories about such matters.

Fortunately, the processor upgrade makers quickly found a way around that hidden feature, and, as far as I know, all the products do work on Blue & Whites once the maker's firmware updates are used. But there's another hidden property on some of these computers that I only discovered through personal experience.

With the usual precautions about discharging my hands on the power supply and using a wrist strap (if one is available) before popping the heat sink that covers the ZIF slot, I proceeded to remove the old module and install the new one. As an added precaution, I pressed in the motherboard reset ("cuda") switch, which lies just below the battery on the Blue & White (the button right below that switch, by the way, is a power switch).

I snapped shut the case, plugged everything in, and restarted. I heard the familiar startup chord, and then … nothing, not even a few "chimes of death." So what went wrong? Did a wayward spark of static electricity do in the card or the motherboard? Just to be sure, I restored the G3 card, and it seemed to go through a normal startup process.

I rang up Sonnet and gave them the equivalent of a "Houston, we've got a problem" report. The technical support person I talked with announced proudly, "Oh, your G3 must have a recessed ZIF slot."

"A what?"

It seems that a few Blue & Whites shipped with a ZIF slot in which the center rows of pins were slightly recessed. As a result, processor makers had to design the pins of their upgrade modules to be just a little bit longer to make proper contact on those units. Unfortunately, the G4 card I had received was one of those rare ones with the shorter pins.

It's not something that's obvious to the naked eye unless you put the two modules side by side and compare them. Best I could do was examine the Apple G3 module and the Encore, and the difference in pin length was subtle but obvious. Why is this so? It doesn't matter. Clearly these computers were designed without serious expectation that third-party processor upgrades would be so ubiquitous (or was it another "secret" way to keep them from working?).

Regardless, a lesson was learned, and a few days later, I had my new processor upgrade and Mac OS X both coexisting comfortably on that old Power Mac.

Summing Up

Although some Apple products, such as the iBook and iMac, aren't eligible for much in the way of upgrades, quite a few are. With a little judicious selection and careful attention to installation, you can gain new features and better performance with your upgrade product.

In the next chapter, I'll review the other part of doing an upgrade, which even an iBook or iMac can handle—a RAM upgrade.

Using Processor Upgrade Cards:
The Good, the Bad, and the Ugly

Chapter 4

The Mac Upgrade Guide: Dealing with RAM Upgrade Pitfalls

Having discovered the tips and tricks of installing expansion cards and CPU upgrades in Chapter 3, now's the time to get to the main event—RAM.

True, installing RAM on your Mac isn't always as easy as you might like, but you should be able to come through those installations like a champ. I have installed RAM in probably one or two hundred Macs over the years (including PowerBooks and iMacs) and have never lost a patient (although I've had, as you'll see later in this chapter, some odd experiences).

However, there's also that old adage that if something can go wrong, very likely it will go wrong at one time or another. I have written this chapter to cover the possible pitfalls of a RAM upgrade and what to do should the worst happen.

Yes, It's All Right for You to Add a RAM Upgrade

In the old days, Apple gave you a stern warning. You could void your new product warranty if you added anything but an expansion card or internal drive to your Mac.

Fortunately, that policy has been liberalized (and certainly it's moot if the warranty has expired). For the newest models, Apple will even give you detailed instructions on how to do a RAM upgrade. If you have a regular Blue & White Power Macintosh G3 or G4, it's so simple, instructions are hardly required.

For the iBook, Apple even put a little label inside the computer itself, so you can see where the upgrade module fits. The exceptions to the rule are those long-retired compact Mac models, such as the Plus and Classic. Opening the case on those models exposed you to the high-voltage video display chassis, and there is a potential shock hazard. Even the manufacturers of displays and televisions warn you not to poke your hands in those places.

CAUTION   *Although just about any Mac can receive a RAM upgrade, take care if your Mac is under warranty. If your Mac is damaged as a result of installing a RAM upgrade, Apple is off the hook. It's your problem. But if you take care in installing the upgrade, this shouldn't be anything to worry about.*

How to Avoid RAM Upgrade Damage

Mac RAM installations are fairly straightforward, once you get past the process of removing the necessary parts to get to the RAM slots, a problem that afflicts the first-generation iMacs (Rev. A through Rev. D). As I said in the previous chapter,

About Those Free RAM Upgrade Offers

With RAM prices plummeting to ever-lower levels (assuming they don't go up again by the time this book is published), a number of dealers (especially mail order and Web-based) offer free RAM with a new Mac. Entry-level PowerBooks and iMacs are eligible for an extra 64MB or 128MB, and the more expensive models get up to 256MB.

The only catch: You have to pay a small installation fee, usually around $30. Is it worth paying $30 for something that doesn't cost all that much more on the retail market? Yes. When the dealer installs the RAM for you, they will generally test your new computer for proper operation and will not ship the unit to you if it doesn't work. Even though you can do it yourself on many Macs in a minute or two (I have it down to less than a minute on a G4), the service charge for the free RAM upgrade is more than worth the bother.

The end result is a new Mac fully outfitted with just about all the memory you'll need without you having to snap the case open. Just remember, though, that the registration presentation that normally comes with a new Mac will not appear when you first boot your new computer. You'll usually find the Register program on your Mac's desktop, if you choose to use it (your warranty is actually verified by serial number and the sales slip, not whether you sent that registration form in to Apple).

How to Avoid RAM Upgrade Damage

you need to take a few precautions to make sure you don't fry your Mac's logic board in the process of installing any other sort of upgrade inside your Mac. That's because all of these electronic components are quite delicate and susceptible to damage by the elements and static electricity.

That's why I recommend using a wrist strap if your memory chip supplier includes one (and if you get one from another purchase, keep it on hand). If you don't have a wrist strap, it's not a catastrophe. Touching your Mac's power supply (after it's shut down, of course, but with the power cord still in place) should be quite enough to drain static electricity.

Here are some other considerations:

■ **RAM retaining clamps are delicate.**   Depending on the kind of Mac you have, the little clamps that lock your RAM in place are either plastic or thin metal. Either way, they are delicate, and if you push, tug, or bend them, they can break off. These parts are not replaceable; if you break them, the RAM slot may not be usable, and you'll have to replace the logic board if you need to install that extra RAM.

■ **Orient the RAM properly.** Each RAM module has something in its design to let you know in which direction it should be placed. You may find separate sets of pins with different widths, for example. Just make sure the pin layout on the module exactly matches the one in the slots, and you won't go wrong. It is possible to force it in the wrong direction, and pay the price of damaging your RAM or the slot.

■ **Don't be embarrassed to ask for help.** While the newest Apple computers are designed for simple RAM installations, the same isn't true for the early iMacs, which were not designed with easy RAM upgrades in mind. If you have doubts, it's better to pay a professional to do the work for you. Many dealers charge a fixed rate for RAM upgrades, regardless of the complexity. A local Mac user group may be able to assist as well. The small amount you pay is a lot less than what it would cost if you damaged something.

NOTE *A RAM supplier's Web site may also have information on installing upgrades. For example, The Chip Merchant (http://www. thechipmerchant.com) has a series of FAQs at their site that cover common Mac RAM installation questions and troubleshooting. NewerRAM (http://www.newerram.com), originally part of Newer Technologies (a now-defunct manufacturer of processor upgrades), has a set of RAM installation instructions in Adobe Acrobat format.*

Checking RAM Compatibility

When you install RAM, it doesn't put up a warning label to let you know that you've installed the wrong chip. The only surface indication is that the pins line up and the chip fits, and that's about it. Arcane items such as voltage requirements and the design elements of the module are not things you can easily detect except, perhaps, for a packing slip or a box or container from the vendor, or a little set of numbers on the module itself. And, more often than not, the packing slip doesn't contain information that's easy to translate. The only way you can test your RAM after installation is to actually boot your computer.

However, if you have the wrong kind of RAM, that may be too late. You could risk damage to the module or perhaps the logic board by installing the wrong type. So I must emphasize that, before you attempt installation, you check the original packaging or invoice to see if it has the proper labeling. If in doubt, call the dealer and ask what you need to do to confirm you have the right product.

Not All RAM Is the Same

Wouldn't it be great if all RAM chips were the same? When you buy a new Mac, you could simply move the module from the old model to the new, thereby extending your investment.

Alas, this is not to be. There are a number of different types of RAM available for Macs of one sort or another, and you cannot mix and match. What works with one model may cause problems with another, even if it looks exactly the same.

Here's a very basic guide to the kind of RAM that's available for recent Macs. Your best approach, when you buy RAM, is to make sure your dealer knows exactly which Mac you have, so there's no room for confusion. Some RAM modules may come in packaging that lists the make and model it's designed for, but since most of the time Apple uses industry-standard RAM for many of their newest models, the label may not be informative.

CAUTION *Using RAM that is not suitable for your Mac could damage the module itself or your Mac's logic board. If you have the slightest doubt about whether the memory upgrade is suitable for your Mac, check the technical specifications that came with your Mac or ask your dealer for assistance.*

■ **DIMMs**   Beginning with the PCI Power Macs, the second generation, Apple went to something called DIMMs (Dual Inline Memory Modules). The larger, 168-pin DIMM modules could be installed in single units, though some of those Power Macs and Mac OS clones benefit from interleaving, if you install identical DIMMs in matching memory banks (Bank A and Bank B).

NOTE *I refer to interleaving for information only, since the models that offer this feature do not officially support Mac OS X.*

■ **SDRAM**   The first-generation Power Macintosh G3 and PowerBook G3 models incorporated still another variation on the memory theme, SDRAM (Synchronous Dynamic Random Access Memory). The word "synchronous" means that the clock speed of this sort of RAM chip synchronizes with the Mac's CPU. Obviously, the size of a RAM upgrade module that fits a PowerBook won't work on a desktop Mac.

- **SO-DIMMs**   This kind of RAM module (Small Outline Dual Inline Memory Module) runs on both G3 PowerBooks and first-generation iMacs. You'll need to check with your dealer as to which sort of RAM is required for your model.

- **PC100 and PC133 DIMMs**   Beginning with the Blue & White Power Macintosh G3 line (and the second generation, or slot-loading, iMacs), Apple went to a type of SDRAM that would support the 100Mhz system bus. PC100, as the name implies, is a standard for RAM used on PCs as well. The year 2001 Power Mac G4s went to a 133MHz system bus and PC133 RAM. As with other types of RAM, you need to make sure you buy a module that supports the model you have. Not all DIMMs are created equal.

CAUTION   *While PC133 RAM should be backward compatible with older models, the same isn't true the other way around. Putting PC100 in a Mac that requires PC133 may result in the failure to boot or frequent crashes. Check the product labels.*

I have not tried to cover all subdivisions of RAM types available on various Macs, and won't even attempt to predict the future. As soon as Apple standardizes on one type of RAM module, it seems they are apt to find still another kind for another model line.

How Do I Know What to Add?

There are many ways to skin a cat, and many logic board layouts to confront, not to mention the kind of RAM chips you need.

If you still have it, the first and best resource is the original manual that came with your Mac or the technical information booklet. If neither is available, check out Apple's AppleSpec database, which is available to view or download directly from their Web site at http://www.info.apple.com/applespec/applespec.taf.

Another helpful resource is a RAM vendor, NewerRAM (at http://www. newerram.com). Not only do they provide a wealth of information at their Web site about the various sorts of RAM available for Macs (and those long-gone Mac OS clones), they also offer a free program, GURU (see Figure 4-1), an easy way to check on the RAM needs of your Mac. You can download the latest version of GURU directly from their Web site.

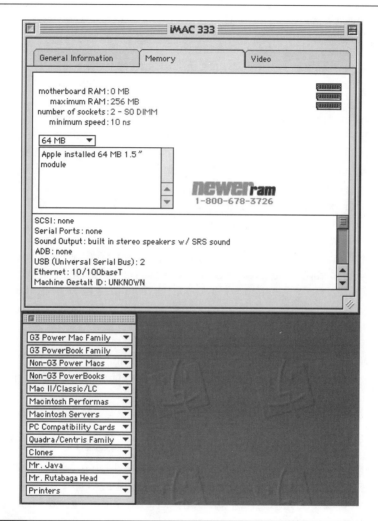

FIGURE 4-1   GURU lets you tap a database of RAM requirements for virtually every Mac, Mac OS clone, and Apple printer.

Why the Price Difference?

RAM prices are volatile, sometimes more so than the price of oil on the world market. You'll find upgrades selling for $50 one week, and maybe quite a bit more (or less) the next. You'll also find widely varying prices from vendor to vendor.

Market conditions in Asia, where a large amount of the world's RAM chip supply is produced, can also affect the process, in addition to natural disasters (such as the major earthquake that occurred in Taipei at the time this first edition of this book was written in 1999, which inflated prices for a while).

So the question arises: Does it make a difference? Isn't memory a commodity product?

Here's a simple guide to memory purchases. Most of the world's memory chips are produced by the same basic set of manufacturers. They are generally produced to meet a similar set of specifications. But it's up to the RAM vendor to test the modules and make sure that they do indeed work as advertised.

When you buy RAM, don't hesitate to shop around, and don't hesitate to negotiate with a dealer, if you're making a large system purchase. Not all prices are fixed, and a dealer may be happy to sacrifice a little profit on a large order to keep a customer.

If you're buying RAM from a dealer that strictly specializes in RAM and other upgrades, you'll want to subject them to the same sort of scrutiny to which you subject any business from whom you want to make a purchase. Check the company out with the Better Business Bureau or consumer agency in their home city. Check online message boards, in newsgroups or on AOL or CompuServe, and see what other customers have to say about these vendors.

You should also consult the product warranty. Some vendors offer "lifetime" warranties, which means they are honor-bound to replace the RAM upgrade module if it fails.

Adding RAM Upgrades to Regular Desktop Macs

You'd think with the easiest-to-use operating system, Mac users would have a relatively easy task when adding a RAM upgrade. But this isn't always the case. Apple doesn't seem to have given due consideration to the consequences of their design decisions in laying out the internal workings of some models.

Here are potential pitfalls:

■ **Nightmare installations**   The Blue & White Power Mac G3, the Power Mac G4, and the earliest modular Macs (such as the II series, the IIcx, IIci, and so on) were conveniently designed for simple RAM upgrades. Not so with the first-generation iMacs, the ones with the slide-out CD tray. Although a straightforward process, you need to remove a subassembly containing the logic board and other components to get at the top RAM slot. A heat sink must be pried open and the processor daughtercard removed from the bottom RAM slot.

CAUTION   *Before you do your RAM upgrade, be sure you have your toolkit handy. Depending on the make and model, you'll need a regular flat-edged and a Philips-head screwdriver (or perhaps a miniature Philips-head for an iBook or PowerBook). If the memory vendor supplied such a tool, be sure to put the wrist strap on either hand, then attach the clip at the other end to your Mac's power supply as soon as the case is opened.*

A Basic RAM Upgrade How-To

Once you get your RAM upgrade, you only need to make a few simple preparations and you're ready to begin the installation process.

TIP   *Apple System Profiler, an application available in Mac OS X's Utility folder, will report on your Mac's actual memory configuration. Before you go to the bother of opening the case and encountering a surprise, check the listing on the opening screen, under Memory Overview, which displays your Mac's built-in memory setup, so you can see which slots are filled and what size RAM is being used.*

The following steps are presented as a general set of guidelines, since almost every Mac model family has a different set of instructions that apply to them. But if you follow the process with care, you'll be able to handle a RAM upgrade on just about any Mac to come down the pike:

1. Shut down your Mac and all attached peripherals.

2. Disconnect *all* external cables from your Mac except for the power cord (you'll see why in a moment).

3. Unscrew or snap open the case. On the iBook or PowerBook, you'll need to remove the keyboard and a heat sink to get at the RAM upgrade slot. Consult your manual or Apple's technical information database for instructions that apply to your Mac if it's not immediately obvious from the layout.

4. Touch the power supply (it's usually a big rectangular box with drilled holes, often having a label indicating its power capacity). This helps drain

off static electricity. If you have a wrist strap, attach the other end to the power supply.

5. Go ahead and remove the power cord; don't have the unit plugged in as you complete the process (or at least turn off the power strip, if the unit is attached to one).

6. If necessary, remove any parts that surround the RAM slots. This situation applies to Apple laptops and the iMac.

7. Locate the empty slots for your RAM upgrade. If they are already filled, you may need to recheck the configuration (see the tip earlier in this section about running Apple System Profiler first).

8. Position your RAM upgrade module so the pins precisely match the layout of the ones in the slot (they'll only install properly in one direction).

9. Place each RAM module in position and snap into place. On some models, you have to insert at an angle, making sure the RAM is seated in the slots, then snap into the upright position (or straight down on an iMac, iBook, or PowerBook). In any case, you may have to gently move a retaining clip aside.

CAUTION *Don't force the RAM module into place. You risk damaging the slot or the delicate pins that enclose it, which would require a logic board replacement.*

TIP *If the empty slot is between other RAM modules, you may want to remove the module in front of the one you want to install, to make installation easier.*

10. Repeat steps 8 and 9 for each RAM module you intend to install.

CAUTION *It's a good idea to stay put for the entire upgrade process, especially on a carpeted floor, where you may give yourself a new dose of static electricity if you walk around the room. Best to do your bathroom visits before you begin.*

11. Recheck the RAM modules to make sure they are properly seated.

12. Reinstall the logic board or any other parts that are required in the reassembly process.

> CAUTION
>
> *In general, it's a bad idea to even try to run your Mac without closing everything up. While some modular models do run with the case open, you risk a possible shock hazard and damage to delicate components if you touch the wrong thing when it's running.*

13. Close the case, keyboard, or whatever parts were loosened during the installation process.

> CAUTION
>
> *Don't be surprised if you have to spend a few minutes aligning the bottom cover on an iMac or the keyboard on an Apple laptop. Just be careful before tightening things down. For example, if the keyboard on the iBook or PowerBook isn't seated just right, you may not be able to put the unit into Sleep mode (although I haven't seen any damage resulting from the misalignment).*

14. Reattach the mouse and keyboard, and then the AC cord. Leave the peripheral jacks alone for now; you just want to make sure everything works properly.

15. Turn on your Mac. You should hear the startup chord and it should proceed through the normal Mac OS X startup process without incident. If everything works properly, go right to the Apple menu, and open the window labeled About This Mac. Verify that the amount of memory listed is equal to the total amount installed.

16. If the RAM installation is successful, shut everything down (if necessary) and reattach your peripheral components, such as hard drives, scanners, and so on. After your memory upgrade has been installed, it's a good idea to spend some time running your favorite programs to make sure that there are no mysterious performance problems.

Adding RAM Upgrades to the iMac

While Apple has made moves toward simple RAM upgrades in their product line, the first generations of iMacs were a throwback to the bad old days of headaches and frustration.

In order to upgrade iMac RAM on these units, you literally have to tear it apart, first by removing the back cover, then by pulling off cable harnesses and extracting the logic board. Worse, if you want to change RAM on the lower slot, you must remove another heat sink and pry out the processor daughtercard. As clever as Apple's industrial design is from the outside, on the inside, it's a hassle to upgrade.

Fortunately, Apple resolved such headaches in clever fashion with the second-generation or "slot-loading" iMacs. With these models, you easily access a RAM or an AirPort networking card slot simply by opening an access panel at the bottom of the unit. You don't even need a screwdriver—you can use a quarter to turn the screw to release the panel.

But here are some things you'll want to consider if you choose to upgrade your first-generation iMac's RAM:

■ **The rear cover can be difficult to remove.** The first part of the RAM upgrade process on those first-generation iMacs is to loosen and remove a Philips-head screw and lift off the back cover. In my experience, they tend to stick, and you may find yourself dragging hard on the pull handle to get it apart. The iMac's polycarbonate case is sturdy, however, so if you have to give it a couple of stiff tugs, don't fret. Tugging too hard, however, may break the pull handle (or the bottom cover assembly), as I learned once. However, replacement parts for the iMac's case aren't expensive.

CAUTION *Once you get the rear cover off, place your iMac screen face-down on a soft cloth or paper towel to prevent the face of the display from being scratched.*

■ **Move the cables out of the way.** Once you've pulled off the back cover, you have to remove several sets of cables from jacks on the logic board. After the cables have been unplugged, spread them aside to give enough room to pull the logic board assembly out. This is a slightly awkward process, as the cables tend to catch on the edges of the chassis.

■ **Pull the logic board assembly out carefully.**   The chassis includes the hard drive and CD drive as well, and you'll want to take care in removing everything to avoid the possibility of damage to any of these delicate components.

■ **Don't tighten the screws too much.**   After you install your RAM upgrade on an iMac, you have to replace a heat sink. Screw everything in hand-tight. Don't use a power screwdriver and don't make things too tight. If the threads are stripped, you'll be in for a repair bill if you need to take things apart again (either for a larger RAM module or in case the RAM upgrade doesn't function properly).

■ **Put everything back together before testing.**   It's all right to leave the back cover off while you test your RAM upgrade for proper performance. But everything else should be placed back in position and screwed together.

■ **Consult About This Mac.**   After you reboot your upgraded iMac, go right to the Apple menu and bring up the About This Mac window to check that the amount of memory is correct. If the numbers don't add up, shut down, take everything apart, and reseat your RAM upgrade module. If the RAM still isn't recognized, remove it, pack everything up, and contact the dealer from whom you got the RAM upgrade.

TIP

If you want further information on installing RAM on a first-generation iMac, you can retrieve two handy technical information documents from Apple's Web site on the subject. The URL for the first part is http:// til.info.apple.com/techinfo.nsf/artnum/n43012. The second part of the instructions shows up as a link on the first page, but is available separately at http://til.info.apple.com/techinfo.nsf/artnum/n43013.

Adding RAM Upgrades to iBooks and PowerBooks

The PowerBook is another Apple product line where upgrades have traditionally been, shall we say, a little dicey. It's not that it is so hard to open a PowerBook's case. But up until the so-called "Wall Street" PowerBook G3 arrived, you needed to use special screwdrivers, of the Torx 8 and Torx 10 variety (with six sides), to undo the screws.

Adding RAM Upgrades to the iMac

NOTE   *An earlier version of the PowerBook G3, which used the same chassis as the PowerBook 3400, still requires Torx screwdrivers to open the case for RAM installation. However, since this model is not supported by Mac OS X, the issue is essentially academic.*

Why Apple would choose such an unusual form factor is anyone's guess, but nonetheless that's the way it is, to quote the famous phrase of a former TV news anchor.

Fortunately, with the arrival of the upgraded PowerBook G3 product line and the iBook, Apple got the idea and took steps to make RAM installations simple. They even provide step-by-step instructions in the manuals, or, in the case of the iBook, inside the unit itself.

Here are some basics about PowerBook RAM installation:

- **Turn it off.**   Many of you keep your PowerBooks in Sleep mode most of the time. Before you do a RAM installation, don't forget to bring the PowerBook back to life, and shut it down. Then remove the battery and any expansion bay or PC card peripherals (assuming you have a PowerBook with an expansion bay slot) before you attempt your RAM upgrade.

- **Protect the screen.**   On some PowerBook models, you will be lifting the keyboard and placing it atop the delicate LCD display. Protect the screen with a paper towel or soft cloth before you rest the keyboard against it.

- **Watch out for paper-thin cables.**   The consequence of the clever miniaturization of the PowerBook is ultra-small components. This is especially true for the connection cables inside, which are paper-thin and subject to easy damage.

- **Look for a loose video cable on G3 "Wall Street" PowerBooks.**   Some of the G3 PowerBooks using 13.3-inch screens suffered from weird screen defects, such as a white vertical band appearing at one end of the display. The cause was traced to a loose video cable. Since the RAM upgrade on these models sits at the left of the video cable, make sure the cable is plugged in tightly while you've got the case opened.

NOTE
If weird screen symptoms don't disappear when you reseat the video cable, contact Apple's customer service department or your dealer for service. In some instances, the cable may have to be replaced with a newer design (I know, it happened to me).

- **Don't force the RAM to fit.**   As I said, the PowerBook's guts are more delicate than other Macs. Don't try to force the RAM module to fit. If you have a problem, contact your dealer for assistance. Even the most complex PowerBook RAM installations can be done by your dealer in less than a half hour, and they shouldn't charge you more than a very basic service fee if you'd rather have them do the job.

- **Don't try to use a PowerBook with an open case.**   You should put everything back together before you attempt to use your PowerBook with its new RAM upgrade.

- **Check About This Mac when you're done.**   As soon as you complete your PowerBook RAM installation, boot your PowerBook or iBook and go right to the Apple menu. Choose About This Mac from the Apple menu and check to make sure that the numbers listed for your laptop's built-in memory are correct. If not, shut everything down, open the case, and remove and reinstall the RAM upgrade. If it still doesn't work, contact your dealer for assistance.

How to Know If RAM Is Properly Installed

RAM installation is usually an either/or process. If you have seated the modules properly in their slots, your final test is to boot your Mac. If it starts up, you know (well, usually) that you've properly installed the RAM upgrade.

However, it's not always clear-cut, and sometimes a slight misalignment of the module in the slot will allow your Mac to boot most times, but sometimes you'll encounter intermittent startup problems. My Case History for this chapter covers one such incident, which actually occurred to one of my clients only a few weeks before I wrote this chapter.

Case History

Intermittent Startups

The problems were vexing to my client. After installing a RAM upgrade, sometimes the Mac wouldn't start at all, and on occasion, all that was heard were the dreaded "chimes of death" (see the next section), as if someone was trying to tune up a musical instrument.

It was clear the Mac was telling the client that there was a hardware problem of some sort. I was assured the RAM was installed correctly, and that the problem was rare. On the other hand, the Mac would crash just a little too often to be normal, so I suggested it wouldn't hurt to check into the situation.

The client was nervous. This was the Mac he used to write advertising copy and press releases; if it went down even for a short time, he'd blow his deadlines.

When I arrived at the client's small suburban office, I shut the system down and pried the cover off the Mac, an entry-level PowerPC that was several years old. I inspected the RAM chips, and noticed that one of the four modules didn't seem to be seated fully. As a precaution, I removed, then reinstalled, all four modules, making sure each component was firmly seated in the slot. I restarted the Mac, and it worked just fine.

Then the client proceeded to work with a few programs that had been generating those awful crashes, and the crashes were gone. I shut down the computer several times, then rebooted with no return of the awful symptoms.

The problem was gone, never to return. That ever-so-slight degree to which the RAM was misaligned was enough to cause unstable performance. However, as you'll see later in this chapter, not all RAM installation problems are cured by simply reseating the RAM.

Interpreting the Signs That Something Went Wrong

When your Mac boots, it goes through a basic routine of self-testing. The hardware is checked, and then your Mac's hardware looks for the presence of a working System Folder. At this point, you'll see your Happy Mac face, which tells you that the first part of the process is done.

But if something is drastically wrong, the boot process will come to a screeching halt (and you can sometimes interpret that phrase literally). Instead of a normal startup process, one of the following symptoms may occur:

- **Chimes of death**   Your Mac's screen will remain dark, and you'll hear several musical tones. They usually signify that the RAM test has failed. This is a catastrophic failure, meaning that one or more RAM chips is not properly installed or is defective. On some models, the sound will more closely resemble that of a car crashing.

NOTE   *Other, less common causes of this problem include defective logic boards, CPU cards, or video RAM. But if the symptoms accompany the installation of new RAM, that's the first place to look for a solution.*

- **Sad Mac**   There are a bunch of Sad Mac messages, but they all signify some sort of hardware-related issue. Sometimes it's hard drive related, sometimes related to RAM problems.

NOTE   *A Sad Mac screen sometimes occurs when a SyQuest removable disk cartridge is inserted in one of their removable drives. The fast solution to this problem is simply to eject the cartridge and restart. Even though SyQuest is no longer manufacturing drives, a Web site is still maintained at www.syquest.com to provide technical support and removable media.*

- **Gray screen**   This sort of problem usually relates to something other than the RAM, such as a problem loading a hard drive device driver, a graphic card problem, a SCSI-related conflict (assuming you have a Mac with built-in SCSI or a SCSI card), or another hardware issue. But if it follows a RAM installation, you'll have a likely cause for the problem.

- **Dark screen**   This symptom may indicate bad RAM, but if the symptom isn't accompanied by one of those dreadful sounds I mentioned earlier, it could signify other problems. These include a logic board, CPU card, or power supply failure, or a bad PRAM battery. Problems with your Mac's graphic card (loose or defective) can also contribute to this symptom, not to mention problems with your Mac's display. I cover this subject in more detail in Chapter 3 and Chapter 10.

Interpreting the Signs That
Something Went Wrong

NOTE   *Before you concern yourself over the hardware, first tighten everything up, and if that doesn't help, go ahead and replace the PRAM (or backup) battery. It is a common cause of such problems, and the PRAM battery is cheap enough to replace.*

Startup Failure Solutions

Sometimes just restarting your Mac may be sufficient to get things working properly, but more often than not, you need to do a little sleuthing to locate the cause of the trouble.

Here are some things to check:

- **Your new RAM installation**   Remove and replace your Mac's RAM upgrade module. Visually check to be sure each module is properly installed. It should be a pretty snug fit, and the pins should be fully or mostly seated in the RAM slot. If anything looks a little loose, you may get total failure or an intermittent failure (see my Case History, earlier in this chapter, for further details). The best solution is just to remove the RAM and reseat the module, making sure it's seated properly. You'll feel a little "clunk" when it snaps in place. If you run into a real problem making it fit properly (and sometimes it takes a somewhat energetic push), remove the module and check with the dealer to make sure it's the right type for your Mac. As I said, you can't visually inspect for internal differences; all you can do is make sure that the pins line up with the slots and the chip is pointed in the right direction.

- **Failure of another component**   Even if you took care in draining static electricity during your RAM installation, if one of the hardware components on your Mac is poised for failure, this could be the time for it to occur. You'll want to remove your RAM upgrade and, if necessary, restore your previous RAM module or modules. Once you slap everything together again, verify for proper operation. If the Mac still refuses to boot, contact your dealer about possible service.

The Difficult Symptoms of Intermittent RAM Failures

When your Mac refuses to boot, at least you know there's a problem, and you have some areas to explore to solve it. But not all RAM-related problems are so easy to spot. In fact, most times, the failure will only rear its head at random, thus making the process of figuring out a cause ever so difficult.

If you've looked at a RAM upgrade or two, you've seen that it has at least several memory chips on it. If even one of those chips fails, completely or in part, you'll begin to experience strange symptoms on your Mac. You'll encounter crashes for no good reason. You'll try each and every one of the diagnostic steps I've covered in this book, to no avail.

Routine test procedures just won't show anything wrong. Your Mac will seem to be working just fine, except for those rare, unexpected crashes.

But if the onset of those symptoms follows a RAM upgrade, you'll have an indication that this may be where to look for a solution to the problem.

A Convenient Method for Testing RAM

Apple dealers use a program from the manufacturer called MacTest Pro to do their RAM tests. It's quite thorough, but as slow as the blazes. Figure on it taking from 20 to 40 minutes per MB of RAM, depending on the speed of your Mac. Imagine how long a typical desktop Mac loaded up with 256MB or 512MB of RAM would take if you ran this sort of test on it.

Fortunately, you don't have to be a dealer to test your Mac's RAM. Your option is a handy program from MicroMat called TechTool Pro. As I explain in Chapter 13, one of the important components of TechTool Pro is its ability to check and repair hard drive directory damage and optimize the drive.

NOTE
There is a free version of this program, called simply TechTool, which is designed to zap your Mac's PRAM and rebuild the desktop (the latter is a function you still need under Mac OS 9.x). The advanced diagnostic features are reserved for the retail version of the product. In addition, Apple will give you a modified version of the program, called TechTool Deluxe, if you sign up for the version of their AppleCare extended warranty program that was introduced in October 1999.

Among the many features of TechTool Pro is the ability to test your Mac's RAM and report if there are any problems. You have a number of test options, depending on how extensive a test you want to run.

Here's how they work (this description applies to version 2 or later):

NOTE
TechTool's RAM tests run most efficiently if you boot your Mac with the Classic OS with extensions off. This is done by restarting and holding down the SHIFT key until you see an "Extensions Disabled" message. If your Mac successfully completes the test, go ahead and restart normally.

1. Go to the System Preferences application, and choose your Classic Mac OS from the Startup preference panel.

2. After restart, launch TechTool Pro.

3. Choose Standard from the Interface menu (the choice will be grayed out if that option is already selected).

4. Uncheck all diagnostic options except for RAM. This will produce a screen such as the one shown in Figure 4-2. The test will also include the PRAM, ROM, and VRAM.

5. If there's a problem with your Mac's RAM or any of the other components being tested, you'll see an onscreen dialog explaining what is wrong and

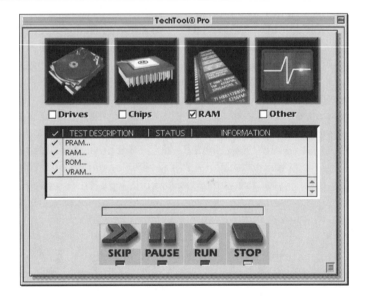

FIGURE 4-2 Since a Mac OS X–savvy version of TechTool Pro wasn't available when this book was written you'll be using the Classic Mac OS version.

what MicroMat suggests you do to solve the problem. If the Mac is all right, you'll also see a report to that effect (see Figure 4-3.). You can read the report on your Mac's screen, or save or print it for later review.

If your Mac is still displaying weird symptoms, and the RAM tests and all your other diagnostic measures produce a big zero, contact the dealer from whom you purchased the RAM for further assistance. At that point, the complexity of the problem may be beyond what you can diagnose in your home or office.

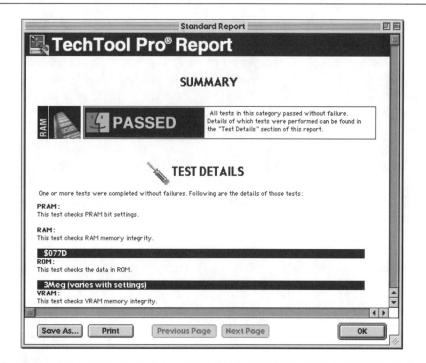

FIGURE 4-3   Tech Tool Pro has successfully completed an extended RAM test.

Case History

The Case of the Temperamental RAM Upgrade

All right, I thought, it's time to take out that old grape 266MHz iMac and see just how well it could handle Mac OS X. I heard the horror stories, for example, one involving a Macworld writer, a truly awful experience that involved chronic crashes, even after several disk formatting attempts.

I didn't have time to endure too many hardships. I decided to give it just one chance; if it worked, it worked. If not, I would just reformat the drive and restore its previous contents. Fortunately, the first part of the setup process went without a hitch. I opted not to concern myself with multiple partitions, and put everything on a single partition. Within a short time, I had Mac OS 9.1 and Mac OS X successfully running.

Unfortunately, performance was dreadfully slow, because this particular iMac only had 96MB of RAM. Sad to think that, at the beginning of 2000, Apple was assuring me that OS X would run fine on an iMac with only 64MB. How things change.

So I went ahead and ordered a 128MB RAM module, which arrived a few days later. While RAM installation on those early-generation iMacs can be annoying, because you have to pull the chassis to get to the slots, it's a pretty straightforward process, which I've got down to just over 10 minutes. Soon I rebooted the iMac—only to have it crash shortly after the Mac OS X desktop loaded.

A restart, a PRAM zap, but still no go. Oh well, the RAM was cheap, maybe it was out of spec. So I rang up the memory supplier and requested a replacement. The next day, I gave it another attempt, and the new chip was no better than the old, despite the assurances of the vendor that the RAM had been tested and was suited for a Rev. C iMac. What to do? Rather than request another replacement, I decided to do the exotic, upon the suggestion of the dealer's technical support staff. First, I installed the RAM module, all by itself, in the iMac's lower slot; this process requires removal of the daughtercard on which the G3 processor resides. Over the next hour or so I managed every possible combination, including putting one 128MB module on the lower slot, the second on the upper slot.

But the startup crashes persisted. Yet, when I restored the original RAM lineup (32MB in the lower slot and 64MB in the upper slot), it worked perfectly. What had started as a casual undertaking was fast dominating my otherwise busy workday as a major crusade. To think I once thought that nothing could be worse than SCSI voodoo.

Just to be sure the dealer wasn't pulling my leg about compatibility, I even went so far as to acquire a RAM upgrade from another vendor, again with assurances it was perfectly suitable for my iMac. Yet even this module failed to yield a successful result. Was this iMac forever doomed to reside in the 96MB zone, or would substituting the 32MB module for 64MB resolve the issue? Some might suggest I just back up and restore the drive with 9.1 and give up on Mac OS X, but stubborn is my middle name.

So I decided to tear down the iMac, thoroughly, from processor card to removal of the VRAM (a single video memory chip on the motherboard). I popped out the backup battery and just put everything aside. After returning to a more productive pursuit (writing a chapter for this book, actually), I returned to the iMac and carefully put everything together. I reinstalled the first two 128MB modules this time, in an all-or-nothing attempt to test the waters. With fingers crossed, I rebooted the Mac, and watched it go through its full startup cycle, all without further trouble.

Since that day, the iMac is running perfectly, with all 256MB of RAM aboard. So what went wrong? Perhaps a little wayward dust caused a poor contact of RAM or VRAM? Maybe the super PRAM zap that resulted when the battery was removed? A case for the X-Files? Or maybe, as one expert I consulted remarked, "It's a personal computer, so you must expect the unexpected."

Interpreting the Signs That Something Went Wrong

Summing Up

In this chapter, you learned ways to ensure your RAM upgrade is successful, and how to handle problems should your RAM installation go awry.

In the next chapter, we'll take our Macs on the road. You'll learn how to prepare for your trip, what you need to take, and, just as important, what to do if you run into a problem.

Chapter 5

Troubleshooting Macs on the Road

This is the typical situation. You have to take a business trip to San Jose, or even Paris or Athens. But you need to work on mission-critical documents for the business presentation, or perhaps finish that special piece of artwork to make the meeting go just right.

Or perhaps you're preparing, at long last, to take the family on a vacation, and you need to stay in touch with your company or personal email. Maybe you just want to have a computer game along in case the kids get bored and need something to do when it's raining or Mom and Dad are busy getting ready for a day of fun and frolic.

In this chapter, I'll give you some hard-won advice on how to maximize use of your Apple iBook or PowerBook—and what to do if things go really wrong.

The Care and Feeding of Laptops

It's sometimes hard to keep up. Apple's product lines change so often; just as soon as you get used to the features and quirks of one product, it's discontinued and another one introduced. If the automobile industry acted this way, you'd have a 2001 model, a 2001.5 model—wait a minute, we do see this sort of behavior in that industry already.

But whether new or old, laptop computers are designed for rather rugged use, far beyond that of a desktop model. This is particularly true with the slim, trim, second-generation Apple iBook, which is clearly oriented toward the consumer and educational market. That doesn't mean you can use them as Frisbees, or that they'll survive a drop onto a hard surface. But it does mean they can wobble around in a case or be moved from here to there, and back again, and manage to survive.

In the next few pages, I'll cover ways to keep your Apple laptop running safe and sound and how to solve typical problems.

Do You Need an Extended Warranty on Laptops?

I normally don't recommend getting an extended warranty, because they don't offer protection commensurate with their cost. For one thing, computers are more likely to fail early in their life cycle or too late for the warranty plan to do any good. Also, such warranties are generally a big profit item for the dealer, which is why they offer them, and they do not necessarily save you enough in potential repair costs to cover what you pay.

But I would ignore that advice when it comes to a laptop. Such computers are subjected to more extreme use than desktops. Therefore they are far more vulnerable to problems. While no warranty will cover you if you drop your laptop or damage the expensive LCD display somehow, other components could fail. If the warranty is inexpensive enough, it may be worth it. For example, the version of Apple Computer's AppleCare Protection Plan available when this book was written extends your new product warranty for three years, and it offers toll-free technical support, extra online support, and a special system diagnosis CD (based on MicroMat's TechTool Pro).

Cleaning Your PowerBook's Display

Yes, I know. Those LCD screens are flexible and flimsy looking, and you wonder what to do if they get a little smudged. Fortunately, they can be cleaned easily. All you need do is turn off the computer, then take a clean, soft, lint-free cloth or paper towel (such as Bounty or Viva) and dampen it slightly.

CAUTION   *Don't even think about spraying any liquid onto the LCD screen.*
I don't need to say anymore.

Wipe the screen gently—don't bear down. If your iBook or PowerBook's screen remains dirty, give it another shot.

According to Apple Computer's technical information document on the subject, you may even try applying a mild glass cleaner (one that doesn't have alcohol or ammonia on the ingredients list) to the cloth or paper towel, or check your dealer and see whether they have a cleaning kit designed for LCD screens. One such product is Klear Screen from Meridrew Enterprises. You can check out the product at their Web site: http://www.klearscreen.com.

NOTE   *These steps apply in equal fashion if you're lucky enough to have an LCD*
display for your desktop Mac.

Making Your Battery Go Farther

Although battery technology has improved over the years and Apple has found newer and better power management schemes, the fact of the matter is that batteries last just so long, and then they give up the ghost. However, that's no consolation if you're not near an AC power source (such as in the middle of a transatlantic flight where you hoped to finish your work or that new DVD before landing).

Obviously, there are no perpetual motion machines for iBooks and PowerBooks— well, at least not yet. So in this little section, I'll give you some advice on how to conserve battery life and what preparations you might take to get a longer lifetime out of your Apple laptop.

Here are some suggestions on how to handle the situation:

■ **Put in a second battery.**   If you have one of the PowerBook G3 models, you have two expansion bays for extra drives or batteries. While you may need one of them for a CD, DVD, or removable drive, if you don't have immediate need of these items, you can remove them and put a second battery in that slot. You get more than double the battery life. I say more, because the expansion bay drive isn't draining any extra juice from the battery.

NOTE   *It's way beyond the province of this book to comment on why Apple ditched the expansion bay slots for its otherwise excellent Titanium PowerBook G4 series. Perhaps they thought the battery was invulnerable; at least you get 30 seconds to change it should it die in flight.*

■ **Remove everything but the battery.**   Following the preceding suggestion, even if you have two expansion bays, there's no reason to keep both of them filled.

■ **Turn off AppleTalk.**   You're not hooked up to a network (unless, of course, you are communicating with another Apple computer using an AirPort wireless networking module), so go to the System Preferences application and click on the Network panel icon. After selecting your Ethernet option from the Configure pop-up menu, click on the AppleTalk tab and uncheck AppleTalk. Now some of the system checks the computer does when AppleTalk is loaded won't drain power. Just remember to turn it back on if you need to network in that fashion with another device.

■ **Avoid disk-intensive applications.**   Mac OS X's advanced virtual memory feature is on all the time; there's no turning it off as you could with the Classic Mac OS. But some applications cause more virtual memory activity than others. If your drive is chugging away whenever you use a program, you can bet that battery life is being reduced, too.

NOTE   *If you don't need to use special formatting when writing a document, you can write it in TextEdit first, then open it in a full-featured word processor later on when you can return to AC power. TextEdit's native format is RTF, which means documents can appear with formatting intact in such programs as AppleWorks or Microsoft Word.*

■ **Buy more memory.**   Mac OS X requires a minimum of 128MB of RAM, but works most efficiently with higher numbers. A "sweet" spot is 256MB of RAM, which reduces disk accesses in many programs, and hence increases battery life.

TIP   *Buying a new iBook or PowerBook G4? Check the dealers for a free RAM upgrade offer of one sort or another. While you may have to pay an extra few bucks (usually $30 or so) to have the dealer install the upgrade, you'll be able to max out RAM on the cheap.*

■ **Use the Energy Saver Control Panel.**   Apple already builds some useful power conservation features into its Energy Saver Control Panel (see Figure 5-1). It's available directly from the System Preferences application. Just click on the Energy Saver icon to bring it up. The standard settings are perfectly fine to give a useful combination of sleep settings for the computer, display, and hard disk. If you want to customize the setting, click the Options tab (as displayed in Figure 5-2) and experiment to your heart's content. You'll do best on the road to keep your hard disk sleep interval, the setting at the bottom of Figure 5-1, as short as possible. If you use software that constantly accesses the drive, there isn't a whole lot you can do anyway.

■ **Reduce brightness.**   Well, I wouldn't suggest you start squinting to see the screen, but bring it down as much as you can without making it hard to see. Usually setting brightness is a simple process of pressing the FN function key plus F1 to decrease brightness and FN-F2 to increase brightness. If in doubt, just check the icons on the keyboard for the proper shortcut.

NOTE   *On some Apple laptops, you'll see a visual indicator at the bottom of the screen showing how high brightness is set.*

■ **Don't use a dark desktop pattern.**   It may look nice on the screen, but dark pixels are "on" when it comes to LCD screens, which means they use more current than light pixels (which are considered "off"). You can choose your desktop patterns in the Desktop panel of the System Preferences application.

■ **If the option is available, allow processor cycling.**   Every little bit helps, and if the processor is asked to do less work, it'll use less juice. Processor cycling is available as an Options dialog box in the Energy Saver preference

The Care and Feeding of Laptops

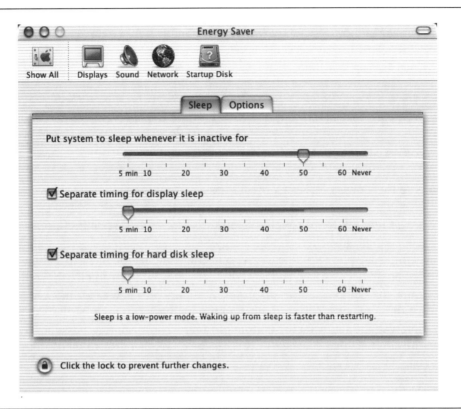

FIGURE 5-1   Choose your energy saving options here.

panel. Just bear in mind that when you select processor cycling, your PowerBook may not perform quite as fast as you'd expect. It may, however, make the difference when it comes to the PowerBook's battery surviving long enough for you.

- **Don't surf the Internet.**   If you're logged on while under battery power, consider getting off as soon as you can. The modem will extract more power to do its stuff.

- **Remove PC cards.**   You can lessen drain of the battery's power simply by removing a PC card or other such device.

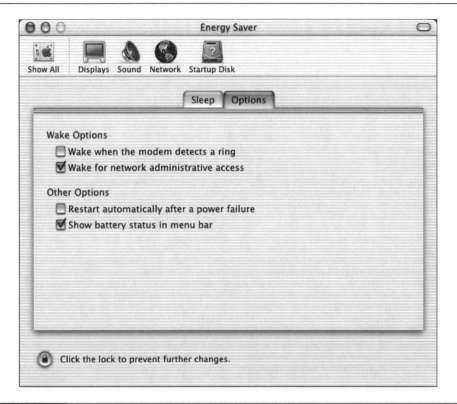

FIGURE 5-2   Customize the settings using this dialog box.

■ **Disconnect expansion devices.**   System resources that access FireWire, SCSI, or USB can drain power, even if those devices are connected to a separate power supply (or may have their own battery power source). My suggestion is that if you don't need them, power down and remove them.

■ **Play it low.**   When you run your PowerBook's or iBook's speakers loud, it may sound better, but it also increases current draw. Headphones draw less power. So if you want to watch *The Matrix* or *The Fifth Element* on your PowerBook's DVD player, and still experience all the great special effect sounds, consider that a good headphone from your favorite stereo store will sound much, much better than the tiny speakers on your computer.

PowerBook/iBook Trials and Tribulations

When it comes to diagnosing system problems, most of the factors that cause incompatibilities with Apple laptops are the same as those that affect other Macs. System extensions may cause crashes in the Classic OS, or one application will interact badly with another.

The troubleshooting steps I describe in Chapters 2 and 18 apply in equal measure to the PowerBook and iBook user. However, these computers have their own little quirks that are worth some extra special emphasis.

- ■ **Crashes when awakening from Sleep mode.**   This has been an ongoing problem in the Apple laptop line under the Classic Mac OS (we've not seen it happen under Mac OS X). You use Sleep mode for its extra convenience, so you don't have to endure a full startup mode to get the computer up and running. But sometimes it just doesn't work. The computer freezes while the screen is starting to display, or it doesn't come up at all. The usual steps to follow are the same as diagnosing any system-related conflict. If you're running the Classic environment, lean out the system extensions you're using. Follow the steps outlined in Chapter 18 for isolating system-related conflicts for both Mac OS 9.x and Mac OS X.

- ■ **Automatic Sleep mode doesn't work.**   If you have an older PowerBook and you're connected to a networked computer, or doing regular Internet log-ins (such as an automatic AOL session), you may encounter this problem. If so, the Mac OS will detect the network activity and not slip into Sleep mode at the specified interval. The solution is to dismount your networked drives, and turn off the automated sessions. If you have AppleTalk turned on in the Network pane of the System Preferences application, turn it off.

- ■ **Trackpad doesn't track properly.**   It's great to be able to mouse around with your finger, but sometimes the clever little device misbehaves. The cursor moves along in ragged fashion or not at all. The usual solution is just to make sure your fingers are dry, not wet or greasy. So even if your hands are sweating because of that approaching deadline, wipe them off before you track, and just use one finger (two fingers fighting each other for mouse motions doesn't help). If performance still isn't right, open the Mouse panel in the System Preferences application (see Figure 5-3). Make sure the mouse tracking speed is what you want, using the slider to change the rate; the factory setting is almost always too slow.

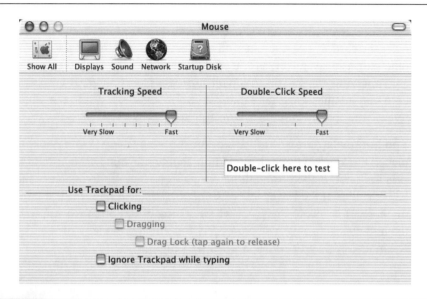

FIGURE 5-3   Choose your Trackpad speed here.

PowerBook/iBook Trials and Tribulations

NOTE   *The mouse speed settings also apply to a regular mouse hooked up to your iBook or PowerBook.*

■ **Battery won't charge.**   If you've had your PowerBook for a while, it may just be that the battery needs to be replaced. But if you have a new battery, there may be another cause. Failure to charge has been put at the doorstep of a bad fuse on the logic board, and, in some cases, a problem with the AC power supply.

■ **Problems with PC cards.**   Those little credit-card–shaped devices, PC cards (also known as PCMCIA), are a relatively inexpensive way to extend the capabilities of PowerBooks. With older PowerBooks, you can use them to add FireWire connections, and you can restore missing features, such as SCSI, on newer models, such as the PowerBook G4. But they have their quirks. The usual way to eject them is to drag the PC card icon to the trash. But sometimes that doesn't work; they get stuck in their slots (it's a tight fit, always). So if it happens to you, try a restart. If that fails, try this: insert a straightened paper clip into the little hole next to the PC card slot and push it in far enough to press the little button inside (the process is the same as force-ejecting a floppy disk or CD). Newer PowerBooks have, instead, buttons to manually eject PC cards. In most cases, this should be enough to eject the card. If not, there's a more drastic way recommended by Apple (and only as a last resort, as you could damage the PC card). Try prying the card out with your fingers or a pair of needle-nosed pliers. If you get the card out, go ahead and take that paper clip and push it into the slot to release the spring (and cross your fingers).

■ **Too hot for lap use.** You're working on your trusty PowerBook. It's placed on your lap (well, it's a laptop computer, right?). And your thigh gets very hot. Is there something wrong? The fact of the matter is that the hard drive is at the lower left of some models, and a lot of heat can build up there. If it gets to the point where it's painful, you may want to have the unit checked. But even a properly functioning model will seem quite warm there. It's great on a cold winter's night.

Changing Batteries on a First-Generation iBook

Switching batteries on a regular Apple PowerBook is a snap, literally. Batteries easily pop out for fast replacement (though sometimes you have to push a latch to ejected it). However, Apple did it differently with the original "clamshell" iBook.

In order to replace the battery on original iBook, you need to get a coin and loosen the retaining screws on the battery door. A quarter-turn counterclockwise is enough to open the door. Then you can pop out the battery, replace it, and tighten the screws.

Fortunately, Apple rethought this awkward setting when redesigning the PowerBook. The slim, elegant second-generation model, which Apple simply calls "Dual USB" in its technical literature, puts the release latch on the battery itself (no cover to remove). Just use a coin to turn and unlock the battery and you can then easily lift it out from the iBook.

NOTE | *The PowerBook G4 has cooling slots at the rear, and a cooling fan will activate if it gets real hot.*

Power Manager Woes

Another common problem with Apple laptops is a corrupted Power Manager. Symptoms may include failure to boot, failure to charge a battery, or the inability to wake from Sleep mode. The Power Manager directs a number of basic functions of the computer, including backlighting, energy saver settings, battery charging, and serial port access. Resetting the Power Manager is done differently from model to model. Here's a brief list of the steps involved in the process for recent models.

NOTE | *You'll find that the steps for these various models are fairly similar, which is a hopeful sign. One hopes Apple will continue using similar power management reset steps for future models.*

PowerBook G3 Series (Wall Street Edition)

1. Shut down your PowerBook.

2. Press the SHIFT, FN (function), CONTROL, and power keys—all at the same time.

3. Count five seconds.

4. Restart your PowerBook by pressing the power button.

PowerBook G3 Series (Lombard or Bronze Keyboard "Pismo" Edition)

1. Shut down your PowerBook.

2. Go to the rear of the computer, and locate and press the reset button. You'll find it right between the modem and external video ports.

3. Count five seconds.

4. Restart your PowerBook by pressing the power button.

iBook

1. Shut down your iBook.

2. Locate the reset button, which is placed at the base of the iBook's display. Take a straightened paper clip and press the button.

3. Count five seconds.

4. Restart your PowerBook by pressing the power button.

iBook (Dual USB Model)

As explained earlier in this chapter, the "Dual USB" designation refers to the totally redesigned form factor, using an elegant, trim case reminiscent of the Titanium PowerBook G4.

1. Shut down your iBook.

2. Locate the reset button, which is situated just above the Audio/Video output port on the iBook's left side, and press the button.

3. Count five seconds.

4. Restart your iBook by pressing the power button.

PowerBook G4

1. Shut down your Titanium PowerBook G4.

2. Look for the reset button; it's placed on the rear panel, between the external video and modem ports. Press the button.

3. Count five seconds.

4. Restart your PowerBookG4 by pressing the power button.

Older PowerBooks Summarized

While older PowerBooks aren't officially compatible with Mac OS X, that doesn't mean some enterprising Mac users won't find a way to do so anyway (just as they've done with older desktop Power Macs). So I'll include this information in case you are willing to test the waters and do something not officially supported.

There are various ways to reset the Power Manager on older models, depending on the kind of PowerBook you have. The processes described are just part of the equation. For many models, you actually need to disconnect the battery and power adapter.

There's not even a reset button on some of these computers. You have to use two straightened paper clips and press both reset and interrupt buttons at the same time for 10 to 20 seconds. On these units, the buttons are usually found inside the rear door.

For more information, pay a visit to Apple's Web site and read their technical information document on the subject. Here's the URL: http://til.info.apple.com/techinfo.nsf/artnum/n14449.

Case History

Is It Dangerous to X-ray a Laptop?

Over the years, I had read differing opinions about whether my PowerBook or iBook could be damaged by the mandatory airport security check. What about the hard drive, I thought? Could the integrity of the data be affected?

For several years, I took the paranoid approach. I asked the security people to do a physical examination instead. All they need to do is have you open the computer, power it up so they see it start and show text of one sort or another, and they'll be satisfied that it's not a repository for contraband or dangerous weaponry.

NOTE *The best thing to do if you must submit your iBook or PowerBook to this sort of check is simply to keep it in Sleep mode, so you can get it up and running quickly. Mac OS X allows the computer to start up within just about a second (a jarring, if certain indicator to the security guard that you really have a laptop computer there).*

On one trip, I noticed the pilot boarding the plane with his laptop (no, it wasn't one of Apple's, but I wasn't going to enter into a platform war discussion with someone who had my life in his hands). I asked him if he ever subjected his computer to special security check.

No way, he said. He just ran the thing through the X-ray machine and he hadn't had a problem, ever.

PowerBook/iBook Trials and Tribulations

Of course, how could I be so dense? I write science fiction stories, so I should have known the elementary scientific principles at hand here: X-rays aren't magnetic. How could they affect the data on my drive? All right, I got the message this time.

On the return trip, I just put the PowerBook's case on the conveyer belt. After the security check, I went to the waiting area, and quickly awakened my precious little computer to be sure it was all right. I suppose I was acting like Jack Nicholson's character in that fabulous movie *As Good As It Gets*. Then again, the character *was* a writer, right?

I repeated the maneuver on a few subsequent trips, and finally just gave up checking and rechecking. I've never had an ounce of trouble, ever. And nobody I know ever has, either. Even Apple Computer, in a technical note on using Apple's products overseas, says, "X-rays and other magnetic radiation associated with X-ray machines only pose a slight potential danger." The only possible risk, they assert, might be to magnetic media, and they are thinking in terms of removable media (such things as floppies, Zip drives, and SuperDisks). My suggestion is to just let the security machines do their stuff and don't worry about it. Even my old-fashioned film cameras have come out of the experience without any damage to the film.

Protecting Your Laptop Against Theft

Although crime rates around the USA are supposed to be down, there is one element where they remain at an especially high level—and that's laptop computers.

According to a survey from Safeware, a company that specializes in insurance policies for computer users, some 303,000 laptop computers (I don't have a breakdown among manufacturers here), with a total value of $906,546,000, were stolen in 1998 alone. As laptops have taken a growing percentage of the PC market, the figures have increased in proportion.

When you consider that it takes months for Apple to sell that many PowerBooks (or iBooks for that matter), you can see the breadth and depth of this problem.

Obviously, this is a great advertisement for getting good insurance, and it's nice to know that more and more firms are recognizing the need to provide computer coverage, especially for home office users.

Despite having an insurance policy at hand, it's far better, obviously, not to have to use the policy. I've experienced a handful of thefts over the years—once a camera, and three times an attempted car theft. Forget about the fact that the lost or damaged items can be repaired or replaced. You feel violated and helpless, and if the item stolen contained valuable information you need for your work, there is the time you must spend recreating all of it, if you can. That's why I emphasize, over and over, the need to back up your files (see Chapter 14)—and I'll say it again at the risk of boring you, because it's so very important.

True, there's not much you can do if you're held at gunpoint or surrounded by a gang of thugs, unless you're a martial arts expert (where's Jackie Chan when you need him?), of course. But there are things you can do to help protect yourself against theft of your iBook or PowerBook—and there are things you can do to help get the thing back if it's taken.

Here are some suggestions:

■ **Be careful in public places.**   If you're at an airport terminal, a car rental establishment, or hotel lobby, for example, don't leave the laptop on the floor or table, even for a second. It wouldn't take long for someone who stalked you to dash on through the crowd and slip away with your computer (even if it's protected in an undistinguished fabric case). Don't put it down. If you have a case with a carrying strap or handle, hold on to it, tight as you can. Yes, I know that an older PowerBook or iBook in a big case can put the weight of the world on your shoulders (thank heavens they are much lighter now), but a few aches here and there are far more comfortable than the pain you'd endure if your computer is stolen from you. If you must set it down, sit on the strap, rest your hand on the case, keep a wary eye on it. And, although laptop cases are convenient, you may be better off putting the case itself into a regular overnight bag or suitcase, so it's not obvious to the onlooker just what you have there.

NOTE   *The striking, colorful design of the original Apple iBook made it a theft magnet. While its convenient fold-down carrying handle makes it easy to carry, you are better off putting it in a case of some sort so it doesn't attract attention.*

■ **Get insurance protection.**   It used to be difficult to get meaningful computer coverage on a home insurance policy, but that is no longer the case. In addition to the company who provided the theft statistics I quoted here (Safeware, a specialist in insuring computers), regular insurance companies such as Farmers Insurance Group offer low-cost riders that cover computers (even for tenants). Be sure your policy is sufficient to cover replacement value of your computer, peripherals, and software (and this can all add up). Make sure there's also coverage for your computer and software when you travel.

■ **Store your laptop in a safe when you leave your hotel.**   I wouldn't for a moment suggest that the staff in a hotel has skullduggery on their minds, or that it's easy to break into your room. But it is a fact that your door will be left open when they're doing their cleaning, and I've seen enough movies showing folks casually walking into a stranger's room under such circumstances (especially those early James Bond flicks with Sean Connery) to be at least wary of the process. So I recommend you check with the hotel and see if they have a room with a safe or can provide secured storage when you're not in the room. At the very least, insist that housekeeping staff close your door when they are making your room ready for you upon your return.

Using Your PowerBook as an External SCSI Drive

In the days of the PowerBook Duo, you could slip it into a Duo Dock and make it into a desktop computer, more or less. PowerBooks with SCSI ports can also be used in a SCSI Disk mode, which allows them to appear as mounted SCSI drives on a regular Mac (the technique requires rebooting under Mac OS 9.1).

NOTE   *At the time this book was written, SCSI Disk mode wasn't supported under Mac OS X, but to use the PowerBook as a hard drive, it doesn't matter what operating system it runs, since the one on your desktop Mac is the one you're using.*

Here, briefly, is how you set it up:

1. Get hold of a PowerBook SCSI Disk Adapter cable. Make sure you get the right cable, as Apple, in its infinite wisdom (I seem to use this phrase often), also designed an almost identical-looking regular SCSI cable, which is used to attach a SCSI device to a PowerBook. Dealers tend to confuse this, so make sure the words "Disk Adapter" are on the package. You can also get a SCSI Dock connector at your dealer, a little module with a plug at one end and a SCSI port at the other, and a switch for either SCSI mode.

2. On your PowerBook, go to the System Preferences application, and choose the Startup Disk panel.

3. Select your Mac OS 9.x system version.

4. Choose restart from the Apple menu.

5. After your PowerBook reboots under your Classic Mac OS version, go to the Apple menu, and access the Control Panels submenu. Choose the PowerBook SCSI Setup Control Panel.

6. Choose a SCSI ID that doesn't conflict with the one on your desktop computer (this is critical).

7. Shut down your PowerBook (don't put in Sleep mode, please) and your desktop Mac.

NOTE
Before you turn off the PowerBook, make sure that the Password Security Control Panel or any other password protection on the computer is disabled. Otherwise, you will run into problems trying to access the drive on another Mac.

8. Attach your PowerBook's SCSI Disk Adapter cable to the SCSI port on your Mac or the one on your last attached device (you may need an adapter plug if it has a different type of SCSI jack).

9. Turn on your PowerBook. Within a few seconds you should see a SCSI icon on the PowerBook's screen.

NOTE
If your PowerBook starts up normally with that cable connected, it means you have the wrong cable, and it's not going into SCSI disk mode. Should this happen, power down and replace the cable.

10. Boot your Mac normally. The PowerBook's disk icon should show up normally on your desktop Mac. If it doesn't, power down and recheck your SCSI setup. SCSI ID and termination conflicts may be present. Should this happen, consult Chapter 15 for further advice on the subject.

Using Your iBook or PowerBook as a FireWire Drive

With the removal of SCSI, PowerBooks (and the latest iBooks) all have FireWire ports. This allows them to run in FireWire Target Disk Mode, meaning the internal drives can be accessed via the FireWire port of another Mac as an external drive.

Protecting Your Laptop
Against Theft

Here's how to use this very compelling, useful feature:

> **TIP**
>
> *It's not just Apple laptops that support Target Disk Mode. The very same feature is available on all Power Mac G4 desktops with AGP graphics slots, the Cube, and the slot-loading iMac (as long as firmware revision 2.4 or later is installed).*

1. Turn off the Mac that's serving "target" drive chores.

> **CAUTION**
>
> *Apple recommends using the AC adapter on your FireWire-equipped iBook or PowerBook, for maximum performance without the danger of running out of "juice" during a copying operation.*

2. Connect your target Mac to the Mac that will serve as host with a standard FireWire cable.

> **NOTE**
>
> *It's not necessary to turn off your host computer to access another Mac via the Target Disk Mode.*

3. Start your iBook or PowerBook, and hold down the T key. Wait until a FireWire icon appears on the screen. Within seconds, the drive's icon should appear on your "host" Mac.

4. When you no longer need to access the target drive, you can dismount it by dragging its icon to the trash (or typing COMMAND-E after selecting the icon) from the desktop or the Finder.

5. Press your iBook's or PowerBook's power button to shut the unit off and then remove the FireWire connection cables.

The Apple Laptop Travel Guide

Forgetting something? When you need to take your Apple iBook or PowerBook with you on a trip (business or personal), you'll want to make sure you have the right stuff, in case of a problem or simply to make your computer run properly in most situations you'll encounter.

The first time I had to take a PowerBook on the road, it was for a purpose that wasn't very pleasant. My wife needed some surgery, and the physician and hospital were in another state, some 250 miles away. Unfortunately, I was also in the middle of a writing deadline, and deadlines aren't concerned with such fine points as family needs.

So I packed my PowerBook, scanner, removable drives, extra keyboard, mouse, modem, and backup tape drive in the trunk, and the entire Steinberg clan took off.

The hotel's housekeeping staff was no doubt startled to see my makeshift home office, but it worked. I was able to spend several hours a day keeping up on that project, with plenty of time for hospital visits. I even managed to take my son for an occasional sightseeing tour, so the trip wasn't quite so boring for him.

A little advance travel planning will do wonders toward making your computer do all the work it can do.

■ **Check overseas phone and voltage requirements.**   If you plan to travel to another country, congratulations. Apple's products are labeled as "universal," designed to work in many international environments. Power requirements generally run from 100 to 250 volts, and current ratings of 50 and 60 Hz. You may, however, need a special adapter plug to access a power line in a particular locale. In addition, Apple won't officially certify older products designed for the USA market for overseas use, although that doesn't mean you can't use them with the proper adapters. Before you visit another country, you may also want to check out a dealer who specializes in international connectivity products. One prime example listed by Apple Computer is TeleAdapt, which you can access on the Web at http://www .teleadapt.com (or telephone 1-877-835-3232). Their product line includes an absolutely staggering array of plug adapters, modem adapters and testers, mobile phone adapters, line filters, acoustic couplers for hotel phones that don't have a separate data port, and security alarm systems.

NOTE   *Apple portable computing products introduced to the market since January 1, 1998, are protected by a worldwide warranty. That means if your recent Apple laptop needs service, you can visit any local service installation during that period for warranty repairs. As far as older models are concerned, well, they'd be out of warranty anyway, and they don't even support Mac OS X.*

■ **Don't break it in on the road.**   If you have a brand-new iBook or PowerBook, you should use it as much as you can before you travel. That way you can check for possible problems that you can fix before your departure. Even with Apple's product warranty (or perhaps an extended warranty), you wouldn't want to have to spend the time away from home diagnosing a system-related problem or having to wait for a repair.

The Apple Laptop Travel Guide

■ **Don't forget a spare battery and charger.**   Even if you don't expect to stretch the limits of the battery, you should be prepared in case of an emergency. For one thing, laptop batteries have a finite life cycle, and may have to be replaced after a year or two of use. Also, if they go bad prematurely, you will be left in the lurch if there isn't a power plug at hand. If you intend to travel to a region with uncertain weather conditions, or visit older hotels with older electrical systems, don't be surprised to encounter a prolonged power outage. In addition to a spare battery, it wouldn't hurt to get a battery charger so you always have a fully charged spare ready to roll. You can get batteries, chargers, and other accessories for recent Apple laptops from the VST Technologies division of SmartDisk (http://www.vsttech.com).

■ **Send your backups to yourself.**   No, this isn't a request that you start talking to yourself, though I have felt that way at times when I've forgotten to take something I really needed on a trip. When you write critical documents that you cannot afford to lose, and you have online access where you are staying, send the file in an email to yourself. That way, in the event your original file is damaged, or if your computer is damaged or stolen, you can retrieve the file when you need it. If you don't want to clog up your mailbox with the added material, see if your online service offers an extra mailbox. For example, AOL and its sister service, CompuServe 2000, both give you up to seven screen names (mailboxes) on each account. EarthLink has a special package with up to six user names, and other ISPs offer similar deals.

■ **Protect your laptop from extreme weather.**   Don't assume your rugged-looking iBook or PowerBook is immune. If you intend to travel into an extreme environment (winter weather or the tropics), pack your laptop carefully, perhaps using a hard-shell shipping case designed for the purpose (check your dealer for product offerings). Keep it away from heat, extreme cold, or moisture. The supplier of international connection adapters I mentioned earlier, TeleAdapt, also has a device called a CoolPad, which keeps the PowerBook elevated from a desk to give it better air circulation (though, frankly, this is a far greater problem with Intel-based notebooks than Macs, because the Pentiums usually generate more heat).

NOTE *While I wouldn't normally suggest you consider a Windows laptop, if you travel into extreme climates often, you might consider buying what is called a "ruggedized" model, such as the GoBook from Itronix (http://www.itronix.com). While the GoBook is big and ugly and expensive (a fully outfitted version was over five grand as of the summer of 2001), it's rated for weather conditions that would do in a lesser laptop, and it can also survive a succession of three-foot falls (at least that's what the manufacturer tells me). When you get home, you can use a Mac/Windows file-sharing program, such as Thursby Systems's DAVE, to transfer document files direct to your Mac.*

■ **Bring a backup drive.**   The reasons that you back up at home or office are doubly important on the road, when there is added risk of damage by the elements or possible theft. You should bring along an extra drive with enough space to store duplicates of your important files, then keep it separate from the laptop computer (so the loss of one doesn't necessarily include the backup device). An expansion bay drive for a PowerBook G3, be it a Zip, SuperDisk, or hard drive, is an excellent choice. The iBooks and G3 PowerBooks with the "bronze" keyboard also have USB ports for extra drives and other devices. Your choices are similar: Zip drive, SuperDisk, hard drive, plus CD writers and tape drives. One USB-based CD writer, the Que Drive, comes with a convenient carrying case that can easily fit into a large laptop case or an overnight bag.

TIP *Another extra drive option is FireWire. Chapter 15 covers the differences between FireWire and SCSI. There are PC card products that will allow a PowerBook G3 to use FireWire drives. Some FireWire drives (including CD burners) don't even require AC power; they're powered by your iBook or PowerBook's FireWire bus.*

■ **Consider a portable inkjet printer.**   If you must produce printed copy, take a look at the products available and see if one is small enough for travel. If you want to save space, you could arrange to fax yourself a copy with your fax modem (but bear in mind a hotel will charge a per page fee for faxes). Another option is to see if there's a local service bureau or printer who could print your documents for you.

■ **Make sure you can access your online service on the road.**
The national services, such AOL, CompuServe, AT&T WorldNet, Prodigy
Internet, and EarthLink have thousands of local access numbers for you
to select, and often a reasonable percentage of those are outside the USA.
It's a good idea to collect these numbers before you travel, so you're ready
to hook up when you arrive. If you have a local ISP without access points
outside your state, consider a Web email service, such as Microsoft's
Hotmail or Yahoo! mail. On the other hand, if you intend to do a lot of
traveling, you may want to rethink your ISP choices for this very reason.

TIP
*Before you leave, it's a good idea to create separate dialing profiles in the
Network panel of the System Preferences application for each locale to
which you're traveling. It's done by choosing New Location from the
Location pop-up menu, and then entering the new information for your
alternate connection setting. If you're an AOL or CompuServe member,
you can create custom connection (location) profiles in the software
provided by these services. Also remember that, under Mac OS X, your
iBook or PowerBook can automatically switch among AirPort, Ethernet,
or PPP connections, depending on which one is active (the faster
connection always gets priority). You can also switch priorities manually
by choosing Advanced from the Configure pop-up menu and then
dragging the listed ports to a different sort order.*

NOTE
*AOL has a Web-based email system, NetMail (also called just AOLMail),
which is designed to provide access to your AOL email if you don't have
access to their regular software. You'll find more information at the
company's Web site: http://www.aol.com/aolmail. EarthLink has a similar
feature, accessible from their Personal Start Page. In addition, some hotels
also offer high-speed Internet access as an extra-cost option, and, if the
ISP the hotel uses is helpful and can give you the right information for
its outgoing mail server, you might even be able to retrieve your regular
email with your favorite email software.*

■ **Don't forget an accessory kit.**   In addition to having an extra battery and
charger at hand, there are some other items you might want to take along.
You'll want to take extra disk media, a SCSI terminator (in case you use
an extra SCSI device), a long modular phone cord (in case your computer
is far from the phone job; again, TeleAdapt can help you here, with one of
their roll-up cords), and maybe even a spare AC adapter.

■ **Consider a separate keyboard and mouse.**   If you plan to spend extra hours on the computer, consider getting a regular desktop keyboard and mouse. Laptop keyboards and trackpads can be an acquired taste, and not everyone takes to them for long sessions. I have found the feel of the iBook's keyboard to be closer to that of a regular keyboard than any Apple laptop I've used (but that's just a personal opinion).

NOTE   *While it's true that keyboards can be a little big for a typical notebook carrying case, they'll fit nicely into a suitcase or overnight bag.*

■ **Choose a case carefully.**   While a thin, attractively designed case may look just great, it may not have enough room to meet your needs. Before you buy a case, try to see it in person (I realize this is a problem if you do a lot of catalog and online shopping). See if there are extra bins and pouches for the extras you need, such as disks, removable drives, and adapter cables. Also check to see if the laptop compartment is well cushioned in case of a bumpy trip. Since Apple's newest PowerBooks have larger screens, they might be a tight fit in older cases. If you do see the accessory case in person, check the product specifications for extra features, dimensions, and so on, so you can be reasonably assured it'll do the job. Order it well enough in advance of a trip so it can be returned in case it's not suitable.

Summing Up

In this chapter, you learned how to make your mobile computing experience safer and more productive. If you want to keep abreast of the latest news and views on Apple laptops, may I suggest you point your Web browser to Jason O'Grady's excellent news and information site, Go2Mac. The URL is http://go2mac.com.

In the next chapter, I'll cover a subject near and dear to my heart, as an old-time commercial typographer, and that's fonts. There's a whole lot more to a Mac's font-handling capabilities than just a few letters and numbers, and the situation is even more complicated in Mac OS X.

The Apple Laptop Travel Guide

Chapter 6

The Weird World of Fonts

One of the Mac OS's core components is its use of fonts. You cannot use a Mac without fonts. Even the basic window and menu bar displayed on your Mac use fonts of one sort or another.

One of the big factors that attracted the graphics industry to the Macintosh platform was the easy availability of fonts and the invention of the PostScript page description language, PostScript fonts, and laser printers.

One would think, then, that fonts would be as easy to handle as other Mac files, but that's not really the case. The proliferation of fonts and new font formats has created a nightmare. The more fonts you have, the more difficult it is to keep them organized. Worse, the arrival of Mac OS X hasn't simplified matters.

Where once you had just one folder, the Fonts folder, to handle, now you five Font folders to fret over. One is in the Classic Mac OS System Folder, and four are managed by Mac OS X.

The purpose of this chapter is to cover the whys and wherefores of font organization and troubleshooting. You'll discover how best to keep up a large font library and how to handle the common problems that affect their use in both system environments.

TrueType vs. PostScript Fonts: What's the Difference?

Before I introduce you to Mac OS X's font management schemes, let's have a little history lesson. In the beginning, fonts came in bitmap form. You had a different font for every size, and what you saw on the screen was reproduced on the page, at least to the limits of those old ImageWriter printers.

Things changed when the clever folks at Adobe invented something called PostScript, which takes the elements of a page and reduces them to math. Accompanying PostScript were PostScript fonts. If you wanted scalable fonts (fonts that would print in all sizes at the full resolution of your printer), you had just one choice, PostScript.

The Anatomy of a PostScript Font

In the old days of traditional computerized typesetting, your fonts came in two parts. There were the actual letterforms themselves, which would be on a thin piece of film or on a floppy disk. Then there was a second part, a printed circuit card or floppy disk that recorded the width values of the fonts. This was the information that told the computer how wide a particular character was supposed to be.

When scalable font technology was introduced by Adobe, they followed the very same design motif. There was a screen font (or bitmap) font, which provided clear display of the font on your screen in a single size, and also contained the width values (or metrics) of a typeface. So the letter M in a proportional font was always wider than the letter I.

The second part of the equation was the printer font, which contained the font "outline" information that allowed the font to be reproduced on your printer in any size you selected. This is the component of the font that scales to whatever size you select, yet retains the same high output quality.

In order for the font to work, you had to install both parts. The screen fonts usually came in several sizes merged together in a file called a suitcase. By giving you extra sizes, the font manufacturer could give you better screen display (at least when you selected those specific sizes). Beginning with Mac OS 7, you would simply double-click on a suitcase file to examine its contents.

In 1989, Adobe came out with a clever solution to give you clear screen display in all available sizes: Adobe Type Manager (ATM). ATM was designed to work with a single bitmap font plus your printer font to generate screen images in the sizes you selected. An added benefit was its ability to use PostScript fonts with non-PostScript printers. Without ATM, whenever you selected a size for which a bitmap font wasn't available, screen display would become extremely poor because the Classic Mac OS's QuickDraw display technology would try to fill in the missing pieces.

NOTE   *In order to view PostScript fonts proper in the Classic environment, ATM is still needed. Apple licensed ATM technology for Mac OS X font display and, according to Adobe, there is no need nor will there ever be a Mac OS X–native version of ATM or ATM Deluxe, the font management version.*

In order for PostScript fonts to work, you simply dragged both files to the closed System Folder icon, and the Finder would put them in the Fonts folder (which was introduced with Mac System 7.1). Under Mac OS X, the locations in which fonts are placed has been multiplied. If you thought you had it sorted out under the Classic Mac OS, prepare to confront a new world. I'll help you make sense of this new situation later on in this chapter, in the section entitled "Mac OS X Is Bursting with Font Folders."

To get back to our discussion: PostScript fonts come in two forms. Type 1 is the most common type. In addition to the fonts you install on your Mac, Type 1 fonts are also installed on PostScript printers.

TrueType vs. PostScript Fonts: What's the Difference?

The other type of PostScript font is Type 3, which is not used as much these days, except for special applications (such as custom logo designs). Type 3 fonts are not as efficiently designed as the Type 1 variety. The file sizes are larger, and they exact greater amounts of printer memory to work; their biggest benefit is their ability to make fonts with grayscale fills and complex characters based on PostScript illustrations. Unfortunately, ATM doesn't support them.

For the rest of this chapter, when I refer to PostScript fonts, I'll be concentrating strictly on the Type 1 variety.

TrueType Fonts Hit the Scene

Back in 1990, the entire subject of fonts on a Mac became more confusing when Apple came up with TrueType. The story goes that Apple resented paying Adobe big licensing bucks to use PostScript fonts, so they decided to come up with their own alternative. And in theory, it's a better alternative, because each TrueType font is a single file, containing both screen and outline portions. You don't have to worry about missing one file or the other.

NOTE *The irony of the arrival of TrueType is that, although a Mac innovation, it was rapidly embraced on the Windows platform, where it appears to have greater popularity, even to this day. The second irony is that, despite their attempt to sidestep Adobe, Apple uses Adobe's PDF format as its 2-D imaging engine for the Quartz layer of Mac OS X. PDF is an open standard, hence no licensing fees are needed.*

TrueType is a scalable font format, too, with the font scaler built into your system software. As a result, you can view and print on any printer connected to your Mac without having to worry about PostScript or Adobe Type Manager. This is a great plus if you have a regular inkjet printer hooked up to your Mac.

And, like a screen font, a TrueType font can live by itself or be placed in a font suitcase, along with other fonts.

The Printing World Gives TrueType a Thumbs Down

TrueType fonts sounded great on paper. And, indeed, they had distinct advantages over PostScript fonts, such as their ability to work on non-PostScript printers and give clear screen display without needing a separate ATM-type program. But they wrought havoc in the commercial printing world. The expensive imagesetters that printers and service bureaus used to make high-resolution output of documents were designed to work best with PostScript fonts. So, even though the Mac operating system could handle TrueType with aplomb, those expensive output devices would choke at the presence of a TrueType font. Sometimes the processing stage would halt, or the output wouldn't provide acceptable results.

And the solutions weren't cheap. In some situations, the actual imagesetter processor's hardware had to be updated to recognize the existence of TrueType, at a cost of hundreds or thousands of dollars. In other cases, it was just a downloadable update. But in either case, it took time for the industry to accept the reality of TrueType.

Even today, PostScript fonts are still the industry standard in publishing. Although the high-end output devices usually work in a satisfactory manner with TrueType, your best approach is to check with your commercial printer before you use such fonts in your documents if you intend to take them beyond your office laser printer.

On the other hand, if you confine your printed output to inkjets and laser printers, or you want to exchange fonts with Windows users, you are apt to fare better sticking with TrueType. Not having to deal with separate bitmap and printer fonts and ATM will definitely make life easier. Even though ATM isn't needed for Mac OS X, juggling bitmap and printer fonts is still a requirement.

Introducing OpenType

As if coping with the vagaries of PostScript and TrueType fonts weren't enough, there's another font format on the horizon—OpenType. Developed jointly by Adobe and Microsoft, OpenType promises to end some of the confusing side effects of the existing font structure.

If OpenType spreads, it'll cure a whole lot of ills. For one, the format covers both PostScript and TrueType fonts, and the actual font file can support either format or both. In a sense, it's a merger of both formats, and there will be no need for separate screen fonts if you opt for an OpenType font with PostScript support. It's all in one file.

Another great OpenType feature is its ability to embed such fonts on a Web page, which helps provide a uniform look and feel for Web pages across browsers and computing platforms.

In addition, OpenType will support extended characters, such as ligatures and fancy letterforms, as well as provide improved character kerning. The latter will go a long way toward making the appearance of type much, much better.

TrueType vs. PostScript Fonts:
What's the Difference?

So What Does OpenType Do for Me?

It won't change your existing fonts in any way. You'll continue to use them as you do now. But once OpenType fonts start appearing on the market, you'll be able to buy them and enjoy the increased convenience and additional features they offer. Mac OS X has full support of OpenType, so you can expect offerings in this format to appear over time.

The Sad Tale of QuickDraw GX

In the early 1990s, Apple announced a new set of technologies that, on paper, seemed just wonderful. It was called QuickDraw GX, and it was designed to not only update the Mac's image display model, but also update how fonts and printing were handled.

When it came to fonts, the character limitations would be history. You'd be able to get and use fonts with all sorts of extra characters, such as swashes (little effects and flourishes that decorate a letter), extended ligatures (such as the combined "ffi" letter combination that you see in high-quality books), and more. Font organization, especially with PostScript fonts, would be eased, since the printer and screen fonts would be combined into a single file (yes, just like TrueType fonts).

QuickDraw GX would also revolutionize the way graphics programs were developed. The core programming routines that covered display and rotation of your drawings would be done behind the scenes by the Mac operating system. Programmers would only have to call up these routines, rather than have to reinvent the wheel and program their own graphic elements. It would make for smaller, less RAM-hungry programs with consistent performance.

And then there was printing. All printers would get desktop icons. Rather than work with the clumsy old PrintMonitor, you could simply drag and drop jobs to the specific printer you wanted to use, and even move documents from one printer icon to another to equalize the load. You could pick different printers from your Print dialog box (no more regular trips to the Chooser).

That was just the beginning. There would be extra printer features, such as the ability to automatically place watermarks on a page, print several small-sized pages on a single sheet of paper (thumbnails), and more.

The theory was truly intriguing, and dedicated graphic designers no doubt waited patiently for the reality. When it finally showed up in the mid-1990s, the reality was not quite as impressive as the promise. QuickDraw GX took up several megabytes of RAM, especially on the then-innovative PowerPC models. It was buggy, it was the source of regular crashes, and software publishers moved at a snail's pace to adopt the technologies. Some blamed the fact that it wasn't a cross-platform technology (and the biggest graphics programs are designed to work about the same in the Mac and Windows environments). Only a very few QuickDraw GX–savvy programs ever came out.

Finally, Apple got the message and scuttled the technology, after borrowing a few elements for the Classic Mac OS, such as desktop printers. But the rest of GX went the way of OpenDoc and other failed Apple technologies that looked great on paper but somehow never worked in the real world.

NOTE
OpenDoc was designed to change the emphasis from the application to the document. You'd create a single document, then OpenDoc would let you use the parts necessary to provide the features you needed (such as a word processing part, a graphics part, or an image editing part).

Yet strangely enough, other elements of QuickDraw GX appear to be present under Mac OS X. Enhanced printing capabilities are offered under the Print Center application; Mac OS X applications designed in the Cocoa programming environment have automatic access to enhanced character features, such as ligatures and kerning; and the Quartz imaging engine, based on Adobe's PDF technology, provides a terrific graphics rendering engine for images and technology. In the end, some of the good ideas of that old, failed technology have made their mark after all.

CAUTION
If you're migrating to Mac OS X from a Mac running an older Mac OS version prior to 9, you'll want to remove all QuickDraw GX components from your Classic System Folder. Apple removed support for it beginning in Mac OS 9.

A Quick Survey of Multiple Master Fonts

Another font technology that hasn't gone a long way is Adobe's Multiple Master Fonts. To explain what this is all about, it may be worthwhile mentioning how fonts were designed in the old days.

Way back when, fonts would be optimized to look good in a single size or a small range of sizes. For example, in relation to their size, you'd make letters tall, wide, and thick for text, to enhance readability, and small and thin for headlines, where you wanted close-knit spacing for optimum appearance in very large sizes.

Font manufacturers actually produced two or more versions of each font to meet these needs. At one time there was even a separate font master for each point size, which simply meant you had to buy lots of fonts to get a reasonable number of point sizes.

With Multiple Master Fonts, Adobe tried to expand upon this scheme by developing a single set of fonts that you could modify in a wide number of ways, to provide the best possible optical appearance. You could even design your own variations on the basic core design, by manipulating the basic letter shapes to be thicker, thinner, condensed, or expanded. The limit was your imagination.

Of course, if anyone tried to match your font alteration for a specific task, it would be a nightmare in the making, since the usual directories of font designs that graphic artists use wouldn't accommodate any such possibilities. And forget about picking them out in a font menu, as the variations were named by adding some numbers to the actual font's name.

Fortunately, or unfortunately depending on your point of view, the technique never really caught on beyond a small set of Adobe font products—that is, except for its emergence as part of Adobe's font substitution technology. Take ATM and a core set of four Multiple Master Fonts, and a database of Adobe designs, and you can simulate many font designs (at least in terms of spacing if not the actual look). This is a great convenience if you just want to get a general idea of how a document looks, without having to go out and get all the fonts you need.

Adobe Acrobat also uses font substitution technology to replace fonts that aren't embedded in the Acrobat file and give the document a look resembling (though not quite matching) the original design.

Mac OS X Is Bursting with Font Folders

With Mac OS X, Apple's attempts to simplify the user interface didn't quite extend to the management of fonts. In fact, there are no less than five default font locations with which to contend.

Yes, I said five font-related folders. Are you now reaching for a hefty dose of aspirin? Let me make it more complicated. Mac OS X is a multiple user operating system, which means different users can have their own personal font libraries. A blessing, or a nightmare in the making?

First I'll tell you about the good stuff. Mac OS X features something called the Apple Type Solution (or ATS), which provides system-wide support for bitmap, OpenType, PostScript, and TrueType fonts. Best of all, the fonts can be used on your local Mac or shared across a network, depending on how and where you place them. Nifty!

But all this flexibility comes at the expense of complexity. Let's have a look at the standard locations for fonts (I'll omit additional locations supported by font management programs under the Classic Mac OS).

- **Default system fonts**   The wonderful collection of fonts that are delivered with Mac OS X are located in the special Fonts folder located inside the Library folder, within the folder labeled System. These are read-only fonts. Under Mac OS X, you cannot delete or add to fonts in this folder. Any font dragged out of it will not be removed, only copied.

> **NOTE**   *The standard system fonts bear a file extension, "dfont." The new file format puts all the information about the font in the data fork (rather than splitting between the data and resource fork, as fonts of old did). What all this "geek speak" means is that such fonts can, in theory at least, translate to other computing architectures. Time will tell how this all plays out.*

- **Standard system-wide fonts**   If you are installing new fonts that can be used by anyone who uses your Mac, you place them in a second Fonts folder, inside the main Library folder at the top or "root" level of your hard drive. Fonts installed in that folder are immediately recognized by the operating system and by Mac OS X–savvy software.

- **User-specific fonts**   Everyone who uses a Mac gets their own personal directory inside the Users folder. There is yet another Library folder inside your Home directory, the folder bearing your name, and inside that folder is your personal Fonts folder. Any font you place inside this folder will be immediately available to you or anyone logging on with your user name and password, and also to the Mac OS X–savvy applications you run. But other users will not be able to run these fonts unless they install them separately. Is there a benefit to this structure? Yes, for the family or business with one user who simply loves fonts and can't get enough of them, and another user who just wants to keep the font menus lean and mean.

- **Network fonts**   If you are involved in a business where fonts need to be shared across a network, you install them in the Fonts folder inside the Library folder, located within the Network. Folks who log onto your Mac across a network (either local or via the Internet) will be able to access the contents of the Network directory, which can also include applications designed for use by a workgroup.

Mac OS X Font Management: Limited to Cocoa Applications

As you know, there are basically two ways to build a Mac OS X–savvy application (in addition to Java, of course). One is Carbon, which uses a set of application programming interfaces (APIs) that allow software publishers to easily port existing Classic applications to the new environment; it also allows many of them to run in older Mac OS versions (at least back to Mac OS 8.6), provided the CarbonLib system extension is installed. The font menu is essentially the same as the one that appears in a regular Classic program. The special font management features of Mac OS X aren't available—well, they weren't available as of the time this book was written (and Apple hadn't announced any plan to change this setup).

The other native programming environment, Cocoa, is descended from the Objective C environment of NeXT, the original Unix operating system on which Mac OS X is based. All applications designed this way inherit the Font Panel (see Figure 6-1).

Using the Font Panel to Select Fonts

With the Font Panel, you can organize your fonts into collections, where you allocate a group of fonts for a specific purpose, such as headlines, body text, or, if you're in the desktop publishing business, even by the name of a client or a specific job.

FIGURE 6-1   Some Mac OS X applications can use this feature for font handling.

Now, it's not always obvious on the surface which application is Carbon and which is Cocoa, but if the Font Panel is available, you'll see a Format menu in the program.

Using the Font Panel involves these basic steps:

1. Choose Font from the Format menu of your Mac OS X/Cocoa application. The keyboard shortcut for this action is COMMAND-T.

2. Choose the font you want from the Family listbox.

3. Select the appropriate style from the Typeface list. What you'll see there depends on the styles available. The standard range consists of Regular (or Roman), Italic, Bold, and Bold Italic.

NOTE *Some "italic" versions of fonts are called Oblique, sometimes because the slanting effect is artificially created from the Roman style.*

4. Finally, pick the size from the Sizes menu.

TIP *Is the size you want not listed? No problem. Enter the desired font size in the text entry field at the top of the size column, and that's the size that will be used.*

5. When you've finished, you can click the Close button to dismiss the Font Panel, although you might just want to keep it handy for more font changes. You can always click the yellow ("minimize") button to keep it around in the Dock for later retrieval if screen space is at a premium (or you don't like window clutter).

Organizing Your Fonts with Favorites and Font Collections

Under the Classic Mac OS, organizing a font library could be a chore. You had to manually add or remove fonts from the Fonts folder (quitting applications before the process and relaunching them after), or use a font management program to organize and activate fonts as needed for a particular document.

While the new organizational features of Cocoa applications under Mac OS X won't actually activate or deactivate fonts, it can make up custom font lists of your library, which definitely eases the process of locating and selecting the fonts you want.

Mac OS X Is Bursting with Font Folders

Here's how to use this feature:

1. Open the Font Panel, as described in the previous section.

2. After selecting the font, style, and size, click on the pop-up menu bearing the name Extras (see Figure 6-2) and choose Add to Favorites.

3. Follow the preceding step for each font you want to select as a Favorite. Once you've created your Favorites, you'll need to expand the Font Panel window with the size bar to bring up the Collections column, which has an item labeled, naturally, Favorites.

Creating an actual font collection is rather more involved than adding Favorites, but the process is pretty straightforward:

1. With the Font Panel opened, choose Edit Collections from the pop-up menu, which produces the Font Collections window shown in Figure 6-3. You'll see several prebuilt collections set up for you by Apple Computer as part of the Mac OS X installation.

2. To make a new collection, press the plus symbol located beneath the Collections column. This action will make a new collection with a prebuilt name, such as New-1, New-2, and so on.

3. To name your collection the way you want, click the Rename button and then give the collection a name appropriate to its use. You can name the collection by purpose, type of font (Serif or San Serif), or in any way that makes it convenient for you.

FIGURE 6-2   Select additional font options from this menu.

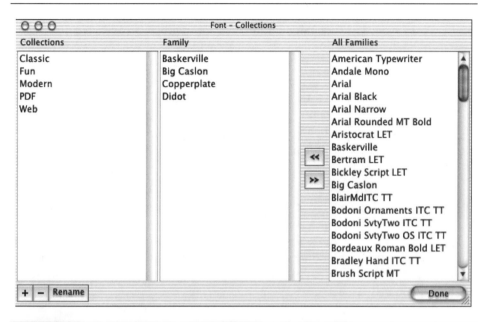

FIGURE 6-3   Here's where you can create and edit font collections.

4. With your collection selected, click on one or more fonts in the Add Families list, and then press the left-pointing arrow to add it to your collection.

5. To remove a font from a collection, select it and click the right-pointing arrow.

6. All finished? Click the Done button to finish the process.

Finding Damaged Fonts

Except in rare circumstances involving hard drive directory damage, you will seldom run into a damaged document. But damaged fonts are another story entirely. Seems as if they turn up at the worst of times, like when you need a font to finish a document. Worse, the problem is not always easy to trace, and it can be easily diagnosed as having a totally unrelated cause.

The Symptoms

When a Mac application is launched, among the things it does while you see the program's startup screen is load a list of available fonts. If one of those fonts is damaged, the program can crash on you right off the bat. In other cases, your program may work just fine, but the font won't print properly, or your printer will hang trying to handle the job.

> NOTE   *While Mac OS X offers more robust stability, it doesn't mean applications won't freeze or quit. As long as programmers are imperfect human beings, that will never change. Fortunately, in just about all cases, you should never need to restart your Mac; however, you will want to restart Classic should a Classic application misbehave.*

It's not always the case that fonts are responsible. For one thing, the symptoms may also have other causes, such as a Classic system extension conflict, a damaged or incompatible program, or a corrupted preference file.

But if you follow through with the standard array of diagnostic steps I've outlined throughout this book and come up with a big fat zero, it's time to consider the possibility that your problem may be font related (and this happens a lot more often than you may expect).

The Cure

A damaged font isn't obvious. The icon doesn't change. It may install just fine, but betray itself by the telltale symptoms just listed.

Here are some ways to check your fonts for damage:

■ **Try Norton Utilities or Drive 10.**   Both programs will check for damaged files as part of the process of scanning your Mac's drive for directory problems. If one or more fonts come up as damaged, delete them and reinstall the fonts.

> CAUTION   *Be cautious about using drive repair utilities that aren't compatible with Mac OS X. You could end up with potential drive directory damage. The latest versions of Norton Utilities will scan Mac OS X drives (although the one I used requires rebooting under Mac OS 9 or from the CD first).*

■ **Use a font management utility to diagnose the fonts.**   Adobe Type Manager Deluxe, Alsoft's MasterJuggler, Diamond Soft's Font Reserve, and Extensis Suitcase 8 FontAgent can all scan for damaged fonts. Use the built-in capabilities of these programs to find the offending files and then replace them with fresh copies.

NOTE

When this book was written, only Font Reserve and Suitcase were due for Mac OS X updates. However, that doesn't prevent you from running them as a font management program from the Classic environment in search of damaged fonts (or to manage a Classic font collection).

- **A virus program works, too.**   The popular virus detection programs Network Associates' Virex and Symantec's Norton AntiVirus will report damaged files to you as part of their scans for virus-related activity.

NOTE

I recommend up-to-date commercial virus software for the ultimate in protection against computer viruses. But if you have a copy of the old, free virus program Disinfectant around, you will be pleased to know it will check for damaged files as part of its scanning process. However, Disinfectant is not useful as a program to detect present-day Mac viruses.

Coping with Font Conflicts

When programs have serious bugs, the results are usually predictable. Applications can freeze or quit The things you need to do to fix those problems are pretty straightforward. The previous chapter and Chapter 18 cover the subject in more extensive detail for both the Classic and Mac OS X environments.

But font conflicts don't manifest themselves in so clear a fashion. They are not the same sort of conflicts that affect regular software, the kind of conflicts that cause system crashes and other untoward behavior. Rather, they are conflicts that result in improper display and printing of your documents, and they can be a bear to handle, unless you organize your fonts carefully.

Case History   **Futura vs. Futura**

Back in the early 1990s, I was working with a graphic design studio with a bank of those high-end printers, called imagesetters, that are used to prepare final copy for offset printing. One of the services offered was to provide high-resolution prints for a number of clients.

A normal job request came down, a newsletter using the Futura typeface. The client had provided laser prints, so we could compare the original with the end result. And that's where the problem began.

On the screen, before the document was sent to an imagesetter, we could see that everything was all wrong. The line breaks were different, and the look of the lettering was different as well. Sizes didn't match. We ran a laser print, and it only confirmed what we saw on the monitor.

There was nothing unusual about the list of fonts used in the document. They specified several different styles of Futura in several different sizes. So we phoned the client and learned one more thing. Their version of Futura came from a different source than ours. We used Adobe's fonts. Shown here is the regular Adobe version of Futura Bold, in 24-point, a popular typeface used for ad display.

Attack of the Rockoids is Coming!

Their fonts came from a company called Bitstream. The Bitstream variation is similar, when shown in 24-point, but notice how the actual width of the letters and even the size differ slightly from the Adobe version.

Attack of the Rockoids is Coming!

Should it have made a difference? Yes, indeed. Even when the names are the same, each font vendor will have its own idea about how the design is executed. The width values of the letters may differ; even the actual size of the letterforms may be a little larger or a little smaller. This means that 12-point from one manufacturer may be a bit smaller or larger than 12-point from another manufacturer. When the two factors combine, you are creating the climate for a font catastrophe.

The final result was that the client was asked to supply their own fonts with their work. This is a common practice with service bureaus that handle this sort of job. If you supply your own fonts, there's no problem in matching things up.

NOTE *Even though font publishers have stringent licensing requirements for their products, those requirements usually affect the number of output devices you use. Just about every font publisher will allow you to send your fonts to a service bureau, as long as the fonts are not used to output any other client's job.*

> The other suggestion is this: If you intend to share a document with another company and need to make sure everything looks the same, check first to make sure their fonts are the same as yours. If not, request that they acquire the fonts or bring them with you if you need to work on a document at their site.

More Font Troubles and Solutions

In addition to mixing the same fonts in PostScript and TrueType form, or simply having a font from the wrong vendor, there are other problems with fonts that can be just as aggravating. In the next few pages, I'll cover some of the usual problems and the usual suspects.

Bitmapped PostScript Font Screen Display

You write something on the screen, and instead of the letters appearing reasonably clear and sharp, the edges are jagged, and it looks like your font consists of a set of large rectangular bricks:

Attack of the Rockoids is Coming!

Here's what to check:

- **ATM requires PostScript printer fonts for Classic Environment**   If you're using Adobe Type Manager to clean up font display, you have to make sure that both the bitmap (screen) and printer fonts are in the same folder. ATM doesn't have any way to look for your printer fonts in another location. Remember, too, that ATM cannot help you print a document with PostScript fonts on a non-PostScript printer without the printer fonts. Mac OS X provides ATM-like font rendering, but you still need to make sure the fonts are properly installed.

NOTE   *If you're using a font manager for your font library, you still have to keep printer and screen fonts in the same folder for them to work properly.*

- **Missing printer fonts**   Double-check to make sure that you indeed have the corresponding printer fonts for your PostScript font sets. Screen fonts are easily acquired, even from Adobe's Web site, but they don't help if the printer fonts aren't there as well.

Coping with Font Conflicts

■ **ATM not installed under Classic**   Even though ATM technology is part of Mac OS X's ATS, when it comes to PostScript fonts, you'll only get clear display on your screen for your Classic applications if you install Adobe Type Manager. Fortunately, the bare-bones version (with the "Lite" moniker) is usually available with Adobe's Acrobat Reader or as a free download direct from Adobe's Web site. If you installed Acrobat Reader and ATM isn't around, check the folder in which Acrobat Reader is installed. For some unaccountable reason, it's often placed in a folder called Fonts, which has nothing whatever to do with the Fonts folder inside your System Folder. Once you locate ATM, drag it to the closed Classic System Folder icon. Now go launch the System Preferences application, click the Classic icon, and then restart Classic. All should be right with your font display (assuming the fonts are correctly installed).

■ **Reinstall the font**   If the font is correctly installed, and you have ATM in place, try reinstalling the font. The original could be damaged.

■ **Check for font conflicts**   Even if the font is correctly installed, mixing PostScript and TrueType versions of the same fonts (such as PostScript Times and TrueType Times) or having several versions of the same face from different manufacturers may produce some very untidy side effects with your screen display and printout of a document. Read the section entitled "A Look at a Classic Font Manager" for suggestions on software that can help you deal with this dilemma.

Bitmap Printing

Poor screen display may be something you can live with if you can get good quality with your printed documents. But if the output quality is bad (even if the screen display is good), then it is intolerable. Here's how to address the problem:

■ **ATM needed for non-PostScript printer under Classic**   Those inkjet printers from such companies as Canon, Epson, HP, and Lexmark do great work on photos and regular artwork, but when it comes to PostScript, they just don't speak the same language. They work just dandy with TrueType fonts, but to use PostScript fonts on such printers, you have two choices. The simplest is just to install ATM (it's free with Adobe Acrobat Reader or at Adobe's Web site, as I mentioned earlier). If you want to handle PostScript graphics (also known as EPS), you'll want to consider PostScript software, which turns your Mac into a real raster image processor (RIP). You can get one of these programs from such companies as Barmy, Epson, and Strydent.

NOTE   *PostScript graphics are simply those created in a program and saved in Encapsulated PostScript (EPS) format. This file format lets you place or import graphics into your document and get the highest possible print quality.*

- **Missing PostScript printer font**   Even if you have ATM installed, you cannot get good quality printouts unless the PostScript printer font is correctly installed in the same folder as the screen font.

- **Font conflict**   If you have mixed PostScript and TrueType versions of the same font, or two fonts of the same name from different vendors, your Mac may just give up and not download the proper font information to your printer. Instead of just getting poor letter spacing, the actual characters themselves may be bitmapped. The solution is to organize your font library (using the suggestions later in this chapter) to make sure you are cautious when you mix or match.

Fonts Missing from Font Menu

You can't very well use a font if it's not appearing in the font menu. Here are the likely causes of this problem and what to do about it:

- **Classic and Mac OS X fonts are separate**   To add to the confusion of handling multiple locations for fonts, you have to contend with the fact that Classic applications will look for fonts in the Classic Fonts folder (or any location activated under a font management program), and Mac OS X software will seek out fonts in that folder and the various locations set aside for them under Mac OS X. So, if a font isn't available in a particular application, you'll need to make doubly sure the font is properly installed in that environment, Classic or OS X.

- **Screen font missing**   Yes, your PostScript printer font may be properly installed in the right Fonts folder, but it doesn't live in a vacuum. Font menus on Mac programs are also based on the presence of the bitmap (screen) font. So if you install a new font and don't see it listed on the menu, double-check to be certain the bitmap font is properly installed (it can either be a separate file or placed within a font suitcase).

Coping with Font Conflicts

■ **Software won't dynamically update font menus**   Some programs, such as QuarkXPress or Adobe's InDesign and PageMaker, are cleverly designed to know when you install new fonts. The font menus will update automatically, though it may take a few seconds for the deed to be done. But many programs are not so smart about such changes. If a newly installed font doesn't appear in the font menu, quit the program and launch it again. If that doesn't work, just restart your Mac or, at the very least, log out and log in again.

■ **Replace preferences for Classic font menu modifiers**   The programs that modify your font menus to organize and clean up display keep preference files as a database of the fonts you've got installed on your Mac. These programs include Adobe Type Reunion Deluxe, MenuFonts, and ACTION WYSIWYG Menus. If you're adding or removing fonts and the font menus don't reflect the changes, locate the preference files (in the Preferences folder inside the Classic Mac OS System Folder) and remove them. Restart your Mac, and the programs will rebuild their font displays.

NOTE   *If the preference files for a font menu modifier program aren't obvious, look for a folder with the name of the publisher (such as Power On Preferences for the ACTION Utilities product line).*

■ **Reinstall the font**   Even if you've checked your font and it comes up undamaged, reinstall it anyway. Font damage is usually easy to detect when it's a printer font, but if a single screen font size in a font suitcase is damaged, programs such as Norton Utilities and TechTool Pro just won't pick up on it.

Font Has Missing Characters or Square Boxes Instead of Letters

This is one problem that has a fairly easy solution. Some low-cost font packages, from companies such as FontBank and KeyFonts, didn't come with the complete character set. You'd get all of your letters and numbers, but such characters as a percentage sign or a copyright symbol were missing. In addition, some fonts are all capital letters, with nothing but square or rectangular boxes in the lowercase positions.

Whether this is a cost-based decision or is due to some other cause, I won't hazard a guess. But it can be downright annoying.

If you're not certain whether the font you have has the full character set, use Apple's Key Caps program (which is installed in Mac OS X's Utilities folder) or my favorite, a shareware program called PopChar Pro (which I sincerely hope will make the transition to Mac OS X by the time you read this book), both of which will check the letters available on a specific font.

Fortunately, if a specific character symbol isn't available from one font, there's nothing to stop you from switching to the Symbol font or another typeface and using the character from that font instead.

> **NOTE** *Our technical editor, Greg Titus (an old hand at programming in Cocoa) says that, at least for a Cocoa application, the missing symbol will be automatically substituted from another font.*

Can't Delete Font in Classic Fonts Folder

This happens every so often. You decide you really don't need a specific font, so you try to trash it. You open your Fonts folder, and attempt to drag the font to the desktop or trash, but you get a message that you can't do so because the file or folder is damaged.

> **NOTE** *You also can't delete a font if any applications are open, so check your application menu. However, in this case, the Finder will put up a very clear message as to why the fonts can't be moved.*

Here's what to do if this happens to you:

1. Check your Mac's drive directory with the First Aid component of the Disk Utility application (you have to start from another drive or the Mac OS X CD) or a commercial hard drive repair program, such as Alsoft's DiskWarrior, MicroMat's TechTool Pro, or Symantec's Norton Utilities. I'll cover the process in more detail in Chapter 13.

2. After the hard drive is checked, and any disk directory damage repaired, open your Classic Mac OS System Folder, and drag the Fonts folder onto your Mac's desktop (don't delete it!).

3. Open the System Preferences application, click on the Classic icon, and restart your Classic environment. The process will create a brand new, empty Fonts folder inside the System Folder.

4. Open the old Fonts folder on your Mac's desktop and remove the font you want to trash. This should work properly this time (if not, try step 1 again).

5. Select all of the remaining fonts and drag them to the new Fonts folder inside the Classic Mac OS System Folder.

6. Trash your old Fonts folder.

7. Empty the trash.

This process has worked for me every time I've been unable to remove a font. I won't necessarily say it's caused by a corrupt Fonts folder or a corrupt font or hard drive directory damage. It can be one or all of these, but at least you'll be able to start fresh with a brand new Fonts folder. Fortunately, such ills aren't prevalent with Mac OS X's four Fonts folders.

Font Organization Tips and Tricks

Fonts are everywhere. They come in low-cost packages, and they are included with various and sundry software boxes from Adobe, Corel, Microsoft (even with their free Internet applications), and elsewhere. In years past, if you wanted a lot of fonts, you had to pay a pretty penny for them, or get knock-offs that offered poor quality or were missing some of the more obscure characters.

Today, without a substantial investment, you could end up with hundreds or even thousands of fonts from here, there, and everywhere. So what do you do with all of them? Just install them on your Mac and use when necessary? It's not that easy.

A Look at a Classic Font Manager

The dilemma of having to load and unload a lot of fonts was especially cumbersome in the days before Mac System 7 came out, when you had to use a clunky program called Font/DA Mover to move screen fonts in and out of your System file. Half the time, the program would crash your Mac, especially when you needed to do a lot of font movements in a single step.

A clever programmer, Steve Brecher, created a solution. It was called Suitcase (see Figure 6-4), and it was designed to open and close fonts, regardless of whether they were truly installed in the System Folder.

NOTE   *After selling Suitcase to the publisher at that time, Symantec, Brecher has apparently retired from the software game and is living a quiet life in Nevada. I heard from him some time during the year 2000, and he had no interest, at the time, in getting back into the "game."*

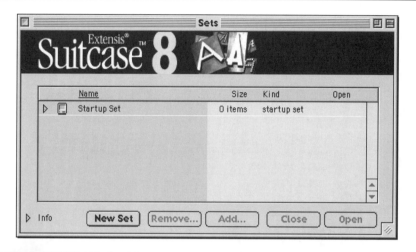

Font Organization Tips and Tricks

FIGURE 6-4 Suitcase helped make font organization make sense.

It worked by fooling "Mother Nature" (in this case, the Mac operating system) into thinking that the fonts were indeed in their proper location, the Fonts folder. Some call the program a clever hack, but I won't use that term.

So all you had to do was create a special folder for your fonts (aside from basic system fonts), then use Suitcase (or one of the other programs that perform this function) to switch your fonts on and off like a light switch.

The fact of the matter is that it was a terrific way to keep your font menus lean and mean and deal with large numbers of fonts, without having to go through the usual installation process.

In addition to Suitcase (which, after going through three publishers, is still going strong and will make the transition to Mac OS X), there's Adobe Type Manager Deluxe (see Figure 6-5) and Alsoft's MasterJuggler Pro.

NOTE

Unfortunately, the arrival of Mac OS X and its new font organizational routine appears to be the death knell for one of those font managers. Adobe, for example, indicated that they would keep the "Lite" version of Adobe Type Manager compatible for Classic, but no native Mac OS X was in the cards. Alsoft was, at the time this book was written, working on a native Mac OS X version of MasterJuggler Pro, described as a "total rewrite."

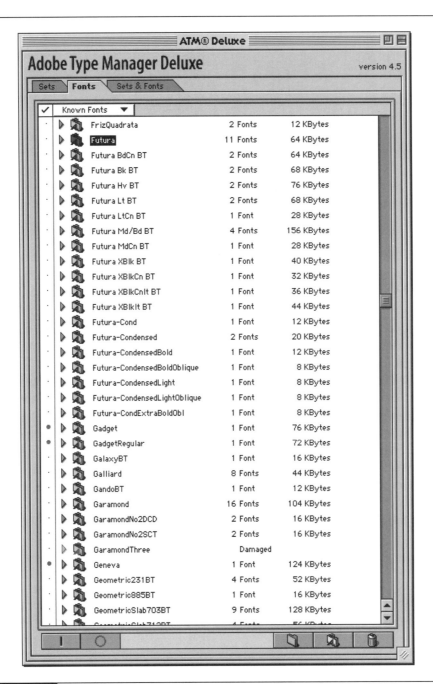

FIGURE 6-5   ATM Deluxe will, unfortunately, never be ported to Mac OS X.

The Font Reserve Alternative

Another font management program, DiamondSoft's Font Reserve, works by putting your entire font collection (except System Folder fonts) in a single, huge database. The program then goes through them and figures out your font conflicts and whether any fonts are damaged.

The advantage here is one of organization. You simply add the fonts to the program's database file, and it sorts them all out for you. It works best, as do the other font management programs, with a large library. The larger your font library, the more valuable one of these programs will be to keep it in tip-top shape.

NOTE   *Font Reserve was in the process of being updated for Mac OS X when this book was written.*

A Handy-Dandy Font Organizing Routine (Using a Font Manager)

If you've got a lot of fonts and need to activate bunches of them at a time, here are some suggestions on how to organize them so you don't run into conflicts and problems launching your applications.

The instructions that follow presuppose that fonts will have to be managed separately in the Mac OS X and Classic environments, and that the native font managers will not necessarily resolve this confusion. This routine assumes you will be using one of the font management programs described earlier. Otherwise, feel free to ignore these suggestions:

- **Keep duplicate font libraries for Classic applications.**   Whether your font management program makes the transition or not, the fact is that, under ordinary circumstances, a Classic application's font menu shows fonts in the Fonts folder within the Classic System Folder, and, when the fonts are opened by a Classic font manager, Mac OS X applications will see fonts in one of the four locations described at the start of this chapter, plus the ones in use by your Classic environment. If fonts are placed in a user's own folder, only that user (or one logged in to that user's account) will be able to use those fonts.

- **Keep the Classic System Folder's Fonts folder small.**   Yes, a mouthful! When you have a font manager, you don't have to put all your fonts in the normal place. The font manager software will do those chores. Just keep your basic set of Apple-installed fonts in your Fonts folder, the ones that you see on your screen beneath icons, in the menu bar, or in titles. These include Charcoal, Chicago, Capitals, Gadget, Geneva, Impact, Monaco, New York, Sand, Symbol, Textile, and Techno. You may also want to leave fonts that you use all the time, such as Courier, Helvetica, and Times. The rest can be placed elsewhere.

NOTE *If you're using Adobe Acrobat, you'll also want to have these fonts installed in your Fonts folder: AdobeSerMM, AdobeSanMM, Adobe Serif MM, and Adobe Sans MM.*

- **Restrict your Mac OS X Font folders to preinstalled fonts.**   While Mac OS X can handle a nearly unlimited number of fonts, there is no sense struggling through endless font menus, nor restricting yourself to Cocoa applications to take advantage of the Font Panel. Use a font manager program to handle all the extra fonts you want to install.

- **Put the rest of your fonts in another folder.**   Aside from the essential fonts, put the rest of your font library in a brand-new folder, which you can call Resources (or anything you like that makes sense to you, such as Other Fonts, and so on). This folder doesn't have to be in the System Folder. It only has to be on a hard drive that is mounted on your Mac when you need the fonts.

TIP *Even if you have to use both a Classic and a Mac OS X font manager (assuming the Mac OS X program doesn't support both environments), there's no reason why they can't point to the very same folder, so you can use the same font library for both environments and save yourself a lot of headaches and potential confusion.*

- **Sort fonts by font manufacturer.**   This makes sorting easy if you have a big font library. Within your Resources folder, create folders bearing the names of the manufacturers of your fonts, such as Adobe, Bitstream, Monotype, and so on. By doing this, it'll be easier to keep tabs on possible font conflicts, which occur when you have more than one font of the same name open.

NOTE *If you can't tell who made the font by looking at the icon, use the Finder's Show Info command and look for a copyright notice. There are no guarantees you'll find one, but it's worth trying.*

■ **Set aside separate folders for each type family.**   This is also a good tip for a huge library. After you subdivide fonts by font manufacturer, set aside a separate folder for each type family. Put Helvetica in one folder, Times in another, and so on. Just remember to try not to mix fonts of the same name from different vendors.

■ **Be cautious about TrueType fonts for professional output.**   Before you decide whether to use a TrueType font, contact the printer or service bureau who will be handling your high-resolution output. Be guided by what they say in terms of font compatibility. And, of course, feel free to seek another firm if the one you call first doesn't give you the services you need.

■ **Be cautious about specifying PostScript fonts for your Web site.**   Just as TrueType fonts aren't a good idea for professional output, the reverse is true on the World Wide Web. The likelihood that a large number of folks will have the fonts you specify is slim, since the basic system fonts for both Macs and Windows-based computers are TrueType. If you keep to those basic TrueType fonts, you'll stand a good chance of providing the best quality font display for the largest number of Net surfers.

■ **Disable fonts you don't need.**   Enjoy the convenience of the font menu manager. Disable any font you have no need for, so your font menus are kept short and your application launch times are as brief as possible.

A Handy-Dandy Font Organizing Routine for Classic Fonts (without a Font Manager)

If you don't have a large font library (that is, more than 100 to 200 fonts), there's probably no need to buy a separate program to manage your font library. But you'll want to keep a few things in mind as you set up your libraries:

■ **Combine font suitcases.**   If you have a lot of fonts from the same family, combine the font suitcases. That way you'll see fewer files in your Fonts folder, and not have to pour through long lists to see what you've installed.

■ **Remove fonts you don't need.**   If you don't intend to use certain fonts, you can move them elsewhere. You may want to create a folder labeled Fonts (Disabled), which corresponds to the folders in which disabled Control Panels and Extensions are placed. Put the fonts you don't need in those folders.

Font Organization Tips and Tricks

 *Those default fonts in the Fonts folder within the System's Library folder cannot be removed under the Mac OS X environment. While they can be removed by rebooting your Mac under your Classic Mac OS, there's no harm in leaving them in their normal locations.*

Quit Applications Before Removing Fonts from a Fonts Folder

Unlike font management software, you usually cannot remove a Classic font unless all open applications have been quit first. If you think you've closed all programs, yet still get the message, check to see if you have any special icon palettes on your Mac's desktop, which are commonly used to launch programs and documents. One example is Apple's Launcher, a standard component of the Classic Mac OS. Yes, it is an application, too, and you can quit it simply by clicking the close box.

Once you quit all open applications, you should be able to remove fonts. If you still get a message that applications are open, restart the Classic environment and try again.

Or just open Extensions Manager, choose a Mac OS (whatever version you have) Base Set, and restart. That should close any hidden or background applications your Mac is using.

TIP *A quick way to open Extensions Manager from Mac OS X is to open the System Preferences application and click on the Classic panel. Click on the Advanced tab and choose Open Extensions Manager from the Startup Options pop-up menu.*

If you're using a Mac OS X application, you'll still want to quit the application before changing the font lineup on any of the Fonts folders. Do not expect them to update dynamically.

NOTE *When I tried removing a font while Apple's Mail application was open, not only did the Font Panel not update, but the program quit.*

Summing Up

In this chapter, you learned about the various font formats on your Mac, how to manage your fonts, and how to deal with font conflicts.

In Chapter 7, I'll cover the trials and tribulations of dealing with graphic files, with special emphasis on Web-based graphics and sharing files with Windows users.

Chapter 7

Dealing with
Graphic File Headaches

“I can't read the file." That's the clarion call of many of the folks who contact me about problems with their Macs. You'd think that the number-one problem a computing consultant deals with would be system-related problems. Considering that application quits and crashes are part and parcel of the personal computing experience, although lessened under Mac OS X, this would seem to be a very logical assumption.

But one of the most vexing problems I deal with on a regular basis is the matter of graphic files. The advent of the World Wide Web and easy Internet access has made it easy as pie to send and receive files. Since the way files are handled differs from one computing platform to the other, it makes for a corresponding number of problems.

The most common complaint is that folks you send your graphic files to cannot read them, or that you cannot read the files they send to you.

A Quick Review of Graphic File Formats

There are dozens of graphic file formats that exist across the various computing platforms. Fortunately, some of these formats are not often used cross-platform, so there isn't much likelihood that you'll encounter many of them. If you do, a shareware program mentioned later in this chapter, GraphicConverter, may serve to help you deal with some of the most arcane types of graphics.

In this section, I'm concentrating on the types of files you're apt to encounter on a regular basis on your travels on the Internet or when exchanging files with your contacts who use the other platform. In addition, I'll list the DOS file extensions that apply to these files, so if you're converting the file to Windows you can attach the appropriate file.

NOTE   *Dealing with graphic file formats isn't the only source of trouble in handling cross-platform issues. I'll cover the subject in much more detail in Chapter 11.*

■ **ART (.art) files**   This is a graphic file format used by AOL for processing Web-based images. It's designed to speed delivery of Web pages to AOL members by compressing graphics in this proprietary format. Unfortunately, this feature can result in the loss of quality on Web-based images, and usually kills any animation that might be present in the original picture. That, in itself, is a real downer, since well-done animation is one of the great joys of visiting a Web site. In addition, you need AOL's software (or Netscape 6, published by AOL's Netscape division) to actually open such images. Even the full-featured GraphicConverter software doesn't read the format. Worse, the file's name isn't changed by the conversion process (so it'll still retain its .gif or .jpg file extension, for example), and you won't know it's in the wrong format until you try to open it. If you're an AOL member, the best way to avoid these problems is simply to turn off the option to compress Web graphics. It's a WWW preference in AOL's software.

NOTE   *When you reinstall AOL's software, recheck this setting. Even though you may have previously turned off the compress feature, sometimes it "resets" itself.*

- **AVI (.avi) files**   This is a Windows-based movie format, designed to compete with QuickTime. QuickTime 4.0 handles such files with aplomb.

- **BMP (.bmp) files**   The Windows answer to PICT. When you use the print screen feature under Windows, the image you capture is saved in this format. Since it is a bitmap format, you can scale it downward (with increased resolution), but when you scale upward, the size of the dots grows larger, and thus image quality suffers.

- **EPS (.eps) files**   The term is short for Encapsulated PostScript. EPS files contain PostScript instructions that require a PostScript printer to produce good-quality output. On a non-PostScript printer, all you get is a low-resolution PICT version. EPS files are normally created by high-end illustration programs and are imported into desktop publishing or word processing documents. This is the only vector format that I'll list here; it's a format that you can scale in any size and still have it reproduce at the full resolution of your output device.

- **GIF (.gif) files**   This is another compressed graphic format, which originated with CompuServe. GIF stands for Graphic Interchange Format. Such files have advantages and disadvantages. One advantage is that they are suitable for Web-based animations, but you are limited to 256 colors (a far cry from JPEG). In addition to their Web capabilities, GIF files tend to work better with text and line drawings, such as diagrams, graphs, and maps, than JPEG. If you're not sure what format to use, try them out on sample documents and see which one looks better.

A Quick Review of Graphic File Formats

■ **JPEG (.jpg) files**   One of the popular file formats used for Web-based artwork. The term stands for Joint Photographic Experts Group, and the file uses compression to save storage space. The compression technique is called *lossy,* because portions of the file are removed, though it takes a lot of compression to reduce image quality to a noticeable degree. However, the quality loss isn't near as great as in the GIF format, because JPEG supports millions of colors. JPEG files work great with photographs, less well with graphics that contain text.

NOTE   *Lossy compression schemes pervade the audio and video world. The ever-popular MP3 music format, for example, uses an encoding technique that not only reduces file size but eliminates data as well (although it's designed to minimize the audible impact). Those DVD protocols that are taking over the home video world also employ an extremely powerful compression scheme to make a complete movie small enough to fit on a 5-1/4 inch optical disc.*

■ **MOV (.mov) files**   This is a format for QuickTime movies. You can open it with QuickTime Player or any other program that can read QuickTime files.

■ **PCX (.pcx) files**   This is a PC format used for bitmap graphics, and it's used for PC Paintbrush and other programs. There are four basic variations of this format, but only the version 5 format supports 24-bit color.

■ **PDF (.pdf) files**   Short for Portable Document Format, this is the native 2-D image rendering format for Mac OS X. Developed by Adobe, this format is also used to distribute electronic documents containing both text and graphics. Mac OS X allows you to convert any open document to PDF format.

■ **PICT (.pct) files**   This was the native Macintosh bitmap file format used for the Classic Mac OS. When you save images to the Mac clipboard, or make a screen capture (using such shortcuts as COMMAND-SHIFT-3 and COMMAND-SHIFT-4), the files are saved in PICT format. This format is not recommended if you wish to send a file to a Windows user.

NOTE   *Some of the original screen capture shortcuts were restored to Mac OS X beginning in version 10.1.*

- **PNG (.png) files**   The promoters of this format called it a successor to GIF. PNG is short for Portable Network Graphics format, and it's designed to offer better file compression and improved image quality (including support for 24-bit color). PNG format is supported by Web browsers that are compatible with HTML 4.0; other browsers just get the GIF variation of the image.

- **SGI (.sgi) files**   This is an image format used for SGI (formerly Silicon Graphics) computer systems. Since SGI workstations are often used in the creation of high-level graphics and movie animations, you may from time to time run across such image files.

- **Targa (.tga) files**   The format was first used by Truevision for their Targa and Vista video capture boards. It's a bitmap file format for high-quality graphics, used in a number of 2-D and 3-D programs.

NOTE   *The Targa capture boards are now marketed by Pinnacle Systems. If you want to explore desktop video editing in more detail, you'll want to read Chapter 19.*

- **TIFF (.tif) files**   The term is short for Tagged-Image File Format. In case you were wondering, the "tagged" aspects are the enhancements made to improve the appearance of the image. TIFF files are commonly used for photographs and other high-quality images. And, need I add, a full-color TIFF photograph can be many, many megabytes in size (which is why such programs as Photoshop require huge amounts of RAM to work efficiently with them). TIFF files are commonly used for creating high-quality printed materials.

- **WMF (.wmf) files**   The term is short for Windows Metafile Format, and it's used for exchanging graphics among Microsoft Windows programs.

How to View PC Graphics on a Mac

As Apple's system software has come of age, the tools to handle files of different formats have grown more robust. For example, when you open a file for which you don't have the original application, Mac OS X will provide a dialog box that you can click and then select an application in which to open that document from among the ones you have installed (see Figure 7-1). As a result, you can usually open those files simply by double-clicking on them—that is, as long as you have a Mac program with which to view the files.

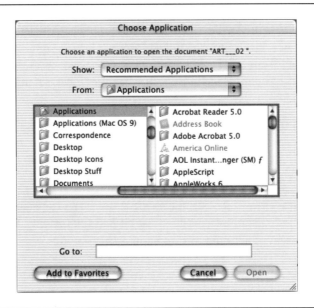

FIGURE 7-1 This is a list of applications recommended by Mac OS X to open this document.

Fortunately, most of the graphic files you're apt to receive are easily read by one or more programs you already have on your Mac.

These are some examples:

- **Adobe Photoshop Elements**   Taking the place of PhotoDeluxe in its Mac product line, this program offers the essential features of Photoshop, and it is quite capable of reading and saving files in a number of graphic formats, both PC and Mac based. You'll find this program bundled with some of the lower-cost scanners from several manufacturers. In fact, you may already have a copy if you have one of those products.

- **Adobe Photoshop**   This is the premiere image editing program, used by professionals in the graphic arts industry. It can read most of the graphic file formats I've described here, including EPS files. A number of scanners include the full or limited function versions of Photoshop as part of the package. If you're lucky enough to get this program, you'll find it a valuable tool to process graphic files of all kinds.

■ **GraphicConverter** This is a favorite of mine. It's a popular Mac shareware program (used extensively to edit the figures for this book), which is capable of reading dozens and dozens of types of graphic files on the major computing platforms (including Unix). I won't begin to list the formats that are supported; the program is updated several times a year with still more supported file formats and more features. A notable exception is EPS, which requires a separate program to rasterize the images (see the previous bullet about Photoshop).

■ **Preview** This program comes with Mac OS X and can handle documents in the native 2-D format, PDF, plus several standard image files, such as BMP, GIF, JPEG, PICT, and TIFF. As a result, most of the image files you get in the normal course of events can be viewed without difficulty.

■ **QuickTime Player** This program can handle the same range of graphic formats as Preview, plus QuickTime movies, Windows-based AVI movies, and many more. Counting the audio and video formats, QuickTime Player can read more than 30 file formats.

■ **Your Web browser** Microsoft Internet Explorer comes with Mac OS X. In addition, another Web browser, OmniWeb, has gained a big following and is preferred by a number of Mac users. Either program can handle the basic image files, such as GIF, JPEG, and PNG, plus the Windows BMP format. OmniWeb manages PICT and TIFF, too.

NOTE *I've made no attempt here to cover all the programs that can read various graphic file formats. There are far too many to list. Instead, I'm concentrating on the ones most often available. If you have other software in these product categories, simply check your documentation for the file formats that are supported.*

As you see, your Mac is probably well equipped to deal with graphic files. Regardless of whether they come from a Web site, email, or another source, here's how you'd view such files:

1. Locate your graphic file.

2. Double-click on the graphic.

How to View
PC Graphics on a Mac

3. If the Mac OS X Finder produces a dialog asking you to select from a list of applications that can read the file, choose an appropriate program (use the ones listed earlier as a guide).

NOTE *When you select a file to use when opening a document, Mac OS X will usually (but not always) remember your choice and religiously use that same program each time a similar document is opened.*

4. Click the Open button to launch the application you select and open the document. If all goes well, you should see your picture file on your Mac's screen in short order.

A Quick Review of Problems in Opening Graphic Files

Even if you have the right programs, it's possible that you will run into trouble when it comes to opening a graphic file. Here are some common symptoms and their solutions:

- **Application doesn't open document.**   Even though an application appears in the Recommended Applications list, it doesn't guarantee it'll open the file. You will want to try different applications to see if one succeeds.

TIP *One way to see whether an application supports the file format is to drag the file atop the icon for the application. If the application's icon darkens, the format is probably supported. Just release the mouse and the application will attempt to open the document—and usually it'll succeed.*

- **Wrong application opens.**   Quit the application and try another application. The Finder may get the message after a couple of attempts. You may also want to change the setting in the Finder's Show Info window for the document in question. Here's how:

  1. Click once on the document's icon to select it, and then choose Show Info from the Finder's File menu or just type COMMAND-I.

  2. Choose Application from the Show pop-up menu, which brings up the window that appears in Figure 7-2.

  3. Click on the radio button labeled A Specific Application under Open This Document With.

4. Click on the application icon preview and choose Add Application.

5. On the next screen, select an application with which to open that document.

If you prefer to have that application open all documents of the same format, click on The Generic Application for Documents of This Type radio button, and then click on the Change Application button to select the new default application.

■ **Try the Open dialog box.**   If all else fails, try opening the application first, then go to the File menu, choose Open, and select the file from the list (you'll probably have to navigate to the correct folder or disk). If the file doesn't show in the Open dialog box, use the program's Insert or Import or Place feature, if available. If the program can open a particular type of graphic file, one of these commands ought to work.

Remember that you can often do things in different ways to accomplish the same purpose. Mac OS X allows you to drag an icon into the Open dialog box and immediately jump to where the file is located. You can also drag and drop the file atop an application's icon, in the traditional Macintosh way.

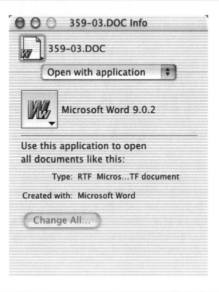

FIGURE 7-2   You can change the application that automatically opens this document here.

How to View
PC Graphics on a Mac

Preparing Mac Graphics to Work in the Windows World

Wouldn't it be nice if all graphics files worked the same way on both Mac and Windows computers?

Alas, it is not to be. On the Mac, a file's format is automatically recognized by the smart Mac OS X Finder, assuming the file's attributes are intact, of course.

> **NOTE** *Our fearless technical editor reminds me that Apple's Human Interface Guidelines for Mac OS X recommend that applications should add the proper file extension to documents if it deals with cross-platform files. As this tendency grows, problems opening Mac files in the Windows world might lessen.*

For other computing platforms, including Windows and other versions of Unix, you have to, in effect, tell the operating system what sort of file it is by using a three-letter extension at the end of the file's name (files saved by applications on those operating systems are already correctly named). Otherwise, the operating system won't know how to handle the files. I'll cover the subject of cross-platform file issues more thoroughly in Chapter 11.

> **NOTE** *Naming a file is half the battle; the file actually has to be saved in the proper format for it to be opened properly. Otherwise, the file may come up as damaged or in the wrong format when someone on another computing platform tries to access it. Don't be lulled into security if your Web browser handles the file, because most Mac browsers check the file's format rather than the extension in the file name.*

So, for example, a JPEG file, a format commonly used in Web graphics, must have a .jpg extension to the file name so the folks who aren't using Macs can access the file. Here's how you can set up your files so users of Windows won't run into trouble in trying to use those files.

> **CAUTION** *When sending files to Windows users, don't use Mac-specific formats, such as PICT. It's very easy to change the file format to something that is compatible without losing image quality.*

File Is in Correct Format

If the file has already been saved in a format that can be read under Windows, just follow these steps (if the naming isn't correct):

1. Click on the file's name to select it and press the RETURN key.

2. Add the proper file extension to the end of the file's name. For example, if the file is called rockoids and it's in JPEG format, you'll rename it rockoids.jpg.

Now you can send your file to Windows users and they'll be able to open it with any program that can read such files.

NOTE

Under Windows, when your document is correctly named, it'll recognize the file as associated with a specific program, so you can double-click on the file and have it open in the proper program. If double-clicking doesn't work, Windows will show a dialog box where you may select an application with which to open the document. Maybe the major computing platforms aren't all that different after all?

File Is in Wrong Format

If the file you have is not already in a format that can be conveniently read by a Windows-based computer, you'll need to not only rename it, but convert it to a format that does work. Here's what to do:

1. Open the file in your preferred graphic program.

2. Choose Save As from the File menu, which will bring up a screen where you can select the format in which to save the file (see Figure 7-3). If the program has no such feature, choose the Export command instead (if available).

3. Choose the file format from the list. Notice that GraphicConverter will automatically pick the file extension for you.

4. Click the Save button to convert the file and change its name.

Now you should be able to send that file to the Windows users of your acquaintance with reasonable assurance they'll be able to open the file without encountering any problems.

Preparing Mac Graphics to Work in the Windows World

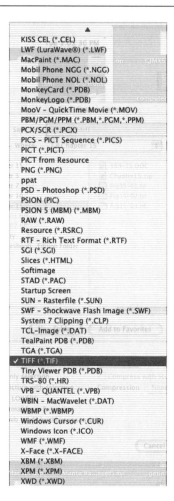

FIGURE 7-3   GraphicConverter gives you loads of options in which to save the file.

Summing Up

In this chapter, I covered the ways to effectively handle graphics problems, so you can freely exchange images with Windows users. This is only a subset of the issues you'll have to consider should you wish to share files with Windows users or if you are on a cross-platform network. I'll cover the subject in much more detail in Chapter 11.

In the next chapter, you'll learn how to install, configure, and troubleshoot your printer.

Chapter 8

Making Your Printer Sing

The highly touted paperless revolution has so far failed to come to pass. Today, you not only print your normal word processing documents, but also Web pages and even those electronic manuals that substitute for real printed instruction books for most products these days.

In fact, there's hardly a Mac out there that doesn't have a printer attached.

But with so many choices, it's hard to know where to begin or what to do when you install your new printer and find it's not working as it should. Mac OS X makes it doubly confusing, because you are, in effect, asked to run a printer from two separate operating systems at the same time: the native system, plus Classic. You are forced to select a printer separately and install software separately (assuming some clever printer maker doesn't come up with a dual installation in a single process).

I've put this chapter together to cover typical problems when working with a printer under Mac OS X and the Classic environments and ways to get it to work properly again.

Installing a Personal Printer

It's amazing what a hundred dollars will buy you in a new printer these days. Such companies as Canon, Epson, Hewlett-Packard, and Lexmark offer great quality full-color printers that can work in a home or small office. Like consumer VCRs these days, they are so cheap that if they break down, there's little problem in replacing them with the latest and greatest successor in that manufacturer's product line.

> **NOTE** *More to the point, the cost of consumables, such as ink, often exceeds the cost of the printer after a replacement or two. You can easily spend far more on keeping the printer running than buying it in the first place, after a month or two of heavy-duty service.*

Here are some things to consider when setting up one of these personal printers (including inkjet models and USB laser printers):

■ **Don't forget to install the printer's software.**   Since Apple left the low-cost printer market, don't expect to find many usable printer drivers on your Mac, except for a handful of preliminary Mac OS X drivers that shipped with the original release of the new operating system and some updated versions for 10.1. Use the installation CDs provided by the printer's manufacturer and look for information about requirements for both Mac

OS X and the Classic Mac OS. Check the setup instructions carefully in case the installer places drivers for several models on your Mac. For example, Epson printers come with serial (or USB) drivers and drivers that work with models with a network card (for LocalTalk and/or Ethernet). In the Classic environment, the latter will have an "AT" in the name you see in the Mac Chooser. Mac OS X's Print Center will usually sort all this out.

■ **Classic and Mac OS X have separate setups.**   The price for compatibility with your older applications is that you literally have to set up your printer to run from two operating systems. When you set up a printer in Print Center, that setting applies strictly to your Mac OS X applications. For Classic applications, you must resort to the Chooser and AppleTalk Control Panels for proper driver and port selection. As more and more native applications arrive, you may find yourself having to cope less and less with this schizophrenic routine, but for now, get used to it.

NOTE

Beginning with Mac OS X 10.1, most USB printers ought to be configured automatically as soon as they're connected, without a trip to Print Center, as long as the proper drivers are installed.

■ **On older Macs, don't forget to turn off AppleTalk in the Classic Environment.**   A serial printer, such as most lower-cost inkjet models, won't work on the printer port with AppleTalk activated. If you are forced to use AppleTalk for a standard network printer, you can handle this dilemma in two ways. One is to connect the printer to your Mac's modem port (if it has one), but then you may have to share it with your external modem if you use an Internet or online service. You could, of course, buy a "port sharing" program or a switchbox to get around this. Or just hook it up to the printer port, and make sure AppleTalk is turned off in the Chooser. For Macs with USB ports, this problem no longer applies (thank heavens).

NOTE

Another symptom of failing to turn off AppleTalk when trying to use a serial printer attached to the printer port is a "serial port in use" message. But, usually, you won't be able to retain the printer port setting for such a printer if AppleTalk is left on.

■ **Remove packing materials before use.**   Be sure that the cardboard, plastic, and/or tape fittings are taken off before you put the printer into service. The delicate inner workings of a low-cost printer are easily damaged.

Installing a Personal Printer

■ **Be careful about third-party or recycled ink cartridges.** My conclusion about this is the same as recycled toner (discussed later in the chapter). Quality tends to be inconsistent. In one example (and I won't mention the brand name in case I just got one bad product), my inkjet printer required repeated head cleaning operations before I could get reasonable quality. By then a large amount of ink was spent, and the money I saved by buying a cheaper cartridge was not worth it.

NOTE *Head cleaning is a process where the ink is systematically sprayed through the printer's nozzles to clean the pathways. It's done automatically when you install new printer cartridges on many models, and you can do it using the printer's software if print quality declines.*

Installing a Network Printer

It used to be that networked printers cost several thousand dollars, and they were only suitable for a large office. However, prices have come down to the point where a network-capable laser printer costs no more than the lowest priced personal laser printers of just a few years ago.

NOTE *I define a network printer as any model that comes with a built-in Ethernet port so you can hook it up to a network consisting of Macs, or PCs and Macs.*

Even if you're using such a printer at home, the ability to seamlessly network with a second Mac may make this sort of product something to seriously consider. Here are a few things to remember when installing and using a network printer:

■ **Use Apple's native laser printer driver unless the printer uses a custom printer driver.** Check the documentation to see if that custom driver is necessary to ensure compatibility with the printer's unique features. Even if you stick with Apple's driver, it doesn't hurt to run your printer's installation disks anyway, as the installer will also usually install a PPD file for the printer (see the section entitled "What's a PPD File and What Do I Need It For?" later in this chapter). There's also the added advantage of good compatibility when Apple updates its system software, since the update will, if need be, include a new version of the driver. That's not always true about the alternatives, such as Adobe's PS Printer (also known sometimes as AdobePS), which had not, as of the date this book was written, been ported to Mac OS X.

■ **Be sure to remove packing materials before use.**   Manufacturers include all sorts of little doo-dads to protect the printer during shipment to dealers and end users. These include cardboard and plastic inserts or pieces of tape. Be sure to check the printer thoroughly to make sure all this material has been removed before you try to run the printer. You will probably have to open various doors and compartments on the printer to locate all of the material (the instruction or setup guide usually explains where to find them). If you fail to remove everything, you may experience paper jams or erratic performance (not to mention the potential to damage the unit).

■ **Rock toner cartridge back and forth before installing.**   By properly distributing the toner, you can be sure that you'll see even print density on your documents.

NOTE   *It sometimes takes a few dozen copies before print quality stabilizes after you install a new toner cartridge. So give it a little workout before deciding there's a problem.*

■ **Be careful about recycled toner cartridges.**   While such products are often advertised as offering superior quality or longevity, my experience has been inconsistent. One cartridge works fine, but the next is unusable. And print quality may differ considerably from the manufacturer's normal range. If you are not preparing your documents for reproduction or for client review, and don't need the absolute best quality, you can save money by buying recycled. In this case, try to stick with a company that offers you consistent performance from cartridge to cartridge.

■ **Consider a used printer.**   You can often get older top-of-the-line laser printers from Apple, HP, and other companies for $200–300, in perfectly usable condition. Many of these printers were designed for large office environments, with life spans of hundreds of thousands of copies before requiring major overhauls. If they haven't been abused, you can expect them to work reliably, year after year without a problem. You should, however, test the printer thoroughly to make sure print quality is good, the unit doesn't make weird scraping or scratching noises, and the paper doesn't jam.

Installing a Network Printer

 *Many older printers made for Macs come with LocalTalk rather than Ethernet ports. So you have to factor in an additional $100 for the conversion module (LocalTalk to Ethernet, from such companies as Asante and Farallon) to allow the unit to work with today's Macs.*

USB vs. Network Printers: Is There a Difference?

A new generation of printers has come to market. In the old days, you hooked up a printer to your serial port (printer or modem or combined), or the Ethernet port. However, current Macs don't have serial ports. In addition to Ethernet, they use USB ports for printer connections and other peripherals.

So is there really a difference? Why buy one over the other? It largely depends on your needs and the performance level you want to achieve. I'll describe some of the differences in the following sections.

Network Printers

A network printer, typically supporting the Adobe PostScript page description language, will usually have its own built-in CPU and memory, meaning it doesn't use your Mac's CPU to run. More important, such printers can be shared across a network by other Macs, and they will be able to correctly handle the output from PostScript programs, such as Adobe Illustrator and Macromedia FreeHand, or documents containing PostScript or EPS graphics with top quality.

NOTE *When I say a network printer "usually" has a built-in CPU, I mean that some don't. There are printers and high-resolution typesetting machines that actually use a Mac or PC to handle CPU chores.*

In general, most networked printers are laser printers, black and white or color. Other networked printers are high-end inkjets or color printers with other technologies (such as dye sublimation) or imagesetters, which provide output on paper or film for the printing industry.

NOTE *Apple's USB Printer Sharing software, which was only available in the Classic Mac OS environment when this book was written, also lets you share personal printers across a network. Such printer makers as Lexmark also offer such features in their drivers (but I didn't have any to try for Mac OS X).*

USB Printers

While some USB printers have come to market supporting PostScript, these printers are simply the descendants of the regular printers you'd attach to your Mac's serial port. We used to call them QuickDraw printers, because they supported Apple's Classic Mac OS native image display language, and could support bitmap or TrueType fonts.

USB printers are not designed to be shared among Macs (unless the manufacturer offers some sort of sharing software as part of the standard installation), although you can get USB switchboxes, which allow you to switch them to work with whatever Mac needs them at the moment. In addition, such printers use your Mac's CPU horsepower to process the files that are being printed, and that means performance may suffer somewhat while a document is being printed.

NOTE *Despite Mac OS X's preemptive multitasking feature, in which the operating system parcels out tasks, you can still expect to see a slowdown while printing to your inkjet, and it's most evident on slower Macs. It's better than in the Classic Mac OS, of course, but not perfect.*

Both USB and serial printers are low cost and deliver great quality, especially when it comes to color photos. For personal use, and limited production needs, such printers make a lot of sense.

Even better, some models, such as a few of Epson's and HP's color inkjets, can be adapted to network use later on by installation of an Ethernet network card or standalone module. But you still have to consider whether or not you need PostScript, which, as it happens, forms the subject of the next section in this chapter.

CAUTION *If you plan on installing a network card in your inkjet printer, you'll want to contact the manufacturer and verify compatibility with Mac OS X first. None of the network cards I tried (for Epson and HP printers) supported Mac OS X as of the time this book was written.*

PostScript: What Is It? Why Do I Need It?

Back in the 1980s, Adobe Systems invented the PostScript language, which reduces the elements of the printed page to math. PostScript is device independent, which means it can work with a printer at its maximum possible level of quality, ranging from a cheap laser printer to the most expensive imagesetters used by the printing industry.

If you just intend to use PostScript fonts with your documents, you don't need a PostScript printer. Adobe Type Manager (which comes free with Adobe's Acrobat Reader) or Adobe Type Manager Deluxe (a retail version that also manages font libraries) can process PostScript fonts and make them work perfectly fine on a non-PostScript printer under the Classic Mac OS environment, such as one of those ever-popular color inkjet models.

In addition, Mac OS X's built-in support for PostScript fonts means you don't have to concern yourself about such issues with native software. In addition, the ability to convert a file to PDF format, Mac OS X's 2-D imaging standard, allows you to submit a complete copy of the document to a friend or business contact that will output on almost any printer, whether it supports PostScript or not.

If, however, you plan on using PostScript (or EPS) graphics in your document, you have no choice. To get the highest possible quality, you need to buy either a PostScript printer or one for which you can add one of those PostScript software programs (which are mentioned in the upcoming section entitled "Using PostScript Software for an Inkjet Printer"). Otherwise, the output quality of documents created in the Classic environment suffers. All those fancy graphics will appear as low-resolution bitmapped images (not very nice).

NOTE *The situation is better under Mac OS X. Native support for PDF means a Mac OS X–savvy application can save a document as PDF, allowing you to print full resolution graphics on any printer. Awkward, but it works, though you may not always get the best in color accuracy.*

Is It PostScript or a Clone?

Just as Apple produced TrueType fonts to, in part, avoid paying licensing fees to Adobe for PostScript font technology, there are printers out there that use PostScript page description emulation technology rather than license Adobe's brand.

The telltale sign is in the printer's specifications. They will list the printer as "PostScript compatible" or talk of various printer language emulations, including PostScript, but won't specifically say anything about Adobe PostScript.

In previous years, this was a problem. You bought a printer that used a PostScript clone, and you were in for trouble. Simple documents, complex documents—sometimes they wouldn't print properly, even though they would work just fine with a printer that used true Adobe PostScript.

Worse, quite often you could not predict which documents would print properly and which wouldn't. Output quality would be inconsistent. Halftones, the dots that make up a photograph, would reproduce poorly at times, and other times it would take extended amounts of time to process even the simplest documents.

However, the quality of the clones has improved, and you don't hear too much anymore of troubles with such printers. I won't argue for or against a PostScript clone, except to say that current Brother and HP printers use clone technology— and I haven't had reports of any problems, either with my own clone printer or the ones used by many of my clients.

If you are, however, considering buying a very old clone printer, I would still urge caution. New printers have become inexpensive enough to make the decision to upgrade not nearly as difficult as it used to be.

Using PostScript Software for an Inkjet Printer

This seems to be the ideal combo. You buy a cheap color inkjet printer, and then get yourself a PostScript program, such as Adobe PressReady (discontinued, but still for sale at some retailers), Birmy PowerRIP 2000, Epson Stylus RIP, or Strydent's StyleScript. All you have to do is install the program and you'll have a genuine Adobe PostScript printer.

NOTE   *Both Adobe's PressReady and Strydent's StyleScript had been discontinued at the time this book was written, which means PostScript options are sadly diminishing. In addition, the remaining contents had not, as yet, been updated for Mac OS X, although Birmy says that a native version is under development, and it may appear by the time you read this book.*

So, do these programs really work as advertised? What are the tradeoffs?

Let me give you the good stuff first. These programs do work! They actually let you use a supported inkjet printer and output your PostScript graphics under the Classic environment. And the quality can be first-rate.

In operation, you normally set up one of your Macs as a server, and the other Macs on your network work as clients, accessing the server Mac for printing. But there are potential liabilities (and solutions) with these programs:

- **They're RAM hungry.**   Although Mac OS X has a great protected memory system, it will still allocate needed RAM for an application. If programs need more than the RAM available, the operating system's advanced virtual memory system goes into play. It's far better than the virtual memory in the Classic Mac OS, but you still can expect slowdowns, unless you're Mac is well equipped with RAM.

■ **Mac OS X versions are missing in action.**   None of the products were available in Mac OS X form when this book was written (although, as already stated, PowerRIP for Mac OS X was in the process of being developed). However, a clumsy workaround is simply to save your document as PDF, and any PDF reader, including Apple's standard Preview application that is part of Mac OS X's installation, will let you print whatever pages you want. You won't get the same color management capabilities as in your graphics application this way, but it'll do in a pinch.

■ **They have to be running for you to print.**   You can't just print your document; you have to launch the software RIP first and keep it running while your document is running. If you quit the program prematurely, your documents will stop then and there, even if they're halfway through your printer.

■ **They will slow down your Mac.**   As with an inkjet printer, a software RIP program uses your Mac's CPU for processing (unlike a regular PostScript laser printer, which has its own CPU and memory). Everything you do will bog down until the printing process is done. Even though Mac OS X's superior multitasking can lessen some of the load, there's just so far you can stretch processor power, particularly on a slower Mac. This can be downright annoying if several Macs are accessing the one that is handling double-duty as a print server.

■ **You'll get slow printer performance.**   Don't expect miracles. Depending on how fast your Mac runs, you can expect it to take minutes (sometimes many minutes) to handle a document that may normally output on an inkjet printer in less than a minute.

■ **You can expect some bugs.**   In my experience, these software RIPs can be buggy, especially if you are working in several programs at once and taking advantage of all the advanced features of Mac OS X. You'll want to restrict the number of programs you run while such a program is handling the printing chores.

■ **Consider a dedicated Mac to run a software RIP.**   This is, in a sense, the same way some imagesetters are run. You set aside one computer to do nothing but process print jobs. That way, you don't run into any performance issues, and the job doesn't bog down any production machines. This is an ideal task for an older Mac due for retirement, but first check the minimum requirements of your PostScript software. For example, the latest version of

Epson's Stylus RIP software requires a Power Macintosh with System 7.6.1 or later. So your older 680x0 Macs won't cut the mustard. The other advantage of this setup is that you don't have to consider whether a Mac OS X version of the RIP will ever appear because, to Print Center, a running RIP will probably show up as just another networked printer (although you'd have to install the proper PPD file supplied with the RIP on all the Macs accessing that printer).

Which Printer Driver Do I Use?

Apple's Print Center makes your choices under Mac OS X rather more simple. Just pick the printer by its name. No more searching for the right driver.

But if you must continue to use a Classic application, you will still confront a potential headache. You open the Chooser to pick a printer; you gasp. There are so many choices. What to do?

Sometimes the answer is obvious. If you have a laser printer, you choose LaserWriter 8, unless the printer requires a custom driver. If you have another sort of printer, you'll want to look over the items in the Chooser for something that resembles the model you have (see Figure 8-1).

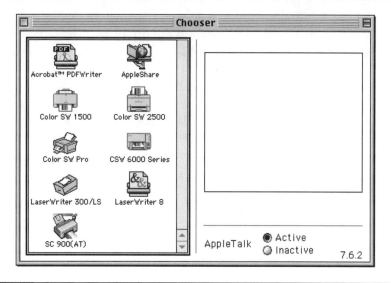

FIGURE 8-1   For the Classic environment, the Chooser is still a necessity.

While some printer drivers are clearly labeled, such as SC 900(AT) for the AppleTalk versions of the Epson Stylus Color 900 series, other drivers may not be quite so easily identified. The best solution is to check your printer's documentation to see what to pick.

> **NOTE** *When you install some inkjet printer software, such as Epson and HP, you'll often find drivers for both serial and AppleTalk versions of the printer. The latter will usually have an AT designation in the level; don't use that one unless you do have a model with LocalTalk or Ethernet ports.*

What's a PPD File and What Do I Need It For?

You buy a fancy new laser printer and it has a number of handy features. These may include extra paper trays, so you can print documents using various paper sizes without rushing to pull paper in and out. Some printers can even be set to duplex, which means you can automatically print on both sides of the paper.

Other printers may include special resolution or image enhancement technology to provide sharper printing or handling photos. Some have the capability of adjusting printer resolution.

In addition, some of the more sophisticated desktop publishing and graphic programs need to know about your printer to give you the best possible print quality.

But your laser printer driver doesn't automatically realize that your printer can do all those wonderful things. The clever folks at Adobe came up with something called a PostScript Printer Description (PPD) file, which is a text document that tells the driver what your printer can do.

If you feel ambitious and want to see just what this file contains, you can open it in SimpleText or any program that can read plain text files, such as Word. See Figure 8-2 for an example of a PPD file for a large office printer from Hewlett-Packard (the 8000 series), which is typical of the breed.

How to Install a PPD in the Classic Environment

In order for your laser printer to work its best, you need to make sure the proper PPD file is selected and installed by the printer driver. Since you are forced to live in two worlds under Mac OS X, there are two ways to install the PPD file.

First, here's how to set up your printer driver to work with your printer in the Classic mode:

> **NOTE** *Don't fret about an Apple laser printer. PPD files are already present for all of its models.*

```
*%================================================
*%          Product Version Information
*%================================================
*ModelName: "HP LaserJet 8000 Series"
*ShortNickName: "HP LaserJet 8000 Series"
*NickName: "HP LaserJet 8000 Series"
*Product: "(HP LaserJet 8000 Series)"
*Manufacturer: "HP"

*PSVersion: "(2014.108) 1"

*PSVersion: "(2014.112) 0"

*%================================================
*%          Device Capabilities
*%================================================
*ColorDevice:      False
*DefaultColorSpace: Gray
*FileSystem:       True
*?FileSystem: "
  save
   false
   (%disk?%)
   { currentdevparams dup /Writeable known
     { /Writeable get {pop true} if } { pop } ifelse
   } 100 string /IODevice resourceforall
   {(True)}{(False)} ifelse = flush
  restore
"
*End
```

FIGURE 8-2   This is the actual PPD file for the author's oversized home office laser printer.

What's a PPD File and What Do I Need It For?

1. If you aren't setting up an Apple printer, locate your printer's software CD and see if there's an installer or PPD file available.

2. If you locate an installer file, run it. The action may include just a PPD or, in other situations, a complete set of software that includes a laser printer driver and printer utilities of one sort or another.

3. If the PPD file is a separate item, select the file and drag it to the closed Classic System Folder. The Finder should tell you it's going to go into the Printer Descriptions folder, within the Extensions folder. If you don't see that message, place it there directly yourself. You don't have to restart your Mac for the PPD to be recognized.

4. If you run the installer, you'll most likely have to restart your Mac anyway (some installers insist on it).

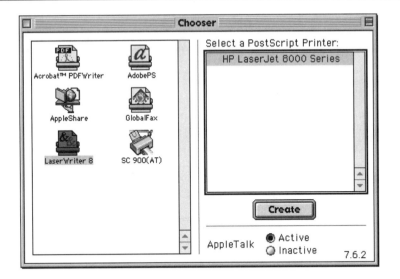

FIGURE 8-3   Select you Classic printer driver here.

5. Once you've restarted, go to the Chooser and select your laser printer driver, as I've done in Figure 8-3.

6. Click on the printer's name in the Chooser window, which will bring up a Create button.

7. Click Create to begin the setup process.

8. The contents of the Printer Descriptions folder will be compared against your printer's characteristics to see if a matching PPD file can be located (see Figure 8-4). If one is found, you'll see another message, Building

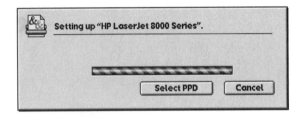

FIGURE 8-4   A PPD is under investigation here.

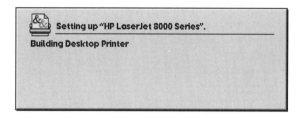

FIGURE 8-5   A desktop printer is being built, but you won't see it under Mac OS X.

Desktop Printer (see Figure 8-5). If the correct PPD is found, you do nothing but wait until the process finishes.

NOTE   *Since there is actually no desktop printer support under Mac OS X, the "building" process is strictly academic. You'd only see it if you restarted under your Classic Mac OS.*

If the correct PPD is found, there's nothing more to do than print your documents. However, sometimes, for one of many reasons, you may find that the driver cannot locate a PPD file, or you get a message that you have to change something on it.
Here's a brief listing of what you can do next:

- **Need to select printer options**   If your printer comes in several configurations, you may see a dialog box in which you have to pick the options that apply to your printer. An example is shown in Figure 8-6. You may have to check your printer's documentation or print out a test or configuration page to see the installed options. Once you've done that, just select the options from the menu, click OK, and the process should finish up in a few seconds.

- **PPD file not listed**   If a matching PPD can't be found, the printer driver will put up an Open dialog box (see Figure 8-7) showing the existing Printer Descriptions folder. You'll then have to pick the correct make and model from the scrolling list, or choose one that's a close match.

- **Choosing a generic PPD**   This may be your final choice. The correct PPD file isn't shown in the list, and you cannot find one on the manufacturer's disks. Until you can search for a solution, select this option. It'll allow you to print regular documents on standard paper sizes, such as legal and letter size.

What's a PPD File and What Do I Need It For?

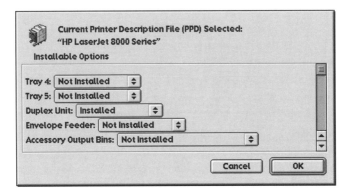

FIGURE 8-6   The PPD is right, but you still have some settings to do before the setup process is complete.

You won't be able to use your printer's custom options for now, but you'll be able to get many normal-sized documents printed.

NOTE   *Here's a great all-in-one source for a PPD file: Adobe's Web site, http://www.adobe.com/prodindex/printerdrivers/macppd.html. Last time I checked, more than 80 printer manufacturers were represented there, and the list is updated regularly.*

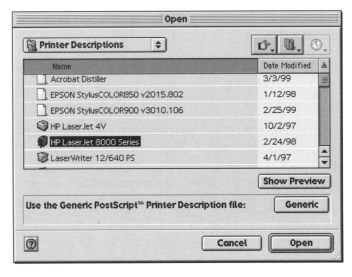

FIGURE 8-7   If necessary, you need to pick a printer from the list displayed here.

How to Install and Use a PPD Under Mac OS X

Under Mac OS X, the actual installation of a PPD file is a little more complicated, and actual use is as automatic as it can be. Fortunately, such manufacturers as HP set up installers to sort it out for you.

The HP PPD files on my Mac are placed as follows (follow the folder path to the end and take a deep breath): Library>Printers>PPDs>Contents>Resources> English.lproj. The last folder's name depends on the language system you're using.

NOTE
The default Mac OS X PPD files, which cover Apple's own printers, are located in the Mac OS X System folder, in the same folder hierarchy as the one just mentioned. In addition, many PPD files for popular PostScript printers from HP and other makers were placed in the same locale, beginning with Mac OS X 10.1.

To use the proper PPD file, just select the correct printer in the Format For pop-up menu in the Page Setup dialog box in a Mac OS X application (see Figure 8-8), and the proper paper sizes will automatically appear in the Paper Size pop-up menu. In addition, the correct options will appear in the Print dialog box, such as the ability to print on both sides of the page, if available, or the ability to switch among paper trays.

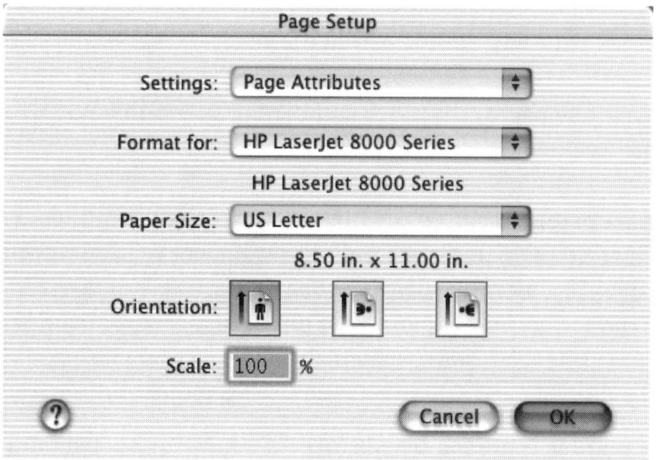

What's a PPD File and What Do I Need It For?

Page Setup	
Settings:	Page Attributes
Format for:	HP LaserJet 8000 Series
	HP LaserJet 8000 Series
Paper Size:	US Letter
	8.50 in. x 11.00 in.
Orientation:	
Scale:	100 %
	Cancel OK

FIGURE 8-8   Once you choose the correct printer from the choices available, that printer's paper sizes become available for your document.

Solving Common Printing Problems

It's a sad fact that most printers don't always know how to tell you when they've got a problem. More than likely they'll put up messages that simply don't make very much sense, and you're left pulling your hair out trying to figure out why your document can't be printed.

An example: You are happily printing away when you see the dreaded warning prompt on your screen. You switch to Print Center (for a Mac OS X application) or PrintMonitor (for a Classic application). Sure enough, you learn the job could not be printed because of an error of one sort or another. Most times, the error will be described in a way that makes little or no sense.

So you go back and recheck your document, or restart your Mac and try again, only to confront the same message. There are two things you can do to see the real error message as the printer driver processes your document:

■ **Change your job logging options.**   When you choose Print from the File menu, you'll find a pop-up menu on your laser printer driver (usually labeled General under Mac OS 9.x or Copies & Pages under Mac OS X). Under Mac OS X, choose Error Handling (see Figure 8-9) or Job Logging under the Classic Mac OS. Choose the Print Detailed Report option, so you can see a real message as to why your document won't print.

■ **Keep Print Center or PrintMonitor window open.**   When you look at the job queue under either program (see Figure 8-10, for example), you can see if a passing error message might explain what's wrong. Sometimes a PostScript error will appear before the generic error prompt is displayed.

Over the next few pages, I'll cover common printer problems, what they signify and the usual means to solve them.

■ **For most printer-related problems**   Try printing your document again if at first you don't succeed. For whatever reason, a second attempt sometimes just works (without rhyme or reason). If it doesn't work, go ahead and turn off the printer, then turn it on again. Sometimes the mere act of resetting the printer (which also clears its memory banks) will help cure the problem and your document will print just fine.

■ **Inkjet printer lettering breaks up**   An inkjet printer should give some visual indication (or flash a light) when a cartridge needs to be replaced. Epson printers, for example, will stop running. But if you see faint lines in

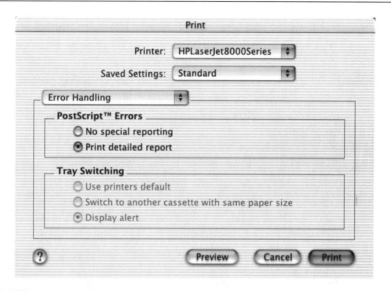

Solving Common Printing Problems

FIGURE 8-9 Printing a report will give you some information about why a job failed to print.

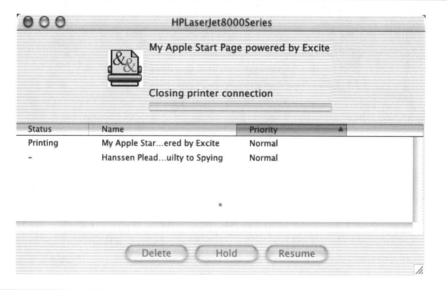

FIGURE 8-10 Several jobs are in the queue in this Print Center display.

letters or photos, you may just have to clean the print heads. Check the documentation for your printer on how to run a cleaning operation. You may have to do it from your Mac, using the printer driver, or perhaps there's a cleaning switch on the unit's front panel. For example, Epson printers include a Utility icon in their printer driver dialog boxes, which you access for maintenance functions. Some HP printers offer similar features in a separate utility program that's installed as part of the regular software installation.

NOTE *If you haven't used your inkjet printer for a few months, be sure to run the cleaning utility that came with the printer (HP puts the HP DeskJet Utility application in Mac OS X's Utilities folder if you run its driver installation program). Over time, ink dries (the manufacturer's documentation might list a time limit of six months or a year); and, when cleaning doesn't succeed, you may have to actually replace the cartridge even though it's filled with ink.*

■ **Inkjet printer text out of alignment**   Try a higher resolution setting and see if the situation improves. Also see if your printer has an adjustment to align the printer heads for best performance. The printer utilities that can clean the print heads will often have a print-head alignment feature of one sort or another.

■ **Inkjet with network card loses connection when you send a job to another printer**   The network cards on these printers have different capabilities in terms of managing a print queue. I have noticed, for example, that HP's JetDirect Ethernet cards can accomplish the task without a whimper. I've successfully sent jobs to an Ethernet-equipped HP inkjet printer and, while it's working on the document, selected another networked printer for another job, without missing a beat. On the other hand, the network card on some Epson printers will lose communication with the printer if you choose another printer to handle a document while it's still at work. The job stops dead in its tracks, and you often have to turn off the printer to reset it before you can output the document again. When you're not faced with a critical deadline, you might want to experiment with the network card's ability to manage jobs after you switch printers and see whether there are any glitches of this sort. If there's a problem, just make sure the inkjet has finished printing before you switch to another printer.

■ **Bitmapped font display**   For PostScript fonts, you may be missing the printer font. You'll want to consult Chapter 6 for advice on how to deal with font-related problems.

■ **Bitmapped graphics**   If you are using an inkjet printer or other printer without PostScript, don't try to use PostScript (or EPS) graphics with your document. The printer won't be able to handle anything but a low-resolution preview image (same as your regular fax software). If you want PostScript graphics, you can consider buying a PostScript software program for such a printer, but, as I said earlier, such programs have their own limitations.

■ **-8133 error**   This is nothing more or less than a generic PostScript error, which tells you there's a problem, but doesn't quite tell you what it is. More than likely, the printer has run out of memory to process your job. You may want to go back to your original document and see if you can make it simpler, using fewer fonts, maybe simplifying the graphic elements in it (if any). If you're using a heavy-duty graphics program such as Adobe Illustrator or Adobe PhotoShop, look for options to "split paths," which help make the document easier to handle, especially if you're planning on using a high-end imagesetter for your document. Turning the printer off and on again, or just trying to print the document again may also help.

■ **Vmerror**   This is one of the easier to understand messages, but not always easy to fix. It's telling you that a PostScript printer doesn't have enough memory to handle your document. At this point, you can consider either simplifying your document (fewer fonts and graphics) or checking to see if you can add more RAM to your printer. Older Apple printers, such as the LaserWriter NT, couldn't handle RAM upgrades and often ran out of memory with complex documents. But most newer laser printers can be upgraded inexpensively.

■ **Limitcheck**   This is an error that indicates the graphics in your document are just too much for your printer to handle. Your choices here include using fewer graphics or the "split paths" option, if available, to make your document easier to work on.

NOTE
If you are using imported graphics in a desktop publishing program, such as Adobe InDesign, Adobe PageMaker, or QuarkXPress, perform special functions, such as rotating, in the original program before you import the graphic. That will simplify the printing process; it may take longer if your publishing program has to do the rotating.

Solving Common Printing Problems

■ **Mac crashes when printing**   Why depends on whether you are printing from Classic or a Mac OS X application. Consult Chapter 18, which covers the process of diagnosing system-related problems. But if all other steps fail, you may also want to consider reinstalling the fonts used in a document. A damaged font suitcase can also cause your computer to crash at some point during the print process.

■ **Printer resets itself when processing a document**   This is the printer's equivalent of a system crash. Something has overwhelmed the printer's memory and caused it to stop working. The usual step to take now is simply to try printing your document again. Most of the time this is quite enough to get your document printed. If the printer still acts up, consider trying your document with fewer fonts and simpler graphics. As a last resort, you may want to reinstall the fonts you're using in the document; damaged fonts can also cause this problem.

■ **Banding and moiré effects on photos and artwork**   This may be a limitation of your printer that you cannot do anything about (other than changing your design to use solid colors rather than fill patterns). You can check your program's Page Setup dialog to see if your program has any way to adjust printer output. High-end graphic programs may; regular word processing programs won't. You may also want to consult your printer's documentation to see if there are any settings you can use to improve the print quality.

NOTE   *A moiré effect consists of unintended regular, geometric patterns across the image.*

■ **Edges of printed document cut off**   You may have exceeded the margins of your printer, but as a test, you can double-check the Page Setup box in the program you're using. For the latest LaserWriter print drivers, a setting of Letter (Small) or Legal (Small), means you're not getting the largest possible size. Choose the plain old Letter or Legal. But on some lower-cost printers, with limited memory, trying to print a legal-sized document to its full dimensions may be too much for the printer to handle. You may want to reduce the size of your document's printed area (it can also be scaled down in the Page Setup box).

TIP   *On a PostScript printer, you can find maximum page dimensions by opening the PPD file with a text editor program. If it shows up in pixels, just divide by 72 to get the right figure. You may also find the exact specifications in your printer's manual.*

■ **Undefined Offending Command error**   This is another of those generic PostScript printing errors that really doesn't tell you what went wrong or how to solve it. It is similar to the -8133 error, and you should take the same steps to fix it. Simplify your document, using fewer fonts or graphics. Use the "split paths" option for high-resolution graphics, if your software supports that capability. You can also try, in succession, restarting your Mac, turning the printer off and then on, and printing the document again to see if the problem repeats itself.

■ **Font substitution on laser printers**   Sometimes your carefully constructed document, with a number of font styles, will come out with sections in Courier, that old typewriter-style font. Should this occur, consider using fewer fonts in your document. If you're printing from a Classic application, check your Page Setup box and look for an option labeled Unlimited Downloadable Fonts under PostScript Options (see Figure 8-11); a similar choice doesn't appear in a Mac OS X Page Setup box. Make sure this option is not checked. Sometimes what it does to help (allow you to use more fonts in a document on a printer that has limited memory) actually causes a font substitution instead. This is especially true if you are printing a document that contains an imported graphic that, itself, uses fonts different from the ones in your regular document. Read Chapter 6 for more information on dealing with font-related hassles.

Solving Common Printing Problems

NOTE   *If you are printing from a Mac other than the one the document was created on, be sure you install the very same fonts (from the same manufacturers) on that Mac, too. If you don't, you will neither see nor be able to print your documents in the correct face. Chapter 6 covers this subject in more detail.*

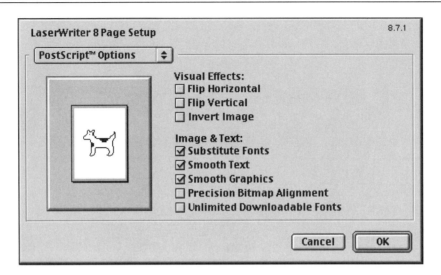

FIGURE 8-11   This option only appears for Classic Mac OS applications.

TIP

If you continue to get font or Courier substitution when printing a document with an imported graphic containing text, try this: Use the same font somewhere in the text portion of the document. Just a single character or word space with that font will be sufficient to ensure it's downloaded to the printer so the graphic will reproduce properly.

■ **Laser printer documents develop splotches or smears**   This may be the symptom of a bad toner cartridge, which is easy to replace. Or it may represent a problem with the fuser assembly, which is part of your laser printer's imaging engine. Your first step should be to replace the toner cartridge before looking into the hardware. If the printer is under warranty, contact your dealer or the manufacturer for further service if replacing a cartridge doesn't solve the problem.

■ **Laser print quality fades at one side of the page or another**   Try removing the toner cartridge and rocking it back and forth. Run a few pages and see if the situation improves. If it doesn't, replace the toner cartridge. This is also a symptom of spent toner.

■ **Laser print documents get very light**   A classic indication that toner is low. First make sure any hardware density settings haven't been changed by accident. Some printers do it via a printer utility, others have a little dial on the printer itself. If that doesn't help, try removing and rocking the toner cartridge back and forth a few times. Sometimes redistributing the toner will get you a little bit longer toner life, but be prepared to replace the cartridge.

- ■ **Laser printer documents are all black**   First, check the toner density setting on the printer. If that's correct, it could be a symptom of leaking toner. I suggest you remove the toner cartridge and replace it, but be prepared to clean out little clumps of toner from the printer itself.

- ■ **Printer can't be found**   Make sure the printer is actually on and that your cable connections are secure. If you're using an older Mac with a serial printer (such as an inkjet), you need to make sure AppleTalk is turned off on your printer port (or use the Mac's modem port, if available). Regardless, Mac OS X doesn't support this setup.

NOTE   *If you're using a switchbox to allow a personal printer to work with different Macs, and your Mac doesn't recognize your printer, be sure the switchbox is set to the right connection.*

Solving Common Printing Problems

Case History
The Case of the Damaged Font Suitcase

This happened to me in the early 1990s. I was working with a large graphic art studio, and we had to produce a critical document for an important client. I had printed the document on the office laser printer, and it looked just perfect. So I decided it was time to send it to the company's expensive imagesetter.

I brought up the PrintMonitor window (we didn't have desktop printing options or the Print Center then). The document contained nothing more complex than a few paragraphs of text in several different styles of type. Piece of cake, I thought.

I watched and watched some more. And nothing happened. PrintMonitor put up a "processing job" message and just sat there for about half an hour.

In frustration, I canceled the job and restarted the Mac. Then I tried printing again, and the same problem occurred. At this point, the studio's management came over and began to fret and worry about the delay. Constant phone calls from their client didn't help their collective blood pressure. They even tried printing the document from another Mac with the very same result.

So why did it work perfectly on the laser printer and not on the imagesetter?

The solution was something we couldn't diagnose directly, because the Macs we had in that studio were all running quickly and reliably, with only a rare system crash. Many larger printers and imagesetters actually come with their own hard drives, so you can store PostScript printer fonts on the output devices themselves. This speeds up performance, because there's no delay in sending the font information to the printer.

On a whim, I decided to remove the fonts that the document required from the imagesetter's hard drive, and downloaded them again from the copies I had on my Mac.

With fingers crossed, I printed the document again.

Within less than a minute, the imagesetter gave forth its regular beep sound and began to print the document without any problems at all.

It seems that one or more of the printer fonts were damaged. But since they were located on a printer's disk, there was just no way to diagnose the problem except to actually replace the fonts.

Hints for Faster Printer Performance

Today's printers offer photo-quality reproduction, and the ability to produce documents you can take directly to your commercial printer and get excellent results.

But despite the promise of faster and faster performance, there are times your printer will just bog down and take seemingly endless amounts of time to handle your documents. Is it something you did, or is the printer just not doing what it should do?

If you are dissatisfied with the level of performance your printer delivers, consider these suggestions:

- ■ **Clean up your document.** If your documents contain a lot of fonts and complex graphics, your printer has to work that much harder to produce them. If you can simplify the document, you may find it'll output much faster and perhaps quality won't suffer.

■ **Use a lower print resolution.**   Inkjet printers offer several resolution options, such as 360 dpi, 720 dpi, and so on. Those extraordinarily high maximum speed ratings of such products are based on the lowest resolution. If you are just printing a draft of your document, or you simply want a hard copy of a Web page for later reference, set your printer to the lowest resolution setting and get maximum speed. You'll also want to compare quality at various settings. For example, a top-quality inkjet printer may only deliver its best reproduction of color photos on a special photo-quality paper, and then take many minutes to handle even a single document. If you don't want the best-quality pictures, and use regular paper, you may find you can save many minutes per page by choosing a lower resolution setting.

■ **Turn off background printing in the Classic Print dialog box.**   Just choose Background Printing from the Print dialog box (see Figure 8-12), and click on the Foreground radio box. Background printing is designed to make you more productive; you can continue to work on your Mac while printing happens in the background. But it can also make your Mac bog down terribly, especially if it's an older model. When you turn off background printing, your Mac will sit there and do nothing but print and you won't regain control until it's over. Since that process gets 100 percent of your Mac's attention, your document is printed more quickly. It may be a good choice if you need to print a long, complex document and you are on your lunch hour. Turning off background printing also sometimes helps when you cannot print a document in the normal way.

NOTE   *The ability to switch off background printing is not offered under Mac OS X for native applications. While Mac OS X's superior multitasking will provide less impact to your Mac's performance, doing heavy-duty work in a graphics program and printing to an inkjet printer (which uses your Mac as the processor) will slow down most Macs, particularly the ones with slower processors.*

Hints and Tips for Upgrading a Laser Printer

The symptoms are typical: your printer seems too slow or it chronically runs out of memory when processing large, complex documents. Is there an answer?

It depends. Many of those out-of-memory messages are related to your system software and are not necessarily the result of a problem or an indication your printer lacks anything. Here are some options you might consider, though, to enhance your printer's performance:

- **RAM upgrade**   At the time this book was written, RAM was still quite inexpensive compared to what it was years ago (but had risen slightly above the lowest levels because of supply and demand). RAM upgrades for many popular printers cost less than $100. A RAM upgrade will give a laser printer the ability to handle more fonts in your document, or speed processing of documents with complex graphics. This is especially true of the lowest-cost models, where RAM allotments are kept to a minimum to keep prices down. On the other hand, the more expensive laser printers generally have more than enough RAM for normal use out of the box. Some years back, I did an office printer survey for *Macworld* magazine. Their test laboratory actually benchmarked several office laser printers with or without RAM upgrades, and found little performance difference between the two. The other consideration: on some printers, you may have to completely disassemble the unit to find the logic board and RAM slots. The time and energy may not be worth the bother, especially if you need to pay a dealer to do the job for you.

- **Duplexing**   The ability to duplex on a printer means it can print on both sides of the paper in a single operation. This is useful if you want to save paper or you want to print a small number of books for office manuals or

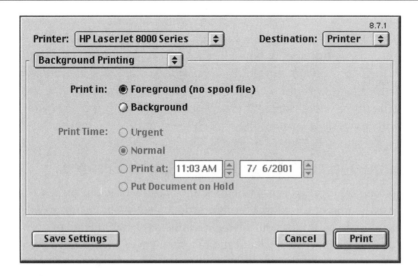

FIGURE 8-12   You can still turn off background printing with a Classic Mac OS application.

other purposes. I haven't seen a downside, other than the increased possibility of a paper jam due to the highly complex paper paths.

- **Extra trays**   If your printing needs require different paper sizes or large amounts of paper, this is a worthwhile option, if not always a cheap one. If you're using a printer with extra trays in a home or home office, prepare for spousal protest. My wife says my laser printer (with a duplex unit and extra trays) looks like an ugly beige washing machine.

- **Optional hard drive**   Some printers are set up to allow installation of a hard drive for font storage. Since print times slow down as fonts are downloaded to a printer's memory, if you handle lots of documents with a large number of fonts, having a hard drive attached to the printer may be useful. On the other hand, compared to the cost of regular hard drives that you connect to your Mac, a printer's drive may be an expensive proposition. In addition, you may be forced to buy the manufacturer's disk upgrade rather than just install a regular hard drive, because of special drive formatting requirements.

How to Fix Paper Jams and Feed Problems

A printer has a lot in common with a copy machine, especially if it's a laser printer. And, as with copiers, paper jams occasionally. Sometimes it's the printer's fault; a little wheel or gizmo has worn out and paper won't travel through cleanly. Or perhaps you just didn't install the paper properly, and it folded on itself as it fed through.

When you face a problem of this sort, here are some suggestions on how to solve them quickly:

- **Be careful when you remove paper stuck inside the printer.**   Whether it's a low-cost inkjet printer or an expensive laser printer with multiple trays, the parts used generally consist of a complex array of levers, rollers, and springs, and it's very easy to damage or loosen one of these parts. So be careful, and don't push and pull things unnecessarily to extract the paper. Generally, the manufacturer's instruction manual will give you suggestions on removing paper jams. Some printers may even have a small diagram located inside the unit that shows you how to clear a jam. Once the paper is removed, check to make sure that little pieces aren't left (as they can often cause further jams).

CAUTION *An indication of our disposable society is the fact that it often costs more to repair an inkjet printer than replace it. So you should be extra careful when attempting to remove a paper jam. If you're not succeeding, contact the dealer or the manufacturer for help.*

- **Smooth and fan paper before you place it in the paper tray.** A jagged batch of paper can often result in paper feed problems. And it's not just the low-cost inkjet printers that are sensitive. More expensive printers may also be sensitive to such problems.

- **Don't mix paper types with inkjet printers.** The paper transport mechanisms of these low-cost printers are as inexpensive as the rest of the product. Having paper of different thicknesses can cause the possibility of a paper jam. This is especially true if you're using so-called "photo quality" paper for the highest quality reproduction. Some printer instruction books recommend you remove regular paper first before putting the glossy stuff in the paper tray.

- **Be especially careful with envelopes.** Each printer varies in its ability to handle envelopes; few do it perfectly. Before you use an envelope, make sure the flap isn't bent or stuck together and consult the manual for the proper orientation (it isn't always obvious). If you live in a humid climate, make sure the gum isn't damp. You wouldn't want to have to extract that stuff from one of your printer's paper-transport rollers. If your printer cannot handle envelopes properly, see if a special envelope tray is available as an option, or consider addressing envelopes the old-fashioned way.

Summing Up

In this chapter, you discovered how to get the most from your inkjet or laser printer, and you discovered the different ways in which printer setups are handled in the Classic Mac OS and Mac OS X.

The next chapter is devoted to input devices—you'll learn how to add and configure a new keyboard, mouse, trackball, and joystick on your Mac.

Chapter 9

Troubleshooting Mice, Joysticks, and Keyboards

O ne of the most jarring differences between Macs and computers with other computing platforms is the standard mouse on our favorite computing platform. It has just one button, compared to two or more buttons for those other input devices. The functionality of the extra button (the right button on a Windows-based PC), however, is available in the contextual menus feature, accessed by a COMMAND -Click on an item.

But back in the old days, it was simple. Your new Mac often came with just a mouse, and you bought whatever keyboard you wanted (though it was often just an Apple keyboard, extended or otherwise). The original compact Macs had a small keyboard, true, but things got better beginning with the Mac Performa series when Apple included one of its low-cost AppleDesign keyboards as part of the package. The practice soon spread to the entire desktop product line.

NOTE   *The 105-key Apple Pro Keyboard and similar products essentially mimic the style of the typical PC keyboard, with added scrolling keys, such as HOME, DOWN, PAGE UP and PAGE DOWN, and 15 function keys. The original Mac keyboard had none of these.*

Nowadays, it may seem there is no reason to buy an input device at all. After all, Apple already gives you what you need to get started. But there are a number of reasons, in addition to replacing defective units, why getting another input device may be important to you.

NOTE   *An input device is defined as any product you use to input something on your Mac, such as a keyboard to input letters, or a pointing device, such as a mouse or trackball, to input clicks and move your cursor to the desired position on your screen.*

Choose Your Own Input Device

The Apple Pro Keyboard and the Apple Pro Mouse sport fairly traditional designs in elegant plastics and have garnered great reviews from Mac users worldwide. But millions of Macs shipped with the original iMac-inspired keyboard and mouse, two input devices that just weren't everyone's cup of tea. The rounded "hockey puck" mouse, for example, is cute but confusing to use, since you don't always know which way is up by feel alone (unless you remember to grasp the cord every so often to be sure). Even though Apple put a little lip at the top of the mouse on some of its later versions, it may not be enough. And the keyboard, while nicely designed for such a compact product, puts its ultra-small page navigation keys in an awkward place (at the top) and is missing several features that users of the extended keyboard are used to. These include those extra function keys and the END key (to take you to the end of a document window).

In addition, you may want to consider buying a trackball, a special "ergonomic" keyboard because of a wrist injury, a joystick for games, or a graphic tablet for drawing. As a result of these needs, there is a growing demand for after-market input devices, as well as devices that can be used to offer enhanced capabilities.

Here's a brief list of the sort of input devices now available:

- **USB mouse extension**   If that round mouse is getting you down, you can buy a little plastic fitting, such as the iCatch from MacSense or the UniTrap from Contour Design. Either device clips onto that clumsy round mouse and makes it look and work just like a regular mouse. Both products come in the usual variety of iMac- and G4-inspired colors.

- **Standard mouse**   If a plastic attachment doesn't suit, you can buy a complete, normal-sized USB mouse for your iMac or Power Mac; obviously the Apple Pro is a compelling upgrade. Or you can get a plain old ADB mouse to replace the one used on older Macs. There are a wide variety of options. Some of the less expensive styles more or less mimic the form factor of the standard Apple ergonomic mouse, such as the Macally single-button mouse. Macally also has a cute alternative, the iSweet, which includes a number of separate covers, to match your iMac's color scheme.

NOTE   *The following products all generally come in both ADB or USB versions, but you'll want to check with your dealer or the manufacturer for a complete list of their offerings. If the product doesn't identify the protocol, look at the plug. An ADB plug is round, while the USB connection plug to your Mac is flat.*

- **Multibutton mouse**   Such companies as Adesso, Belkin, Interex, Kensington, Logitech, Marlow Data Systems, Macally, Micro Connectors, MicroSpeed, XLR8, and even Microsoft offer a whole array of mouse products that offer two, three, or four buttons. The supplied software (assuming it's been upgraded to support Mac OS X) adds extra functions to these buttons, which let you automatically launch applications or bring up Apple's Contextual Menu. The latter function, in effect, mimics the right-mouse button on a Windows mouse. Some models even include a scrolling wheel, letting you dial your cursor's position for ultra-precise movements.

NOTE   *A regular USB mouse designed for the Windows platform may often work just fine on a Mac without any extra software. The multibutton types, though, will not provide any extra functions unless you can find a Mac driver for the product. In addition, Mac OS X has built-in support for the extra buttons and the scroll wheel on many input devices. But not all manufacturers designed their products to use this capability without extra software installed.*

■ **Trackballs**   A trackball is, simply stated, an upside-down mouse. The little ball that moves is at the top rather than the bottom; so instead of moving the entire pointing device, you just whirl the trackball. Some folks find moving a trackball to produce less wrist strain than a traditional mouse; others just find it more convenient. Whatever your preference, you'll find a reasonable selection of trackballs from many of the same manufacturers as a regular mouse-type product. They start with the famous Kensington Turbo Mouse, one of the earliest trackballs and still being produced, and that company's Orbit, a smaller trackball that some prefer (including your long-suffering author). Most trackballs have two or four switches, which can be programmed via software for additional functions.

■ **Joysticks**   This product is designed to turn your Mac into a true gaming machine. You use the joystick to handle the traditional cursor movement chores, or to perform functions required by a regular game. I have one client who actually preferred to use a joystick over his regular mouse, and he had no interest in computer games of any sort.

■ **Graphic tablet**   If you want to use your Mac for graphic design work, you may find that having a mouse or trackball emulate a pen and pencil may not provide the precision you need. A graphic tablet literally uses a pen-like device that you use to draw your pictures on a flat panel that mimics the function of a drawing pad. They are pressure sensitive, which means that the lines you draw on the tablet become thicker and wider as you bear down. If you purchase a device of this sort, of course, you may still prefer to have a regular mouse around for regular pointing chores.

Choose Your Own Input Device

NOTE *One of my publisher's fearless editors once suggested that a graphic tablet is also very useful for cutting and pasting parts of images in such programs as Adobe Photoshop. It makes it far easier to trace the sometimes convoluted outline of a picture in order to select it.*

■ **Trackpads**   If you like the approach used on the iBook and PowerBook, where your fingers walk on a trackpad to provide cursor movement, you may be able to find a standalone version you can hook up to a regular Mac. I say "may" because none of the trackpad products I have seen demonstrated through the years seem to have made it into the Mac catalogs I consulted while writing this book. If you do run across one of these devices, it may be worth a try—that is, if you like this input device approach.

■ **Wrist and mouse pads**   While not pointing devices, these are accessory products you may find useful. Both are designed to orient your wrists in a position that's designed to relieve stress. I won't presume to recommend any of these items, except to say that my teenaged son began to use a wrist pad when he developed minor aches and pains. The symptoms have since departed, and he uses his wrist pad all the time when he's working on his iMac or the modified Blue & White G3 we both share for extra work. On the other hand, when I have to do something on his computer, I move the wrist pad to the side. (I hate them, and my wrists have yet to complain about it, so maybe I am strange.)

■ **Replacement keyboards**   If your old keyboard has expired, you'll find a ready market of replacements. You can buy one of Apple's "Pro" models, or choose products from many of the same companies that make mice and trackballs. Most of these keyboards resemble the Apple products in some fashion, and can be considered low-cost alternatives (but try them out first).

■ **Ergonomic keyboards**   This variation on the keyboard theme is designed to incur less wrist strain. Such keyboards are typically divided into three or four segments of keys, each segment fanning out at a slight angle to provide greater keying comfort. This type of keyboard is an acquired taste. I know of some folks who swear by them, but I have spent way too many years on the traditional keyboard, and I usually just curse at such keyboards whenever I have a chance to try them. My suggestion is that you work with one of these devices first to see if you can become accustomed to it.

■ **Combo keyboards**   One interesting keyboard alternative comes from DataDesk Technologies: the TrackBoard. This is a line of products that includes an integrated three-button trackball fitted onto the keyboard itself. Some models include a numeric keypad, while others are designed so you swap the trackball with the keypad.

CAUTION   *The so-called "QuickSilver" Power Mac G4 sports an optical drive without an Eject button. That function is taken over by the EJECT key on the Apple Pro Keyboard. If you decide to use a different keyboard with this model, you will need to check with the manufacturer whether or not the Eject function is available via a keystroke.*

ADB Input Device Cautions

Have you ever accidentally pulled the ADB plug from your Mac or mouse? You plug it back in and what happens? Most times, response is slow; your mouse cursor seems to just take forever to move across the screen. A restart will usually fix the problem, but the symptom should raise a warning flag.

The ADB version of plug-and-play requires you to shut down before you remove or attach any devices. Apple Computer gives a stern warning about this. The risk is not just erratic performance. When you plug and unplug an ADB device, there could be a brief short circuit, and that short circuit has the potential of damaging the input device or your Mac. In the latter case, that can mean replacement of the logic board (unless you have a spare ADB port to use).

If you do pull the plug by mistake, restart your Mac right away. Even if it works out all right, don't think you can do it over and over again with impunity. Although I've not personally encountered an ADB port failure as a result of plugging devices in and out, I have read the warnings and tried my best to heed them, since they are based on actual technical considerations. Just be careful!

NOTE   *Mac OS X doesn't change this situation, since the limitation is hardware dependent, and not dependent on the operating system you're running.*

Installing Input Devices

The arrival of USB on the Mac has greatly simplified the process of installing an input device, but that doesn't mean you can just add as many as you want, without observing a few cautions.

If you have one of the older-model Macs that sports ADB ports, there are very specific problems that you'll need to consider before you hook up such devices.

ADB Input Device Installation Guidelines

When it comes to installing an ADB device on your Mac, you'll follow some of the very same steps you use when you install a SCSI device.

First, turn off your Mac; don't take chances here! Then unplug the ADB product you want to remove, and add the new devices. ADB devices are daisy-chained, one after the other. If any of the cables are too short, contact your dealer about getting an extension cord. If your unit has special features beyond that of the regular keyboard and mouse, such as programmable keys, you'll need to install some software first, and shut down. Restart after hooking up the device. You'll also want to take a few important precautions (see the next section) as to how many devices you can add in safety.

CAUTION   *Don't expect your input device software to work unless it's specifically compatible with Mac OS X. You'll want to check with the manufacturer of the product for information. Without software, you may be able to use the input device, but you may lose access to special features, such as extra buttons, programming function keys, and a scroll wheel.*

USB Device Installation Guidelines

You have lots more freedom with USB ports. You can, in theory, daisy-chain up to 127 separate devices on each USB bus. On the other hand, real-life considerations, such as the amount of bandwidth the device needs to run at full capacity, make this number largely a pipe dream. In practical terms, you can hook up any reasonable number of input devices you can reasonably expect to need. And you can add a host of other devices to the USB chain, as explained in the section entitled "How to Handle the USB Connection."

NOTE   *The original iMacs and Blue & White G3 Power Macs had a single USB bus, with two ports (thus, a 127-device limitation). The second-generation (slot-loading) iMacs and G4 Power Macs have two USB buses, hence a limit of 254 devices (at least that's the theory).*

Setting up a USB device isn't terribly hard. You plug it into a free USB port on your Mac, iMac, iBook, or later generation PowerBook. If there's no free USB

Installing Input Devices

Case History   **The Case of the Frozen Mouse**

This happened to me when I visited a small advertising agency. I was busy updating several of their Macs, and one of the graphic artists asked me to help her solve a problem with a frozen keyboard. I followed her to her Mac, a model of recent vintage, and gave it a workout.

The Mac started perfectly normally, but as soon as the system software finished loading, everything was frozen. I restarted the Mac with extensions off (SHIFT key held down at startup) to no avail. Frozen tight as a drum.

I checked mouse and keyboard movement as the startup process progressed, and right after the Happy Mac face appeared, they both locked up.

I plucked out a copy of the Mac's system software CD and restarted directly from the CD. Same problem. Finally, I shut everything down, and located a spare mouse in an accessory box and replaced the one installed on that Mac. Then I restarted.

The computer booted perfectly; everything worked just fine. Mouse and keyboard action were completely normal. While you might not expect a defective mouse to affect other devices on the ADB chain, in this case, even the keyboard failed to work.

port, you need a hub. With a large USB chain, there are some cautions that are explained in the last section of this chapter.

Once the unit is attached, go ahead and install any necessary software. A restart shouldn't normally be necessary, because of the superior plug-and-play architecture of Mac OS X. If you run into any problems, check the section in this chapter entitled "USB Problems and Solutions" for further assistance.

Test Drive Your Keyboard First

When you buy a new car, you usually take it out for a spin first, especially if you haven't had experience with that particular make and model. This is understandable, considering how expensive even compact cars are once you add a few necessary options to the mix.

But it's very common for folks to buy a keyboard without trying it out first. You see a nice-looking keyboard at your dealer or in a catalog; the price is right and you buy it, without a second glance. When you get the item home, you may find it's not quite what you wanted or expected. The keys are too springy, too mushy, or awkward to the touch. You find yourself making more errors, even if you are an experienced, skilled typist. At the end of the day, your hands feel fatigued, as if your workday has expanded way beyond your expectations. So what do you do?

Keyboard quality is a matter of personal taste. What I like, you may despise. My absolute favorite Mac keyboard is the Apple Pro Keyboard, the very one that you get on all new desktop Macs and the iMac. It's the closest match to my prior favorite, the AppleDesign keyboard, which shipped on pre-USB Macs. I like the soft touch and responsive action of these two models. Though I'm not a fan of the original iMac-inspired USB keyboard, it was designed with a similar touch. Others hate that keyboard for the very same reasons, preferring a springier feel. (To show you just how opinions may vary, I reviewed the Cube for CNET, and pronounced the keyboard excellent. Another writer reviewed a Power Mac G4 for CNET, a model with the very same keyboard, and said it felt "spongy." To each his own.)

The best solution, if you can, is to try out a keyboard first at your dealer before you take one home. You may have to work with several before you find the one you like, but you'll be rewarded with more comfortable keying and, no doubt, fewer typos to correct.

> NOTE
>
> *Test driving isn't just meant for keyboards. If you want to use an alternate pointing device, say, a trackball or a mouse with a different design, give it a try also. Regardless of what your friends or published reviews may state, it's your personal preference that's involved here. Buy the product you like best, even if it didn't get high marks from other users.*

Installing Input Devices

Dealing with Long ADB Chains

The ADB chain is designed to handle up to 16 daisy-chained devices. This would, in theory, seem to present some terrific possibilities for expansion. Imagine having a mouse for regular work, a joystick for games, a graphic tablet for artwork, and perhaps a second keyboard if you or another user needs one of those ergonomic keyboards to avoid or deal with a wrist injury.

Unfortunately, the theory doesn't always work as well in practice. For one thing, proper performance of the ADB port depends on having enough current with which to drive each attached device. If there's not enough current, you may experience erratic performance or the device may simply refuse to function.

Since each ADB device has different electrical requirements, I won't hazard a guess as to where you'll reach the limit, except to just quote Apple Computer, from their technical information document on the subject: "The practical limit is three or four devices."

If you have one of the older Macs with two separate ADB ports, you're in luck. If not, you'll need to be more judicious about the number of devices you use at any one time.

ADB Device Problems and Solutions

In addition to the limitations on the number of input devices you can place on an ADB chain, there are other possibilities for conflicts and problems. Following are some of the common problems you'll encounter with an ADB device and their solutions:

- **Keyboard is dead.**   When you type something on the keyboard, nothing happens. It appears to be frozen, even though the mouse continues to function. Before you assume it's the keyboard, check the cables first. ADB cables sometimes loosen easily. If the ADB cable is disconnected, try shutting down with the mouse, by selecting Shut Down from the Apple Menu. Once your Mac is off, make sure the cables are properly connected and restart. If the keyboard is plugged in, restart your Mac with extensions off (SHIFT key held down at startup) and see if it works. If the keyboard is still dead, restart with your system CD. If that's not successful, try another keyboard cable if you have one or, if possible, another keyboard. Since a new keyboard is fairly inexpensive, you shouldn't fret too much over a bad one, even if the warranty is history.

- **Some keys aren't functional.**   There may not be much you can do about this symptom. Few keyboards allow you to change individual switches. But first, you'll want to remove the keytop if possible (usually a small flat-head screwdriver can be used to pry it off). Then clean out the switch assembly and surrounding area as much as possible. Sometimes a little electrical contact spray (such as the type Radio Shack sells) can be helpful. If none of this succeeds in making the key work, it's time for a new keyboard.

- **Mouse motion is erratic.**   The once smooth motion of your mouse is now jerky. You move the mouse around, and the cursor either stays put, or it jumps with a start to the other end of the screen. This is usually a symptom of a dirty mouse ball or trackball. On a regular mouse, you should be able to pry open the ring at the bottom. It'll either snap out, or you'll rotate it partway to loosen it. When you open the ring, let the mouse ball drop into your hand or on a soft surface (such as the mouse pad). You can use isopropyl (rubbing) alcohol and a cotton swab to clean the mouse ball, and also the little roller assemblies inside the mouse assembly. A trackball has a similar layout (check the instructions for removing the ball if it's not obvious) and similar cleaning steps. If cleaning doesn't help, contact the manufacturer; it's probably time for a new one.

NOTE *The arrival of optical mice, such as the Apple Pro Mouse, has made the trackball cleaning chore a thing of the past. All you normally have to do is wipe off padding at the bottom of the mouse (if one is there) on occasion for continued good performance. Even mouse pads are passé.*

■ **Mouse button stops working.** If you have a regular mouse, this is usually an indication that it's time to get a new unit. However, such manufacturers as Kensington can fix or replace the mouse buttons on their input devices for a small fee. Check the product warranty or contact the manufacturer for assistance. I remember one instance in which my original Kensington Turbo Mouse had a defective button, just a couple of months out of warranty. At the time they were located in New York City, not far from my office (they have since migrated to the West Coast). I brought in my Turbo Mouse, and for a small service charge, they fixed it and had it ready for pickup that afternoon.

■ **Cable or ADB port is defective.** If all else fails, it may be the ADB port itself that's defective. Unfortunately, Apple dispensed with twin ADB ports many model revisions ago, thus eliminating one possible solution. The remaining choice, beyond a possibly defective keyboard, is the cable. If your keyboard has a second ADB port, try that; also see if you have a spare cable (assuming it's not hardwired into the keyboard, as with the AppleDesign model). If all else fails, restart the Mac and see if ADB functionality returns. Should none of these steps help, a trip to the repair shop may be in order.

■ **PowerBook or iBook trackpad fails.** First, you'll want to consider your trackpad posture. You should use just one finger and not your entire hand when you use a trackpad. Be sure your finger is dry, not wet or oily. You may want to keep a paper towel at hand if you live in a damp climate. If you are using your trackpad properly and you still experience jerky cursor movements or the trackpad stops working, restart with extensions off to see

Installing Input Devices

if a software conflict is possible. Consider zapping the PRAM or resetting the unit (check out Chapter 5 for information on how to reset the power manager on an Apple laptop).

■ **Software conflicts.** Multibutton mice and graphic tablets use special software to provide their unique functions. You'll want to keep abreast of software updates that may address your problems should something happen when you update system software.

NOTE *The arrival of Mac OS X brought with it a flurry of updated utilities for hardware, some of it not in final form. Your prerelease drivers may work but only in a limited way. Best thing to do is check with the publisher for the newest releases.*

■ **Numeric keypad stops working.** You prefer to use the numeric keypad for number entries or special functions (such as document navigation in Microsoft's Office software). Suddenly it stops working. What's wrong? If your Mac has a regular keyboard with a NUM LOCK light, make sure it's glowing. If it isn't lit, press the NUM LOCK key on the keypad and see if it lights up and starts working again. Bear in mind that not all programs support the numeric keypad. You'll want to check the documentation or Help menu if you're not sure.

■ **Poured liquid on your keyboard.** When I worked in a design studio as production manager, I was near paranoid about keeping liquids away from the Macs, but on rare occasions someone would spill coffee or a soft drink on a keyboard. Should this happen to you, shut down your Mac and peripherals. Remove the keyboard, and turn it over onto a paper towel or cloth to drain the excess liquid. Then turn it upright and, if you can, pop off the keys, then use an absorbent paper towel to remove as much liquid as you can. I've heard of folks actually pouring a light stream of water onto a keyboard to wash off spilt coffee or other liquids, but I recommend caution about any such step. Just give the keyboard plenty of time to dry before you try it out. Sometimes the cleanup process works, but don't be surprised if you need to buy a new keyboard.

NOTE *I was very surprised to see a print ad showing someone sitting at a computer table with coffee cup being held right above the keyboard. An accident waiting to happen, or someone just trying to sell new keyboards? I hesitate to guess which.*

Using USB on an ADB Mac

If you're lusting after the Apple Pro Mouse or Pro Keyboard, but you have an older Mac (such as the Beige G3 model) with ADB ports, don't feel left out. A number of manufacturers have USB adapters that'll fit in your Mac's PCI slots. Such companies as Belkin and Keyspan are among the peripheral makers who offer these products.

Once installed, the cards use your built-in USB software to work with the mouse or keyboard of your choice. Some of these products are combo cards, meaning they'll deliver support for FireWire, too.

> NOTE   *Some of those expansion cards support a new USB standard, USB 2.0. Although not officially incorporated into Macs shipping at the time this book was written, the newer USB standard promises to deliver performance levels of up to 480Mbps, compared to 400Mbps for FireWire. In theory, this sounds great, but until Apple supports the standard, don't expect a large number of USB 2.0 products to appear for Macs.*

How to Handle the USB Connection

When Apple introduced USB for the first iMac in August of 1998, a lot of folks complained. What about all those keyboards, mice, trackballs, pointing sticks, graphic tablets—all those things that Mac users had added to their Macs, things you needed for work and play?

To add to the confusion, it was a fact that USB had already been introduced on the PC platform and hadn't gone very far. The lack of support in terms of new products on that other platform was really unfortunate, as USB is an Intel-based industry standard that provides real plug-and-play. And that's something that Windows users usually only get a glimpse of.

You can attach and disconnect a USB device without having to turn off or restart your computer, except when a software driver is necessary. And you can add up to 127 daisy-chained devices per USB bus, although there are practical limitations to that figure (I'll get to this in a moment).

In addition, you aren't limited to input devices on a USB chain. There are USB storage devices (removable, regular hard drives, CD writers, and tape drives), inkjet and laser printers, digital cameras, scanners, modems, and interfaces for displays (to name some of the products that are shipping).

How to Handle the USB Connection

The iMac, Blue & White Power Macintosh G3, the G4, the "Bronze" PowerBook G3, the PowerBook G4, and second-generation iBook all have two USB ports; the original "clamshell" iBook has one. If you need to add extra devices, you can buy a USB hub to provide additional ports.

USB Has Its Limits

The USB silver lining, however, has a few clouds. A USB bus is capable of up to 12Mbps speed, but any device that hogs a large amount of that capacity will impact performance on the rest. For example, you can add plenty of undemanding products such as input devices on a USB chain, but you cannot expect a hard drive and removable drive to both function at their performance limits at the same time, since either will tax the limits of the USB protocol.

So you can expect performance to deteriorate if you copy files from your USB Zip drive to your USB SuperDisk drive or USB hard drive. This may be particularly noticeable in mouse performance while the copying operation is in progress.

This limitation is partly addressed with the Power Macintosh G4 and second-generation iMac models (the so-called "slot-loading" versions), which have two separate USB buses, rather than two jacks sharing a single USB bus. These newer USB designs also let you boot from a USB drive (a feature lacking in the earlier Apple USB products).

The other limitation is power. The USB bus provides enough power for a few low-power devices such as keyboards. Other USB products have their own power supplies. But if you add enough low-power devices together, they may exceed the current offered by the USB port, so you need to buy a hub to provide the extra ports and (where powered) extra current.

USB Problems and Solutions

The advent of USB on the Mac has not been without a few teething pains. But for the most part, the adoption of this peripheral bus has been fairly trouble-free.

If something is wrong, however, your Mac will put up a message about it. Here are some of the error problems you'll encounter most often:

- **Not enough power to function**   As I said in the previous section, any non-powered USB device will draw current from the USB bus. If there's not enough current to power all the attached devices, your Mac might put up a warning prompt. If you have a USB device with an AC adapter, you'll need to make sure it's plugged in and the unit is turned on (if it has a power switch—many don't). If the device doesn't have a power adapter, try connecting directly to the Mac, iMac, PowerBook, or iBook, rather than daisy-chaining. Or consider using a self-powered hub, which should (when plugged in) provide the additional juice necessary to make the extra device function.

■ **Not enough power for all functions**   This error message is a subset of the one just described. It indicates that the device is partly functional. The solutions are essentially the same. If the product has its own power supply, make sure it's plugged in and the unit is turned on. For nonpowered devices, try plugging directly into the computer's USB port or use a powered hub.

■ **No driver available**   If your USB device requires special software, you may get limited functionality under Mac OS X, but then again it may not work at all. Mac OS X drivers are installed as kernel extensions in a folder called, conveniently enough, Extensions. It's located in the Library folder within the folder labeled System (as opposed to the System Folder of previous Mac OS versions), as shown in Figure 9-1. See if there's a file there bearing the label of the manufacturer of your USB device. If not, check with the box that shipped with the product, the company's Web site, or VersionTracker.com for updates.

TIP   *Mac OS X actually has built-in support for a wide variety of USB devices; unfortunately documentation about the full extent of this support isn't complete. The best way to check is just to try the product out. If it works all right, you don't have to concern yourself about extra software.*

■ **USB device connected to hub not recognized**   Some USB hubs (early Macally designs are an example) do not open a connection port until a device driver actually recognizes a peripheral connected to it. Since USB devices are not all created the same, this may cause a problem in using some devices. If you have a spare USB port on your Mac or keyboard, try hooking up the device directly rather than to the hub (or switch things around if you can). Otherwise, contact the manufacturer for a version of their hub that keeps the ports open all the time.

■ **Liquid on your keyboard**   The same possible solutions that I described in the section about cleaning a wet ADB keyboard apply here as well. Just keep your fingers crossed that the process will work (sometimes it doesn't).

How to Handle the USB Connection

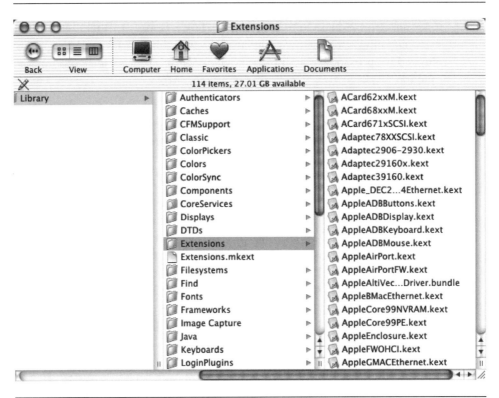

FIGURE 9-1 Yes, Virginia, there is an Extensions folder in Mac OS X.

NOTE

As USB support evolves under Mac OS X, you should expect to pay regular visits to a manufacturer's Web site for software updates. One convenient source of update information and links I've mentioned several times in this book is http://www.versiontracker.com.

Summing Up

Although Apple is being justly criticized for the kinds of input devices they offer on many recent Macs, it's good to know you have choices. And, as long as you don't have an older input device you need to use, the switch to USB is definitely a big improvement over the way things were.

In the next chapter, I'll cover an output device—your Mac's display.

Chapter 10

The Monitor Is the Window of the Computer World

To many Mac users, the monitor and the computer are one and the same. It's no doubt an outgrowth of the original compact Mac, released back in 1984, which placed everything except for the keyboard and mouse in a single case. Millions of iMac and laptop owners would no doubt agree.

The reason? Well, the first thing you see when you turn on your Mac is the monitor. So it's very easy to think that you are looking at the Mac itself, and not another device. It's very much the same image conveyed as when you look at your TV. But the fact is, for most Macs, the monitor you see is a separate product, quite often produced by someone other than Apple Computer, with its own set of opportunities or problems (or both).

When you want to upgrade your Mac, a brand new monitor can give you a new way of looking at the computing world. The picture can be larger and sharper, providing your Macintosh with a much-improved workspace.

Monitors, however, especially larger-sized CRT models, do not usually arrive ready to run their best out of the box. You frequently have to spend at the very least a few minutes setting them up properly.

> **NOTE**   *LCD displays, especially Apple's, are gaining more popularity. While they don't usually require as many setup steps as the CRT variety, there are adjustments sometimes needed for these, too, as you'll learn later in this chapter.*

The purpose of this chapter is to guide you through the essentials of setting up and configuring your new monitor. I'll also cover some of the problems you might encounter with both new and old models, and how you can make them perform at their best.

Display Selection Hints

There are dozens of manufacturers of computer monitors, and the selection and specifications can easily cause your eyes to glaze over. Aside from all the buzzwords and fancy-sounding names, don't buy a monitor just on specs alone. It's a good idea to actually look at a monitor already set up and running to see if it looks right to you.

Even if all specifications are the same, color accuracy and the quality of the picture will vary from one model to the next. Even minor adjustment variations and production differences may result in distinctions between two monitors of the same make and model. I'd recommend you check your favorite Mac magazine or review-oriented Web site (such as CNET.com and ZDNet.com) for information about the latest products.

To help you pick the right type of monitor, here are some of the common terms you'll see and how they may affect the quality of the product you buy:

■ **Aperture grill**   This is an alternative to shadow mask technology (mentioned later), which is typically used in Mitsubishi's DiamondTron, Sony's Trinitron, and products from such companies as Apple, Miro, NEC, and ViewSonic (to name a few examples). The technology employs alternating red, green, and blue phosphors in lines, rather than individual dots. The lines are separated by a series of thin wires, which are referred to as aperture grills.

NOTE   *To cement the relationship that had long existed, NEC and Mitsubishi finally combined forces in the display area, marketing all their products under the NEC/Mitsubishi name.*

■ **CRT**   This term is short for cathode-ray tube. It is the conventional type of monitor, which uses a large vacuum tube as the screen, the same as your regular television set.

■ **Dot pitch**   This measurement describes the size of the little dots that make up your picture. The lower the figure, the sharper the picture (assuming all other elements of the monitor are well engineered). Just about anything with a dot pitch of .30mm or less should give a good-quality picture (but you'll want a lower dot pitch if you use a very high-resolution setting).

■ **Flat screen**   There are two basic types of flat-screen monitors, and it's easy to confuse one with the other because of the common use of the term. Some of the newest CRT-based monitors have a flat-front surface, without the slight end-to-end curvature typical of lower-cost products. Though such monitors cost more, you usually (but not always) get a more accurate picture, free of curves or edge distortion. The other type of flat screen uses LCD technology, same as Apple's PowerBooks and the iBook. LCD monitors will also sometimes be referred to as flat-panel monitors; and because of the price of raw materials, they can cost much more than a CRT monitor of similar size. LCD prices, however, have been in a free fall for a while, so some of the smaller screen units are downright affordable.

Display Selection Hints

NOTE

Apple's own LCD monitor line includes the Apple Cinema Display, a costly wide-screen 22-inch model with spectacular image quality. It's designed as a companion for the Power Macintosh G4 series. If you have a spare two-and-a-half grand on hand (this is the latest, lowest price when this book was written), it is definitely worth exploring. I had a review sample from Apple for a brief period of time (for a review I wrote for CNET), and I really regretted having to give it up.

- **Maximum resolution**   This is a manufacturer's specification, showing the maximum pixels per inch of which the monitor is capable. The typical monitor, however, will tend to look fuzzy at this resolution, and the text will be just too small.

- **Screen size**   This is the size of the actual picture tube used in the monitor, as measured diagonally. The image size you really see will typically be an inch or two less on CRT display. The screen size on an LCD display is identical to the specified size.

- **Shadow mask**   This is the more commonly used monitor technology, which utilizes phosphors arranged in a triangle, with red, green, and blue at the corners. The screen used to separate individual phosphor dots is called a shadow mask.

- **Stripe pitch**   On an aperture grill monitor, this specification will give you an indication of the sharpness of the image. It measures the distance between two lines of the same color.

- **Viewable image**   This is the actual size of the monitor's picture, measured diagonally from end to end. Not that you actually tilt your head when you look at the screen, of course.

- **Analog versus digital**   Digital is in, and while it may not make a big difference for a CRT display, it can accomplish wonders with LCD models. By going straight digital, the extra analog conversion process isn't required, and color accuracy and picture sharpness is kept at the highest possible level. You need a digital video card, too (such as the ATI or NVIDIA graphic cards that come with new Macs), and sometimes an extra cable (as some makers don't think to provide them), but this combination will pay off, particularly with larger LCDs. If you don't want to spring for digital, get a model with both connections, and just upgrade later.

If you want to hook up a digital LCD display without Apple's ADC connector to a new Mac, you need to buy an ADC to DVI adapter plug. Belkin makes one, selling at just under $40.

Installing a New Monitor

For sheer weight and bulk, the CRT monitor is probably the largest purchase you're apt to make for your Mac (except, perhaps, for some of the bigger workgroup printers). Even a 17-inch CRT model, which is quite common nowadays, may weigh from 50 to 60 pounds. Large monitors tilt the scales at 70 to 80 pounds. These are not trivial products that you can easily move from place to place. More than likely, you'll want them to be installed in one position and remain there until you move or redecorate.

The exceptions to the rule are LCD monitors, which are relatively light compared to CRTs and are much, much thinner.

Here are some preliminary steps for setting up your new monitor:

1. Unpack the box carefully, and, if possible, keep the box in storage. If you have to return the unit for repair or replacement, you need to ship it in a container that can protect the unit. Displays are delicate instruments, and they are easily damaged in shipment.

2. Locate cables and adapter plugs, if any.

3. Check the manual for special setup advice, such as using the monitor as a USB hub or taking advantage of special features, such as built-in loudspeakers.

4. Shut down your Mac system.

5. Clear the desk or table on which the new monitor will be installed.

6. Seat the monitor on your desk or table.

If you have a larger CRT monitor, get someone to help you lift it, unless you pump iron and are in excellent physical condition. A monitor is not something you want to accidentally drop. I once observed a monitor fall from a shipper's dolly during delivery, cracking the picture tube. It was not a pretty sight.

7. Plug in all cables from the monitor to the Mac and to the wall outlet. Displays typically come with so-called PC-type connectors (called VGA, short for video graphics array), consisting of three narrow rows of 15 pins, or Macintosh style, which places the 15 pins into two wide rows. If your Mac has the older Mac-type jacks, you will need a converter connector to use a VGA cable. Fortunately, such converters are often supplied with monitors or as an inexpensive option.

NOTE   *Some monitors come with a special AC cable that will plug directly into your Mac. The advantage is that the monitor will come on automatically when your Mac is turned on, and shut off when your Mac is turned off. If you are using a large monitor (19 inches or larger), you may want to first check your Mac's specifications as to how much power it can deliver to an external monitor.*

CAUTION   *Apple's own displays, all of which are LCD now, use a connection scheme called Apple Display Connector (or ADC for short), which combines AC power, a USB connection, and digital video in one plug. Great monitors, convenient wiring scheme, but they only work with Apple's Power Mac G4 line or the Cube, unless you're willing to pay $150 or more for a special ADC to DVI adapter module (which also requires a display card with DVI or digital output capability, such as the ATI Radeon).*

8. Turn on your Mac system, including the monitor.

If all goes well, the picture should flash on within 15 seconds to a minute, and your Mac will begin its startup sequence. You should expect, though, to have to perform a few picture adjustments to get good performance from most monitors, especially larger ones.

If the monitor simply won't work properly, check the last section in this chapter, which covers common monitor problems and the usual solutions.

Making the Picture Look Right on a CRT Monitor

You've installed your new monitor, and now you turn it on for the first time and something doesn't quite look right. It's too dark, the picture tilts to one side, square objects are rounded. Or you have an old monitor, and you've just gotten used to the defects. Is there no way to fix the picture without calling in a service person?

Just about every computer monitor out there has some sort of picture adjustment capability. Sometimes it's just brightness and contrast, but at least you have a starting point. Even the little iMac has a lot more than that, if you take a look at the possibilities.

NOTE *All recent Apple displays, plus the one on the iMac, are adjusted courtesy of the Display panel in the System Preferences application under Mac OS X. Click on the Geometry tab to gain access. If you have an Apple LCD model, you can set brightness and ColorSync profiles, but that's it.*

Most monitor adjustments are quite clearly labeled with an icon or label that specifies the kind of adjustment you're producing. Some models will even produce an onscreen display to simplify matters (see Figure 10-1). Adjustments range from the simple to the very complex, with all sorts of possibilities in between. If you follow these steps (and refer to the monitor's manual if there are big differences), you should be able to get top performance for your monitor.

Making the Picture Look Right
on a CRT Monitor

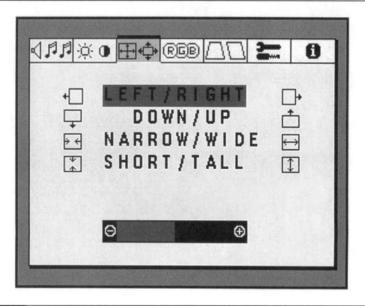

FIGURE 10-1   The onscreen adjustment panel you see here is from an NEC display, but the ones for other manufacturers are quite similar.

> **NOTE** *The notable exceptions to the rule are LCD monitors, which provide essentially perfect geometry and usually just require adjustments for brightness, contrast, and color accuracy.*

Where Are Those Adjustments?

Display adjustments are provided as a set of either knobs or buttons. The latter are usually accessed by calling up a menu of some sort. If you have an AppleVision monitor or iMac, you can also do the adjustments using the Displays panel in the System Preferences application (see Figure 10-2 for an example).

If the specific monitor adjustment isn't identified by a clearly labeled control, you may find a button labeled Menu, Proceed, or Select that lets you toggle or move through various types of settings.

In the next few pages, I'll list some of the common and not-so-common adjustments available for a regular monitor and for Apple's iMac. You can easily extend these descriptions to apply to almost any available model.

> **NOTE** *LCD displays, particularly when using an analog monitor connection, have a few of their own setup oddities, which are also described in this chapter.*

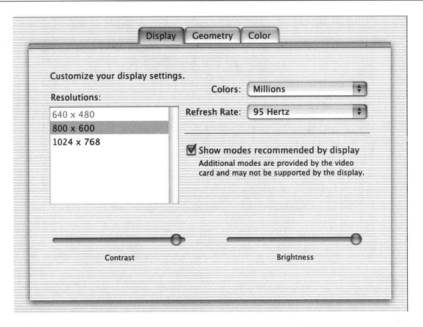

FIGURE 10-2   Click on the Geometry tab to get the best possible picture from your monitor in this Mac OS X preference panel.

Before You Adjust Anything

While brightness and contrast have pretty obvious effects, the changes wrought by geometry and other calibration settings may not be quite as obvious. Before you change anything, you might want to consider these:

- ■ **Look for a "default" or "reset" button.**   If you get too far afield and your monitor's picture looks worse than ever, you may want to get things back to the factory settings. Most monitors have a button that will change things back to the shipping configuration. Sometimes the reset sequence may require pressing two buttons, so check the monitor's manual. For the iMac, a click on the Factory Default button on your Geometry setup screen will do the trick.

- ■ **One setting affects another.**   The geometry settings, which affect the shape of the picture, are sometimes dependent on other settings. You fix one thing, another setting is changed as well. You should make your adjustments a little bit at a time to make sure the changes are what you want. I sometimes wonder how TV service people manage to keep a clear head after having to deal with these things day after day.

- ■ **Write down what you've done.**   Take a writing pad or open a word processing document on your Mac. As you make an adjustment, note what setting you started with and what you ended with. Some monitors put up a numeric display as you make adjustments, so you can easily go back to the original setting.

- ■ **Avoid adjusting anything inside the monitor.**   Some of the settings (especially those involving the early Apple color monitors) are located directly on the unit's chassis. When you open up your monitor's case, you will be exposing high-voltage components that can give you a nasty shock. Such adjustments are best left to a service agency. Worse, if something is damaged, the product warranty won't cover it. Limit yourself to the adjustments you can do using the front, side, or rear controls (or the Geometry preference panel, for some Apple products).

- ■ **Don't expect perfection, especially on larger monitors.**   I have never seen a perfect CRT monitor, one that offers precise geometry across the screen, perfect convergence, and so on. As long as cathode-ray technology dominates, it's going to be imperfect. The larger the monitor, the more difficult it is for the circuitry to keep things precise. Expect a few imperfections and learn to live with them.

NOTE   *Although offering perfect geometry, LCD monitors have their own limitations. With larger screens, color brightness may vary from one end of the screen to the other. Even the otherwise excellent Apple Cinema Display exhibits such symptoms. Such monitors may also have one or more dead pixels (meaning the little dots that make up the picture). Most times, such little blemishes aren't noticeable, but if there are enough of them, a manufacturer will generally replace the unit (or the monitor portion, if on an iBook or PowerBook).*

■ **If all else fails, get help.**   If your adjustments still fail to get you a picture you can live with, contact your dealer or the manufacturer for assistance. Some manufacturers offer a fast replace option, which means you'll get a replacement unit within a day or two if the original is defective.

Display Adjustments by the Numbers

Now that you're ready to dive in, here's a list of common monitor adjustments, including the ones you make on your iMac. With this guide, you should be able to make almost any monitor perform at its best in just a few minutes.

The following list includes adjustments that you can make on a wide variety of monitors; if they apply strictly to an LCD display, it'll be noted. Some will have similar settings and labels; some won't. Armed with this information, simply go through my step-by-step adjustment scheme, and you should come out with a great-looking picture in a few minutes.

NOTE   *It can take a computer monitor up to half an hour to warm up fully, during which time monitor adjustments may change. Make sure the monitor is on for at least this amount of time before you begin.*

■ **Color depth**   This adjustment can be made via the Displays panel in the System Preferences application or, if you choose the option, as a menu bar icon. For maximum color accuracy with graphic programs, choose millions of colors, if available. You may find lower color depths if your Mac's video monitor hardware doesn't support that resolution.

■ **Resolution**   As with the color depth setting, this adjustment is made from the Displays panel in the System Preferences application or the Displays menu bar icon. It sets the number of pixels monitored by your monitor. An ideal setting for the iMac or similar-sized monitor is 800 x 600; for a larger monitor, try 1024 x 768 or 1152 x 870; the Apple Cinema Display's normal setting is 1600 x 1024 (wow!). If one of these settings isn't shown, try the nearest equivalent. Not all Mac monitors have all the resolutions you may want to try.

CAUTION   *If the quality of your picture deteriorates sharply when you choose a specific resolution setting, try a lower figure. It may be that the monitor you have isn't sharp enough to show a higher resolution. LCD displays work best at their "native" resolution, which you'll usually find in the manual or product specification sheet. Otherwise, it has to interpolate the proper resolution, which reduces picture quality.*

TIP   *Does your picture turn black when you pick a new resolution setting? More than likely your monitor or the Mac graphic monitor hardware doesn't support it. Usually if you leave well enough alone for a few seconds, the Mac will revert to the previous resolution. If not, restart and zap the PRAM (the process is described later in this chapter). Some Mac graphic cards may require that you press a key (such as R) at startup to reset resolution to something the monitor can support.*

■ **Brightness**   This setting controls the overall brightness of your monitor. The best starting point is halfway between the darkest and lightest settings. If you're not using ColorSync to adjust the monitor to a specific range, use whatever adjustment feels comfortable to you.

NOTE   *As the monitor ages, the adjustments you make may drift. You may want to redo these adjustments approximately once a year or whenever you move the monitor to a different place in your home or office. Apple says its monitors have circuitry designed to correct color as the unit ages, but most of these models haven't been on the market long enough to see how well this technology works.*

■ **Contrast**   This setting controls the image's brightness compared to the background. The usual setting is the highest, and that's what the ColorSync setup suggests. But if it seems too extreme, feel free to experiment with something you prefer.

■ **Convergence (CRT only)**   Your color image is made up of three colors: red, green, and blue. If the three colors aren't properly aligned to form a single combined image, text and pictures on your monitor may be fringed with blue or red. There will typically be a vertical and horizontal adjustment. Some monitors include additional convergence settings to control each corner of your monitor.

- **Size and position**   These adjustments affect the height and width of the picture on your monitor. An example of such a setting appears in the Geometry panel in the System Preferences application on an iMac.

NOTE   *No doubt you'll be tempted to stretch your picture as much as possible. Depending on the type of monitor you have, image sharpness may deteriorate at the very edge of the image, or you may exceed the image area (in which case, the edges of the picture will be clipped).*

- **Geometry (CRT only)**   These settings handle the curvature and angle of your monitor image. Here's a list of the ones you'll find most often:

  - **Pincushion**   This setting affects the inward or outward curvature of the image at either side of the monitor.

  - **Pincushion balance**   This setting controls the amount of left or right curvature and is used with the preceding setting to help refine the image.

  - **Parallelogram**   This setting adjusts the left or right tilt of the side of your image.

  - **Keystone (or trapezoidal)**   This adjustment will increase or decrease the size of the image at the top or bottom, to make a perfect rectangle.

  - **Rotate**   This setting will tilt the entire image clockwise or counterclockwise.

NOTE   *The tilt of the image on a CRT monitor depends on your monitor's position in relation to the Earth's magnetic pole. So if you turn the monitor around when moving it to a new location, be prepared to redo this setting.*

  - **Corner correction**   Some monitors, especially with larger screens, let you adjust the corner geometry of the image so if one corner seems misaligned, you can hone in on a more precise setting.

  - **Linearity**   If this setting is available, you can use it to make sure squares and circles are perfectly proportioned or as perfect as a modern computer monitor will allow. You'll probably want to have a ruler handy to measure the results.

■ **Sharpness**   This setting controls how clear your image will look. The most accurate adjustments are done with small text. Look at the text from corner to corner to get the best compromise. On LCD displays connected with an analog rather than digital connection, a similar adjustment, called "Phase," will adjust picture clarity, especially for text.

NOTE   *Since monitors aren't perfect, don't expect to find your text to be equally sharp from corner to corner and top to bottom on a large monitor. Just try to make it as close as possible. If there's a wide variation, contact the manufacturer or dealer for additional assistance.*

■ **Moiré**   This setting controls the wavy pattern you may see on your monitor, especially on grayscale or color images. The setting, if available, will reduce the effect.

How to Make Your Display Adjustments

Now that you have covered the basics on what monitor adjustments do, here's how to perform the settings so you can set up your monitor like a pro.

Adjusting the iMac and AppleVision Displays

Under Mac OS X, the System Preferences application is used to make most of your monitor settings onscreen. Here's how you do it:

1. Go to the Dock and click on the System Preferences application icon and then click on the Displays preference panel.

TIP   *If you just want to make brightness and contrast adjustments, you will usually find they are on the initial Displays dialog box (otherwise they are on the ColorSync setup screen). If you plan on performing a ColorSync calibration, you can leave these settings alone for now.*

2. Click on the Geometry tab, which brings up the settings screen shown in Figure 10-3.

3. Click on the radio button that represents the kind of adjustment you want to make.

Making the Picture Look Right on a CRT Monitor

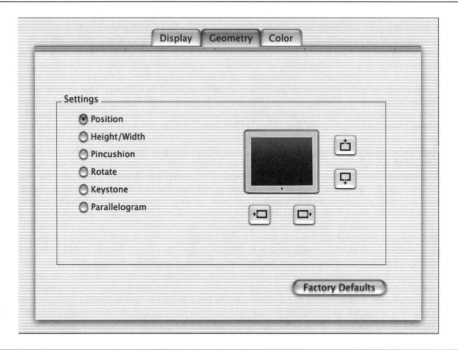

FIGURE 10-3   Begin the geometry adjustment process here.

4. Click one of the arrows and hold down the mouse to make the adjustment shown on the icon (as shown in Figure 10-4).

5. Repeat steps 3 and 4 for each setting you want to make.

6. Once your settings are the way you like, choose Quit from the System Preferences application menu, or click on another icon to make a different type of setting.

Adjusting Other Displays

If you have a monitor from Apple or another manufacturer that doesn't benefit from geometry settings in the System Preferences application, you should be able to make a reasonable set of adjustments.

Here's what to do:

1. Check the bottom, side, or back of the monitor for a control panel, knobs, or buttons.

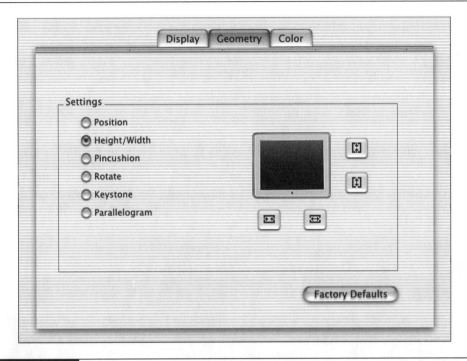

FIGURE 10-4   Adjustments move in the direction in which the arrows are displayed.

NOTE   *If you cannot locate any monitor settings, consult your manual or contact the manufacturer or dealer for advice. Nearly every monitor I've ever seen has had at least a brightness and contrast setting of some sort (with the exception of the current iBook or PowerBook models and Apple's own line of LCD monitors, for which you can only adjust the brightness).*

2. If your monitor produces an onscreen monitor panel for settings, click the button that activates this feature. It may be called Menu, Select, or Proceed, to cite some common examples of an adjustment entry switch. This onscreen menu will produce a monitor of adjustment options.

3. Use the appropriate button to move back and forth or up and down through the settings menu. Once you select an adjustment to change, you may need to click the settings entry button again to activate it.

4. Move the adjustment buttons or knobs to adjust the setting to your taste.

5. Once you have finished making a specific adjustment, look for an Exit or similar button to leave the settings screen and move back to the main menu.

CAUTION *On some monitors, you have to use a Save option to store the settings you make; otherwise, they will vanish when you exit the settings screen. Check the manual for information on whether your changes must be stored to remain active.*

6. Follow steps 3 through 5 to continue to make your monitor adjustments.

7. Once you have completed your settings, press the switch that exits the settings panel (and it may indeed be called Exit). On some monitors, pressing the adjustment entry button once you're at the main menu will exit the screen.

Can You Use Unsupported Graphic Cards with Mac OS X?

In the year before the now-departed 3dfx Interactive first released graphic cards for the Mac, it staged an all-out campaign to win the hearts and minds of Mac users, particularly those who were active gamers.

First the company hired some Mac programmers, then it produced a set of prerelease software to "flash" the PC versions their Voodoo graphics to make them run on Macs. Over time, they issued updates, and finally announced plans to make real Mac graphic cards.

The Mac Voodoo5 5500 and 4500 cards both came out in the year 2000, but the company encountered business problems and eventually folded, after selling assets to arch-rival NVIDIA. As a result, drivers for these products won't be upgraded to be compatible with Mac OS X unless a third-party company wants to get involved, and prospects for that seem doubtful.

In the initial releases of Mac OS X, only graphic cards from ATI, ix Micro (a now-defunct company that used to sell products to Apple), and NVIDIA are supported. If you have a graphic card from another company still providing products for Macs, such as Formac, you'll need to contact the company about its plans. At the time this book was being written, Formac was still working on the updated drivers for Mac OS X.

As far as other graphic cards are concerned, unless someone can provide a set of generic drivers, the prospects for support seem dim. Fortunately, the Macs on which Mac OS X is officially supported have perfectly capable built-in graphics capability.

NOTE *Most monitor settings windows are designed to vanish from the screen if you don't use them after a minute or two. So don't be surprised to find it's gone if you're called away from your monitor for a short time.*

Adjustment Problems/Solutions

All things being equal, the adjustments I've just described are likely to make a noticeable improvement in the way your monitor looks. I've seldom seen a monitor that won't benefit from a little tweaking here and there. Even the models with so-called "Auto Adjust" capability cannot take into account every possible installation or graphic card or how you position the monitor in your work area.

If the adjustments don't work, here are more things to consider:

- **Degauss the monitor (CRT only).**   If there's a stray magnetic field, such as that caused by putting a small magnet or regular loudspeaker too close to the monitor, it may distort the picture, leaving blotches at either or both sides. Click the Degauss button to restore the picture to its normal condition. If no such button is available, turn the monitor off for a few seconds, then turn it on (you don't have to restart your Mac).

- **Reset to factory defaults.**   If the settings are too far out of whack, you may find it difficult to bring things back to normal. If the monitor has a reset switch of some sort (it may require pressing two buttons on some models), use it to return to the settings the unit shipped with. On the iMac and AppleVision monitors, the setting is labeled Factory Defaults in the Display preference panel of the System Preferences application.

- **Get help.**   If you cannot get a satisfactory picture, don't hesitate to call the manufacturer or dealer for assistance. If your monitor is new, or refurbished, it could be defective. Most new computer monitors have product warranties of one to three years.

Using ColorSync to Calibrate Your Display

As you've seen so far in this chapter, there are quite literally dozens of ways you can adjust your monitor. And any single adjustment may affect another adjustment in a less than favorable fashion.

But even after your picture is clear and sharp, and the squares are straight rather than circular, and the brightness is relatively equal from one end of the screen to another, it doesn't mean the colors will match.

Color matching may not make all that much difference if you just want to surf the Web, keep a checkbook, write some letters, and draw some pictures. But if you intend to actually print the documents you create on a color printer, and you want to use color, having a monitor that has reasonably accurate color matching is quite important. And it can be a real time and money saver, especially if it helps prevent a nasty surprise when you see the printouts.

ColorSync: Its Limits

In the next section, I'll guide you through a typical monitor calibration using Apple's ColorSync technology. But before I go on, I should point out that while these adjustments will get you in the ballpark, if your work requires high-end graphic design and expensive color printing, it is probably not enough.

Here are some additional issues to consider:

- **Calibrate input and output devices, too.** The monitor may be set up just right, but if you are scanning and printing in color, you'll want to make sure that these items are calibrated as well. You'll want to check the installation disks for ColorSync modules. These modules are typically placed in the Profiles folder, within the ColorSync folder in Mac OS X's Library folder on the top level of your hard drive.

NOTE   *Any preference files placed in the Library folder inside your Users directory will only apply to a single user, not to all users of your Mac. It's not a recommended location for Mac OS X installations.*

- **Consider calibration hardware.** If you intend to use your Mac for high-quality graphic design and output, you may want to buy a separate calibration device, which will provide the most precise color matching. Contact your monitor's manufacturer or your dealer for information about these products.

Calibrating Your Display with Apple's Display Calibrator

As with previous versions of the Mac OS, Mac OS X includes software to provide a pretty decent level of color calibration, courtesy of the Display Calibrator application and ColorSync technology. This program is especially useful when you're calibrating your input, monitor, and output devices for top-quality graphic work. For regular work, frankly, this is nothing you need fret over.

To calibrate your monitor, follow these steps:

1. Set the room lighting to your usual needs. The presence of sunlight in the room will affect the accuracy of the settings, so you may want to close the blinds for a more accurate result (unless you usually prefer to have sunlight brighten your work area).

NOTE   *If you prefer to open and shut the blinds as the workday progresses, feel free to create separate profiles for each lighting condition. One of the great features of ColorSync is the ability to create as many profiles as you need.*

2. Go to the Dock, click on the System Preferences application, and, when it launches, click on Displays.

NOTE   *If you've removed System Preferences from the dock, just go to the Utilities folder and double-click on the Display Calibrator application.*

3. Click on the Color tab, which brings up the Display Calibration Assistant, as shown in Figure 10-5.

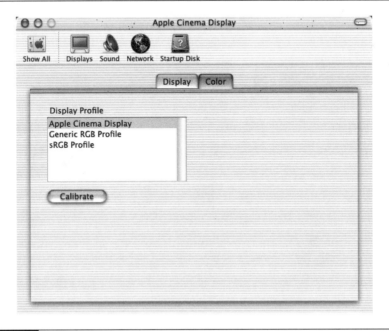

FIGURE 10-5   You'll begin the color calibration process right here

4. Choose a color profile from the list that most closely matches the make and model of your display. If it's not shown, choose a generic profile (don't worry, you'll still get a good result).

5. Click the Calibrate button, which brings up a screen labeled Introduction, which explains what you're about to do. Click the right arrow to continue (see Figure 10-6) or the left arrow to return to a previous setup screen.

NOTE   *You'll want to perform this adjustment with the Expert Mode checked. The extra options allow for adjusting the color balance of red, green and blue. With this option unchecked, the adjustment is strictly grayscale.*

6. Set your display's contrast to the highest setting.

NOTE   *On some Apple displays, it's possible that some of the setup screens will be bypassed, and the Display Calibration Assistant will allow Apple's built-in ColorSync calibration to do the work.*

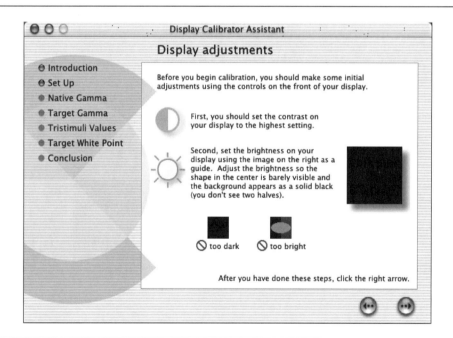

FIGURE 10-6   This screen is used to set brightness and contrast.

7. Adjust your brightness setting to produce a perfect black square, with just a faint oval in the center. Click the right arrow to move to the gamma (color intensity) setting, which brings up the screen shown in Figure 10-7, where the color balance for the three primary RGB (red, green, and blue) colors is adjusted.

NOTE   *For Apple displays, plus the iMac, iBook, and PowerBook, you'll be able to set brightness (and sometimes contrast) via sliders on the Display adjustments page. Otherwise, the adjustments have to be made by the controls available on the monitor itself.*

NOTE   *This can be a somewhat difficult setting. You need to move the sliders back and forth until the Apple illustration in the center vanishes, for the most part, in the background. You will probably want to move your chair back until you're roughly two feet from the display to get this setting right. It will never be perfect, but when it's close enough, you'll barely be able to separate the Apple shape from its surroundings.*

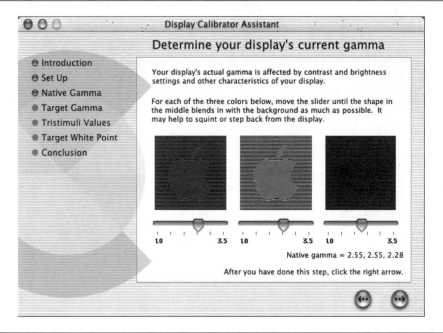

FIGURE 10-7   Take your time with the gamma setting, since it is critical for accurate color display.

Using ColorSync to Calibrate Your Display

8. When you've finished making your color settings, click the right arrow to bring up your target gamma screen, as shown in Figure 10-8.

9. Your target gamma (midtone setting) is set based on the purpose for which you're using your display. The middle setting (1.8) is the one used on most Macs. If you must match the monitor's gamma to PCs in your company, choose 2.2 instead. Click the right arrow to move on.

10. In the next setting, you'll select a specific display from the scrolling list. The choice you make is designed to provide ColorSync with the most accurate information about the range of colors your display can show. If you don't see the right model, pick the one closest to it. Most models within a manufacturer's line will handle colors similarly. Click the right arrow to continue.

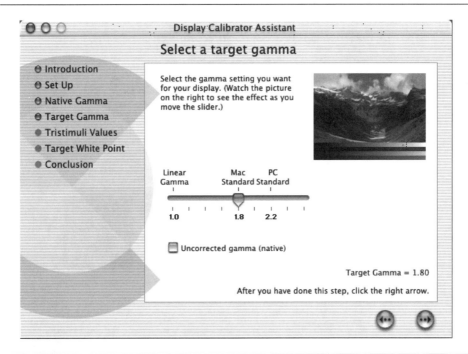

FIGURE 10-8   Choose your target gamma from the settings shown.

Using ColorSync to Calibrate
Your Display

> **TIP**
>
> *Feel free to use the left arrow to cycle through the setup screens of the
> Monitor Calibration Assistant to double-check your configuration.*

11. On the screen shown in Figure 10-9, move the slider to the point that
corresponds to your display's white point setting, which adjusts the accuracy
of the white image on your display. The setting you pick here will depend
on the sort of lighting in your work area. Click the right arrow to move on
to the final step.

> **NOTE**
>
> *I find that the D65 setting seems to work best with an Apple LCD display;
> otherwise, choose something in the 9300 range for good white balance.*

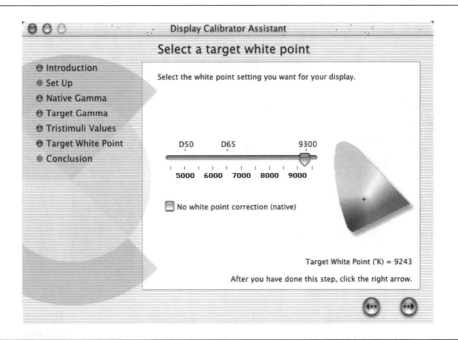

FIGURE 10-9   This screen is used to specify your white point setting.

12. The journey is just about over. On the final screen (see Figure 10-10), you name your profile, as I've done, then click the Create button to make it so.

13. Choose Quit from the System Preferences application menu to finish the process (or click on another preference icon to make other settings).

NOTE *Since the settings you make now will change as your display ages, you'll probably want to recheck them every few months.*

Hints and Tips about Multiple Displays

There are some very good reasons to add a second monitor—if your work desk is big enough. You can "mirror" or duplicate the picture on the other monitor: this may be a good choice if you wish to see the material at two different sizes at the same time.

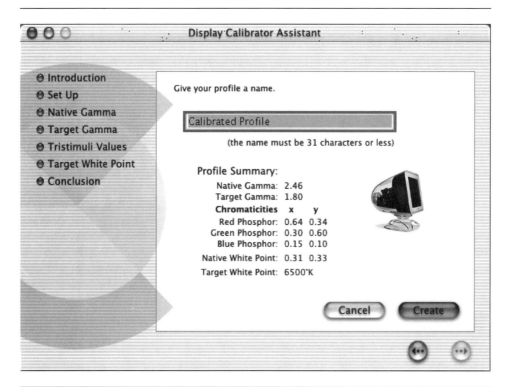

FIGURE 10-10   Give your profile a name, and then create your display's profile.

But the most frequent purpose for adding another monitor is to extend your Mac's desktop. Graphic designers and architects and programmers find this feature especially useful. It's like having one huge monitor that spans several feet in width.

Whether you can support one feature or both depends on the kind of Mac you have. Here are some hints and tips about using more than one monitor on your Mac:

- **Are you limited to mirroring?**   The iMac DV has a standard VGA plug for a second monitor, but it's just for mirroring. The same is true for many PowerBooks with a video monitor port and the new, 2001 edition low-profile iBook. Check the instructions for your Mac to see whether such features are supported. If your computer has a Video Mirroring Control Strip when you boot under Classic OS, check it to see whether you can switch between these modes.

- **Move the menu bar to the startup monitor.**   You can adjust your extended desktop with the Displays panel in the System Preferences application. You will see an icon for each monitor. For the menu bar to appear on a particular monitor, click and drag the menu bar on the monitor icon to the one you wish to use, if it's not already there. You can move the monitor icons around in relation to each other to set where your extended desktop goes.

- **Can you use a TV as a monitor?**   Look for an RGB output on your graphic card. If it's not there, consider getting a graphic card with this feature, such as the Radeon from ATI Technologies, the same company that supplies the chips for Apple's onboard graphic controllers (the Apple-bundled version lacks the TV-out feature, unfortunately). Just remember that your average computer monitor is designed to deliver more accurate and sharper pictures than a television (which is why, size for size, they cost so much more). There are also outboard converters available (from such firms as Focus Enhancements) that can convert your Mac's monitor output to work on a regular television—and that's useful for special presentations where a very large screen is necessary. (If you happen to have a Titanium PowerBook, it comes with an S-Video-out port standard.)

- **Consider a two-headed graphic card.**   Are two heads truly better than one? Well, the folks at ProMax Technology would want you to think so. The company, a supplier of systems for the video-editing market, is also selling a product called DH-MAX, which is a Matrox graphic card modified for Macs. It has two VGA ports, for analog displays, and will work in the AGP port of any recent Power Mac G4 (but it's probably too large for the Cube).

Hints and Tips about Multiple Displays

However, based on pricing at the time this book was written, it may be cheaper to buy a second graphic card—unless, of course, you don't have enough free slots on your Mac to accommodate an extra card (which is a good reason to consider the two-headed card).

NOTE   *The top-of-the-line "QuickSilver" Power Macintosh G4 released in the summer of 2001 includes a version of the NVIDIA GeForce2 MX graphics card called "TwinView," which lets you connect separate monitors to its VGA and ADC ports. The TwinView card can also be added as a build-to-order option for the rest of the G4 desktop line.*

What's Wrong with My Picture?

You have adjusted everything to perfection, but you are still not satisfied with the picture. Or the picture suddenly changes for the worse. Or you simply want to install an old monitor on a new Mac and something goes wrong.

Most times, a few adjustments are enough to get your monitor working the way it should. In the final portion of this chapter, I'll cover common problems and solutions. There are so many possible Mac and monitor combinations that it's impossible to cover the more obscure issues. If your problem isn't addressed here or solved by the steps I've outlined, contact your dealer or the manufacturer for assistance.

An Old Display on a New Mac

Your trusty old monitor works just beautifully. Clear, sharp pictures. Geometry is straight. It cost you a bundle, and you'd like it to last a good, long time. Then you trade in your Mac for a new model, and suddenly the monitor stops working. The picture is blank. Is there any hope for that old, trusty friend?

Yes, there is. The most recent Mac models can work with most Mac monitors and just about any PC monitor with VGA support. But you may have to jump through a few hoops to get them to work. Here's what to do:

■ **PC monitor support**   This is really a piece of cake. As long as the monitor has a standard VGA port, you can buy an inexpensive Mac adapter at your local computer store. Recent G3 Power Macs and PowerBooks already have VGA jacks, standard issue, as do some graphic cards. Just plug the monitor in normally and start your Mac, and you should be able to get a usable picture. The moral of the story is that if a computer dealer says such a monitor won't work on your Mac, they're probably wrong.

- **Sync on green monitors**   Older Mac monitors used a technique called "sync on green," which is the process of combining the green signal with the synchronization pulse. Shorn of the technical goodies, support for this feature was removed from the onboard video of Macs beginning with the Quadra series back in the early 1990s. There are two ways around it. One is to get a graphic card that supports the feature (such as the one from Formac, and you'll want to make sure Formac has their Mac OS X update out first), but that doesn't help if your Mac has no place to put a graphic card (as with a PowerBook). The other solution is Griffin Technology's Mac Sync Adapter. You can buy the adapter plug from a dealer or order directly from the Nashville-based company from their Web site: http://www. griffintechnology.com. In fact, the head of the company, Paul Griffin, built the company on selling these adapters, which give your old monitors a new lease on life. The company has since expanded to support missing features in other Apple products, with ADB and serial port adapters for the iBook, iMac, Blue & White Power Mac G3s, Power Mac G4, and Cube.

Curing Common Picture Irregularities

Whether the problem occurs when you set up a new monitor or it shows up suddenly, more likely than not, there is a conventional solution. Following are a few common symptoms and their equally common solutions.

Faint Lines on Screen

If your monitor has one or two faint horizontal lines across the screen, check the specs. Displays that use aperture grill technology, such as those using Mitsubishi DiamondTron or Sony Trinitron picture tubes, will have those faint lines on the screen. It's part of the assembly of these units and it's perfectly normal. You'll learn to ignore them after a while. If the lines are very dark or vertical, or aren't straight, have your monitor checked by the dealer or manufacturer.

Shrinking Picture

Over time, as components on your monitor age, the picture may shrink. If you have a size adjustment, you can easily extend the height and width to their original size. If

What's Wrong with My Picture?

such adjustments aren't available, or do not accomplish the desired effect, contact the dealer or manufacturer for service.

Color Changes and Artifacts

■ **Black-and-white or grayscale picture suddenly appears.**   Check your color depth settings, either in Displays docking or on the Displays panel of the System Preferences application. See if you accidentally switched the setting.

■ **Color depth changes.**   Some games will only run at 256-color setting. If your monitor setting changes abruptly when you play a game, don't despair. It'll probably change back when you quit the program. If not, you'll need to switch it back manually, using the Displays icon on the menu bar (if active) or the Displays panel of the System Preferences application. Most games, however, will put up an alert box about this, which you must OK to make the change. If the game doesn't put up an alert, but monitor performance bogs down, you should try setting the color depth to 256 colors anyway to see if the setting helps.

■ **Color changes when switching programs.**   Some programs handle the Mac's color palette differently than others, so this effect may be normal. It's more likely to occur, however, when you are using a lower color depth, such as 256 colors. The problem ought to rectify itself when you quit the program.

■ **Color artifacts appear onscreen.**   If you see splotches of color on the screen in a particular program, switch to another program or to the Finder to see if the problem disappears. Some programs may interact strangely with certain Mac video hardware, particularly if it's a Classic Mac OS application rather than native to Mac OS X. If the problem begins to affect all of your programs and the desktop, check your Mac's video hardware or software to see if there's the potential for a problem. A call to the manufacturer's technical support department is a good idea.

Unavailable Color Depth Settings

When you install a larger monitor, you may face a problem. You were using millions of colors, and now, at the resolution you pick, you only have 256 or thousands available. If this happens, it may just mean that your Mac's video hardware doesn't support the setting. If your Mac or video card can handle a video memory upgrade, it's time to think about that possibility. If your Mac can support separate graphic cards, you may want to buy a new one. To get millions of colors from a 19-inch or larger monitor, for example, you need at least 4MB of video RAM for a graphic monitor; since every graphic card out there has at least 16MB, this is pretty much a nonissue.

> **NOTE**   *I'm using the term "video RAM" in the generic sense here. A number of different types of RAM are used for video monitors in various Mac models and graphic cards.*

Picture Too Large

You install a larger monitor and suddenly everything on the screen, from windows to text, is just too large. You will probably want to check the Display menu bar icon or the Display panel of the System Preferences application for a higher pixel resolution setting. This will reduce the size of the items monitored on your screen.

Screen Blacks Out Momentarily

When your Mac is starting up, it will load software that provides the selected display resolution on your display. When this happens, the picture may briefly black out and then return; it doesn't always happen, so don't be concerned if there's no such symptom. Sometimes the actual monitor size (resolution) will change as well. This particular phenomenon is quite normal.

Slow Screen Redrawing

- **There are too many pixels.**   When you get a larger monitor, or increase screen resolution and/or color depth, your Mac's video hardware has to work harder and draw many more pixels to create a screen monitor. That's apt to make your screen monitor slower. You may want to try a lower screen resolution setting (which makes images look larger) or choose a lower color depth to speed up performance. This sort of symptom is particularly noticeable on an early-generation iMac or Beige Power Macintosh G3, both of which had slower ATI graphics chips.

- **The video drivers are missing.**   Mac OS X ships with video drivers that should work with most ATI, ix MICRO, and NVIDIA graphic cards. Other companies will provide software for their products, assuming they are Mac OS X savvy.

- **The video drivers are not installed.**   Should you have a graphic card that didn't ship with drivers for Mac OS X, it may work, at least insofar as producing a picture is concerned. But don't expect fast performance.

Unstable or Rapid Scrolling

If these simple changes don't work, contact the manufacturer or dealer to check the unit.

- **Check the video cable at both ends.**   Make sure it's seated properly. If the cable connector is loose, shut down the system before you tighten it.

- **Make sure the Mac video adapter plug settings are correct.**   If you have a Mac video adapter plug with dipswitches, see if there's a label at the bottom showing settings for specific types of monitors. Some of these plugs came with a separate information sheet or card that explains what settings to make for a specific monitor or display resolution. Again, shut down your system before making these changes.

NOTE   *Older games, running in the Classic environment, may produce less-than-desirable video performance, particularly with older Mac video hardware. You might want to see if your favorite game has made the transition to Mac OS X, or look for other options.*

Fuzzy, Blotchy Picture

- **Move computer speakers farther away from the monitor.**   While speakers designed for use with a computer should be magnetically shielded to prevent such symptoms, sometimes it's just not enough.

- **Degauss the monitor.**   This function helps remove stray magnetic fields, which can cause blotchy effects on your monitor. Some monitors have a special switch for the purpose, but usually just turning the monitor on and off (you don't have to reboot your Mac) is sufficient to provide the degauss effect.

- **Try the "moiré" control.**   This will help eliminate the crosshair lines that may appear on the picture. Not all monitors have this control.

■ **Adjust sharpness and convergence.**   Check adjustments affecting sharpness or convergence and see if the picture is improved. If not, consider sending the monitor to the manufacturer or dealer for service.

Bouncing Picture, Wavy Patterns

If these solutions don't work, have the monitor checked by the manufacturer or dealer.

■ **Is there electrical interference?**   The most common cause is an electrical interference. If you have a vacuum cleaner or other heavy appliance running, turn the appliance off and see if the problem is gone. If it is, consider moving the appliance to another outlet and see if that helps.

■ **Move the monitor.**   Sometimes proximity to fluorescent lights will cause monitor oddities.

■ **Try another outlet.**   If you're adjacent to an office that uses lots of appliances (such as a dental office), transport the monitor to a different position or to a different electrical outlet and see if it helps.

Missing Colors, Tinged or Discolored Picture

■ **Zap the PRAM.**   Sometimes the monitor settings get corrupted. Zapping the PRAM is done by holding down the COMMAND-OPTION-P-R keys at startup. You then wait for at least two startup "tones" to sound on your Mac. The net effect is to restore some of your Mac's settings (such as monitor depth and startup disk choices, among others) to factory defaults. If these settings are corrupt, monitor irregularities and even system crashes may result.

■ **Select another monitor resolution or color depth setting.**   Perhaps your monitor or graphic card doesn't support your selected configuration.

■ **For AppleVision monitors**   Some of Apple's 15- and 17-inch monitors have a hardware defect that will cause a color problem. A common defect is a red-tinged image that appears intermittently or just stays put. If you encounter this sort of difficulty, contact your dealer or Apple's customer service department and inquire about their special warranty program affecting some of these units. If the customer service department doesn't have any information for you, insist on speaking to a supervisor about it.

What's Wrong with My Picture?

NOTE

Extended warranty programs usually have an expiration date, usually 7 years from date of purchase, but it doesn't hurt to complain after that date, especially if your defective product developed its problem just after the warranty expired.

No Picture

Your monitor is set up correctly. You have the proper sync adapter, and everything is all plugged into the right place. You turn on your Mac, and there's no picture. Is it the Mac, the monitor, what?

Here are some likely scenarios and their solutions:

- ■ **It's not on.**   This may seem to be a simple solution. But the power switches on some monitors will depress slightly when you turn them on. If you don't push them in far enough, they pop out again and your monitor is off. If the switch won't stay engaged, take the unit in for service. Some monitors will show a small, rectangular LED light when they're on.

- ■ **The lithium battery is dead.**   Your desktop Mac has a little lithium backup battery that's used to power the parameter RAM (PRAM). Such settings as date and time, monitor resolution and screen depth and network settings are stored there. If the battery goes bad, not only will those settings revert to factory defaults, but your Mac may not start up at all. You'll have just a dark screen. The battery itself is fairly cheap ($10 to $25, depending on the Mac model you have) and can usually be replaced in a few minutes. You can check the battery with a simple voltmeter, or just remove it for ten minutes and reinsert it (sort of a super PRAM zap). If the latter doesn't help, replace the battery.

TIP

You don't have to buy one of those backup batteries from an Apple dealer, or even Apple's own chain of retail stores. I found one for a Power Mac G3 at a Radio Shack, clearly labeled for Apple computers, at less than half the regular price charged by the computer stores. I doubt there's a dime's worth of difference between the Radio Shack and the official version (which usually has a manufacturer's name that isn't clearly recognized anyway).

- ■ **A graphic card is loose.**   If you move your desktop Mac around, the graphic cards may slip out of their slots slightly. Before taking everything to the repair shop, shut everything down, open your Mac, and reseat the card or cards. Then power up everything and restart the Mac. This should restore your picture.

■ **Video cables are loose.**   Shut down the system and reattach the cables. Sometimes cable contacts are oxidized and don't make good contact. The act of loosening or removing them and then reinserting and tightening is usually enough to fix the problem.

> **NOTE**
>
> *There are a few so-called "boutique" computer cables available at some dealers, with gold-plated plugs and so on. They are comparable to the high-priced connection cables you can buy for home stereos, because they cost a lot more than the regular brands and seldom provide any real benefits.*

■ **It's the wrong kind of monitor.**   While Macs can use VGA-style PC monitors in addition to Mac models, you cannot, for example, use monitors designed for the Apple II or some other older computers that don't support current standards.

■ **There's a bad graphic card.**   There's no way to test for this, except with another graphic card. Most manufacturers guarantee their product from three to five years, and replacement cards are fairly cheap nowadays. But until the replacement arrives, your Mac will be without a video monitor, unless it also has internal video.

■ **There's a bad logic board.**   If the Mac only has onboard video (the iMac, for example), you've no choice but to have it replaced.

■ **The power supply is bad.**   Same answer. The power supply will have to be replaced.

■ **The power supply on the monitor is bad.**   This sort of repair may cost a couple of hundred dollars at the very least, and is only done by specialists, perhaps only at the manufacturer's own facility.

> **NOTE**
>
> *Before you decide whether to repair that old monitor, you may want to price a new model. The cost of monitors today is but a fraction of what it was only a few years ago. For example, the money you used to pay for a 14- or 15-inch monitor will now get you one with a 19-inch monitor. Even LCD displays are becoming downright affordable.*

What's Wrong with My Picture?

Summing Up

In this chapter, you discovered how to set up and adjust your new monitor, and how to fix problems when they occur. You were also shown how easy it is to set up Apple's ColorSync so you get more accurate color display.

In the next chapter, we will pay a visit to the Windows world, and you'll learn how to integrate your Mac in a Windows environment and how to use Windows and even PC applications on your Mac.

Chapter 11

Help with Mixed Mac/Windows Offices

When Apple CEO Steve Jobs puts Apple Computer in the same league as a BMW or Mercedes-Benz in the automotive world, it's a clear admission that the Mac occupies a small minority of the personal computing world (although a very significant minority in terms of influence). Obviously the vast, vast majority of PCs out there operate under Windows. Though it's true the Mac platform has made great strides in recent years, and has reclaimed a huge amount of its former glory with clever new products such as the iMac, iBook, Titantium PowerBook G4, and Power Mac G4, it's a cross- platform world out there.

Many offices have computer systems from both platforms, and even home-based systems may have a Mac and PC at hand. Others use Linux or another flavor of Unix.

It's hard getting people who speak different languages to work in harmony, but it can be done. And the same is true for personal computers. It may take a little work to make things work properly, but it can be done, and done successfully.

Making Macs and PCs Communicate Peacefully

Direct from the factory, Macs are equipped to work with many Windows files without having to install special software or translators. It's also possible to network computers from both platforms; in fact, it's not uncommon in many businesses to use a Windows or Windows NT (or Windows 2000) computer as a file and/or print server, and use Macs for regular production work.

To make things work more efficiently, beginning with Mac OS X 10.1, Apple included an SMB client application in the package, which allows you to network with Windows NT, Windows 2000, and Unix-based SAMBA file servers without having to configure special software or options. The process is the same as accessing any other file share (even that Mac across the room). All those headaches in running Microsoft's Services for Macintosh, for example, are history.

Accessing DOS or Windows Files on Your Mac

Being able to read Windows files is not a new trick for Apple. For several years, the Classic Mac OS included a program that helps you translate Windows files so Macs can read them. In addition, the program lets your Mac read PC floppies, and such removable media as Jaz, Zip, and SyQuest, as easily as you read a Mac disk.

Originally, the program was PC Exchange, and, with Mac OS 8.5, it became File Exchange, which also incorporated the functions of another file access program, Mac OS Easy Open (see Figure 11-1).

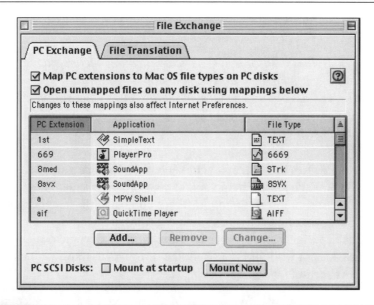

FIGURE 11-1   File Exchange, part of the Classic Mac OS.

For Mac OS X, Apple simply decided to put all this capability under the hood, so you don't have to configure a specific program to gain the ability to open files created on other computing platforms. As long as you have a Mac application (Classic or Mac OS X) that supported the file format, you'd be able to open a document without having to jump through hoops or crossing your fingers.

Solving File Opening Problems

Even though Mac OS X offers extensive compatibility with many types of documents, nothing is perfect, and at times the process of double-clicking on a document won't yield the desired result.

Here are a few common scenarios that you might encounter along the way:

- **You cannot open a file by double-clicking on it.**   If the Mac OS X Finder doesn't deliver a choice of applications that might open your document (see Figure 11-2), do this: First launch the application you want to use first, then use the Open dialog box to locate and open the file. You may have to change file-opening options from a pop-up menu in the Open dialog box, though. For example, in Word 2001 there's an All Files option that is very powerful and can manage to extract the text from a great many types of files.

NOTE   *If opening files created in a Classic application becomes a chronic problem, consider rebuilding the desktop on your Mac. It can cure a variety of ills of this sort (yes, desktop rebuilds can still be done in the Classic environment). The subject is covered in much more detail in Chapter 18.*

- **Document files have strange characters or they're garbled.**   If opening the file directly doesn't help, look at your program's documentation and see if there's an Insert, Import, or Place command that can be used. Such functions will often activate special file translators a program can use to read the special characteristics of many types of document files. If this choice doesn't work, try to use another program to translate the file (see the next section for details).

- **Disk is unreadable.**   When your Mac can't read the contents of a disk, you may get a message asking if you want to initialize the disk. Don't do it! This operation will wipe out the data on the disk. While you may just want to do that as a last resort, you should first click Eject, and then restart your Mac. If that doesn't work, try running the First Aid component of the Disk Utility application (in the Utilities folder), or a commercial diagnostic/repair program, such as Alsoft's DiskWarrior, MicroMat's Drive 10, or Symantec's Norton Utilities on the disk. For more information on using these programs to repair or recover a disk or drive, read Chapter 13.

There is no application available to open the document "32702F.doc ".

Choose Application...   OK

FIGURE 11-2   Click Choose Application to see if you can find a program to open the document.

CAUTION

Except for Disk Utility and Drive 10, the disk diagnostic programs mentioned here, as of the time this book was written, could only examine a Mac OS X disk when booted from a Classic Mac OS. And older versions of these utilities should not be used.

NOTE

Every time you start your Mac under Mac OS X, all available drives are scanned automatically. So it shouldn't be necessary to check your standard hard drives (the startup drive, in fact, cannot be scanned at all) unless you encounter problems with damaged files.

■ **CD can't be read.**   All Macs supported for Mac OS X shipped with their own CD drives. If you were able to install Mac OS X on your Mac, there should be no problem using the drive to read regular CDs (and DVDs, if supported). If the drive suddenly stops working, restart your Mac. If that fails, recheck the cables that connect your drive to the Mac's motherboard (shut it down, of course, before trying this). If you have a Mac with an unsupported installation of Mac OS X, it's possible the drive came from a third-party dealer, in which case Apple's native drives may not fully support the device. Should this occur, call the publisher of your CD software and see if they plan on releasing a Mac OS X version.

■ **File extensions are missing.**   On the Mac, the Finder can keep track of documents and the applications to which they link by virtue of creator (name of application) and file type (type of document, such as word processing file or spreadsheet file). But in the rest of the computing world, a document's format is identified by a three-letter suffix or extension. So, for example, a Word document bears the .doc extension. An AppleWorks document bears the .cwk extension (yes, AppleWorks is also available for Windows). The Mac OS X Finder sorts all this out, so usually you don't need to concern yourself with whether a file has the correct extension or not. If you find that the file extension that was here yesterday is gone today, use the Finder's Show Info command to check. Select the file, choose Name & Extension from the Show Info window's pop-up menu, and see whether Hide extension is checked (see Figure 11-3). There's also a Finder Preferences option, "Always Show File Extensions," which will make them appear all the time.

Making Macs and PCs Communicate Peacefully

FIGURE 11-3   This Show Info window is fine; file extensions aren't hidden.

How to Change File Mapping

If double-clicking on a DOS or Windows file brings up an application that won't do the job, you can easily change the file mapping (the program used to open a document) using Mac OS X's Show Info feature.

Here's how it's done:

1. Select the icon for the file in question and choose Show Info from the Finder's File menu.

2. Choose Open with Application from the pop-up menu (see Figure 11-4).

3. Click on the icon that represents the application that presently opens the document (it'll say "no application available" if the Mac OS X Finder can't locate one). Figure 11-5 shows the list of suggested applications.

4. Once you've selected an application from the list, you'll be returned to the Show Info window. Now there's one more decision to make. Would you like to have all documents of this type open in the application you selected? If so, click Continue (see Figure 11-6).

5. Choose the program you want to use to translate the file.

FIGURE 11-4   You can change the application that opens documents of this sort here.

6. Click the Continue to make the change; click Cancel if you want to reconsider.

7. When you're done, click the close button to dismiss Show Info.

Networking Mac and Windows Computers

When it comes to accessing a regular network printer on a cross-platform network, the issues are not complex. The printer will appear in the Chooser for Classic

FIGURE 11-5   Choose an application from the list or click Other for more choices.

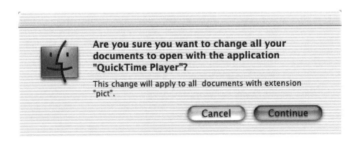

FIGURE 11-6 Make your decision here about opening other documents of this type with the same application.

applications and in Print Center for Mac OS X applications, and you set it up without regard to whether Windows users can access it as well.

But if a Windows computer is doing chores as a print server (that is, storing print jobs and feeding them to the printer), the situation is more complicated. The same is true if you want to share files across the network with your Windows counterparts.

Depending upon the sort of Windows network configuration you have, there are different ways to share files. These will be covered in the next few pages.

Windows Services for Macintosh Not Needed

Things have changed. Once upon a time, if your network used the server version of Windows NT, Windows 2000 Server, and Advanced Server, you had to use a set of tools called Services for Macintosh to allow Mac users to access your network. While the setup process was fairly straightforward, typical of Windows user configuration, it involved lengthy trips through dialog boxes and many options to consider to make sure things were set up properly.

Beginning with Mac OS X 10.1, Apple eliminated the need for a special software solution to make Macs access a Windows server. By including SMB support, it made it possible to connect to Windows NT, Windows 2000, and Unix-based SAMBA file servers simply by using the very same Connect to Server feature used to access another Mac on your network.

This sheer simplicity not only means that you don't have to go to network school to put Macs on a multiplatform network, but it helps dispose of the argument that Macs are not suitable for corporate use.

Making Macs and PCs
Communicate Peacefully

TIP

When you bring up the Connect to Server dialog box from the Finder's Go menu, the Windows or Unix file shares should be listed when you click on the network label (such as Local Network). If it's not there, manually enter the IP address or name of the server using the prefix smb:// in the Address text field.

Setting Up DAVE for Mixed Networks

However, you don't have to have a Windows server on your network in order to allow your Macs to network with Windows PCs.

For small networks especially, you may want to consider a Mac program that lets you directly access a Windows network: DAVE from Thursby Software Systems. You can get more information about the program and a time-limited demonstration version at the company's Web site: http://www.thursby.com.

DAVE lets your Macs connect directly to Windows computers using NetBIOS (Network Basic Input Output System). Installing DAVE is as simple as double-clicking on the installer program and restarting your Mac at the end of the setup process.

Once you have installed DAVE, though, it has to be configured. There's never a free ride when it comes to cross-platform networking.

To configure DAVE, follow these steps:

NOTE

The following setup information is based on a pre-release version of DAVE for Mac OS X. Some of the setup information may change from preview to final release.

1. Install DAVE by launching its installer and following the prompts.

2. When the installation is complete, the handy DAVE Setup Assistant launches (see Figure 11-7).

3. The first thing you have to do is enter your Administrator password to make DAVE do its stuff (click the lock at the bottom of the Setup Assistant Window).

4. Once you have entered the password, click Continue to move through the Setup Assistant (click Go Back to recheck a previous setting). Over the next few setup screens, you'll be asked to make sure your TCP/IP network

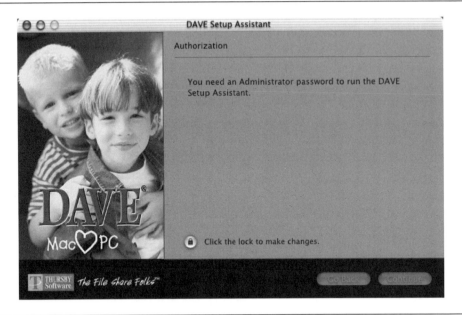

FIGURE 11-7   Follow the prompts to make your Mac play nice with a Windows peer-to-peer network.

connection is correct, and then you'll need to configure your Mac's name, and enter the name of the workgroup or domain of your Windows network.

NOTE   *You'll need to look at the Network Control Panel of your Windows network for some of the requested setup information.*

5. At the tail end of the process, you'll have the option to decide whether to share your local files on the Windows network. If you select that option, click Continue to launch the DAVE Sharing preference panel (see Figure 11-8).

6. Click Start to activate DAVE Sharing.

7. Choose the appropriate security level, whether it should apply to the Share (volume or folder) level or the User level.

8. To share something on your Mac, click New Share, then select the folder or file you want to share. You'll be asked to give the Share a name, and then set read and write access for various users.

FIGURE 11-8   Configure DAVE Sharing in this panel, installed as part of Mac OS X's
System Preferences application.

9. To access a Windows shared item on your Mac, launch the DAVE
Explorer application, which was placed in your Mac OS X Applications
folder (see Figure 11-9).

10. As soon as DAVE Explorer opens, it'll check your network to see what
computers are available. To access a Windows computer, click on its
name, and you see the list of folders being shared (by default it'll be the
MYDOCUMENTS folder).

11. Click on the item, then click the Mount Share button. Once you enter the
correct password, the shared folder will appear as a network volume on
your Mac OS X desktop.

12. Now to see your Mac's shared folders on a Windows PC, just open the
Network Places directory. Under Windows Me, which I used for this book,
double-click on the Entire Network icon to bring up a list of computers
sharing the network.

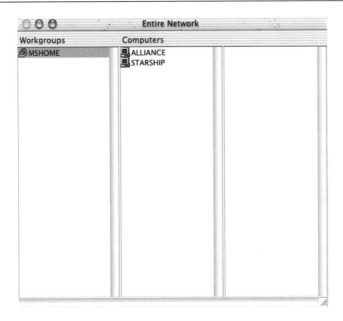

FIGURE 11-9   Here's the Entire Network that you have configured so far.

13. When you see the name of your Mac, double-click on the icon, and then click on the shared folders to see the list of files that can be shared across the network (see Figure 11-10).

14. Once you're finished working on your shared Windows folder, you can eject it, same as a hard drive, to send it away. Just launch DAVE Explorer to select it and bring it back.

Troubleshooting Mixed Network Problems

On a Mac, networking is usually fairly easy. You can connect other Macs courtesy of your Mac's Ethernet port.

To activate File Sharing, simply open the System Preferences application, and choose the Sharing panel. With the File & Web tab selected, click Start under File Sharing to activate the feature on your Mac. If your Macs are running a Classic Mac OS version, the option is available via the File Sharing or Sharing Setup Control Panels.

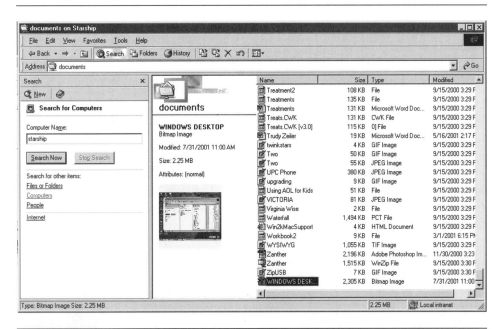

FIGURE 11-10 The Documents folder on one of the author's Macs is now seen on a Windows Me desktop.

CAUTION *It's a good idea to double-check the Computer Name on each system on your network. Even though Mac OS X can recognize another Mac via IP number, be sure there is no naming conflict. To change the computer name, just click sharing off, rename the computer, and turn it on again.*

The wrinkles begin when you also need to connect to Windows users on the very same network. You'll find that the setup process that works so easily on a Mac computer isn't quite so easy in the Windows environment.

Common Cross-Platform Networking Problems and Solutions

The issues of setting up a Mac/Windows network can be complex, and even if you follow all the convoluted dialogs and setup procedures, there is still potential for trouble.

Over the next few pages, I'll list some typical problems and solutions to make your cross-platform network function properly. As you'll see here, these are not user-friendly issues, and you may need to pore through manuals or consult a systems administrator (if your company has one) to troubleshoot the system. These are intended as basic guidelines to follow:

Make Sure Your DNS Servers Are Up to Date

On TCP/IP networks, Windows-based PCs rely primarily upon WINS and their NetBIOS Master Browsers to provide them with the capability to match a specific computer name to its IP address. But Macs, like their Unix cousins, rely upon DNS to match a computer's name to its IP address.

DNS (Domain Name Service) is the system that, like WINS, keeps track of the names of computers and their IP addresses. However, unlike WINS, which dynamically learns the computer's name and IP address from each computer as it boots up, DNS must be manually configured. This means that the DNS server's listing of computer names and their IP addresses can become inaccurate when a computer's name or IP address is changed. So, if you are having trouble connecting servers on the network from your Macs, the first thing you should check is your DNS servers to make sure they are functioning and their databases are up to date.

Check Your AppleTalk Setup and Your Routers

A router is a device that directs network traffic. When setting up a router you are, in effect, tying together two or more AppleTalk networks.

When you have trouble accessing computers outside the segment of the network on which you are located, take a look at the router or the switch that controls the link between your AppleTalk network and the other AppleTalk networks in your installation. Here are some diagnostic steps to follow:

- **Check your network protocol.**   One of the first things you should look at is what network protocol you are using to reach the other parts of the network. If you are using AppleTalk, you need to make sure that AppleTalk is enabled on the adjoining segments of the network or that the routers are set to transfer AppleTalk packets through the network using TCP/IP. You will also need to ask the simple question: are there any other segments of the network that use AppleTalk?

- **Check the other configuration settings.**   If there are other AppleTalk networks on your network and they are set up to communicate properly, you should look at the other settings you've used. In the old days—well, just a few years ago actually—when Macs tended to be quite chatty while communicating via AppleTalk, it was pretty common to install access lists on the routers so that certain types of AppleTalk traffic was blocked. Unfortunately, many routers still have these access lists installed despite the fact that modern Macs are nowhere near as demanding upon the network as they used to be. To check if an access list is blocking your Macintoshes from reaching the various resources on your network, look for access lists that would impact AppleTalk. On a Cisco router, this means looking for access lists that range from 600 to 699, as these are the AppleTalk-related access lists. Examine the various access lists and make sure they are configured in such a way as not to block your access to the resources you are trying to reach.

NOTE   *When it comes to network traffic, AppleTalk is referred to as being chatty because it constantly sends out network requests asking for updates on the network setup. The problem became more manageable as Apple improved AppleTalk performance beginning with Mac OS 8, and as more and more high-speed Ethernet networks were established.*

■ **Check the TCP/IP setup.**   If you are using TCP/IP to communicate, you'll want to make sure TCP/IP is configured properly on the Mac. If you are using DHCP to obtain a valid IP address for your Macintosh, you should check to see that it has acquired a proper one by opening the Network pane of the System Preferences application, choose your Ethernet or AirPort network, and see what IP address it has grabbed. If the address you get is in the range of 169.254.0.0 to 169.254.254.255, you have a problem with the Macintosh not being able to communicate with the DHCP server. The most common cause of this problem is that the router that controls this segment of the network is not configured to forward DHCP packets from one segment of the network to another. On Cisco routers, this command is called IP Helper. As I said at the beginning, we are getting to the real nitty-gritty of network management issues with some of these issues.

■ **Look at the default gateway.**   If your Macintosh is communicating properly with the DHCP server and getting a valid IP address, you should check if the router has a default gateway set up for the segment of the network on which your Macs are residing. Forgetting to set a default gateway is a very common error that happens when a network engineer sets up an AppleTalk-only network and then goes back later to add in support for TCP/IP or other network protocols.

■ **Look at the routing table updates.**   Aside from these common problems, you should make sure that the router controlling access to your segment of the network is receiving regular routing table updates. These updates tell the router where to send data so that it will reach its intended destination. If the updates aren't current, your data can be sent off into "never-never land." Another common issue you should check is that the Ethernet switch to which your Mac is connected has an up-to-date ARP cache and that the port settings for your Macintosh are set to the proper values. While modern switches are very good at determining what Ethernet speed and duplex settings are appropriate, they can sometimes choose an incorrect value or be set incorrectly by hand.

Troubleshooting a Mixed Network

The key to isolating and exterminating network problems on a mixed Mac/Windows network is to figure out if this is a Macintosh problem, a Windows problem, or both. First, you'll want to see if the problem affects computers from both platforms.

If the problem is affecting only your Windows-based PCs, you should focus on those portions of the network that are used only by Windows. For example, Windows uses TCP ports 135–139 to handle a variety of inter-computer communications as well as file transfers via NetBIOS. If your Windows-based computers have trouble sending and receiving files via NetBIOS, make sure there are no access lists on the routers that might be interfering with the movement of this traffic.

On the other hand, if the problem is Macintosh based only, you should look to see whether it is related to AppleTalk—that is, you're having trouble sending files between Macintoshes and to AppleTalk-based printers. If your troubles are limited to AppleTalk, take a look at the routers to make sure they are properly configured for AppleTalk. You should also make sure that AppleTalk information is being properly routed over the network, so the router knows how to direct AppleTalk traffic from one AppleTalk network to another.

TIP   *Mac OS X also networks via TCP/IP. If you have recent Macs that allow TCP/IP file sharing, you should use that feature rather than AppleTalk. Performance will be better and the AppleTalk-related issues that affect a mixed network can be minimized.*

How to Handle a Windows Emulator on a Mac

It would seem like a dream come true. All you have to do is install some software, and you convert your Mac into a Windows computer. Is the dream of having two computers a reality, or is there some hidden shortcoming that isn't being revealed in the advertising for these products?

Before I get into details, let me tell you that the most popular software solution, Connectix Virtual PC, works pretty much as advertised. You install this program and set it up according to instructions, and, presto, you have a real Windows environment on your Mac.

NOTE   *What about FWB's SoftWindows? The program has been discontinued by the publisher and will never migrate to Mac OS X. Fortunately, you can just buy the Virtual PC application and have it recognize your SoftWindows disk image file, which means you can remain up to date without paying a lot of extra money.*

You can use that Windows environment to run your favorite Windows programs and games. What's more, Virtual PC is designed to emulate an Intel-based computer, rather than just an operating system. This means you can go ahead and install other operating systems with the program. These include Unix-based systems (such as the Intel version of Linux, the popular open source operating system that's giving Microsoft fits).

NOTE   *Open source means that the computer code used to make the operating system is freely available for programmers to use or modify. Apple Computer has released part of its OS X operating system as open source, too, under the name Darwin (though it doesn't include the proprietary Mac OS user environment).*

In addition to software, there used to be hardware-based solutions as well. These solutions actually put a PC logic board inside your Mac, using the PCI slot. The cards contained an AMD or Intel processor and a logic board with various components that allow it to interface with a Mac environment.

At one time, even Apple Computer produced such products, but no more. Both Apple and the sole remaining DOS on a Mac hardware company, OrangeMicro, have discontinued such products, so Mac OS X compatibility is extremely doubtful, unless an enterprising independent programmer wants to tackle the task.

At this point in time, the sole solution to run Windows on a Mac under Mac OS X is software.

How PC Emulators Work

Virtual PC works by setting aside a part of your hard drive to make a big file that is used to emulate a PC drive. On the Mac side of the world, all you see is one very big file. When you use the Windows emulator, it's accessed as an actual PC drive.

To enter the PC world, just launch the program. Since Virtual PC can support a number of PC operating systems, your default operating system will launch, or just put up a window where you select one to open. You then switch in and out of this program the same way as any other program (see Figure 11-11).

Virtual PC is set up to map the PC environment to your Mac's various connection ports, so you can share drives, modems, network and Internet connections, and printers. The version of Connectix Virtual PC being shipped when this book was written also was designed to support USB.

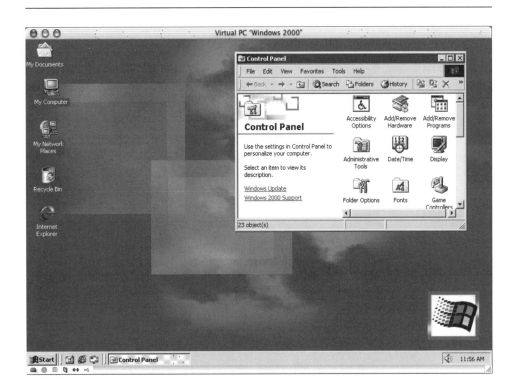

FIGURE 11-11   Windows is running under Mac OS X, courtesy of Virtual PC.

A Look at Windows Emulator Performance

Just how good is the imitation compared to the real thing? When it comes to software, there is no free ride. Here are some considerations:

- **They're RAM hungry.**   Windows emulation software requires lots and lots of RAM, first to cover the emulation software's overhead to do its magic, and then to act as RAM for the PC environment. You should figure on allocating a minimum of 48MB to your PC emulator for adequate performance. Although Mac OS X has a highly advanced virtual memory system, having enough real RAM is best, and the more you have, the better PC emulation will be, within the limits of what your Mac's processor can handle, of course.

- **They need big DOS files.**   You should figure on allocating between 250MB and 1GB of hard drive space for a Windows emulator. And since speed is dependent on the drive you have, consider a faster hard drive if you want to spend a lot of time emulating Windows.

- **They're slow.**   Even on the top-of-the-line Power Mac G3 and G4 (and Virtual PC is optimized for the G4's Velocity Engine), performance won't even come close to the cheapest PC you can buy today. Expect low-end Pentium performance across the board on a fast Mac, although these programs feel zippier than the raw measurements indicate because the publishers optimize such functions as pulling down menus. It's fine for doing some Internet surfing and running a word processing program. But when it comes to playing games, you may not be quite as satisfied with the level of performance.

If you have the need to run Windows programs with better performance, you may want to consider going all the way and buying a low-cost Windows computer. Even the very cheapest model will run much faster than a Windows emulator on a dual-processor Power Mac G4. You will, however, have to consider the inconvenience of using a separate display, keyboard, and mouse. However, if you need some serious Windows-based computer power to handle programs that just aren't available for Macs, this may be your only option. As I explained earlier in this chapter, with a program such as DAVE, you can actually set up a fairly inexpensive cross-platform computer network without a terrible amount of fuss and bother.

NOTE

Since modern-day PCs support USB, you might save space and use your keyboard and mouse for both computers (switchboxes are available). If you are using one of Apple's current LCD displays, though, there may be a problem. Apple uses a proprietary connection scheme, ADC, to connect a monitor to your Mac. To use such a monitor on a PC, you'd need to spend from $150 to $200 for an ADV to DVI adapter, and have a graphic card on the PC with DV (digital) video capability.

An All-Too-Brief Primer on Windows Troubleshooting

When you use a program that emulates Windows, or one of those DOS cards, you have indeed departed from the Mac operating system in large measure, and you'll no doubt be faced with an interface you have to get used to, and a new set of problems that may rear their ugly heads.

In this section, I'll cover some common Windows-based diagnostic steps. If you find your particular problems are rather more complex than I've dealt with here, may I recommend you get yourself a copy of *Windows 98: The Complete Reference*, by John Levine and Margaret Levine Young, from Osborne/McGraw-Hill. Just about any question you may have about the subject is answered in this 1,000-page book.

NOTE

The steps described in the next section can, in large measure, be applied to Windows Millennium, which is only a minor update to 98. The arrival of Windows XP, however, may bring with it new possibilities for mischief.

Windows Crashes at Startup

When your Mac crashes in the Classic mode, a common diagnostic procedure is to restart Classic after selecting a Base set in Extensions Manager or starting with Extensions off.

If you run into problems with Windows, you're apt to encounter a process that's roughly equivalent: Safe Mode.

If you have a severe crash, your Windows-based PC might actually start up in this mode. You can also enter it in rather a tricky fashion:

1. Restart Windows.

2. As soon as you see a message similar to "Starting Windows 98," or any recent version of Windows, press F8. You have to react fast to see this message, as it may zip by before you notice.

3. You'll see a Windows 98 Startup menu, and you'll be faced with six choices. Type the number **4**, then press ENTER to invoke Safe Mode.

Safe Mode supports only the very essential functions of Windows—the keyboard, mouse, display, and disk drives—and your screen size is limited to 640x480. If you successfully start up in this mode, more often than not, you'll be able to restart normally, and that, as they say, is that.

Otherwise, you may have to do some further troubleshooting. We'll cover a few more steps next.

The Windows Variation of the Force Quit

The Windows program you are working in suddenly hangs or crashes completely. You may or may not see an onscreen error prompt. Regardless, here's a way to close the program (as I said, similar to the force quitting on a Mac):

1. When the program hangs, press CTRL-ALT-DEL (this is the DEL key on the Extended keyboard, not the DELETE key). This will bring up a Close Program dialog box.

2. Locate the name of the offending program, select it, then click End Task. That should close the program.

3. If the program isn't closed, after a few seconds, you'll get another Windows dialog asking if you really and truly want to close that program. You should OK this message.

4. Should the program finally give up the ghost and quit, it's a good idea to restart Windows. Better to be safe than sorry, especially if you need to use that program again.

5. If you cannot quit the program this way, press CTRL-ALT-DEL two times, which should force Windows to restart. At the next restart, Windows will run its equivalent of the Mac's Disk First Aid, ScanDisk. And like the feature that first premiered in Mac OS 8.5, your Windows drive (or drive image in this case) will be scanned and errors will be fixed.

How to Handle a Windows Emulator on a Mac

NOTE   *As much as we like to credit Apple Computer with many of the major innovations in operating system flexibility, it's a fact that Apple has not had any qualms about borrowing a feature here and there from that other operating system. Running a disk check after a forced restart is cited as one example, although the feature actually made its debut under Unix. Another example is Contextual Menus, which is similar to the right-mouse-button feature under Windows, and I won't remind you about the way the Force Quit window is implemented in Mac OS X.*

A Look at Windows Troubleshooters

If you continue to run into problems in the Windows environment, you may also want to consult a set of tips and tricks provided for your benefit by none other than Microsoft. They're part of the Windows Help menu and are known by their collective name, Troubleshooters.

To access this feature follow these steps:

1. Open the Windows Start menu and choose Help. This will bring up the Windows Help menu.

2. Click on the Contents tab. This will produce a list of available topics.

3. For Windows 98, select Windows 98 Troubleshooters. This will bring up a list of topics for you to explore.

4. When you've found a suitable topic, click on it to select it.

5. On the right pane, you'll see a listing of typical problems. Click on the one that seems to apply, then click the Next button.

6. For each step of the way, you'll be asked some questions and based on your Yes or No responses, you'll be given proposed solutions. The steps described ought to help for most reasonably conventional problems.

NOTE   *If you are dealing with a Windows environment using Virtual PC, there are a number of hardware issues you are not apt to encounter. However, the software-related matters ought to apply to a number of the situations you will confront.*

In Defense of Your Mac

It's very true that Apple has found plenty of methods to shoot themselves in the foot. In the years before Steve Jobs returned to take over management of the company, Apple Computer managed to introduce so many related models that it took a scorecard to figure out the differences. They also squandered resources on technologies that few people bought into, such as OpenDoc and QuickDraw GX.

Although Apple's prospects have improved tremendously, especially since the iMac hit the marketplace in August 1998, there are still firms that, for this and other reasons, are seriously considering abandoning Macs and moving to the other platform.

If you are facing this situation, you will find the next section interesting. It has a rather Mac-centric view of the computing world, because that's the world I work in most often. But it will also give you some realistic information about the two platforms that you can use to examine the situation.

NOTE   *To be perfectly fair, I do have occasion to use Windows PCs, as product reviewer and technology journalist. The more I learn about both platforms, the more I can appreciate what is right or wrong about either.*

The Truth about Mac System Stability

No doubt you've heard the arguments. Some folks say a Mac is more stable than Windows, others say that Windows blows the Mac out of the water. As with anything as complex as a computer operating system, there are many variables at work here. There are plenty of examples where the usual assumptions just don't apply.

However, in the next few paragraphs, I will cover some of the basic issues that determine stability on both platforms. The biggest difference you will notice when moving from the Macintosh to Windows or from Windows to the Macintosh is how easy it is to destabilize each operating system, particularly if you're using a Mac that hasn't migrated to OS X yet.

The Mac View of the Windows Environment

Mac users often find themselves aghast at how the installation of a simple application or update can render a perfectly functional Windows-based PC completely useless.

Even under the Classic Mac OS environment, Macintosh-based applications and utilities seldom installed a large number of files directly into the operating system or replaced commonly shared files with a version of their own. However, many Windows-based applications do. Since Windows utilizes a large number of interrelated files to function properly, having an installer install the wrong version of a file or delete a critical file during installation can easily render Windows inoperable.

> **NOTE** *To be fair, I should point out that some Mac installers do from time to time toss stuff in the System Folder without regard to whether there are newer, better versions there. But more often than not, you'll just find two different versions of the same files (such as an older and newer version of AppleScript or QuickTime). It's not difficult to locate and then trash the older version. Fortunately, Mac OS X minimizes the number of files installed on a system level. The most common way to run even a system-related utility is as a Login application, automatically launching during the login process (similar to using the Startup Items folder under the Classic Mac OS). As a result, system-related difficulties are minimized.*

Likewise, the sheer number of files and the myriad ways they interact with each other make it nearly impossible to determine exactly what went wrong on a Windows computer and how best to repair it. While the addition of uninstall utilities with many applications has helped, they do not always restore the PC to its original state. Unfortunately this means that when something goes badly wrong with Windows, you almost always have to do a completely fresh re-installation of Windows. Then you will probably have to reinstall all your application and utility software in order to get the PC back to a working condition.

In the earlier section entitled "A Look at Windows Troubleshooters," I just scratched the surface to help you deal with the basics. If you have to do a major troubleshooting task on a Windows-based PC, you're apt to find that the entire time-consuming process makes a clean install on a Mac seem to be simplicity personified.

The Windows View of the Mac Environment

Windows users coming to the Macintosh will be surprised to find that there are far fewer components to the average Mac application or utility. This means that installing and removing Mac applications and utilities is a far simpler process in general than it is on a Windows-based PC.

Macs are, as a general rule, harder to crash than a Windows-based PC for two reasons. First, because of its Unix-based underpinnings, Mac OS X is far more resilient to the ills that can bring a personal computer down (to be fair, so is Windows 2000 and Windows XP). In addition, Apple has greater control over the hardware and software, and thus the ability to make sure things work properly, than does Microsoft. Although Apple's tight integration of the hardware and operating system is sometimes criticized because it grants the Mac user fewer purchase options, in this case, it works as an advantage.

Under the Classic Mac OS, a great many problems that a Mac user will encounter can be traced to either a bad extension or control panel, a bad font, or perhaps a bad application or application preference file. Since the Mac OS is inherently less complicated than Windows, due to the lesser number of files in the operating system, it is usually far easier for a user to diagnose and resolve problems without having to reinstall the operating system. I cover this subject in more detail in Chapter 18.

Under Mac OS X, troubleshooting is usually less of an issue. If an application quits constantly, reinstalling or just looking for an upgrade can often cure the problem. And, as with the Classic Mac OS, removing a damaged preference file can do a world of good.

Since you can continue to use your Mac if a Mac OS X application crashes or quits, the need to constantly restart is limited to a system update from Apple or the rare program that does require such a process.

NOTE *The vast majority of Mac OS X applications are bundled in package form, where all the disparate elements of the program are placed in a single folder that can be double-clicked to launch the application. That minimizes application clutter and makes installation and removal a snap.*

To be fair, Microsoft's industrial-grade operating systems, Windows NT and Windows 2000 (and Windows XP, which is based on the Windows 2000 kernel), are usually far more robust and significantly harder to crash than the Classic Mac OS or Windows 95/98/Me. While Windows NT and 2000 suffer many of the same flaws that affect Windows 95/98/Me users, by relying upon a large number of files and settings to function properly, they are also designed to survive most software crashes without bringing down the entire operating system.

To the average user, this means that Windows NT will, for example, either fail completely—producing what is known as the blue screen of death—or will just shrug off the error and keep on running. Windows 95/98/Me, when confronted with a similar system error, will almost always cease to function (but, of course, that's also true of the Classic Mac OS).

In Defense of Your Mac

This fact of life isn't lost on Apple. For years they have been working to deliver better stability to the Mac operating system. The arrival of Mac OS X has sharply reduced the number of errant system problems, although many will persist if you must continue to use Classic applications.

Is the Mac Really Slower?

You compare the horsepower. On the one hand, you have all those Pentiums advertised with 1.5 to 1.8GHz CPUs and, on the other hand, Macs in the 500 to 867MHz range (the numbers of both ends of the equation will continue to rise over time).

On the surface, then, it would seem that Macs are noticeably slower than their Windows counterparts, at least if you just examine the megahertz figures.

But evaluating computer performance isn't as easy as that.

Since Steve Jobs took over as Apple's CEO, Apple almost always introduces their new computers with a big flourish, and benchmark tests that are designed to show their computers running much faster than Windows-based systems with up to twice the CPU ratings. The problem with benchmarks is that they don't apply equally to all computer functions.

For one thing, performance doesn't just depend on raw megahertz or gigahertz, but also on how much data the CPU can actually process, and how fast—and that is a complex issue, depending on how the CPU is designed and how it performs in the real world. Computer performance also depends, to name a few examples, on the performance level of the other elements of your computer, such as the logic board, the hard drive, the video display hardware, the CD drive, and the efficiency with which a program is created.

The fact of the matter is that some programs manage to work better on the Mac and others better with Windows (no blame is being assigned here, of course).

So every time Apple produces a benchmark showing how the Mac does something faster, a Windows user will come back with their own benchmark showing how one of their computers has excelled in one task or another.

As a practical matter, if you use your Mac strictly for such things as financial transactions, word processing, or surfing the Web, a little performance advantage one way or the other won't make you any more productive. But if you want to play high-energy games or deal with programs that do complex rendering tasks (such as image editing, 3-D design, or editing video), you'll want to eke out every possible increment of performance.

Competition is at work here. As quickly as Apple touts superiority, Windows-based systems get faster, too. By managing to leapfrog each other, the performance level of personal computers continues to grow, and the state of the art hits a higher plateau. And the next Mac you buy will likely be much faster than the one it replaces.

> **NOTE**   *It's not just Apple talking up the megahertz myth anymore. Even AMD, whose Athlon processors have fallen behind Intel in the gigahertz race, has been repeating the "size doesn't always matter" mantra.*

Where to Find Mac Software

When I first bought a Mac, I included in the package much of the software I expected to use on a regular basis, so I was able to get up and running without having to buy anything extra. And today the consumer model Macs, the iMac and iBook, come with a nice selection of software you can use to get started. These include AppleWorks, Apple's great little integrated program featuring word processing, spreadsheets, database, and simple illustration components, plus the software you need to access the Internet. At times, dealers will also set up special packages that include a software selection.

But one way or another, you may find that you want to expand your horizons or you need a special type of software for a particular purpose. You visit your local Mac dealer and find the cupboards bare, or close to it. There are a handful of utilities, a few games, and maybe a copy of the latest Microsoft Office.

You ask the salesperson for more, and you may get this typical response, "Sorry, there isn't much Mac software available."

Did you make a mistake? Choose the wrong computing platform? Does Windows begin to tempt you?

Well, the truth is, there are thousands of Mac programs available, and not just mainstream software that's designed for a mass audience. There are dedicated Mac programs for legal offices, dentists, physicians, and other special purposes. But you won't typically find a decent section at most local dealers (though a few, such as CompUSA and Apple's growing chain of retail outlets, which first debuted in 2001, have well-stocked software bins).

Most Mac users go to mail order catalogs to buy software, from such companies as MacConnection, MacMall, MacWarehouse, and MacZone (to name just a few popular examples). When you pick up one of those catalogs, you'll find thousands of programs listed. But even a local dealer can usually order a program that isn't regularly stocked.

NOTE

If your dealer doesn't have the software you need, you may want to check Apple's Web site for information on more than 18,000 available Mac products: http://guide.apple.com. The site splits the information up into a number of hardware and software categories. If the product is listed, you'll see details about how to contact the manufacturer for more information.

So before you visit the other side of the computing platform, do a little checking first. In most cases, the program you need will be available in Mac form.

NOTE

I'd like to offer a very special thank you to Pieter Paulson, who has collaborated with me on several writing projects, for his help in writing this chapter. Pieter is an experienced network administrator who has supported a number of mixed platform networks in his long career.

Summing Up

The problems with making Mac and Windows computers work together in reasonable harmony are not insurmountable. Although it may take a little troubleshooting to get all the pieces to work together, it is a task that will be worth the rewards in being able to share files and printers across even the largest personal computer networks.

In the next chapter, I'll deal with another issue that can rear its ugly head whether you share files with Windows users or not. And that's the subject of computer viruses.

Chapter 12

Do You Have a Computer Virus?

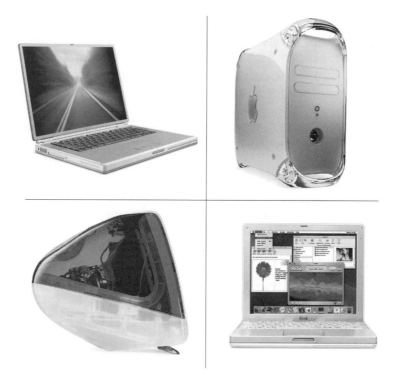

Computer viruses are part and parcel of our folklore. From news stories to the world of show business, virus authors play various roles in our society, mostly as a threat to computer users everywhere. However, in two notable celluloid examples, virus authors were actually the heroic figures who saved the day.

In the top-grossing science fiction movie *Independence Day,* one of the brave heroes, a cable TV technician portrayed by Jeff Goldblum (the same actor prominently featured in a number of Apple's "Think Different" commercials), used a computer virus to infect the aliens' computers and make them vulnerable to attack by Earth firepower. Naturally, it's never explained just how a simple laptop computer, in this case an Apple PowerBook, could somehow interface with an alien operating system without a direct connection and spread a virus. Perhaps the aliens were using a futuristic version of Apple's AirPort wireless networking system?

Another popular movie, *The Net,* featured Sandra Bullock as a computer programmer whose identity had been stolen by an evil industrialist. To get back at her enemy, she infected the villain's evil software with a virus.

In these two fictional cases, the computer virus was the good guy, the secret weapon that allowed our heroes to defeat the bad guys. In the real world, however, a computer virus isn't so nice. A computer virus may simply put up a silly message on your computer and be done with it. Or it may alter or damage your precious application and document files, even your system software. Worse, a virus may actually wipe out your files or erase your hard drive.

In addition to the havoc they wreak, writing and spreading computer viruses is a crime in just about any civilized location in the world. There have been notable cases through the years in which virus authors were caught, tried, and convicted.

Even if just a childish prank, the presence of computer viruses is a threat to everyone, whether you use a Mac or a PC.

Are Computer Viruses a Danger to Mac Users?

On the PC side of the computing universe, virus strains number in the thousands, with more being discovered almost every day. This is one of the perils of being the majority platform.

That's not to say that Mac users are immune to such problems. In addition to the rapid spread of Microsoft Office macro viruses (as discussed in the next section), the newfound popularity of Macs, iMacs, and iBooks has brought with it the consequence of renewed interest in writing viruses for our favorite platform.

From the early days of the Mac, some very potent viruses have infected our platform, and you need up-to-date protection. No doubt about it.

Case History

My First Close Encounter with a Virus

I remember this as if it were yesterday.

After migrating from a design studio to Mac-based desktop publishing in the 1980s, I went and bought myself a Mac system for my home. I had hoped to resume my writing career and perhaps do a little telecommuting, so I could stay home and get paid for it.

It was the spring of 1989, and the hot Mac of that era was the IIcx, which sported the fastest Mac-based microprocessor, the 68030. It's hard to believe that I thought of the computer as incredibly fast, but that's how technology changes.

I set up the system and worked hard and long to install software. I downloaded programs from the Internet, but the problem really originated when I brought home a small utility program (the name isn't important) from a local dealer.

I installed the program, and then I tried to create a new document in QuarkXPress. Now XPress is one of a number of programs that's classified as "self-checking," meaning that it'll refuse to run if it's modified in a suspicious fashion, such as might occur when infected by a virus.

I launched QuarkXPress, and got a warning about a possible virus infection. Then it refused to run. Now I was startled. A virus infection was something I hadn't seriously considered on a brand-new computer, and so I hadn't bothered to get any virus detection software.

I cleaned up all the files I could think of. I even reinstalled system software and the affected program, but it didn't work. I still got the virus warning.

Finally, I wiped the hard drive clean, and reinstalled everything from scratch. As soon as I was up and running, I logged on to an online service and downloaded a shareware virus detection program (it was Virus Detective, no longer being produced).

It reported that I was still infected with the nVIR virus, but it was able to eradicate it from my Mac and some infected disks. And then I found the cause: that little utility I had purchased from a local Mac store was apparently infected at the factory. (They told me it was a shipping error.)

The moral of the story: Even when you buy commercial software in a reputable store, check it anyway. Sometimes mistakes are made, and there's no reason for you to have to suffer as a result. If you do find the presence of a virus on any software you buy, tell the store and the publisher immediately, and ask for a clean copy.

Are Computer Viruses a Danger to Mac Users?

The Real Dangers of Cross-Platform Viruses

The nice thing about Microsoft Office programs is that you can view and edit them on both the Mac and Windows platforms.

The nasty thing is that they make Macs vulnerable to infection by the thousands of macro viruses that infect such applications as Excel and Word. Microsoft's macro feature is valuable. It helps you easily automate repetitive steps and handle complex formats at the click of a button (or via a simple keystroke). But with convenience comes a danger, that the very same avalanche of macro viruses may infect your Mac also.

Fortunately, on our side of the computing universe at any rate, such virus infections primarily hurt your documents, not your application or system files. As noted in the following section on Mac viruses, a common Word macro virus may somehow password-protect your document (with a password you don't know, of course) or make it impossible to save the document as anything but a template.

> **NOTE**
> *You'd be very surprised to hear the strange places macro viruses turn up. I've gotten infected documents from advertising agencies, publishers, and, in one case, a company who made DOS conversion hardware for the Mac. Most of these folks were surprised and thankful I discovered the problem (except for one company, whose name I'd prefer to forget).*

Fortunately, such problems are easily remedied. Current Mac virus protection programs will handily diagnose and dispose of macro viruses, and they are updated regularly as new mischief-makers do their dirty work.

> **NOTE**
> *It should be pointed out that a number of Microsoft Office macros on the Windows platform use Visual Basic code that isn't supported on the Mac version of the program. This lessens the danger to Mac users. But if you transfer those infected files back to the Windows platform, the infection will transfer as well, so protecting yourself from macro viruses is still very important.*

> **TIP**
> *Another potential virus threat is an AppleScript virus. Please see in Chapter 23 the section entitled "AppleScript Virus Causes Havoc" to learn about a real-world example of such an infection.*

PC-Borne Viruses and the Dangers to Mac Users

It's true that a virus designed to infect the DOS and Windows operating systems won't harm your Mac, but there are notable exceptions to the rule. And they apply if you decide to emulate the PC operating systems on your Mac.

Windows Emulators

When you install Connectix Virtual PC, you are definitely working in a Windows environment, even if it shows up in a separate application window.

NOTE
The same holds true when you install a DOS card, such as the ones that Apple and Reply used to sell, and the ones manufactured by Orange Micro. None of the DOS cards, however, were certified for use under Mac OS X as of the time this book went to press, by the way, and even Orange Micro's line has been discontinued.

Since you are actually running PC operating systems, those special environments are nearly as vulnerable to a PC virus as a regular PC. That means your PC application, document, and system-related files can be infected by one of those many thousands of viruses that lurk on the other side of the computing world. That means you need to get virus protection software.

NOTE
If there's an exception to this cross-platform problem, it's viruses that affect low-level drivers and hardware that aren't part of the emulation software. So in that regard, a Windows software emulation solution may have an advantage.

But the Mac programs mentioned at the end of this chapter won't run in a PC environment. For protection, you need to buy one of the Windows-based virus detection programs and install them. Fortunately, the very same publishers of Mac virus software, Network Associates and Symantec (and others), have virus programs for you.

If your exploration of DOS and Windows extends beyond mere curiosity and you really intend to do productive work using files acquired from others or surf the Internet, you'll want to buy virus software and keep it updated as needed.

If you want to learn more about running Windows on a Mac, please read Chapter 11.

The Real Dangers of Cross-Platform Viruses

How to Know If It's a Virus or a Software Problem

Your favorite Mac applications (usually ones in the Classic environment) are crashing constantly; you've restarted the Classic environment so many times that your fingers are getting tired opening and closing the System Preferences application (or you just leave it open all the time). You can't get any work done, and it's most definitely hair-pulling time. The question that may be foremost in your mind is whether some nasty computer virus is at work here, and what do you do next?

Fortunately, the instances of Mac computer viruses are small. The vast majority of Mac computing problems can be traced to more conventional solutions, such as system extensions conflicts (for the Classic Mac OS), the need to reinstall your Classic operating system software, or issues with hardware peripherals, such as SCSI chain oddities.

Unless your Mac displays a classic virus-based symptom, the best advice is to look elsewhere for a solution. Many of the chapters in this book cover troubleshooting for various elements of your Mac user experience, and you'll want to read the ones that apply to your situation.

Mac Viruses and Their Effects

Some viruses just put up a silly message. Others can damage files or even your hard drive directory. Whatever the symptom, ridding yourself of the virus is paramount, because you never know whether a silly message may camouflage a more serious problem with your Mac.

The following is a brief look at some well-known Mac computer viruses and their most common symptoms (current virus software can detect all of these):

NOTE   *I have not tried to be complete in these descriptions. I'm just summarizing the basics for their historical value. And I don't pretend to cover all known Mac viruses here. In addition, some of the older viruses, such as nVIR, are relics of the non-PowerPC era, and may not be as dangerous to today's software. Moreover, ones that may still cause damage would likely affect only the Classic rather than Mac OS X environment (but even Unix-based viruses would be a threat as Mac OS X use grows). Since the popular virus protection programs protect you against all of the viruses described next anyway, this is not an issue you need to consider.*

- **ANTI Virus**   This virus infects primarily non-PowerPC (680x0) applications, but the damage may not be sufficient to cause a problem running a program unless the application itself has self-checking code, which means it won't run if there's an unauthorized modification. If an application is infected, it's best to replace it rather than let your virus software repair it.

- **AutoStart Worm**   This Mac-borne virus turned up in 1998 after a period of quiet on the Mac platform. It's called a "worm" because it doesn't actually alter a program or document file to pass itself around. Rather, the worm duplicates itself from disk to disk on vulnerable systems. The virus itself will add invisible files to your drive, which will result in mysterious hard disk activity. Some data files may also be overwritten with random data. A fast way to protect yourself against the virus in your Classic Mac OS is to turn off the AutoPlay feature of QuickTime in the QuickTime Settings Control Panel or with the CD-ROM Control Strip. This won't help if you're already infected, so you need to check all your disks with virus software as well. The worst part of it all is that a few commercial program CDs actually shipped with AutoStart, until fast solutions were found (don't worry, the disks were quickly recalled by the publishers).

> NOTE
>
> *I remember a brief one-month period in which nearly half my clients could cite at least one or two instances of succumbing to this irritating virus.*

- **CDEF Virus**   This virus primarily infects System 6–type desktop files, so it's not an issue with Mac OS 7 or Mac OS 8.

- **CODE 1 Virus**   The primary effect of this virus is to rename your startup drive to "Trent Saburo." It may also cause unexplained system crashes.

- **CODE 252 Virus**   This virus was designed by someone with mischief on their mind. It appears when you launch an infected application or system file between June 6 and December 31 of any year. The message it displays is as follows (and no, it doesn't erase any disks):

```
You have a virus.
Ha Ha Ha Ha Ha Ha Ha
Now erasing all disks. . .
Ha Ha Ha Ha Ha Ha Ha
P.S. Have a nice day
Ha Ha Ha Ha Ha Ha Ha
(Click to continue. . .)
```

- **CODE 9811 Virus**   The effects of this virus are rather severe. It hides your applications and replaces them with files that have gibberish titles, such as "FIDVCZWGJKJWLOI." Your desktop backdrop will also take on an aspect of electronic worms, and you may see a message stating, "You have been hacked by the Praetorians." What makes this whole mess doubly confusing is that this message only seems to affect about 25 percent of the infected installations, and only appears on a Monday. Definitely a Blue Monday.

- **CODE 32767 Virus**   This virus supposedly attempts to trash documents once a month, but it hasn't spread widely.

- **Flag Virus (also known as WDEF C)**   This virus will infect system files and apparently overwrite a WDEF resource of ID 0 in your system, which may cause problems with some files.

- **INIT-M Virus**   This virus is particularly destructive. It will appear on a Friday the 13th, and can damage files and folders. The names of files are changed to random strings containing just eight characters, and names of folders will have one to eight characters. The most serious problem, though, is that the file type and creator information (used by the Finder's desktop files to link documents to applications) are altered, and the creation and modification dates become January 1, 1904. Another symptom: The name of one or more icons on your Mac may be changed to "Virus MindCrime."

- **INIT 17 Virus**   This pesky critter will spread to the System file and applications. When an infected Mac is restarted, you'll see the message, "From the depths of Cyberspace." The virus can also cause unexplained crashes and other untoward symptoms, especially on older 68000 Macs, which begin with the Mac Plus and Mac SE and end with the Classic.

- **INIT 29 Virus**   This very old Mac virus (dating back to 1988) can infect all sorts of files, from documents to applications and operating system components. The virus seems to be System 6 specific, and can spread very easily, though it doesn't seem to do any serious damage.

- **INIT 1984 Virus**   This virus is similar in its effects to INIT M. It can also cause crashes on very old Mac models, such as the 128K.

- **INIT 9403 Virus**   This is a particularly destructive strain. Once it infects your Mac, it can proceed to erase disks. Fortunately, it was only discovered in Italian versions of the Mac OS, and all current virus detection programs will eradicate it.

■ **MacMag Virus**   This very old virus (1987) also bore the names Aldus, Brandow, Drew, and Peace. MacMag would damage system files, and was spread via a HyperCard stack named "New Apple Products." The virus was designed to self-destruct, so you probably won't have to worry about it, unless you have a really old Mac and operating system without virus protection.

■ **Macro viruses**   These are rampant because of the widespread use of Microsoft Office programs, such as Excel and Word, on the Mac. They are also cross-platform, which means that both Mac and Windows users can be infected (though the Windows platform is more vulnerable to such viruses). While Windows users can encounter corrupted system files, the most common symptoms on a Mac include mysterious password-protection of a document, and making it impossible to save a document as anything but a template.

■ **Mac.Simpsons@mm Virus**   This is an AppleScript virus, bearing the title "Simpsons Episodes," which is similar to the PC "worms" that afflict email software. The affected applications are Microsoft's Entourage and Outlook Express. When the script is executed, the email applications are launched, and the virus is copied to everyone in your contact list accompanied by a message about alleged secret episodes of the Simpsons TV show.

■ **MBDF Virus**   This is a Trojan Horse virus, spread through such games as 10 Tile Puzzle, Obnoxious Tetris, and Tetricycle. Once it infects a Mac, MBDF will go on to damage both Classic application and system files. If the system is damaged, you'll have to do a clean reinstallation.

■ **MDEF Virus**   This virus has also been given the names Garfield and Top Cat. The virus infects application files, which beep when you run them. Beyond that, there doesn't seem to be any particular damage.

■ **nVIR Virus**   Similar to Scores (which is described next), nVIR will infect the System file. Then, once you run an application, it'll be infected as well. One of the symptoms includes a voice message, "Don't panic," which you'll hear if you have Speech software installed on your Mac.

How to Know If It's a Virus or a Software Problem

■ **Scores Virus**   This virus has also been known as Eric, NASA, San Jose Flu, and Vult. Its most notable symptom is a change of icons for your Note Pad and Scrapbook files, both located in the Classic System Folder. Instead of having their distinctive icons, they change to blank sheets of paper with turned-down corners. And they don't change if you rebuild your Mac's desktop. Aside from spreading from application to application, after the initial infection of your system, Scores doesn't appear to do any serious damage.

■ **The SevenDust Virus**   This is a particularly threatening virus strain, and it's also known either as MDEF 9806 or MDEF 666. There are several strains, two of which may actually erase nonapplication files on your startup drive. One variation of SevenDust actually masqueraded as a video acceleration extension under the name Graphics Accelerator (with a nonprinting file prefix that would make it load first). What makes that doubly confusing is that there is a genuine Apple system extension named Graphics Accelerator, which is used for Macs equipped with ATI video chips or ATI graphic cards. The real extension was later renamed ATI Graphics Accelerator, which should avoid the confusion. Besides, the latest virus detection programs will find the fake.

■ **T4 Virus**   This is another one of those Trojan Horse variations, which came embedded in a game called GoMoku. Once infected, the virus spreads to your applications, including the Finder, and it also tries to alter your System file. Once infected by T4, programs cannot be repaired, and the changes to the System file prevent extensions from loading at startup.

■ **WDEF Virus**   Back around 1989 and early 1990, I was working as a consultant with a graphic design studio. During a period of several weeks, just about every floppy disk we handled there had been infected by WDEF, which infects desktop files (the ones used by System 6). The net result of the virus was not serious, but it was downright annoying nonetheless. Fortunately, the advent of System 7 in 1991 and the new forms of desktop files effectively put the kibosh on that virus, since it won't affect the later generations of Finder desktop files.

■ **ZUC Virus**   This virus was designed to infect applications, and causes the mouse cursor to bounce around erratically across the screen when you run an infected application. The virus can also alter the desktop backdrop and cause strange spurts of disk activity. It can infect Macs across a network.

Is Mac OS X Immune to Ordinary Mac Viruses?

The $64,000,000 question, one I asked of David Loomstein, Mac product manager for Symantec's utility product line. His answer was mixed. Macro and AppleScript viruses have the potential of affecting applications in both the Classic and Mac OS X environments.

In addition, virus software available when this book was written required separate programs and installations for the two systems.

But what about regular Mac viruses? Loomstein said there was "almost no chance" of such viruses affecting Mac OS X or a native application. However, the Classic environment may indeed be vulnerable to virus infections, particularly the SevenDust, CODE 9811, and MBDF strains.

What's more, some of the very first computer viruses affected the Unix platform, so it is quite possible virus authors will want to spread their mischievous deeds to Mac OS X, too. That's why it's just as important as ever to have robust and up-to-date virus protection.

Choosing and Installing Virus Protection Software

When you fight computer viruses, it's a moving target. Virus authors deliver their nasty tricks without warning, at any time. You never know when a new virus strain may emerge—witness the AutoStart virus that infected Mac users after years of the relative absence of new viruses on our favorite computing platform.

In order to protect yourself against the unexpected, the best thing to do is buy up-to-date virus protection software and keep it updated with new detection strings.

With regular software, there's no problem in using an old version, as long as it works with your present Mac and operating system version. Mac OS X's Classic environment is a godsend, because many programs that will never see the light of day for the new operating system may still run just fine. But not so with virus software.

The publishers are notorious for removing support against older versions after a few years, which means you are left unprotected against current strains of older viruses. And some programs are simply no longer available. Among the casualties of various software company mergers and departures are such products as Dr. Solomon's Anti-Virus ToolKit, McAfee VirusScan, and Rival.

Even the freeware and shareware market has changed. Back when I first got a Mac, I used Virus Detective, which was retired by its author when it became too time consuming and costly to update. Alas, shareware users usually don't pay the fees to a program's author. In addition, John Norstad's venerable free virus program, Disinfectant, was similarly retired because its structure didn't allow it to recognize the latest virus infections, such as so-called Trojan Horse and macro viruses.

Comparing Norton AntiVirus and Virex

As of the time this book went to press, two long-time virus programs were still being published: Norton AntiVirus from Symantec (successor to SAM, Symantec Anti-Virus Utilities for Macintosh) and Virex from Network Associates. In addition, a new virus application, Intego's VirusBarrier, was competing hard for market share, and MicroMat's TechTool Pro also incorporated virus detection capabilities as part of a comprehensive system diagnostic and repair package.

NOTE   *As a point of history, the original programmer for SAM, Paul Cozza, was also the programmer for MasterJuggler, one of the early font management programs. Programming chores for both programs have since been assumed by others, and last I heard, Cozza was enjoying a fairly lucrative retirement from Mac programming, living, in part, on the royalties earned from the sale of these products (maybe I'm in the wrong business).*

A quick gander at present-day virus programs will show that they are more similar than different. They are regularly updated for newly discovered viruses, and get regular updates to fix problems and improve performance. You will not go wrong with any of them.

Here's a rundown of what these programs offer.

Norton AntiVirus

The version of Norton AntiVirus (see Figure 12-1) that shipped when this book was prepared, version 7, included these notable features above and beyond basic detection of the presence of computer viruses:

■ **Auto-Repair**   The program can be configured to automatically repair infected or damaged files (though this measure isn't always 100 percent effective).

■ **Check for suspicious activity**   The program is normally set up not just to check for known viruses, but also for activities that may indicate the presence of an unknown virus strain.

■ **Compressed files**   Files compressed in a number of popular compression protocols will be automatically expanded and checked by the program.

■ **LiveUpdate**   This feature allows you to check Symantec's Web site automatically to retrieve program and virus string updates.

■ **SafeZone**   You can set aside a location on your hard drive for automatic scanning. Whenever a file is copied to that location (either from the Internet or another drive or network), the program will check it for the presence of viruses.

■ **Scheduled scans**   You can configure the program to do a full scan of your Mac's drives at regular intervals.

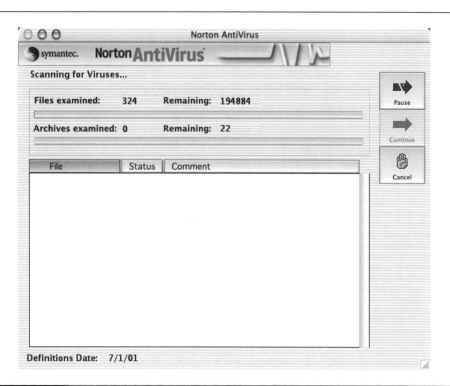

Choosing and Installing Virus Protection Software

| FIGURE 12-1 | Norton AntiVirus was one of the first virus utilities to make the Mac OS X transition. |

> **NOTE** *At the time this book was written, background and scheduled virus scans were limited to the Classic Mac OS version. These features were scheduled to be added to Mac OS X at a later date.*

Virex

The next contender in the virus protection market, Network Associates Virex, was also at version 7 when this book was written. This program (see Figure 12-2 for a preview of the Mac OS X version) can also scan for known viruses and the presence of virus-related activity. Here are the additional features:

> **NOTE** *As of the time this book was written, Network Associates was still offering public beta tests of its Mac OS X version. As a result, the interface and features may not be quite as described here (for example, background scanning had not yet been implemented on the version I used for this book).*

- **Contextual menu support** You can access Virex's features with a CTRL-click of a file.

- **Diagnose Compressed Files** This feature is limited to files compressed in Aladdin's StuffIt format (Norton AntiVirus, in contrast, supports several compression formats).

- **Electronic updating** As with Norton AntiVirus, the program can be set to update itself directly from the publisher's Web site. It works in concert with the program's Schedule Editor to check for new detection strings on a regular basis.

- **Repair** The program can be configured to repair or delete infected files without asking.

- **Scan-At-Download** When you download files from the Internet, or retrieve them from a network, Virex goes into action to check the files.

- **Schedule Editor** Configure the program to do a full scan of your Mac's drives at regular intervals.

- **Use Heuristics** The program uses its internal logic to check for virus-related activity and report back to the user.

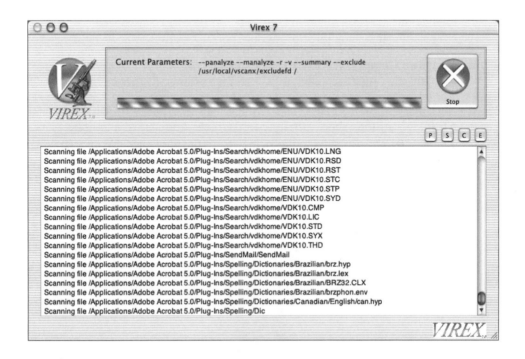

FIGURE 12-2   Virex7 offers a standard range of protection and detection features.

Choosing and Installing
Virus Protection Software

VirusBarrier

Considered the new kid on the block among virus detection utilities, this application (see Figure 12-3) sports a compact attractive interface that makes it easy to configure. Following is a product description, based on the Classic Mac OS version I've been using regularly.

NOTE   *Intego assured me when I was writing this book that the feature set and interface of the Mac OS X version of VirusBarrier would be essentially the same as the Classic Mac OS edition.*

■ **Nonintrusive**   The promise of all virus programs. Its background scanning activities were designed to be virtually unnoticeable (though it took a few versions before it got there).

■ **Automatic repairs**   If a virus infection is found, the program can remove the infection automatically. The program's progress log will indicate whether such infections could not be repaired.

■ **Diagnose Compressed Files**   As in the case of Virex, VirusBarrier can only scan files compressed in Aladdin Systems' StuffIt format.

■ **NetUpdate**   Another stab at the popular method of updating virus software. All Intego utilities share this function, which can retrieve and update applications and virus detection strings from the publisher's Web site.

■ **Drag and drop scanning**   Just drag and drop a file, folder or drive on the application's icon to initiate a scan.

■ **Menu bar icon**   The Classic Mac OS version puts up a convenient menu bar icon to allow you to activate Intego's utility software from a single location.

FIGURE 12-3   VirusBarrier was in the progress of taking the path to Mac OS X when this book was being written.

TechTool Pro

MicroMat's TechTool Pro 3 does it all, hardware—including hard drives; system conflicts; and, yes, virus protection (see Figure 12-4). Unlike the competition, however, the version I examined for this book had not as yet been updated to catch Word macro viruses, though this was promised in a later release.

Virus Program Oddities

Virus programs are highly tied into your Mac's system software, because they are designed to carefully check for suspicious activity and the presence of known virus strains.

As a result, as Apple updates its Mac OS, from time to time virus programs are rendered incompatible. Here are some common symptoms of virus detection activity that you just have to expect (because you need the software unless your Mac operates in a closed universe):

■ **Slow icon dance at startup in Classic Mac OS environment**   This is particularly noticeable with Norton AntiVirus as Classic boots. The program carefully checks your system extensions for the presence of viruses, so you hear a lot more churning of the hard drive and see icons move more slowly at startup. This is a normal consequence of how such a program runs.

■ **Applications take longer to launch**   The larger the program, the greater number of support files, and the longer it takes for virus software to scan everything to make sure the files are clean. Again, it's the price you pay for protection.

■ **Scanning prompt when you insert a floppy or other removable media**   You can turn these options off, but viruses are commonly spread through floppies and removable media, so you should make sure the program is configured to scan both kinds of disks.

NOTE   *Virus programs normally scan floppies automatically as part of their default settings. Although Mac OS X didn't support standard Mac floppy drives, the floppy capability of the SuperDisk and other third-party floppy-based drives were supported.*

■ **Mysterious application quits in Classic environment**   Check the publisher of the virus software for possible updates. In one example, when Mac OS 8.5 first appeared, you'd get crashes whenever you

FIGURE 12-4   The Classic version of TechTool Pro can check for viruses that may infect the older Mac OS.

copied files across a network. Both Norton AntiVirus and Virex required updates to fix the problem. Fortunately, Apple's system Read Me files will generally inform you about this.

> **NOTE**   *As an example, the arrival of Mac OS 9 forced Network Associates to deliver a 6.0.1 update to the Virex software to quash some incompatibilities. Since Mac OS X's Classic environment uses Mac OS 9.1 and 9.2, you can expect the same sort of difficulties in that environment unless you get the update.*

Summing Up

Computer viruses can be annoying or dangerous, but with up-to-date virus protection, it's a problem you can cope with. It's a good idea, however, to tell your contacts right away if you happen to get an infected disk from them. It's part of practicing "safe hex," as one of the original virus software programmers used to say.

In the next chapter, I'll introduce you to a full-fledged hard drive maintenance and repair program.

Chapter 13

Keeping Your Hard Drive Healthy and Happy

Can you imagine a Mac without a disk drive? A Mac without a disk drive is like a car without fuel. It sits there, looking just fine, especially the latest model with its innovative case design, but it doesn't do anything else. And you didn't buy a Mac just to look at it.

In order for the Mac to do something, you have to have something to read and write data from: a disk drive.

A Brief Primer on Cataloging a Disk Drive

It was a whole lot easier with phonograph records! When you wanted to find another selection, you just picked up the tone arm and placed it on the right spot on the record (of course, you had to check the label to know where the song was). With a cassette deck, you just have to wind the tape to the right location, press Play, and listen.

With computer drives, these basic access techniques won't work.

For one thing, a computer's drive is more complex than a record or cassette tape. However, it uses a technology not far removed from tape. Recording tape is made up of a flexible plastic material with a metal coating. The coating is usually iron oxide, more commonly referred to as rust. You record on a tape using a little part called a recording head. This head is a powerful magnet, and it magnetizes the little iron particles as it passes over the tape. On a cassette deck, the way the tape is magnetized represents the electrical pattern of the voice or musical signal being fed to it (that's why it's called *analog*). With computer data (called *digital),* the input is reduced to binary ones and zeros, and it can consist of any kind of data, from music to your document files, your computer's programs, or Mac OS X.

A floppy disk looks like a combination of recording tape and a record. If you move aside the plastic shutter of your floppy, you'll see a flexible round disk in there. Both sides are coated with the same sort of material as your magnetic tape. A Mac's floppy drive (where you still find them) uses magnetic heads to record and read from both sides of the floppy disk (which is why older floppies are sometimes called *double-sided*).

NOTE   *With floppy drives no longer being supported on Macs, you may wonder why I even mention the subject. Well, this is partly for background. Besides, some current drives, such as the SuperDisk and Zip, do use floppy-based media.*

Hard drives use a similar principle, only the magnetic coating is placed on a rigid platter. There are usually several platters in a single hard drive. As the drive spins, the magnetic heads float above the drive platters, suspended by a cushion of air, which helps prevent wear and tear to the drive. Cassette tapes, as you recall, do wear out eventually.

In order to store huge amounts of data on a hard drive, the files are put in a very small amount of space (and it gets smaller all the time as hard drive technology improves). To make the drive write and read your files faster, the platters spin much faster. It is common for today's hard drives to run at speeds from 5,400 rpm to 10,000 rpm (or faster!).

Hard drives have a dangerous combination of compactness and flexibility. With data stored in a microscopic space and spinning at a high rate of speed, even a little particle of dust can cause a disaster. That's why hard drives are made in a special place free of contaminants, called a clean room.

It's All in Little Pieces Rather Than Big Ones

Another big difference between an LP or CD and a hard drive is the way the information is stored. On both the LP and CD, you have one long, spiral track that goes from the outer rim to inner rim, and vice versa (well, actually, on a CD, it's from the end to the beginning). On a hard drive, the tracks are concentric, one inside the other. The heads use a little motor assembly to step from one track to the next.

It's hard to picture what those tracks look like, except that they are very small and not visible to the naked eye, unlike your LP record. Hard drives can have 600 tracks per square inch and more, and you can expect this number to increase over time as technology improves.

Each of those tracks is made up of little pieces called *sectors*. Each sector contains up to 512 bytes of information.

Erasing and Formatting: What's the Difference?

With the departure of the Finder's Special menu, the Erase command has migrated to the Disk Utility application under Mac OS X. To access it, you need to launch the application (located in the Applications folder, under Utilities), click the Erase tab, select the disk or volume, name the disk, and click the Erase button; you'll see the option shown in Figure 13-1.

For a floppy drive, Erase Disk performs two functions. First, the tracks on the floppy disk are set up to receive data. This process is called formatting or *low-level*

A Brief Primer on Cataloging a Disk Drive

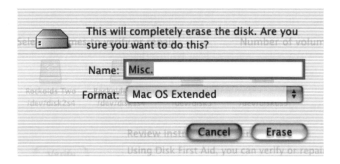

FIGURE 13-1   A familiar Mac OS command is in a totally new place under Mac OS X.

formatting. The second step is to write a directory on the hard drive, which sets up a blank catalog file. This process is often called *initializing*, and it's the final step of the formatting process.

With a hard drive, the Erase command only does one thing—initializing. It wipes the drive's directory (the list of files it contains) clean and installs a new one. But, as you'll learn later, that's enough to wipe out all information about your old files and write new ones on the drive.

When your drive is initialized, the formatting software puts a little invisible file on your hard drive, called a driver. This file is used to "talk" back and forth with your Mac when it wants to read and write files to the drive.

Which Formatter?

When you buy a new Macintosh computer, the drive is already formatted with Apple's own disk formatting software. Originally it was called HD SC Setup. The most recent version was named Drive Setup, whose functions have been divided into two places in the Disk Utility application. The first, described in the previous section, is for formatting a drive. The second, when you click on the Drive Setup icon (see Figure 13-2), lets you partition a drive into two or more volumes. I'll get into partitioning later.

Disk Utility can definitely handle the basics. It will initialize a hard drive and divide (partition) the drive into smaller pieces. However, it may not work with some drives not supplied in an Apple product.

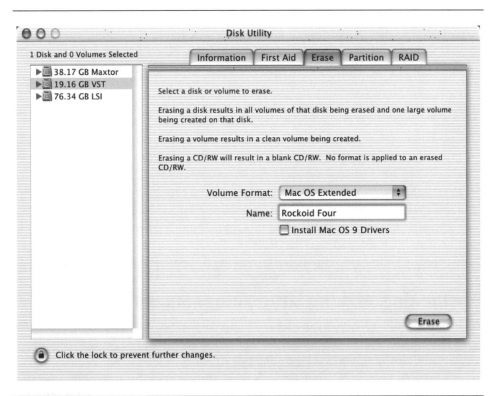

A Brief Primer on Cataloging a
Disk Drive

FIGURE 13-2   Drive Setup is just one feature of Mac OS X's Disk Utility application.

CAUTION   *Officially, Apple's disk formatting software is designed to work strictly with an Apple-label hard drive; however, most drives in Apple computers these days are essentially the same devices used in other PCs. Just about any IDE or FireWire device should be fine, although you may run into problems with some older SCSI drives.*

In previous versions of the Mac operating system, when you install the latest versions of the Mac operating system, the installer would dutifully try to update the hard drive. If the drive was formatted with something other than Apple's software (or is recognized as a non-Apple drive), you'll see a warning notice about it.

However, with Mac OS X, it's a whole new ballgame. As long as your drive is formatted in Apple's HFS+ format with a disk formatter that's compatible with Mac OS 9, it shouldn't present any problem. Apple's disk analysis tools won't attempt to hijack the drive, nor put up any message warning you of a problem.

CAUTION   *FWB, publishers of Hard Disk ToolKit, say the latest versions of its software (and a Mac OS X version was under development when I talked with them) will work fine for Mac OS X installations. If you're using any other disk-formatting program, you might want to check with the publisher first.*

In fact, there's nothing wrong with buying a non-Apple drive. The dealers who sell these drives get products from the very same companies Apple uses to buy its own drives. These include IBM, Maxtor, Seagate, and Western Digital. The drives usually come preformatted, and the dealer will give you a program (on the drive itself or on a CD) that you can use to format the drive whenever it's necessary.

Partitioning: Making Little Things Smaller

With a large hard drive, you can often organize files more easily if you divide your drive into smaller pieces. The process is called partitioning. The process usually requires initializing your drive (meaning the directory is wiped out, so you need to back up your files first). Then the disk formatting software creates a number of smaller pieces, or volumes, from the same hard drive, each of which has a separate directory and a different name (such as Mac HD One, Mac HD Two, and so on). The partitioned drive shows up on your Mac's desktop as separate drives, with a separate disk icon for each volume.

NOTE   *Older versions of LaCie's Silverlining have a feature that sometimes lets you partition a drive without losing any files. But it can often take a couple of hours or more to run this procedure, and you still need to have a backup of your files in case something goes wrong.*

The Drive Setup component of Apple's Disk Utility and just about all the third-party disk formatters can be easily set to create hard drive partitions. But remember, *you must back up your data when you partition a drive, as the directory or table of contents of the drive is wiped clean.*

NOTE

If you'd like to explore hard drive technology in more detail, you may want to get a copy of FWB's Guide to Storage, *by Norman Fong. The book used to be supplied with FWB's Hard Disk ToolKit formatting software, and can also be purchased directly from FWB. If you have an older version of Norton Utilities from Symantec, you'll also find a very good hard drive guide as part of the package. Unfortunately, newer product manuals from Symantec are limited to strictly instructions on using the software.*

Organizing All This Stuff

With your regular cassette deck, when you search for a particular selection, you press the deck's control buttons to shuttle the tape back or forth to reach the exact point where the information is stored. This is fine for a music tape, although it can take several minutes to get from here to there. In the early days of computers, all the data was stored on huge reels of tape, and you had to wind them back and forth to find the files you wanted. Of course, you don't get very much work done if you have to wait five minutes every time you want to open a new file, launch a program, or connect to an online service.

NOTE

In the days before floppy drives, however, we had to put up with such waits to access and edit a file. At least we all had credible excuses when the boss dropped by and asked why we weren't working.

The amount of information on a computer's hard drive is incredibly large (don't forget there are at least 600 tracks per inch on a modern hard drive), so imagine how long it would take to get from one place to another if you looked for it the old-fashioned way. Instead, a special place has been set aside on your hard drive to record the locations of all the files, so you can access them quickly.

Hard Drive Directories: You Can't Tell a Book by Its Cover

Data on your Mac's drive isn't all stored in one piece. It's divided into little segments; and, depending on how big the file is and how much space is available on the drive, it may be stored in different spots all across the drive.

In order to find your files, a hard drive has a directory, somewhat similar to a book's table of contents. It tells the Mac what files are available and where they

A Brief Primer on Cataloging a Disk Drive

are located. Before you look at the makeup of this hard drive directory, it's important to know that all this information is consulted in the blink of an eye, no matter how big your drive or where the files are located.

The File Manager

What's a File Manager? Well, under Mac OS X, it gets rather more complicated than with the Classic Mac OS, because of the larger range of file systems supported. Under Apple's Unix-based operating system, there is something called the VFS (for Virtual File System), which is a component of the Darwin core. The VFS is the system that is used to handle your files. One level handles the file systems, the other the storage devices you have connected to your Mac.

VFS is called into play to check your hard drive's directory structure, locate files when you wish to find them, call them up on your screen, modify files, delete files, and update your drive's directory about all the changes that have been made.

Roughly similar in function to what the File Manager did for the Classic Mac OS, VFS goes into action every time you attempt to access a file. It's used when you double-click on a document or program icon, or when you use the Open or Save dialog boxes in your favorite word processing program. VFS is even used when you access a Web site from your Internet provider or online service, because the Web artwork is cached or stored on your hard drive.

The Master Directory Block

The first level of information in your drive directory is called the *Master Directory Block*. It's a part of a drive that is your guidepost to its contents. It records your drive's name, its size, how much of it is filled, and even where your System Folder is located (so it knows where to find it when you boot your Mac). Most important, it shows how much space is still available, so you cannot save a file that's too big for your drive to handle.

The Volume Bit Map

Once VFS learns how much space is available, the next thing to determine is what part of your drive is filled and what part isn't. A Mac file is made up of little pieces, and not every piece of the file is in one place. The larger the file, the more likely it'll be made of lots of pieces in different parts of your hard drive. So the *Volume Bit Map* is consulted to see which blocks have data and which don't. Once the locations are determined, the file can be written to your drive. Remember, all this happens in the blink of an eye, faster than you can even think about it.

NOTE   *When a file is split into pieces at separated locations on a drive, it's considered fragmented. In theory, optimizing the drive, which puts all the pieces of a file adjacent to each other, may speed up performance. This is dealt with in more detail later in this chapter.*

NOTE   *When you trash a file and then empty the trash, the actual file itself doesn't just disappear, at least not then. All that happens is that the blocks that are filled with the file are marked "empty" by the Volume Bit Map so new files can be written on those blocks. This is why file recovery software can sometimes bring back files you've deleted by mistake.*

A Note about Trees   In the following sections, you'll see that the word *tree* is often used to describe a specific disk cataloging function. That is how the file system is organized. Just imagine one large tree, with many branches, each of which has many more branches.

Extents Tree (or B-tree)

The next stage in keeping track of files is which block carries what file or part of a file. That's the job of the *Extents Tree.* This portion of your drive's catalog allows your Mac to call up the file and have it reassembled into its original form, whether you saved it five minutes ago, yesterday, or five years ago. It's very much like assembling the pieces of a gigantic jigsaw puzzle, because the pieces may be scattered all over the drive.

The Extents Tree consists of two parts. One is called an *index node,* which is used by the Mac to find the information stored. Then there's the *leaf node,* which contains the information itself.

The Catalog Tree

Now we're getting somewhere. You've seen how the files are stored; the next step is to find them. As shown earlier, the file is found in the blink of an eye, and only really large files take time to appear on your Mac's screen. In order to locate that file, the *Catalog Tree*—the Mac equivalent of a library's catalog file—must be consulted. This directory records all the information necessary to keep tabs on your file. The Catalog Tree stores the name of the file, the folder it's placed in, its position on the desktop, and how big the file is. In short, it stores all the information needed to find the file, bring it up on the screen, and make it possible for you to modify or replace the file as you continue to work on a document.

Putting It All Together

When you tell your Mac you want a file, it goes to work behind the scenes to consult the catalog, and find out if the file exists and where it exists. Then it puts it all together, and the file appears on your screen. That's well and good. Once you see your file, you may want to do some work on it, changing a word or two in a word processing file, updating your illustration in a drawing file, or moving things around or creating new pages on a page layout program.

Once you've changed the document, you will want to save it, so the latest version is available next time you need to see it or print it. When it comes time to save the file, VFS has to go back and not only figure out where all the elements of the file are stored, so they can be replaced, but it has to find new locations on your drive to store the new material.

If you run out of spaces, you'll simply get the message that there isn't enough room to write that file. In that case, you'll have to save it to another drive, or go back to the Finder and remove files you may not need (after making copies of them on another drive, if you plan to use them later on).

When you save a file for the first time, it's similar to putting a new book in a library. A new catalog entry has to be made for the file; the catalog has to be consulted for file locations to store the new file; and the catalog has to be updated with all of this information so the next time you need that file, it's there for you to call up—again in the blink of an eye.

HFS

Apple's HFS (Hierarchical File System), which began to be replaced in Mac OS 8.1, is one technique used to organize these files. Using this system, you are able to store files in multiple levels for efficiency and convenience. For example, you can put folders at the top level of a drive (let's call it the first level), then store files inside those folders (the second level), and nest still more folders within the main folder, continuing with still more levels of files and folders. When you look at a diagram of this file storage system, it looks like a tree with many branches, each of which can lead to more branches.

The neat thing about this system is that you can change it at any time. If you decide you really don't want a file to be put in one folder, you can drag it to another, or make a new folder and put the file in that one instead. And all the time the Mac's clever filing system is figuring out where all this stuff goes, so you can retrieve it whenever you wish.

NOTE
I mention HFS just for reference; you can't install Mac OS X on an HFS volume, even though such volumes can be read under the new operating system.

HFS+

There's one thing that's certain about hard drives. Each year they get bigger, faster, and cheaper. Ten years ago, an 80–100 megabyte hard drive would cost over one thousand dollars. Today, a quarter of that amount will buy you a hard drive of 75GB or greater capacity.

Having drives with hundreds of times the capacity isn't a luxury, it's a necessity. Apple's operating system software and the application software you use have grown in an equal fashion. A decade ago, you could fit an entire System Folder on a floppy disk; today, you have to use a CD. The actual System Folder for Mac OS 9 routinely exceeds 400 megabytes in size (mine is just shy of that) and is often much larger.

NOTE
Greg Titus, our long-suffering technical editor, says his System Folder is 740MB large. I hate to ask him what he's running.

Worse, you need 1.5GB of free space to install Mac OS X, and the completed installation consumes more than half that amount of storage space.

Having all this extra capacity has its downside, though. When Apple created the HFS file system, they divided a drive into 65,000 pieces or blocks. The number is the same regardless of the size of your drive. A little mathematics will show that this scheme becomes rather inefficient with a big hard drive, because the smallest amount of space a file can occupy increases in proportion to hard drive size. For that typical 20GB drive very common on new Macs, one single file, with just a couple of words in it, will fill over 300 kilobytes of space on the drive.

If you have lots of little files on your drive, such as the cache files that are created when you use your World Wide Web browser, you can see that you're wasting a lot of space on that drive. This is one reason why many users partition their drive—use their hard drive software to divide the drive into smaller volumes so the smallest file size isn't so high.

Apple has an even better solution, called HFS+, which is also known as the Mac OS Extended format. The most important new feature is that, instead of

A Brief Primer on Cataloging a Disk Drive

dividing the drive into 65,000 blocks, the number has increased to the billions (2^{32} to be precise). The file that would be 128K under the Mac OS Standard (or HFS system) is now 4K under the new file system.

As you can see, if you have lots of small files, Apple has given you lots of extra breathing room. When you switch to the Mac OS Extended format, you'll find many megabytes of additional space.

HFS+: The Disadvantages

All new Macs ship with drives formatted in HFS+ format, but switching an older model (or just a drive formatted the old way) isn't so simple. In order to convert from HFS to HFS+, you must initialize your hard drive under the new format. That means you will have to back up all your files first. Apple's Disk Utility and the newest versions of non-Apple disk formatting software can easily handle this process. They all offer an option to initialize your drive in Mac OS Extended format. And even if your software doesn't have the option, it's still available. Just select the drive volume you wish to convert, launch Disk Utility, and click the Erase button. Select Mac OS Extended from the pop-up menu and click the Erase button. In a few minutes, the drive's directory will be rewritten in HFS+ format. When you copy files there, they'll be smaller.

Here are the other disadvantages to HFS+:

■ If you have a Mac network with older models, you cannot use an HFS+-formatted drive as a startup disk with a 680x0 Mac. A second drive, without a System Folder, can be formatted in HFS+ format, though.

■ If other Macs in your home or office are using versions of the Mac OS prior to 8.1, the folks who use those Macs won't see the files on an HFS+ drive. Instead, they'll see a "wrapper," a blank directory showing nothing but a Read Me file from Apple telling you how to access the files (basically, that you need to be running Mac OS 8.1 or later, or the files have to be shared across a network from a computer running the new system versions).

■ In order for the drive's directory to be displayed properly in the Classic Mac OS (or on another Mac with an older system), you also need Apple's Text Encoding Converter Extension in the Extensions folder and the Text Encoding folder in your System Folder. If you're using Extensions Manager or a program such as Conflict Catcher to manage your Classic system extensions, you will need to leave these items intact and not move them.

HFS and Mac OS X

Getting more mileage from your hard drive is not the only benefit of HFS+. There's yet another benefit that helps users of Mac OS X: bigger file names. HFS+ was designed to allow for 255-character file names. Of course, you'd need really large Open and Save dialog boxes to accommodate file names that big, but it is the wave of the future.

Just imagine what it would be like to have a file named "This is the silly poem I wrote last week in response to a request from my boss to come up with a new advertising slogan by March 2, 2002." And even that file name leaves several dozen characters left to fill.

How to Convert to HFS+

There are actually two methods of changing your drives to HFS+. One is a serious issue, since you have to initialize the drive. The other is simple, since it can switch over your drive in place.

Here's how the two options work:

- **Initializing**   To convert to HFS+, you have to start your Mac from another drive or your system CD. First, make sure all your files are backed up. Then the simplest method is to launch Disk Utility, click on the Erase tab, and select the drive from the list of mounted volumes. This will bring up an option similar to the one shown in Figure 13-2. Select Mac OS Extended (the official name for HFS+) from the pop-up menu, then click the Erase button. In a few minutes, your drive will be initialized in the new disk format, and you're ready to roll.

- **Using software to convert "in place"**   Initializing your hard drive is definitely a big event. You have to be prepared to restore your files, and you'll want to devote the better part of the afternoon to the task (or maybe longer). The other way to do it is with HFS+ conversion software. Your two options (as of the time this book was written) were Alsoft's PlusMaker and Power On Software's SpaceDoctor. Both programs will, essentially, rewrite all your files in HFS+ format in place, without the need to initialize the drive and restore the files. However, no program is perfect, and you should always have a recent backup around in case something goes wrong. I cover the subject of backups in the next chapter.

A Brief Primer on Cataloging a Disk Drive

NOTE   *The versions of these utilities examined when this book was written only work if you reboot your Mac under Mac OS 9.x first. But the converted volumes should work fine when you return to Mac OS X.*

The Impact of the UFS File System

The advent of Mac OS X delivers yet a third drive formatting option, known as UFS (short for UNIX File System). This is, of course, the same file system used under Linux and other Unix-based operating systems. You can format your hard drive in this fashion as part of the actual installation of Mac OS X.

However, Apple basically recommends that you avoid UFS unless you just like to experiment, because the HFS+ environment will be more comfortable for most Mac users. UFS is mainly useful if you're porting Unix software to the Mac environment or you're running your Mac as a server. Because UFS handles huge numbers of small files with less overhead than HFS+, it also makes a better choice for handling email and Usenet newsgroups.

NOTE   *UFS is also self-defragmenting, so you will not need to fret over file fragmentation and, in fact, never need to run an optimization program.*

Here are a few areas where UFS differs and why you might want to avoid it:

- **Case sensitivity**   Under HFS+, case doesn't matter in a possible file naming conflict. You can't have a file named "Rockoids" and another named "rockoids" on the same drive. However, UFS is case sensitive, so, yes, you can have both files. This can be the source of endless confusion.

- **AirPort's not compatible**   At least for the initial releases of Mac OS X, Apple's marvelous AirPort wireless networking system isn't compatible with UFS. Of course, that, as with all operating system conflicts, might change.

- **Can't run a UFS volume under Classic Mac OS**   That's right. If you're hoping to reboot your Mac on occasion under Mac OS 9.x, forget UFS. The Classic Mac OS won't recognize UFS, and your drives won't mount.

If you're willing to accept its limitations, and you plan on developing applications for the UNIX, however, you might just want to test the waters. My suggestion, however, would be to do it on a separate drive, so you have a choice.

What Can Go Wrong with a Drive and How to Fix It

Despite all the complexities of keeping track of thousands and thousands of files on those ultraminiature hard drives and removable devices (such as Iomega, Orb, and CD-R products), most times the process works just about perfectly. You can locate and access your files in an instant and seldom encounter a problem unless you run out of room in which to store a file.

But things can go wrong—bad things—and as a result there is a potential to lose your data. As hard drives become larger, the amount of data you may lose grows ever larger and the impact far more serious.

How a Simple Shut Down Command Protects Your Drive

When you shut down or restart your Mac, it goes through a few seconds of disk action, which writes files stored in the drive's cache and in RAM. It also does other bookkeeping chores that keep your Mac's file system up to date.

Bad things may happen if you don't do the normal shutdown routine—for example, if your Mac crashes (a rarity under Mac OS X, but it could still happen on occasion), and you have to restart by shutting off your Mac and turning it on again. Or if you restart with the "reset" switch (which is a little switch with a triangle inside it on the front or side of many Macs or by the keyboard combo COMMAND-CTRL-POWER ON). If the restart process isn't done normally, all that file cleanup (which clears cached files and other data) doesn't happen. So the disk's directory may not be properly updated or may be damaged.

Sometimes a problem may be caused by forces that have nothing whatever to do with your Mac. There may be a power outage, or a spike sent across your power line (perhaps during a thunderstorm) interrupts the transfer of data to your drive. Or you simply make a mistake and turn off a power switch (something you could do on older Macs), thus shutting down your Mac before it has a chance to update the drive properly.

Whatever the reason, the files may not be properly cataloged. Even one missing or extra byte of data is enough to set problems into motion. Minor damage may not be noticeable right away, but as you continue to write or change files on your drive, you may find that files may suddenly disappear, or they may be damaged (so you can't open them).

Sooner or later, you may find not only files disappearing, but also the entire drive. As I said earlier, the Master Directory Block is the entranceway to your drive's catalog. If the directory is damaged, strange things can begin to happen. One possibility is that a portion of the drive with files on it may, by mistake, be marked as being available for new files. When you write new files to your Mac's drive, the new file overwrites part or all of an older file that you still need. When you try to access that file, it won't be there. Or you'll get a message indicating there's something wrong with the file.

Over time, the problems may become worse. One day the drive may become unreadable, and you may see a little disk icon with a question mark when you try to boot your Mac.

Other Causes of Problems

Hard drives are electromechanical devices. As I pointed out earlier, the mechanical complexity of your typical hard drive is awesome, and the drive is subject to regular wear and tear. Drive manufacturers will rate a drive as having several hundred thousand hours of useful life ("mean time between failures," they call it), but that doesn't mean all units will last that long. Some will fail much earlier. One possible symptom is the onset of bad blocks, where data cannot be written or retrieved from the drive. And accidents can happen. Your computer is dropped to the ground while it's running, and there's a head crash (the drive's heads strike and damage the drive platter). Whatever the cause, hard drives can and do fail eventually. That is something you should expect, though usually they last for years without trouble.

Protecting Your Files

One of the best ways to ensure that your files are safe is to have more than one copy. It's a good idea to do a regular backup of your valuable data. If the files are mission critical (financial data, for example), you may want to have an extra copy of your files at another location, as protection against a fire or weather disaster that may damage your computer.

I'll cover the subject of backups in more detail in the next chapter.

A Guide to Partitioning Your Drive

As noted in the first part of this chapter, the HFS file system wasn't very efficient for large hard drives, such as the ones that are commonplace in today's Mac OS computers.

The bigger the drive, the bigger the files. So when you had a large hard drive, it was convenient to partition the drive, which is simply dividing the drive into smaller segments. Apple's Disk Utility and all the third-party disk formatters can do the work, but it requires reformatting the drive. Once you do that, each segment or partition mounts on your Mac's desktop as a separate volume.

You can set aside one partition for your System Folder, another for your applications, a third for document files—whatever method of organization suits your purposes.

Since Apple introduced HFS+ beginning with Mac OS 8.1, you could actually get away with not partitioning at all. In fact, Apple ships all its computers with a single partition, even on models with 60GB drives and larger. On the other hand, if all your files are in smaller partitions, in theory, access times are faster. So you may still want to partition your drive (I gave it up when HFS+ came on the scene). Each of the available disk formatting programs has its own interface for doing the task. I'll show you how with Apple's Disk Utility, since that program will support all Apple products and even some non-Apple drives.

1. Back up your files first.

2. Restart your Mac using another hard drive (after selecting with the Startup Disk panel in the System Preferences application) or with your Mac OS X CD.

3. If you restarted from your Mac OS X CD, the installer application will launch.

4. Go to the installer's application menu and choose Open Disk Utility.

5. With Disk Utility opened, click on the partition button, and select the drive you want to partition (see Figure 13-3).

6. The easiest way to proceed is simply to click on the Volume Scheme pop-up menu (shown in Figure 13-4), then choose the number of volumes you want to create.

7. If you want to customize the sizes any further, you may click a partition in the Volumes window and drag the edges of the volume to fit the size you want.

8. Once you have selected the number of volumes into which you want to divide a drive, use the Partition command to divide your drive into small pieces.

9. If you want to partition other drives in the same fashion, select each drive, separately, then repeat steps 6 through 9.

10. When you've finished, choose Quit from the application menu and OK the restart prompt.

What Can Go Wrong with a Drive and How to Fix It

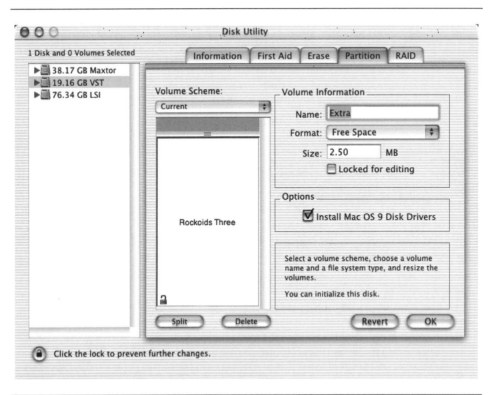

FIGURE 13-3   Select a drive before proceeding.

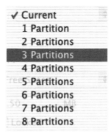

FIGURE 13-4   Pick a partition, any partition.

NOTE *If you're using a third-party hard drive formatting program to partition your drive, follow the directions in that program, after rebooting from another drive.*

What's a Bad Block and What Do I Do about It?

Hard drives are not perfect, and over time, one or more of the microscopic blocks on the drive may become unusable as the drive platters age. Once that happens, minute portions of the drive may no longer be able to hold a magnetic charge. You write files and get a message about a "write error," or parts of a file already stored on your drive become damaged (a "read error"), and the file cannot be accessed.

Fortunately, the hard drive diagnostic/repair programs I'll be discussing in this chapter can do surface scans to check for such problems. They may even be able to mark the blocks as "used"—in other words, they already have data, so new data won't be written to them.

But the best solution for this problem is to back up and do a low-level format of your hard drive. This process will wipe out all of the data, and the formatting software will generally mark bad blocks so they will be inaccessible for writing files.

NOTE *The low-level format option was missing from the version of Apple's Disk Utility used when this book was written, but it is available from older versions of Drive Setup, if you reboot under Mac OS 9.x, or you can use a third-party disk formatting utility.*

Is Optimizing Truly Necessary?

The theory goes that as you add and remove files from your Mac's drive, the little pieces that files are made of become more and more scattered across the drive. This is called *fragmentation*, and if there is enough of it, your hard drive will take longer to access the files, thus slowing performance.

Is there a solution to the problem? Well, of course, you could initialize the drive, then restore your files in a single operation so they won't be fragmented. But that's quite an extreme step to take just to cure a little fragmentation problem.

Fortunately, two of the major hard drive diagnostic/repair programs mentioned in this chapter, the Speed Disk component of Norton Utilities (see Figure 13-5) and TechTool Pro, offer a more practical solution, by optimizing the drive. The publishers of DiskWarrior have another product, PlusOptimizer (Figure 13-6), which performs the same function. These programs are designed to basically rewrite the data on your hard drive so all elements of a file are adjacent to one another, in theory speeding up hard drive performance.

NOTE   *The latest versions of these programs can optimize a drive on which Mac OS X is installed, but, of course, you must boot from the publisher's own CD or from another drive running Mac OS 9.x. If you aren't sure whether the version you're using will work properly with the new operating system, check with the publisher first.*

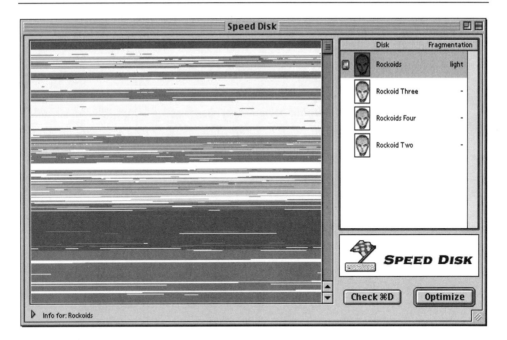

FIGURE 13-5   The Speed Disk component of Norton Utilities will optimize a directory and the files on your hard drive.

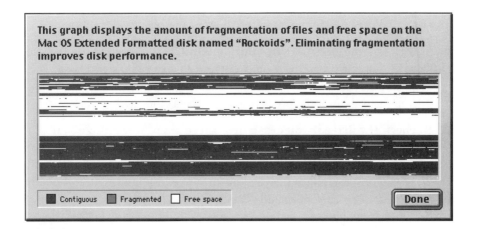

This graph displays the amount of fragmentation of files and free space on the Mac OS Extended Formatted disk named "Rockoids". Eliminating fragmentation improves disk performance.

■ Contiguous ■ Fragmented □ Free space   [Done]

FIGURE 13-6   PlusOptimizer performs a single function, but does it well.

So the question arises: since hard drives access files in milliseconds, does it really matter if it takes a few more to bring up a file?

Well, if you deal mostly with a small number of files, you could probably run your Mac for years and not experience any severe problem. Frankly, it'll take a lot of file manipulation to severely fragment your hard drive.

On the other hand, if you work with large image files (such as the ones you scan or create in a program like Adobe Photoshop), you may find that, indeed, a large amount of disk fragmentation develops, and occasional optimizing (about once a month) is probably a good idea.

Drive Optimizing Tips

If you decide you do want to optimize your hard drive (it's also called defragmenting or defragging), you'll want to make sure that you have a ready backup of your data. (See the next chapter for details on creating backups.) I don't want to alarm anyone, but I have seen accidents happen once or twice in the last 15 years and it never hurts to be careful.

Once you decide you're ready, start with these options:

■ **Check the hard drive first.**   Use Apple's Disk Utility or one of the commercial hard drive repair/diagnostic utilities. If your drive's directory is corrupted, things can definitely go wrong while all the data is being written during optimization. While the optimizing software will normally check the drives before the process begins, it's best to be cautious.

■ **Start from another drive or your system CD.**   The commercial hard drive optimizing programs usually come with a separate startup disk. While, in theory, it's possible to optimize the drive without dismounting it (removing it from the desktop), the process may not be as thorough.

■ **Recheck the drive if you crash or if there's a power outage.**   If something happens to interrupt the process of optimizing your drive (one of those infamous rolling blackouts, perhaps?), be sure to run your hard drive diagnostic/repair utility and make sure everything is all right before continuing. The current lineup of optimization programs have built-in safety checks to protect against this sort of thing (such as not deleting a fragmented version of a file until the optimized version is copied to your drive), but you should definitely check the drive anyway. Then, if the optimizing process didn't finish, go ahead and resume the process.

How to Cope with Drive Directory Problems

Keeping your hard drive happy and healthy is a matter of preventive maintenance. You cannot do anything to stop the forces of wear and tear, but there are things you can do to make sure your valuable files are protected.

Run Regular Diagnostics

To avoid potential problems with your hard drive, you should check it regularly with a disk diagnostic program, such as Apple's Disk Utility, at least once a week and after a system crash.

NOTE   *When you restart under Mac OS X, all your available hard drives are checked as part of the startup process. But since many users of Mac OS X may keep their Macs running for days or weeks without a restart (just using the Sleep function when the computers are not in use), running Disk Utility on occasion manually isn't a bad idea.*

Here's how to run a standard Disk First Aid check of your drive:

1. Locate Disk Utility in your Utilities folder (this is where Apple's system installer usually places it).

2. Double-click on the program to launch it, and click on the First Aid tab, which brings up the screen shown in Figure 13-7.

3. Click on the icon of the drive you wish to check (hold down the SHIFT key to select more than one volume).

4. Click Verify to check the drive's directory.

5. Click Repair to also fix any hard drive directory damage that's discovered (this is the better choice).

6. If drive damage is found and fixed, run the program again to make sure one problem didn't hide another (it happens).

7. When the program has done its work, choose Quit from the application menu to close the program.

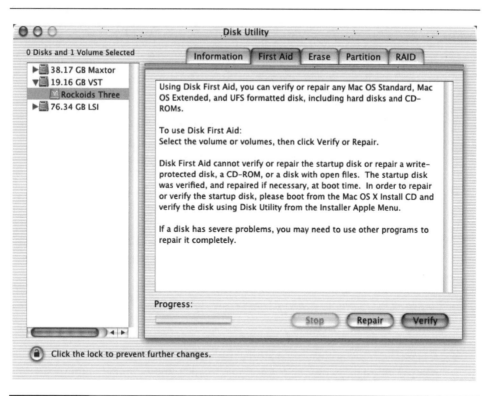

FIGURE 13-7 This is the successor to Apple's venerable Disk First Aid.

How to Cope with Drive Directory Problems

NOTE   *Disk Utility cannot examine the startup drive. The only way you can fix a problem is to reboot from another drive volume, or run Disk Utility from the Mac OS X Installer application, after restarting from the CD (it'll be available from the installer's application menu).*

Using Other Drive Diagnostic Utilities

The advantage of Apple's Disk Utility is that it comes free with your Mac OS computer or the latest system software version. Because it's free, though, it may not be quite as thorough as the commercial programs. They promise to catch more problems and fix them, thus justifying the purchase price.

Here's a quick overview of the available options:

- **Norton Utilities for the Macintosh**   Symantec's Norton Utilities is one of the best-selling Mac programs, with good reason. It has been around for years in various forms (it's the survivor of the merger of three products, including MacTools and Public Utilities, from companies Symantec took over) and has provided generally reliable performance. Beginning with version 5, the diagnostic/repair component, Norton Disk Doctor (see Figure 13-8), can match Apple's ability to diagnose and repair problems on a startup drive without having to dismount it first.

NOTE   *Norton Utilities 6, the version shipping when this book was written, can diagnose hard drives with Mac OS X on them provided you run from a Mac OS 9.x startup disk or the program's supplied boot CD.*

- **TechTool Pro**   This program is a descendant of MicroMat's original diagnostic utility, MacEKG. In addition to checking, fixing, and optimizing your hard drive, it'll run checks of a Mac's other systems, such as the CPU, cache, RAM, serial ports, and so on. Dozens of checks, in fact. It's a great way to check for potential hardware problems before they get out of hand.

NOTE   *According to the publisher, TechTool Pro 3.0.4 or later can work fine with a Mac OS X volume, when booted from the Mac OS 9.x environment or the publisher's startup CD.*

- **Drive 10**   A single-purpose utility for Apple's new operating system, MicroMat's Drive 10 (see Figure 13-9) is designed to locate and repair directory problems under Mac OS X. However, it cannot fix a startup disk, so you'd need to reboot with the publisher's startup CD or from another volume.

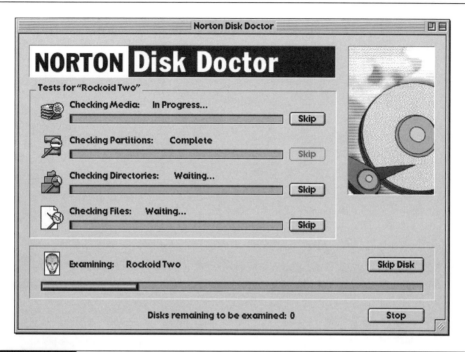

FIGURE 13-8   A Mac OS X version of this program may be out by the time you read this book.

- **Alsoft's DiskWarrior**   Called a "one trick pony" by reviewers, this program does its single trick very well indeed. The other programs are designed to fix hard drive directory damage. DiskWarrior (see Figure 13-10) is designed to actually create a brand new drive directory with optimized performance and replace the old one (after fixing whatever damage it finds). The only downside to this program is that you cannot check your startup disk. You need to use the program's boot CD or another drive to run it.

Bundles, Dates, and Other Problems

Norton Disk Doctor will not only check for drive directory problems and fix them, it can also check for problems with individual files. If a file is damaged, it'll report that fact (but all you can do is replace the file, since damaged files cannot be fixed). It'll also report some very arcane issues, such as whether bundle bits or Finder dates are correct or not. Bundle bits are only of concern if a file icon doesn't show correctly on your Mac's desktop; otherwise it's nothing important. If Norton Disk Doctor

FIGURE 13-9   Drive 10 is busy checking one of the author's hard drives.

reports any of these problems, use the Fix All option in the Disk Doctor screen to repair what it finds and don't worry about any of it. TechTool Pro has a similar set of fixes, called Finder Info, and provides similar results.

It's also normal for one program to interpret a date or bundle bit problem differently than another. I call it the case of the "dueling bundles." As I said, let the program fix the problems and don't fret about it.

Does It Make a Difference If You Don't Have SCSI?

Not to the Mac operating system. All new Macs use some form of ATA hard drive, with the exception of some of the Power Macintosh computers you order via the Build-to-Order program at the Apple Store or through your local dealer. At one time, an ATA hard drive was slower than its SCSI counterpart, in addition to being somewhat cheaper. This is no longer true with the latest ATA protocols—now it's both fast and cheap.

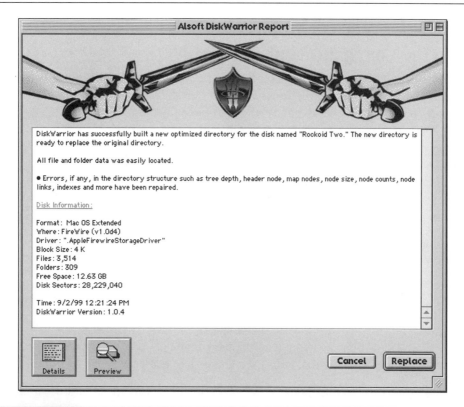

DiskWarrior has successfully built a new optimized directory for the disk named "Rockoid Two." The new directory is ready to replace the original directory.

All file and folder data was easily located.

● Errors, if any, in the directory structure such as tree depth, header node, map nodes, node size, node counts, node links, indexes and more have been repaired.

Disk Information:

Format: Mac OS Extended
Where: FireWire (v1.0d4)
Driver: ".AppleFirewireStorageDriver"
Block Size: 4 K
Files: 3,514
Folders: 309
Free Space: 12.63 GB
Disk Sectors: 28,229,040

Time: 9/2/99 12:21:24 PM
DiskWarrior Version: 1.0.4

FIGURE 13-10   DiskWarrior can also diagnose your Mac OS X volume.

In addition, Apple's computers also support FireWire, a super-fast interface developed by Apple that lets you hook up external drives without need of setting IDs or termination. You can even hot-plug a device (after dismounting the drive icon by moving it to the trash).

NOTE *First-generation FireWire-equipped desktop Macs, the Blue & White G3s, remain the only models that will not allow you to boot older versions of the Mac OS from a FireWire device. In addition, you cannot run Mac OS X from either a FireWire or USB device, though this may, of course, change in a later OS update.*

How to Cope with Drive
Directory Problems

Checking Mac OS X's Startup Disk
via the Command Line

Under normal circumstances, you probably won't need to do this, but if you don't have a Mac OS X installer CD or disk repair CD on hand, this might be a way to handle a problem that doesn't seem to be getting fixed.

True, Mac OS X does a disk check during the boot process, but this procedure takes you right to the command line, at startup, and may help get you out of jam (or at least give you a visual indication of what's going on under the hood, as it were).

1. Restart your Mac, and press COMMAND-S. You will see a text display scroll up on your Mac's screen.

2   When the scrolling process is done, type this command, exactly as I've typed it:

    ```
    fsck -y
    ```

3. Press the RETURN key. In the next few moments, there will be a series of status lines showing the progress of the disk check. If the drive directory is repaired, you'll see a message that it has been "modified."

4. If repairs are done, run the same command again, repeating it until the "modified" result no longer appears.

5. To reboot your Mac, type the following command, followed by the RETURN key:

    ```
    reboot
    ```

Unless you are looking for a RAID setup (one in which two or more drives are used as one, which is available in FireWire or SCSI trim), there is no need to be concerned that you have an ATA drive, except for the lack of capability to add a number of extra devices. Performance ought to be similar, and the Mac operating system will handle any of these drives in exactly the same way.

NOTE *The Power Macintosh G4 series is set up to allow you to add a second ATA drive, but that's a far cry from what the other drive interfaces permit.*

Whether ATA, FireWire, or SCSI, you can back up, reformat, optimize, or check the drive without having to be conscious of the drive interface it follows.

Case History

The Case of the FireWire Drive Slowdown

You can never quite predict the things that'll make a hard drive misbehave.

A case in point was a mysterious performance slowdown with the FireWire drives I have connected to a Blue & White Power Mac G3. With the first release of Mac OS 9 installed, I copied some files to one of the FireWire drives, and it took maybe five or ten times longer for the process to finish.

I tried another FireWire drive with the same result. I then subjected the drives to complete tests with all of the hard drive diagnostic programs I had at hand, and they came up with a clean bill of health.

It was positively weird!

Finally, I tried Casady & Greene's great extension management utility, Conflict Catcher to see if it could pinpoint a possible conflict. I ran the program's Conflict Test, and did a quick benchmark of a FireWire drive's performance after each restart. After about 15 minutes or so, Conflict Catcher flagged the USB drivers for an Imation SuperDisk drive as the culprit.

Sure enough, disabling the drivers cured the FireWire drives' slowdown. What's more, I discovered something else. Without thinking to reactivate the software, I inserted a SuperDisk into the SuperDisk drive and it worked anyway, just as it did before.

Why?

Although it hadn't been documented as extensively as it should have been, beginning with Mac OS 9, Apple incorporated support for many USB devices in its USB Device Extension, which is part of the standard installation on any USB-equipped Mac. It even recognizes an Iomega Zip drive. So I didn't need the SuperDisk drivers after all, and their presence played havoc with other elements of the Mac OS (the FireWire software included). A little testing also showed that having the SuperDisk drivers installed would also make the SuperDisk drive behave erratically even on Macs without FireWire (such as a first-generation iMac), sometimes not working at all, not to mention an increase in system crashes in the Classic environment.

While updates to the FireWire and SuperDisk USB drivers permanently resolved the problem, don't be surprised if you encounter oddities of one sort or another when switching between the Classic and Mac OS X environments. Even though the list of supported devices under Mac OS X is extensive, there is always the exception, particularly with a less-popular drive mechanism. Don't say I didn't warn you!

What to Do If Hard Drive Diagnostic Programs Fail

There's only so much a hard drive diagnostic program can do to fix directory damage and restore your data. It will try to rebuild or (in the case of DiskWarrior) replace the directory.

But there are situations where diagnostic software just won't work for one reason or another. It will report that directory damage cannot be fixed, or the problems will simply reappear each time you run a scan.

Here's a brief listing of those situations and possible solutions or alternatives (if any):

- ■ **Make sure your SCSI chain is safe and sound.**   As I state in Chapter 15, using SCSI peripherals, such as drives, scanners, and whatnot, is not a cut-and-dried process. Even if you follow the rules to the letter, things may go wrong. If you have a Mac with a SCSI chain, double-check that all devices are properly connected, that termination and ID setups are correct, and that all devices are left on while your Mac is in use.

■ **Try another disk repair utility.** If Disk Utility can't fix a problem, give the job to DiskWarrior, Drive 10, Norton Utilities, or TechTool Pro (or vice versa). What one can't fix, the other might. Even if the disk damage is fixed properly, it never hurts to run a second scan to see if the problems return.

■ **What if the problems recur?** If you see the same disk directory problems over and over again, it's usually a good time to bite the bullet and reformat the drive (but first try the step mentioned in the next section). Directory problems can only get worse; they do not disappear.

Corrupted Device Driver

If the hard disk driver is damaged due to a crash, the drive may become inaccessible, or you may see the dreaded prompt asking if you want to initialize the drive when you boot your Mac (just say no!).

If you cannot recover the drive with a disk diagnostic/repair program, try one of the following:

For Drives Formatted with Apple's Disk Utility

1. Restart your Mac with another startup drive or a Mac OS 9.x CD. If you're booting from a CD, hold down the C key at startup, which will allow the Mac to boot from the CD drive.

NOTE   *The version of Disk Utility that came with the first releases of Mac OS X did not include an Update feature, largely because standard device drivers are already part and parcel of the operating system.*

2. Locate the Utilities folder on the CD and open it.

3. Look in the folder for Drive Setup and launch the program.

4. If your drive appears normally on the list of recognized devices, select it.

5. Use the program's Update function (in the Functions menu) to update the drive.

6. If the Update function isn't available, consider reformatting the drive, after checking low-level format under Initialization Options. Be sure you have a backup for your files first, since they will be gone for good.

Mac Doesn't Start from a CD?   If you cannot get your Mac to boot from the CD, and it starts from your hard drive instead, open the Startup Disk panel in the System Preferences application and select the CD as the startup disk.

You'll also want to make sure that your Mac supports the operating system version on the startup disk, especially if it came with one of the disk diagnostic/repair utilities. Make sure the version is the same or later than the one on your Mac's original CD. If not, contact the publisher of the utility program to see if they have a later CD for your Mac. Generally they'll just charge you a modest shipping and handling charge to send a new CD, if one is available.

For Drives Formatted with Non-Apple Formatting Software

If you bought your hard drive from a dealer, it was likely formatted with a non-Apple disk formatting utility. Should this be the case, check the packaging for a formatting disk or contact your dealer about getting formatting software. Once you have acquired such software, follow this process:

1. Restart your Mac with another startup drive or (if it came with one) a CD containing your disk formatting software. If you're booting from a CD, hold down the C key at startup, which will allow the Mac to boot from the CD drive.

2. Locate your disk formatting software on the CD and launch it. You'll see a screen similar to the one shown in Figure 13-11 (using FWB's Hard Disk ToolKit).

3. If your drive appears normally on the list of recognized devices, select it.

4. Use the program's Update function to update the drive.

5. If the Update function isn't available, consider reformatting the drive, using the Format (not Initialize) function. Remember that the process will wipe out any files on the drive.

The Dangers of Leaving Hard Drive Damage Unfixed

If your hard drive seems all right, despite the report of those disk utilities, you may be inclined to leave well enough alone.

True, your Mac may run fine and dandy, for now. But over time, you'll encounter such symptoms as frequent system crashes, particularly during a file copying operation; and, perhaps, one day you'll find files disappearing or damaged.

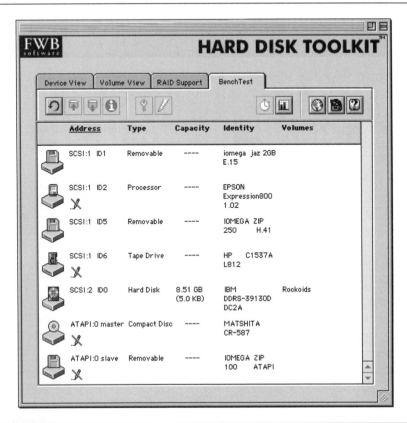

FWB software		**HARD DISK TOOLKIT**™			

Device View | Volume View | RAID Support | BenchTest

Address	**Type**	**Capacity**	**Identity**	**Volumes**
SCSI:1 ID1	Removable	----	iomega jaz 2GB E.15	
SCSI:1 ID2	Processor	----	EPSON Expression800 1.02	
SCSI:1 ID5	Removable	----	IOMEGA ZIP 250 H.41	
SCSI:1 ID6	Tape Drive	----	HP C1537A L812	
SCSI:2 ID0	Hard Disk	8.51 GB (5.0 KB)	IBM DDRS-39130D DC2A	Rockoids
ATAPI:0 master	Compact Disc	----	MATSHITA CR-587	
ATAPI:0 slave	Removable	----	IOMEGA ZIP 100 ATAPI	

FIGURE 13-11   Here is a recent version of FWB's marvelous disk formatter.

Worse, you may even experience a hard drive crash. It's not the same thing as dropping the drive on the floor. It simply means the directory has been so badly damaged that your drive is no longer accessible. You may even see a message on your screen asking if you wish to initialize the drive.

When you get to that point, it may be past the point of no return. The hard drive diagnostic/repair programs can resurrect a crashed drive, but not all the time.

The best advice is this: if your hard drive has directory damage that can't be fixed, back up your files and reformat the drive.

Drive Hardware Failures

If you find that your diagnostic software and your disk formatting program cannot find the drive (and everything is set up properly), there's the possibility the drive mechanism itself has failed. Despite those huge claims of extended lifetimes, this is something that can happen at any time. And it's also something that no diagnostic/repair program can fix.

If your drive failed, and it's still under warranty, the dealer or manufacturer can arrange to repair the unit. But they usually cannot recover your files, unless they offer that service as a special option.

If you do need to recover data that's not been backed up, prepare to pay upward of $2,000 to recover a drive with many gigabytes of files. That's one reason (aside from the time you are left without your files) that you will want to make sure your data is properly backed up.

> **NOTE**   *It's beyond the scope of this book to recommend a hard drive recovery service. One that I've read about is Drive Savers, at http://www. drivesavers.com). They claim to be able to recover files from all the major computer operating systems. In addition to recovering hard drives, they can attempt to recover files from damaged floppies and removable media.*

Summing Up

Now that you've discovered how to keep your hard drive healthy and happy, you'll want to go right to the next chapter, where I cover the steps to take to protect your files should the worst occur. It's all about backups.

Chapter 14

Foolproof Backup Techniques Explained

L et me cut to the chase. The files on your Mac aren't safe, so when it comes to safeguarding the document files you create on your Mac, one copy is never enough.

As you have seen so far in this book, the likelihood that your Mac will crash is very, very high, particularly if you must continue to use applications in the Classic environment. They do not inherit Mac OS X's industrial-strength stability. While most crashes are annoying, the risk that you will actually lose more than your recent work isn't all that much.

But there are times when you'll find yourself in a situation where your precious data could be lost. One typical example is when you save your document. It doesn't matter if it's your novel, an important spreadsheet, or your checkbook program. When you click Save, your software will remove the old version and replace it with the new one. But what if something goes wrong at that very moment? What if you have a power failure? What happens next?

Why Backups Are Necessary

It doesn't take a lot to make your file unrecoverable. With a paper document, ripping off a piece of a page or spilling a soft drink on it doesn't hurt very much. You can even tear it in half and fix it with tape.

But computer files are much more sensitive. The loss of even one of those bits and bytes that make up a computer file may be enough to make it impossible to open. While some programs (such as the Office 2001 for Macintosh program suite) can handle slightly damaged files, there's the very real possibility that you will not be able to recover your document. It's not a large possibility, but it's ever present, so it's a good idea to take some precautions so that you will be able to preserve as much of that data as possible.

In addition, there are other reasons why your files may be lost. Here's a brief list of the causes:

■ **Software conflicts**   As I explain in Chapter 2, there are plenty of software conflicts on your Mac. What Mac OS X has done is reduce such conflicts at the system level, but applications can still do plenty of mischief. Some are minor, resulting in minor cosmetic or performance irregularities, but others can cause the application to freeze, or quit. If this happens when you're saving a document, the document may be damaged beyond repair.

- **Viruses**   The newfound popularity of the Mac platform has produced a new set of virulent Mac viruses. While some are silly pranks, others can cause crashes or perhaps corrupt your documents. Some of these viruses are designed to target users of Microsoft's Office Software for the Mac. You'll want to read Chapter 12 for more information.

NOTE   *While the only Mac viruses that appear to survive the migration to Mac OS X are macro or "script" viruses, the danger of a new brand of Unix-based viruses is ever present (viruses, after all, were first developed under Unix).*

- **Hard drive directory damage**   The catalog file of your hard drive is delicate enough to be damaged by one crash too many. Over time, as your drive wears, files may also become damaged due to bad blocks, or the drive mechanism may simply fail. Whatever the reason or symptom, you may find your precious files can't be retrieved. I cover some avenues of recovery in Chapter 13, but they focus more on fixing the drive directory than on getting any individual files back. The prospects for the latter are, to be perfectly blunt, rather remote.

- **Power outage**   You are saving a file and the power goes off, thus corrupting the file (or even the hard drive). UPS devices, which provide surge protection and battery backup, can help. But they have a limited amount of backup time, and repeated outages may reduce the chance of being able to shut down your Mac and preserve your documents.

NOTE   *The need for a battery backup has become much more necessary in this day of rolling power blackouts in various parts of the country.*

- **Theft**   No further description is necessary. Despite the finest burglar alarm systems, we are all vulnerable to household or office theft of one sort or another.

NOTE   *I don't want to minimize this threat. One of my clients, who resides in a gated community in an affluent section of Phoenix—with a security guard present at all times—experienced a theft that resulted in the loss of all of his computer equipment. His insurance policy paid for the loss, but without backups, he now has to spend days in an effort to rebuild all his critical files.*

Why Backups Are Necessary

■ **Fire**   Even heat damage or water damage as a result of fire fighting efforts could damage delicate drive mechanisms or media.

■ **Flooding**   Whether you live in an area where floods are common or not, heavy rains and other unexpected weather conditions can cause serious problems. Water damage to your computer could have catastrophic results. I faced such a threat shortly before the original edition of this book was written, when heavy rains caused pools of water in two rooms of my home (fortunately my home office remained dry).

■ **Earthquakes**   A moderate quake can shake things about sufficiently to cause damage. At the very least (even if your Mac doesn't topple over), the hard drive could experience a head crash (where the read/write heads strike the surface of the drive), thus resulting in lost files.

So what do you do?

NOTE   *If you use your Mac strictly for play or recreation (whatever you prefer to call it), and don't create documents you need to preserve, perhaps you don't need a backup after all. New Macs come with a CD labeled "Restore," which is designed to put your Mac's hard drive in the exact shape it shipped from the factory. If the drive is corrupted beyond repair, you can use this disk to erase the drive and put all the old files back, and you've got what is, in effect, a new computer.*

How Big Companies Back Up Data

Your bank, your favorite Internet provider, and big businesses around the world all treat computer data in the same fashion. They understand there are risks of losing that data, and so they back up the files on a regular basis, often using "mirroring" techniques (see the section "An Overview of Backup Media," later in the chapter), to make simultaneous duplicates of files on separate media. Copies are also stored offsite, in the event their computers are damaged for one reason or another.

They really have no choice. Imagine, for example, the consequences if a bank's financial data, including the information about your account, was suddenly lost, or if a company lost all its business records.

Case History

Too Little Too Late

This really happened to a client of mine.

One morning I got a frantic phone call from a small magazine publisher. The Mac G3 on which they produced the publication wouldn't start up properly. All they saw was a disk icon on the screen with a flashing question mark. As we discuss in Chapters 13 and 15, it's a classic symptom that a startup drive with a working System Folder can't be found.

The client tried running Norton Utilities and Apple's Disk First Aid to no avail (this happened in the days before Mac OS X arrived). The startup drive wasn't visible—period. Weeks of work, an entire special issue of the magazine was on that drive and now they couldn't get to it.

"How old is your most recent backup?" I asked.

"What backup?"

The sad conclusion: I was able to help them restore the drive with a disk diagnostic program, but many of their files were lost. Had they invested in a backup strategy, they would have been able to recover all or most of their files in a relatively short time. As it was, they had to work around the clock for days to recreate everything.

A few weeks later, the client called and asked for advice on buying some backup drives, which they promptly followed. I've heard no complaints from them since that original unhappy event.

Backups: How, What, and When

There is no precise backup strategy that will work for everyone, but you should be able to use the information here to develop a plan that will be convenient and offer the amount of protection you need.

Over the next few pages, I'll cover various methods to safeguard your files. Basically, there are two ways to back up your data: manually and automatically.

- **Manual backup**   The fast-and-dirty way to back up your files is simple. You simply set up another drive or removable device. Then you drag the icon representing files or folders you want to copy to the other drive. That way you have the precious extra copy. The big shortcoming is that you have to manually select which files to copy over, and there's always the possibility of making a mistake. In addition, a number of Mac OS X system and program-related files are actually invisible, and since you can't see them, you can't copy them.

- **Automatic backup**   Programs such as Retrospect and other solutions I'll mention later in this chapter allow you to perform your backups at predetermined intervals. All you have to do is have your backup media in place and, if you don't need to switch media when it fills to capacity, you can go home or to dinner, and your backup will proceed without your presence.

Backup Software Choices

There used to be a number of backup programs for the Mac. In addition to Retrospect, you had FastBack and Redux, to name two popular choices. The major hard drive utilities, which then included MacTools and Norton Utilities, also included backup modules.

Times have changed, however. FastBack and its sibling, FastBack Plus, were casualties of the purchase of the publisher, Fifth Generation Systems, by Symantec. Shortly after Symantec acquired MacTools, their main rival in the disk utility business at the time, they also removed the backup utilities from that program and Norton Utilities. Then they killed MacTools as well.

Fortunately, there are good backup options, so you don't have to lament the loss of these programs.

> **CAUTION**   *If you still have copies of one of those discontinued backup programs running on your Mac, and it still works properly, you may continue to use it strictly for a Classic Mac computer. But do not expect to be able to run the backup software successfully under Mac OS X, nor will the backups include the "hidden" files that are part of the system installation. If you want to reboot under the Classic Mac OS, and you don't want to back up Mac OS X system–related files, it might be all right to run such programs. But you should consider up-to-date alternatives.*

Retrospect Express and Retrospect

Many of the backup tape drives you buy include a copy of Retrospect Desktop Backup or its lower-cost sibling, Retrospect Express Backup. Dantz Development has kept up to date with new Macs and new system versions. They have also added more great features with every release, which is why they get top reviews from the Mac publications. They are proven and tested in both small and large companies, so you can use them with confidence. Here's a brief overview of what these programs offer:

- **EasyScript**   This feature allows you to create an automatic backup plan without knowing any programming language or how to script. When you run EasyScript (see Figure 14-1), Retrospect will guide you through the simple steps. You just answer a few questions, and you're ready to do complicated automatic backups of a single Mac or an entire network.

- **Extensive support for backup media**   Whatever backup drive you pick, more than likely Retrospect will support it. Everything from tape drives to Zip drives is included (except in Retrospect Express Backup, which doesn't support tape media). And as new drives come out, the publisher will generally provide a special update to support the product.

- **Network backups**   The regular "Desktop" version of Retrospect also comes in a version called the Retrospect Network Backup Kit, which allows you to back up the files from an entire computer network. If you dabble in the Windows platform, you'll be pleased to know there's a Windows version with a similar set of features.

- **Internet backups**   If you want to do an online backup (and you'll need to check the limitations), you'll be pleased to know that Retrospect can handle these chores for you as well, with the same level of efficiency.

- **Simple interface**   Once you set the program up, all features are visible from the simple tabbed interface (as shown in Figure 14-2). You don't have to consult a complex manual to get up to speed. The commands are labeled in plain English, and the online help can take you through the more arcane aspects of a backup strategy.

NOTE   *Retrospect has a useful if time-consuming technique to ensure your backup is robust. It's called "compare," and the function is activated automatically once a disk has been backed up. While you can defeat this option as a preference, I recommend that you let it run. It's an important ounce of added protection that's designed to give you peace of mind.*

Backups: How, What, and When

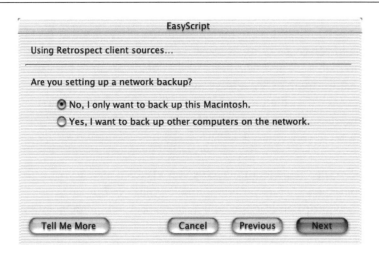

FIGURE 14-1   EasyScript means easy automation of your backup routine.

FIGURE 14-2   The Classic face of Retrospect will change only slightly for Mac OS X.

FWB's Backup ToolKit

This application's mirror mode makes a perfect copy of the original; incremental mode copies only the files that have been changed since the previous backup. The mirror evolutive feature makes a perfect copy of the contents of a disk or folder, as well as saving the previous versions—so that you can easily restore an older version of a file.

Intego's Personal Backup

Personal Backup, originally published by ASD Software, can do pretty much all of its stuff from a single screen. Once installed, you can do "on demand" backups whenever you wish, using the program's handy menu bar command. You can also set up an automatic schedule for regular backups.

Another handy feature is its ability to simply synchronize files between two drives. That's particularly useful if your iBook and PowerBook do heavy road warrior duty, and you need to make sure that the laptop and the desktop Macs both have the latest copies of your documents.

TIP   *A great feature of Personal Backup is its ability to record keystrokes. That way, if you lose the file, you'll have a backup of the text that you can use to help rebuild the document.*

Connectix CopyAgent

Unfortunately Connectix has, as of the time this book was written, decided not to attempt to update the program for Mac OS X. While it will still run if you boot from a Classic Mac OS version, it will not be able to copy the various invisible files placed on your hard drive as a result of the Mac OS X installation.

AppleScript and Backups

Under the Classic Mac OS, you were able to use a fascinating feature of AppleScript, Folder Actions, to make automatic backups to another drive or networked volume. The initial releases of Mac OS X didn't include a version of AppleScript that supported this clever technique. However, in the event the feature returns, you'll be able to designate an open folder to perform a specific scripting procedure, and use one of Apple's prebuilt scripts to make it so.

An Overview of Backup Media

Before you set up your backup plan, you'll want to decide where to put the files. One thing you should *not* do is copy the files to the same drive as the original. The point of the backup is protection in the event something goes wrong—not just with the file, but with the drive itself, whether it affects just one file or all of them.

Here's a quick overview of the kinds of backup media available as of the time this book was published, along with advantages and limitations. As time goes on, you'll find that clever manufacturers will devise variations on these themes, or even come up with ideas that are completely different from anything you see here.

- **Floppy disks**   The original backup medium, especially when Macs were young. And even with newer Macs and iMacs, where you can buy an external floppy or SuperDisk drive, it's neither robust nor efficient. Imagine how many 1.4MB floppies it would take to back up the contents of even a 3GB hard drive (which is small by today's standards). The mind boggles. Aside from the inconvenience, floppy disks are prone to failure, especially if you try to use them over and over again. For a small document file or two, they'll probably do, especially to transport the file to another location. For backup purposes, you'll probably want to look elsewhere.

NOTE   *Just as important, the first releases of Mac OS X didn't support the internal floppies on such models as the original "beige" G3, which otherwise is compatible with the new operating system.*

- **Extra hard drive**   Whether the drive is located inside your Mac or attached via the FireWire, SCSI, or USB port (whatever applies), this is a useful, convenient place to store your backups. The big limitation is portability. It isn't practical to put the drive in a safe place if it must be regularly available to receive those backup files.

NOTE   *While it's easy to partition a drive (divide it into multiple segments), it's not a terribly robust way to protect your data. If a problem is serious enough to take down the drive, all partitions will be history.*

- **Mirroring data**   Special software packages, supporting RAID (Redundant Array of Inexpensive Drives), have a feature that "mirrors" or duplicates the files you save across two or more drives. That way, if one drive goes bad, there's another, identical file that you can use on the other drive. Mac OS X's Disk Utility application has RAID support.

- **Removable drive**   These products come with such names as Jaz, Orb, Peerless, SuperDisk, SyQuest, or Zip, but they are all designed to perform in a similar way. The drives use a media that acts like a floppy disk, because you can remove the media when it's filled, and replace it with another one to receive more files. Capacities range up to 20GB (and no doubt bigger drives will be forthcoming), similar to many regular hard drives. And, of course, you can store the media in another location for protection. Although some of these removable devices use hard-drive–based technology, they are usually somewhat slower and potentially less reliable, since the drive mechanism is more susceptible to dust.

- **Magneto-optical drive**   Such a drive uses optical disk technology (somewhat reminiscent of a compact disc), which ensures longevity. If you want to keep your backups for several years or more, this option (or a CD recorder) might be useful. The disadvantage of this technology is that it's rather slow compared to a hard drive (though faster than Zips or CD recorders); but as a tradeoff for a robust backup, it may be worth the time and trouble.

- **CD-R or CD-RW**   These two methods are based on conventional compact disc technology, same as that used with your regular audio CDs. The advantage is permanence. When was the last time any of your audio CDs failed? If you want to store your files for years and years, you'll want to think about this method. If you're lucky enough to have a recent Mac, you may already have a built-in CD burner and be able to use Apple's Disk Burner software to make quick, convenient copies, just by dragging and dropping. Some non-Apple CD burners will also function with this useful utility. Otherwise, you need special software to "burn" or create a CD. With the third-party programs, however, you cannot just drag the files to a mounted disk icon and have them copy over. It can also be quite slow compared to most other backup media. Figure on it taking 15 to 45 minutes for a 650MB CD, depending on how fast the CD recorder runs. But it's a cheap way to go. CD blanks are less than a dollar each. The CD-RW variation uses more expensive media and allows you to write on the disc over and over again (usually up to 1,000 times), but older CD drives won't read the discs.

- **DVD-RAM**   This technology is based on DVD, the high-quality videodisc format. You can store over 5GB of data on it when you use the higher-density media. Its major limitation is that, as of the time this book was being prepared, there is more than one way to skin a cat, and no guarantee that the media created on one drive will work on another, since competing technologies exist.

■ **DVD-R** First making its debut on the Mac with the SuperDrive, the feature was, up to the time this book was written, limited to making movies, not copying data. However, data copying is a logical extension of the technology, so this is a possible alternative backup method. Stay tuned.

■ **Tape drive** There are several types. One of the popular varieties is DDS (Digital Data Storage), which is based on DAT (Digital Audio Tape) technology. Tapes are cheap but not as robust as other media. And they're generally slow compared to other backup media, though newer tape drives give pretty decent performance. Finding even a single file may take a while, since the tape has to be shuttled back and forth in the drive to locate a special item (same as your audio cassette player). And this isn't the only inconvenience. With the exception of a special utility, Optima Technology's DeskTape Pro (which was being updated for Mac OS X when this book was written), you cannot mount a tape on your Mac's desktop. You need special backup software, such as Retrospect, to write and retrieve files.

■ **Network drives** If your Mac is located in a business environment, you may be able to use the networked drives or servers for backing up. Some companies will have a special strategy in place for such actions, however, so you'll want to be sure you aren't putting files somewhere where they are neither welcomed nor assured of safety.

■ **Internet backups** This new option is a consequence of the new generation of Power Macs, iMacs, iBooks, and PowerBooks, which don't have standard floppy drives. Rather than buy something extra, you upload your file to an Internet backup service, which provides secured access and stores your files. Assuming the service backs up *their* files regularly, it is a nice option, but you also have to consider how long it'll take to upload your file to this remote location. Unless you have high-speed Internet access, such as a cable modem or DSL, it may take hours to transfer even a small number of document files. The well-known free option is iDisk, a feature of Apple's iTools that gives you 20MB of free storage space. If you need more, Apple offers it as an extra cost option.

NOTE *Rather than subscribe to an Internet backup service to store your files, you could upload them to a family member or trusted friend for safekeeping on their computing system. Of course, you would want to make sure they have a robust backup method in case something goes wrong at their end of the backup chain.*

Your Regular Backup Plan

No doubt about it, backups can be a pain. You have to stop what you're doing and remember to make an extra copy or two of your precious files. And if you're busy creating one of those files, approaching deadlines make it easy to forget something or just plain put it off until you have the time. Unfortunately, without an ironclad strategy, that time may never come. It's so easy to say, "I'll do it tomorrow." Unfortunately, if you lose that file today, tomorrow is too late.

Here's a suggested daily backup strategy you can use, with or without extra software. All you need is a separate backup drive to which you copy files:

- **Use a program's AutoSave or Backup option.**   Check the Preference dialogs in your favorite software to see if either or both options are available. If there's the choice to save a backup to another drive or drive partition, consider using it.

- **Make extra copies of critical documents.**   While working on a file, drag a copy of the document icon to another disk, or just use the Save As option in the File menu to make an extra copy.

NOTE *If you are using the Save As feature, you may want to place that extra copy on another disk, in case something happens to the original drive.*

- **At the end of the workday, back up critical files.**   You can use a backup program for this purpose or do it manually.

NOTE *Among those "critical files" is the Preferences folder inside the Mac OS 9.x System Folder and your Mac OS X Users folder. These two folders contain most of your personal program settings, including those involving your Internet connection. If you have multiple users working on your Mac with extra user accounts, there are separate copies of these folders for their settings, too.*

■ **Make full backups at least once a week.**   Over time, no doubt you've customized your Mac in many ways. You may have changed the desktop pattern, adjusted mouse tracking speed, and made a load of settings to the various programs you use. If you had to recreate all the things that make your Mac friendly and comfortable to use, it could take hours. But if you have a complete backup of the contents of your startup disk, at the very least, you'll be able to restore everything to the way it was without a lot of fuss or bother.

■ **Store backup files in a safe place.**   Your backup media is subject to the same risks as the originals. In the event of fire, flood, or theft, they can be lost as well. Big firms often place a copy of their backups offsite. A secure location, such as a bank vault, might be useful if you want the maximum amount of security. But even a friend's or mother-in-law's home will do. The point is to have another copy somewhere else if the first is damaged or stolen.

■ **If you travel, take a copy of the backup with you.**   Pack it in your suitcase or laptop carrying bag. That way if you come home to find disaster has struck, you'll be able to get up and running quickly. Computers, printers, and scanners can be replaced (good insurance is a must), but it may take hours, days, or weeks to recreate your missing data.

NOTE
I always take this advice to heart. Before leaving on a trip with my iBook or PowerBook, I bring a tape with the most recent complete backup of all my files. Often I will also bring a CD with my current document files, in case the ones on my laptop become damaged in transit and I need to use another computer. (This happened to me, in fact, when I visited the Macworld Expo in January 2001, and found out that my iBook's disk drive had failed.)

■ **Label your backup media carefully.**   When you need to restore a file, it can be especially vexing to have to waste time searching through disk after disk to find the one you need. If possible, print out a directory of a disk's contents (clearly, you can't do this with a tape drive).

■ **Don't use the same media over and over again.**   Removable media, from tapes to cartridges, may wear out over time. The best way to maximize life span is to have several disks run in rotation.

- **Recycle media.** Older disks that contain files you no longer need can be placed back into action, but if the disks are especially old, you may find it safer to simply purchase a new set.

- **Consider CD-based backups for long-term archiving.** While traditional disks and tapes may wear out over time, optical-based media can last for many years. If you anticipate you might need that file five years from now, a CD or DVD recorder or magneto-optical drive may be something to consider as an extra backup tool.

- **Don't expect to be able to just copy your Mac's hard drive under Mac OS X.** Because it's a multiple-user operating system from the ground up, Mac OS X has a complicated method of protecting the contents of a drive from just being copied. As a result, the attempt may deliver a message that you don't have sufficient "write" privileges to copy the disk. You need dedicated backup software to perform the task; otherwise, you have to select and copy over just the individual files to another drive.

What Do You Back Up?

There are several strategies you can use when you decide to back up your files. Whether you do it manually or use a dedicated backup program, you'll want to consider which options provide the best combination of safety, speed, and flexibility.

- **No-frills backup** You have your original system software and program installation disks at hand, so you may not feel it's important to make duplicates. You can just back up your document files and your Preferences folder, the ones you make with those original programs.

- **Full backup** In this scenario, you back up everything on your drive. While it may take a lot of extra time to do, there's the added advantage of being able to conveniently restore your Mac to something approximating the shape it was in before catastrophe struck. This means that all of the custom settings you've done—from fancy desktop patterns to more subtle aspects of your Mac user experience, such as mouse tracking speed and a program's preference settings—are in place.

- **Incremental backup** You use this method to back up strictly the files that have changed since your last backup. Backup software is capable of sorting all this out in the event you need to restore your files.

Backups: How, What, and When

Application Backup Features

In addition to backing up all your files to a central location (another drive, removable disk, or tape), there's another backup option you'll want to consider.

Some programs offer an automatic backup or automatic saving option as part of their preference settings. That way you can be assured there's a second, recent copy around somewhere in case your original file becomes damaged and unusable. I'll cover two popular choices next.

Word's AutoSave/Backup Option

If you are a regular user of Word for Mac OS X or Word 2001 (or even the previous version, Word 98), you'll find a handy feature hidden in the Preferences settings that will help you protect your valuable documents in the event of a problem. A similar preference is available for PowerPoint, but, unfortunately, not for versions of Excel prior to the Mac OS X upgrade. Here's how to use it:

1. Choose Preferences from the Tools menu.

2. Click the Save tab, which brings up the screen shown in Figure 14-3.

3. To have an extra copy of your document, click the Always Create Backup Copy check box. Once this setting is made, you'll have an extra copy of your document file with the prefix "Backup of" in the same folder as the original.

4. If you want to make it possible to recover a document if you crash while saving it, click the Save AutoRecover Info Every check box, and specify the interval. Ten minutes, the default, should do just fine. Once the setting goes in effect, if you open a document that's been damaged, Word will use the AutoRecover information to restore it to its original shape (and you'll see an onscreen dialog about it).

5. Click OK to put your settings into effect.

QuarkXPress's Not-So-Secret Backup Feature

The well-known desktop publishing program QuarkXPress has a very robust but seldom-used backup option. The feature is of vital importance, as all recent versions are known to corrupt documents on occasion. While most of these problems may be due to other causes, such as problems on the SCSI chain, they are no less vexing.

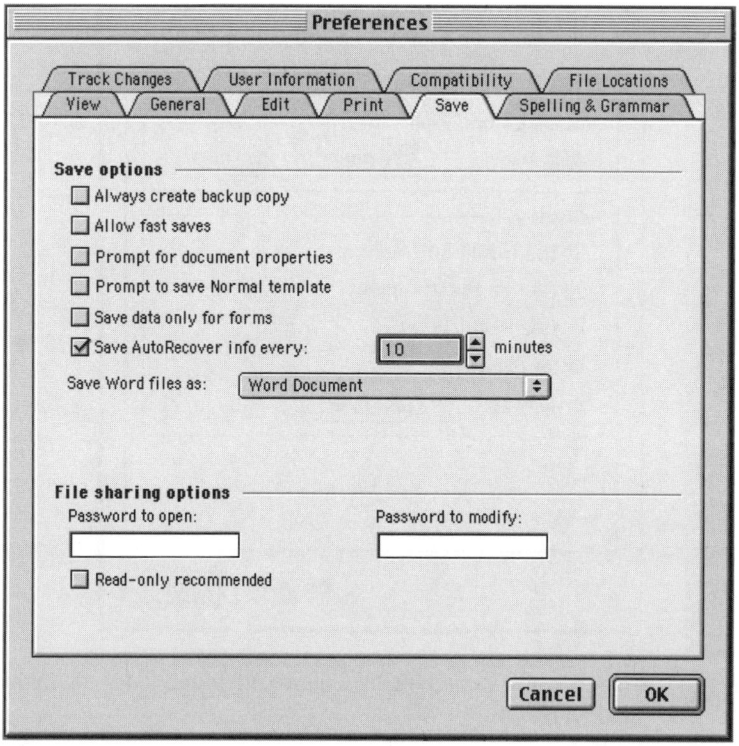

Preferences

Track Changes \\ User Information \\ Compatibility \\ File Locations
View \\ General \\ Edit \\ Print \\ Save \\ Spelling & Grammar

Save options
- ☐ Always create backup copy
- ☐ Allow fast saves
- ☐ Prompt for document properties
- ☐ Prompt to save Normal template
- ☐ Save data only for forms
- ☑ Save AutoRecover info every: 10 ⬍ minutes

Save Word files as: Word Document ⬍

File sharing options
Password to open: Password to modify:

☐ Read-only recommended

Cancel   OK

FIGURE 14-3   Word 2001's automatic backup feature can be a useful means
of protection.

Backups: How, What, and When

NOTE   *When I say "seldom-used," I'm not exaggerating the point. I have worked with many users of XPress, and not one of them has ever so much as looked at this particular preference. (I'm using the word XPress here to refer to the program, and Quark to refer to the company; this is the official way, although I know many people refer to the program itself as Quark.)*

The following steps will help you automatically save and back up your XPress documents:

1. Launch QuarkXPress. You do not need to open a document at this point.

2. Choose Preferences from the Edit menu, and select Application Preferences (the first one on the list). This will bring up the dialog shown in Figure 14-4.

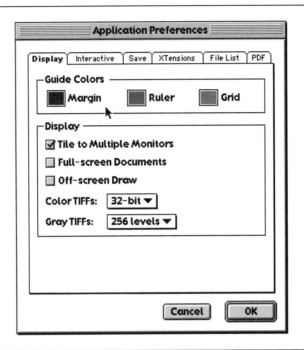

FIGURE 14-4   A number of cool preference features are found in this dialog box for
QuarkXPress 4.

NOTE   *As this book was being written, QuarkXPress 5 was under development for both the Classic Mac OS and for Mac OS X. Previews of the new program indicated that all or most of the features I am describing here will be retained in a redesigned Preferences dialog.*

3. Click on the Save tab, which will bring up the screen shown in Figure 14-5.

4. Check Auto Save, then pick the interval. The default is 5 minutes.

5. Check Auto Backup, then indicate how many revisions you want to have. The default is 5, but you're better off with 1 or 2. Otherwise, you'll have a lot of extra files around that you don't need.

NOTE   *If you choose the option to make more than a single backup file in QuarkXPress, you may find your destination folder filled with extra copies. Every so often, it's a good idea to prune the folder of unneeded files.*

6. Select the Destination for your backup. The default, the Document folder, just compounds the risk, in case something goes bad with your drive. So click the Other Folder radio button.

7. In the dialog that appears, select the drive or folder where you want to place your backups. You may want to use the option in this dialog to create a new folder, giving it a label that makes it easy to find later on. One example may be "XPress Documents Backups" (or "Quark Documents Backup," if you prefer).

NOTE *If your Mac has a second attached drive, you may want to place backups there. A networked Mac or server may also be a good backup choice, but it may slow down when doing a save operation—especially if you're not on a high-speed network.*

8. Click the OK button to store your settings. From here on, all documents you create in QuarkXPress will be saved or backed up as you specified. Auto Backup files will have the original filename, plus suffix, beginning with the number (#) sign to indicate how many backed-up files have been created.

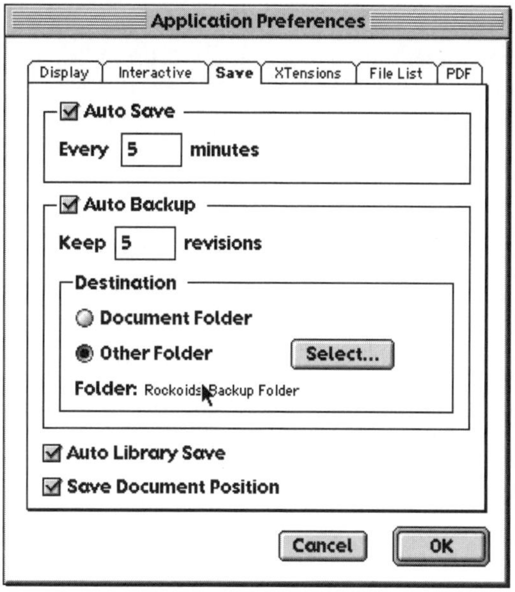

FIGURE 14-5   Specify your document backup options here.

NOTE

If you run across a damaged QuarkXPress file, and even the backup doesn't work, there's another solution. MarkZWare, a publisher of Quark XTensions (add-ons) offers a product, MarkZTools, that can recover many damaged XPress documents. You can learn more about the product by visiting their Web site at http://www.markzware.com.

How to Restore Your Files

Whatever backup technique you use, you should make sure that you *can* restore your files should the worst occur. In schools and large companies, they often conduct fire drills to test performance in the event of a real emergency. You should consider a similar test with your backup routine. You'll want to know, in advance, that the files you're backing up are available at your beck and call when you need them.

Test Driving Your Backup Strategy

To examine the efficacy of your backup program, you should consider running a drill by actually restoring something. Here's one way you might accomplish this task:

1. If you're doing a manual backup, or a backup in "Finder" format (meaning the backed-up files appear in the same form as the originals), simply copy a few document files back to your drive, to a location different from the original. You don't want to actually replace any files; you just want to see if they are in good shape.

2. Open the files, and make sure that what you see matches the original file. More than likely, if you can open the file normally, you should have no problem.

3. If the file fails to open, review your backup plan, and the next section, to address problems with the backed-up files.

4. If you're using a backup program, such as Personal Backup or Retrospect, simply use the Restore function in the program, and select a handful of files to restore to your drive. Again, you don't want to replace any existing file—just make sure that you actually have a good copy of the files available in the event you really need them later.

If your test works, you can feel fairly confident that your backup routine is going to be successful.

What If the Backup Goes Bad?

There can be no greater source of disappointment and frustration than trying to restore your files and finding out that your backup has gone bad. You engage the Restore operation on your backup software, or simply try to copy over files you've backed up manually, and you get a message that there's a disk error or a warning that something's wrong with your backup program's "storage set."

It's frustrating, true, but it doesn't have to mean that you won't be able to restore at least some of your files. In Retrospect, for example, there are tools to fix the backup directory, known as the Storage Set. The Storage Set is your catalog of all the files you've backed up, and Retrospect needs this file to track the progress of your backup and retrieve files when necessary. While the process I'm going to describe here won't fix a bad disk, it will allow you to recover the files that are still available.

Fixing a Bad Retrospect Storage Set

If Retrospect can't recover your files, you'll see a message about it onscreen when you attempt to restore one or more files. Usually, it'll indicate that the contents of the Storage Set don't jibe with the actual backup files. Quite often this happens if your Mac crashes at some point in the backup process, though a damaged Storage Set file will trigger the same message.

NOTE   *Retrospect stores the Storage Set files in the same folder that contains the original application. As an ounce of protection, you ought to make duplicates of these files on another drive or removable disk. While the sets can be recreated in the event the original drive is lost, it can be a time-consuming process you will probably want to avoid.*

Here's how to address the problem, using recent versions of Retrospect (this description is based on a preliminary edition of the Mac OS X version):

1. Make sure the first or only disk of your backup is in the backup drive.

2. Launch Retrospect.

3. Click on the Tools tab, which brings up the screen shown in Figure 14-6.

4. Click on the Repair button, which produces the dialog shown in Figure 14-7.

5. The decision you make now depends on what sort of problem message you saw when you tried to restore a file. If it stated the catalog was out of sync with the backup, click the first option. If you don't have a Storage Set, you can recreate one using the data on your backup media, by clicking on whatever option in Figure 14-7 applies.

6. If your backup has additional disks, you'll see an onscreen prompt asking you to insert those disks (usually the previous disk will be ejected, but you may have to click an Eject button to do this). When you state there are no additional backup disks, the dialog will conclude with an onscreen acknowledgment that you can OK.

7. Depending on how badly your Storage Set catalog is messed up, it may take anywhere from a few minutes to a few hours to recreate or build the file. But the best prevention against a bad backup is to have more than one. That way, if a fragile disk goes bad, another disk will be available for you to get your documents back. When it comes to backups, three times is definitely a charm.

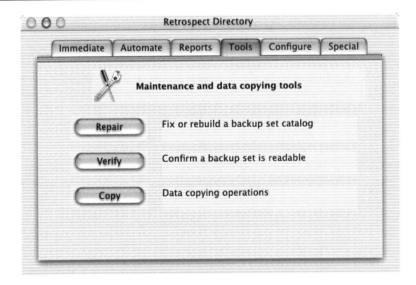

FIGURE 14-6   You can configure and fix storage sets here.

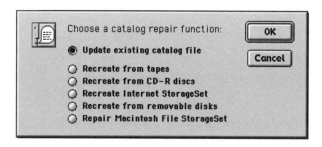

FIGURE 14-7   The storage set can be repaired from this dialog box (this is the Classic Mac OS version).

Other Backup Recovery Methods

If your actual backup disk or tape is at fault, rather than the backup catalog, there are no guarantees you'll get it back, which is why I suggested you have extra backups.

This is especially true if your backup is on a tape, which can only be read by special software, such as Retrospect. When these disks go bad, your regular file recovery and repair programs, such as the ones I describe in Chapter 13, just won't function.

> **NOTE**   *When you use a tape drive, follow the manufacturer's recommendations about using cleaning disks to keep tape heads clean. For example, DDS drives should be cleaned about every 15 hours. Retrospect can be set to remind you of this cleaning interval. If you fail to run the cleaning disks regularly, you may subject your backup to read/write errors, and the potential for corrupted or lost files.*

Abbott Systems to the Rescue

An old-line Mac utility publisher, Abbott Systems, offers two programs that can help you recover damaged or trashed documents. One of them, CanOpener, is designed to open almost any document file and retrieve the contents, even if the original program cannot access it. While a complicated financial document or desktop publishing file may not be recovered in its original form, basic text and pictures can often be found.

> **NOTE**   *Although not updated for Mac OS X, the two applications from this publisher seem to work just in the Classic environment.*

Another program from this publisher, RescueTXT, can be used to track text on files you've accidentally deleted. This may be the court of last appeal should a hard drive recovery program, such as Norton Utilities or TechTool Pro, not be able to retrieve a file.

NOTE *Norton Utilities and TechTool Pro work best if you install them before you have a problem. Both programs will catalog your deleted files and your hard drive directory and update the catalog regularly, which makes recovery easier in the event of trouble later on. They work far less reliably if you have to use their recovery tools without having first installed the software before your drive went bad.*

You can check out the Abbott Systems product line at their Web site: http://www.abbottsystems.com.

Diagnosing Backup Problems on a Large SCSI Chain

Here are some steps to follow should you be unable to retrieve a backup from a SCSI device in a setup with several drives attached:

1. Check your SCSI chain. Make sure all attached devices are on and that termination is turned on or attached to the final device on the chain (the one at the very end).

2. If you need to move any devices to different positions, shut down your Mac, then your attached SCSI devices, then move the devices. Be sure to observe proper termination and SCSI ID settings.

3. If you still cannot get your backup device to retrieve files or run properly, shut down your Mac, then the SCSI devices.

4. Set up the backup drive as the only SCSI device on the chain. Be sure to switch on termination, or install a termination block, whichever applies.

5. Turn on the backup drive, then the Mac.

If these steps don't help, and you're using a conventional removable drive, such as a Jaz or Zip, run a disk diagnostic utility, as described in Chapter 13.

CAUTION

Before you run a disk diagnostic program with a removable drive, check the manufacturer's recommendations in the manual or Read Me file. You wouldn't want to make matters worse, unless, of course, the media is useless. In that event, even a risky method may be worth the risk.

NOTE

If you cannot make a backup drive work on your Mac, there may be an alternative—that is, if you have an extra Mac around to which you can attach the drive. Just set up the drive on the other Mac, and see if you can retrieve the file that way (you may have to install the backup software, of course). If it works, you can network the two Macs to access the files, or just copy them to another drive, if available.

Summing Up

Backing up your data may seem an unneeded chore until you lose one of your valuable files. This chapter covered backup techniques using all types of media. One of these techniques is bound to work well in your situation.

The next chapter covers one of the principal causes of headaches and aggravation on a Mac, the SCSI chain; Mac OS X has not eliminated the oddities that occur with SCSI. You'll learn the best methods to set up a SCSI chain and the telltale signs of trouble.

What If the Backup Goes Bad?

Chapter 15

Storage Device Technologies: Dealing with SCSI Chain Hassles

The Mac's version of plug-and-play is a terrific engineering feat, especially when compared to the failed efforts on the Windows platforms. I cannot tell you how many times I've set up Mac hard drives, networks, and printers in minutes, only to face hours of debugging to do the very same things on the PC side of the platform.

But that doesn't mean the Mac is the bee's knees when it comes to total freedom from setup hassles. For one thing, SCSI—once Apple's primary peripheral bus to connect such things as CD drives, hard drives, and scanners—needs, shall we say, a little work to make things operate correctly.

Sometimes you have to just set it up and pray that it'll work properly, which is where the term "plug and pray" comes from.

I've devoted this chapter to SCSI chain setup, diagnosis, and how to add extra devices, in the hope it'll make your encounters with SCSI voodoo less frustrating.

Fortunately, with its recent models, Apple has moved totally away from SCSI except as an option. New Macs, iMacs, iBooks, and PowerBooks come with ATA drives as standard issue. In the future, you may even see internal FireWire drives, although so-called FireWire drives today are largely ATA devices with a special printed circuit board for conversion. Before long, the problems you encounter here will be history once you upgrade your Mac and peripherals. But even if you have a new Mac, you may need to add SCSI capability (where possible) to handle those older scanners, removable drives, and other peripherals.

At the end of the chapter, you'll also read about the technologies Apple has adopted that are free of many of the limitations of SCSI. As you update your Mac and your accessories, you'll be pleased to know there's truly light at the end of the tunnel.

How to Organize the SCSI Chain

If you follow a few basic setup procedures, you should be able to get most SCSI chains to work properly—most of the time, that is. Here are a few of the basics to consider:

> **NOTE**   *A SCSI chain is simply a collection of two or moreSCSI devices on a single SCSI bus.*

- ■ **Keep SCSI chains short.** In theory, you can have cable lengths with a total of over 19 feet on a plain-Jane SCSI chain, but in practice, there are limits. For one thing, that figure also includes the actual cable inside a drive mechanism, which can add up. Figure on a foot or so for every device.

NOTE

High-speed SCSI chains, such as SCSI Wide, require much shorter cable lengths. Consult the information provided with your SCSI accelerator card for specifics on this subject.

■ **Don't forget termination.**   The first and last devices on the SCSI chain (regardless of SCSI ID number) need to be terminated. Your Mac provides termination at the beginning of the chain, so you only need to add it at the end. Some SCSI devices require a terminator block, but others use pushbuttons, DIP switches, or little bitty buttons to switch termination on or off. Mechanisms from APS Technology, Iomega's removable drives, and some scanners from such companies as Umax all offer a termination switch of some sort. If a quick glance at the device doesn't give you an answer as to how termination is to be set, consult the manuals or call the manufacturer for assistance. I won't even try to cover all of the confusing possibilities here.

NOTE

I'll repeat this a couple of times in this chapter: The older PowerBooks that came with SCSI capability didn't generally supply enough termination power for a well-performing SCSI chain (especially if there's more than a single device). The manuals for those models usually suggest double termination (at the beginning or middle and the end of the chain).

■ **Watch out for duplicate SCSI ID numbers.**   If your Mac has some internal devices installed, there are several ways to check this out. You can run the Apple System Profiler application, or one of the hard disk formatting utilities, such as Anubis, Hard Disk ToolKit, or Silverlining Pro, to check for each device on the chain. You can also use SCSI Probe, which is available from many Web sites, such as http://www.versiontracker.com. Normally, the internal drive on a Mac is set at ID 0 (I've seen different ID numbers for replacement drives, though this is easily changed), and the CD-ROM drive is set at ID 3. Apple's internal SCSI Zip drives are set at ID 5.

CAUTION

Be extremely careful about using non-Apple disk formatters with Mac OS X. You'll want to consult the publishers first about when or if they are compatible. For now, consider Apple System Profiler your first line of defense here.

■ **Keep all attached SCSI devices on.**   I know, you're not using that scanner, and you don't want to wear out the bulb (many of them are difficult and costly to replace). But many scanners are set to power down their bulbs after a period of disuse, and, in any case, the bulbs usually last for thousands of hours. The problem here is arcane, and involves matters of proper termination power, correct voltage on the SCSI chain, and that sort of thing. In some cases, leaving off a connected device won't do anything bad. But you may also experience unexpected system crashes and damaged files. The best advice is to keep all attached devices on. If you don't intend to use a device except on a rare occasion, power down, remove it from the SCSI chain and power up again (don't forget to change termination if necessary).

A Handy Guide to SCSI Voodoo

In the previous section, I explained how SCSI devices are supposed to work. The word "voodoo" is used when it comes to SCSI chains, because sometimes setting things up as advertised isn't quite successful. Drives don't show up, you get frequent crashes, or data ends up damaged.

Why It's Necessary to Keep SCSI Devices On

The telephone call was frantic. A client couldn't boot his vintage Power Mac, and he had to complete a business proposal.

I rushed over to the site and ran Alsoft's Disk Warrior and Symantec's Norton Utilities (see Chapter 13). The drive had various and sundry disk directory errors that were fixed, but, sad to say, a whole folder was filled with damaged files.

After the drive's directory was repaired, I performed a clean installation of the client's operating system and had them up and running in a short time. But I noticed something amiss in his setup. He had two devices on the SCSI chain, a scanner and a Zip drive. The scanner was off. He said he only used it once a week and so he didn't think he wanted to waste the electricity.

The scanner was turned on, and the Mac restarted.

After I talked with the client a few minutes, I realized that since he had decided to turn off his scanner when not in use, his Mac crashed much more often. And there was that folder containing damaged files to deal with. He agreed to leave his scanner on and has had no problems since then, although it took him quite a few hours to recreate the damaged graphic files.

Frustrating, yes? But if you follow a few troubleshooting steps, you'll usually get things to run correctly. I say usually because there are exceptions that defeat the best efforts of humankind to resolve.

CAUTION *Before you change anything on your Mac's SCSI chain, turn everything off. And before you reboot your Mac, turn on all attached SCSI devices first. No exceptions! You could damage your Mac's logic board or one of your devices if you try hot plugging (although there are some devices available from hard drive vendors that promise to do this sort of thing).*

- **Use an extra terminator.** Yes, I know. I said that only the beginning and end of the SCSI chain are supposed to be terminated. But this doesn't necessarily work on large SCSI chains (with several devices and cables stretching the length limits) or with PowerBooks. PowerBook manuals usually have a special section on SCSI hookups. For other Macs, place a pass-through terminator in the middle of the chain and see if it helps improve performance.

- **Use an active terminator.** These devices help regulate the current on the SCSI chain and will sometimes compensate for devices that don't supply proper current or electrical variations among cables. Some models will even include a power brick, which is used to help supply extra juice to help regulate a SCSI chain with a PowerBook and similar products.

- **Use cables from the same manufacturer.** In theory, a cable is a cable, but products from different manufacturers may differ slightly in electrical specifications. It may not mean much if you have only one or two items on the SCSI chain. But on a large SCSI chain, small differences may account for a lot. If all else fails, try buying a new set of cables from one manufacturer.

NOTE *I'm not a fan of boutique cables since (as with the cables you use on your home stereo system) you seldom, if ever, get better performance in exchange for the higher price you pay. Cables from major companies, such as Belkin, work just fine in any installation.*

- **Move devices around.** For whatever reason, some SCSI devices work best in a specific position on the SCSI chain. Sometimes a manufacturer will make a suggestion as to positioning in their manuals. An example: some scanners work best at the very end of the SCSI chain, others work best at the beginning. You need to experiment and move things around to

A Handy Guide to SCSI Voodoo

see if the proper combination can be found. Just remember to change SCSI
ID numbers where needed (so they don't conflict) and move termination to
the last physical device on the chain.

■ **Change SCSI ID numbers.**   A SCSI ID number doesn't have to be
   consecutive. Number 6 doesn't have to be after number 5. You can reverse
   the numbers if you desire (just make sure they don't conflict).

Do Drives Really Last for 500,000 Hours?

It's very common for hard drive manufacturers to quote incredible lifetimes for their
products. They usually range from 200,000 to 500,000 hours MBTF (mean time
between failures). Considering that 200,000 hours would amount to more than two
decades continuous operation, more than anyone might realistically expect to use
their Macs, this would be the equivalent of a lifetime warranty (imagine what
500,000 hours means?).

Yet drive manufacturers seldom warranty their products for more than three to
five years. So, do you take it seriously?

Well, consider this. Just because a hard drive manufacturer quotes an average
doesn't mean a specific hard drive won't fail before that. Hard drives and removable
devices tend to be more trouble-prone because of all the delicate mechanical parts
involved. My suggestion is that you treat your drive as if it might fail at any moment
(which can sometimes be the case) and have regular backups. You can also use a
hard drive maintenance program to be certain there's no damage to the delicate
hard drive's file directory. Chapters 13 and 14 cover these subjects in more detail.

Case History   Mixing and Matching SCSI Cables

Just a few years ago, I went through the hassles of SCSI voodoo when trying to
configure a Mac with a big SCSI chain (six external devices including removable
drives, scanner, and tape backup drive). The symptom was classic. I tried to copy
a large file to and from any drive, and the computer locked up tight as a drum.

I went through the standard array of remedies. I moved SCSI devices around,
and changed SCSI ID numbers. I swapped cables, and switched a few from some
extras I had on hand. Even an active terminator was used.

The SCSI chain worked if I removed any single device, but all together there was no way to avoid the problem. I checked and double-checked everything to be absolutely certain that the setup was correct. Even a second terminator wouldn't fix it.

Finally, on a suggestion from a technical support person at APS Technologies, a big hard drive vendor (now a division of LaCie), I replaced the cables. All of them. Now maybe you could be cynical about it and assume they just wanted to sell me cables. Maybe so. But after replacing the old cables with the new ones, the problem was cured, immediately, never to return. The new cables did it!

Internal vs. External: What's the Difference?

Yes, they're cheaper. And no doubt that is one reason to favor an internal hard drive, but there are complications. For one thing, even if your Mac can handle more than one drive inside, you have to pop the case, remove brackets, and fiddle with hard-to-reach cables (how many of you have ended up with scraped fingers dripping blood as a result of poking for those little-bitty cables?). And even when that's fairly simple, there are the drive mechanisms themselves.

Whether the mechanisms are regular hard drives or removable devices, such as a CD writer, Jaz, or Zip drive, there are other little complications to consider.

For one thing, you have to decipher a sometimes unclear diagram to see if the proper SCSI ID and termination settings are set on the drive. You cannot always depend on the manufacturer or reseller setting up these mechanisms properly.

NOTE *I don't want to name names, but I've always specified the kind of configuration I want when ordering a new internal SCSI drive, and seldom does the vendor adhere to those suggestions. A word to the wise.*

Here are some things to consider when buying an internal hard drive for your Mac:

■ **Consider an accessory cooling fan.**   If you really need that big hard drive, contact your dealer and see if they can set you up with an accessory cooling fan. Such vendors as APS Technologies offer such a product, which usually attaches to the drive itself. It can make a big difference in hard drive reliability.

■ **You need a new faceplate for a removable device.**   If you want to add a SuperDisk, a Zip drive, or some other device for which you have to remove the media, you need to replace the faceplate on your Mac with one that will match the open slot on the mechanism itself. Your dealer can probably handle your needs (or check with Proline, at www.proline.com, for a fine line of such products). On some Mac OS clones, all you need to do is pop a small faceplate, and leave the removable mechanism with its front showing, without a cover.

> **NOTE** *The QuickSilver G4 Power Macs come with a cover with a pop-out insert on the bottom front drive tray that's supposed to be Zip-drive ready. Check this out before you go looking for a replacement faceplate.*

■ **Make sure you can really add an extra mechanism.**   If your Mac doesn't have an extra drive bay, or if it's got an internal ATA chain and no capability, you may not be able to add extra devices without a separate SCSI accelerator card (see the section that follows).

> **CAUTION** *Check the manual that came with your Mac as to what and how many internal drives it supports. Don't assume that, because someone you know got it to work, it'll work that way for you. Sometimes Apple will modify motherboard designs, so one production run may differ from the other.*

Making Sense of SCSI Jumper Settings

When you install a new internal SCSI hard drive, it's often on a wing and a prayer. Even when you ask your hard drive vendor to set it up for you, there's no guarantee it was done properly, so it's best to check.

Internal drives use jumpers (small plastic pieces with metallic lined holes in them) to set SCSI ID settings and termination. Unfortunately, not all drives are made equal, and not all settings are clearly explained on the drive mechanism or on the documentation (if there is any), so you may find yourself installing a drive that's not properly configured for your Mac.

> **NOTE** *Older hard drive mechanisms set termination with a resister pack, a long, thin part that actually plugged into the drive. While removing the pack (usually two resistors with many pins) would turn off termination, the process often broke the delicate pins, so reinstalling was usually out of the question. Nowadays termination is on the controller card for the drive and almost always activated or deactivated with a jumper.*

Here is a bit of advice to get you set up properly. If your questions aren't answered here, I'd suggest you call the drive vendor or the manufacturer for specifics about their products. In addition, the Web sites for the major manufacturers, such as IBM (http://www.ibm.com), Maxtor (http://www.maxtor.com), and Seagate (http://www.seagate.com), provide illustrations on proper setup for a specific model drive.

SCSI Termination—Off or On?

If your internal drive replaces one that's already in your Mac, you'll want to make sure termination is left on. Look for a set of jumper pins with the label "TE" under them. Make sure that a jumper is placed over the two pins in this row to keep it on; remove the jumper to turn them off.

> **TIP** *Jumpers are small enough that even those of you with small, nimble fingers might find them a challenge. I find that a small needle-nose pliers (available at any hardware store) is usually sufficient to handle the tiny things. Just don't apply too much pressure to the jumper or the pins, or something may break.*

Typical Jumper Settings for SCSI ID

Once you've taken care of termination, there's another thing to check, and that's SCSI ID. If the drive is to replace your internal drive, you'll want to keep SCSI ID 0. If not, you'll need a jumper to change the setting.

Setting SCSI ID is simple. Where a pin is supposed to be on, you just place the jumper between the top and bottom pins. Where it's off, you put no jumper in that position.

Table 15-1 shows typical SCSI ID settings for a typical internal drive (based on a popular line of Quantum mechanisms, the Atlas II). I have included the settings for SCSI IDs 8 through 15, for SCSI Wide and faster mechanisms, which have the additional capability when used with a corresponding high-speed SCSI card. Standard, nonwide SCSI drives will have only three ID pins, so column A3 may safely be ignored for such devices.

> **NOTE** *Don't have enough jumpers? Call your dealer or the manufacturer. If you have extras, put them in an envelope and store them in a safe, easy-to-remember place. Or just install them on any two bottom or top halves of an unused set of pins. As long as the top and bottom aren't "linked," they won't affect the drive's performance.*

Internal vs. External: What's the Difference?

Drive ID	Pin A0	Pin A1	Pin A2	Pin A3
ID 0	OFF	OFF	OFF	OFF
ID 1	ON	OFF	OFF	OFF
ID 2	OFF	ON	OFF	OFF
ID 3	ON	ON	OFF	OFF
ID 4	OFF	OFF	ON	OFF
ID 5	ON	OFF	ON	OFF
ID 6	OFF	ON	ON	OFF
ID 7	ON	ON	ON	OFF
ID 8	OFF	OFF	OFF	ON
ID 9	ON	OFF	OFF	ON
ID 10	OFF	ON	OFF	ON
ID 11	ON	ON	OFF	ON
ID 12	OFF	OFF	ON	ON
ID 13	ON	OFF	ON	ON
ID 14	OFF	ON	ON	ON
ID 15	ON	ON	ON	ON

TABLE 15-1   SCSI ID Jumper Settings

Determining the Kind of Drive Mechanism That's Installed

If your drive is already in a case, or it's installed in your Mac, it won't be clear what make and model are being used. Even the model Mac you have isn't a determining factor, as Apple will shop for drives from several vendors, and use any that meet their basic capacity and performance specifications.

Here's a quick (and free) way to check out what hard drive you have: visit Adaptec's Web site (http://www.adaptec.com) and check their Macintosh download area for a copy of their version of SCSI Probe.

SCSI Probe is used to look at your Mac's SCSI chain and see which devices are on it, as you'll see in Figure 15-1. The SCSI Buses pop-up menu at the top can be used to check on devices installed on a particular SCSI bus, if your Mac has more than one.

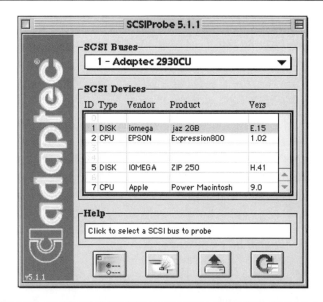

FIGURE 15-1   This is one of the SCSI chains on the author's vintage Power Mac G3

NOTE   *Yes, I know. SCSI Probe was not available in Mac OS X trim when this book was written; perhaps it'll never be. But it's nevertheless a useful utility.*

TIP   *Another possibility is the Apple System Profiler application that is stored in the Utilities folder under Mac OS X. Just click on the Devices and Volumes tab in the application to see the list and location of attached peripheral devices.*

The Safe Way to Install a New Internal Drive

Once you've got the SCSI termination and ID settings configured, here's what to do next:

1. If you're installing a removable drive or other mechanism that requires a special driver, install the software before you install the drive.

2. Power down your Mac and all attached SCSI devices.

3. Remove the case, following the instructions in your manual (most recent Macs have information about adding internal drives).

CAUTION   *If you don't have instructions and your Mac's innards seem too intimidating, don't be afraid to ask a dealer or local Mac user group to assist. There's no sense struggling and possibly breaking delicate cables if the process seems unclear to you.*

4. Touch the power supply or use a wrist strap to ground yourself . `

5. Install your mechanism in a free drive bay, as appropriate. I won't detail the steps here, as they vary from model to model. Your owner's manual should explain how this is done. If you cannot locate the instructions, check with your dealer or visit Apple's Knowledge Base Archive Web site (http://til.info.apple.com) and do a search for your specific type of Mac.

NOTE   *Make sure you have the proper bracket assembly (if one is needed) before you attempt to install a new drive.*

6. Look for a free plug on your Mac's internal SCSI cable. Be prepared to manipulate and push and pull the cables to get them in position. There are too many models (counting Apple products and Mac OS clones) to detail the procedure or the best way to make it function. The key here is that you make sure you are not tearing the ribbon cable (it's delicate) and that you are not bending it sharply.

7. Plug the power cable (the smaller, white one) into the drive.

8. Once installation is complete, close up your Mac, restore all cables, and boot your Mac. If your new drive isn't recognized (a hard drive icon should appear on your Mac's desktop), power down and recheck the mechanism and the installation. It is possible the drive simply was never formatted (see the next section), but if you still cannot get it to work properly after trying to format the drive, don't hesitate to contact your dealer or the manufacturer for assistance.

Not Formatted?

It's a sad fact that some vendors sell hard drives for Macs without formatting them first, and sometimes they'll charge you extra for the software. Before you buy a new drive, ask the manufacturer or vendor to make sure the drive is already formatted for your Mac before you attempt to install it. Insist that they give you formatting software (even if it's an extra cost item) in case you have to reformat the drive later on down the road.

On many occasions, you can use Apple's Drive Utility application, in the Mac OS X Utilities folder, to prepare (format) your drive, using its Drive Setup feature. But with a mechanism without an Apple label this is not guaranteed. The watchword is that if it works, fine, and if not, seek out a third-party, Mac OS X–compatible disk formatter. There's no middle ground.

The Safe Way to Install a New External Drive

The nice thing about an external drive is that you don't have to worry about little jumpers to set, nor do you have to play around with delicate ribbon cables.

1. If you're installing a removable drive or other mechanism that requires a special driver, install the software before you install the drive.

2. Power down your Mac and all attached SCSI devices.

3. Check the instructions that came with the drive for information on setting proper SCSI ID numbers and termination. I won't try to discuss the various combinations of pushbuttons, DIP switches, and other controls here.

4. Install the proper cables from your Mac or other SCSI device to the new drive.

NOTE   *To make matters doubly confusing, some manufacturers don't take into account that a new device may not be the only one on the SCSI chain, so they'll give you a set of cables with the assumption it'll hook directly to your Mac. Be prepared to have to purchase additional cables if the product doesn't have what you need.*

5. Power on the SCSI devices, then boot your Mac.

6. Check the operation of your new device. If it's a regular hard drive, its icon should appear on your Mac's desktop. If your new device isn't recognized, power down and recheck your installation. Follow the SCSI chain configuration suggestions I made in this chapter, and if that doesn't work, contact the dealer or manufacturer for assistance.

Internal vs. External: What's the Difference?

The PowerBook SCSI Port: What Were They Thinking?

I sometimes wonder what sort of logic a company might use in developing a particular feature or in having it work a certain way. It might be someone's inspiration, or a decision on the part of a product development and/or marketing team, or even a focus group, where actual users make the choice.

Such actions come to mind when I get occasional phone calls from folks who still manage to have problems mounting a PowerBook's drive on their desktop Macs. Apple made this possible via a feature called SCSI Disk Mode, but then managed to make its implementation confusing enough to cause consternation on the part of users and dealers alike.

Until SCSI was abandoned in the 2000 models (which have FireWire ports instead), Apple used a space-saving SCSI jack with 30 pins, called HDI-30. Then they developed two types of cables. One of those cables, known as the SCSI System Cable, is used to attach a SCSI device to your PowerBook. At one end is a plug with 29 pins (note that one is missing). At the other end is a standard Centronics 50-pin SCSI plug. The other cable is called SCSI Disk Adapter Cable, and it has the 30-pin plug at one end (no pins are missing) and the same style Centronics 50-pin SCSI plug at the other. This is the one used to make your PowerBook act as a SCSI device when connected to your desktop Mac by way of the last SCSI device on the chain, or with a 50-pin to 25-pin adapter so it attaches right to your Mac.

If your PowerBook is outfitted with the proper cable (and the particular design supports SCSI Disk Mode), when powered up, you'll see a SCSI symbol with the selected ID number parading across the screen. If you use the wrong cable, it just boots normally, though if the other end is attached to a Mac, you might have problems getting it to start.

If you've gone through this hookup process, you know that remembering to get the right cable for the right purpose isn't intuitive. But if you aren't sure, just look at the HDI-30 plug, and see whether it has a missing pin or not.

Or get one of those PowerBook adapter plugs, which have a standard 25-pin SCSI jack at one end and the HDI-30 plug at the other (all pins intact), but use a switch to choose the SCSI mode you want. Better.

When Apple introduced FireWire on its PowerBooks, they did learn something from this little technique, called Target Disk Mode. This method allows the drive on these and other FireWire-equipped Macs that support the feature to mount as a external drive on another Mac.

Adding a SCSI Accelerator Card

When Apple offered Macs with built-in SCSI ports, the question of adding a SCSI expansion card was moot for most users. You didn't need one unless you wanted the largest, fastest hard drives for graphics and video production.

But the newest Power Macs don't include SCSI as standard equipment. So if you intend to add a SCSI device, you are forced to go shopping for an expansion card.

Fortunately, you can buy a basic SCSI-2 card for as little as $50 from most Mac dealers. Manufacturers of such products include Adaptec, AdvanSys, ATTO, Formac, Indeo, and Orange Micro. It's an inconvenience, but one you can deal with. Besides, you may be able to find better solutions using another high-speed peripheral bus, FireWire, and be rid of SCSI hassles forever.

> **CAUTION** *Before using a SCSI card, be certain the product is compatible with Mac OS X. This is not guaranteed, and older cards may never receive the necessary updates for proper performance. If the card isn't compatible, you may want to begin to think about an ATA or FireWire device instead before you buy another SCSI card.*

Single Channel vs. Dual-Channel

Why choose one over the other?

If you have slower SCSI devices, the SCSI chain will slow down accordingly, even if faster drives are connected. If you want to use both fast and slow devices and not have to buy two cards, consider a dual-channel version. It's akin to having a two-in-one card. You can put your slower SCSI devices on one channel, the faster ones on the other, and get the maximum level of performance from each.

SCSI Speeds Compared

Before you select a SCSI card, you'll want to see what sorts of drives you want to use. That is the key to the type of product you'll want to select. You wouldn't want to get something that isn't suitable for your application, and then have to buy another card later on.

> **NOTE** *I won't describe installation of a SCSI card here. Your Mac's manual will have instructions about installing internal cards (if there are slots for them), and Chapter 3 provides hints and tips on ensuring a successful setup.*

Adding a SCSI Accelerator Card

Here's a brief list of six popular SCSI protocols and their potential (a potential that isn't always realized, of course):

It really doesn't make a lot of sense to buy a high-speed SCSI card with low-speed devices; they won't run any faster. You should choose the card based on the drives you have or the ones you intend to buy.

- **SCSI-1 or SCSI-2**   All Macs with external SCSI ports (and most Macs with internal ones) support this protocol, which offers a maximum data transfer speed of 5MB per second. This is just fine for smaller drives, scanners, CD drives, and many removable devices, including SyQuest and Zip drives.

- **SCSI-2Fast**   Maximum speed is 10MB per second. This is good enough for larger hard drives and Iomega Jaz drives. The cheapest SCSI cards offer this capability.

- **Fast/Wide SCSI-2**   The performance level doubles, to 20MB per second. For larger, speedier hard drives, you'll want a SCSI card that provides at least this level of performance.

- **Ultra SCSI**   With a maximum potential of 40MB per second, there are few SCSI drives that'll exceed its capabilities. For anything but the most demanding tasks, this is the card of choice.

- **Ultra-2 SCSI**   This level of performance, up to 80MB per second, is recommended for desktop video and large graphic files. You'll also want to use an Ultra-2 SCSI card for RAID drives.

RAID (short for Redundant Array of Inexpensive Drives) lets you use two or more mechanisms to act as one, which helps speed up hard drive speeds noticeably. Among several RAID protocols, there's also one for "mirroring," which simply means that files are written to two drives at the same time. If one fails, you always have an identical backup. Under Mac OS X, Apple's Disk Utility provides RAID support for multiple devices.

- **Ultra 160**   The top of the line for SCSI as of the time this book went to press, promising throughput of up to twice the speed of Ultra-2. Ideal for content creators and RAID installations.

A Quick Guide to Solving SCSI Chain Problems

The biggest problem with SCSI chains, aside from the need to be a little careful about setup, is that the symptoms of a SCSI chain problem aren't always obvious. Quite often, they'll masquerade as a system extension conflict or a problem with your system software, so you end up having to spend extra time doing a suitable diagnostic routine.

To begin with, for any system crash problems, I suggest you check over the steps I describe in Chapter 18. If they don't help, perhaps these symptoms and solutions will help you arrive at an answer.

NOTE
The Drive Setup component of Mac OS X's Drive Utility application will support many recent hard drive makes and models. But if you have a drive that doesn't have an Apple label or that didn't ship with an Apple product, you may need a third-party formatting program, such as CharisMac's Anubis, FWB's Hard Disk ToolKit, or LaCie's Silverlining (also available as Silverlining Pro). However, as of the time this book went to press, Mac OS X support for those programs wasn't available. If all else fails, get another drive.

Mac Freezes When Copying Large Files

This is a classic symptom of a SCSI chain problem. I suggest you refer to the SCSI voodoo steps described earlier in this chapter to address this problem. A bad hard drive mechanism can also cause this symptom, but that requires a call to a dealer or manufacturer for additional help.

Mac Freezes with Gray Screen When You Boot

This is another prime example of a SCSI problem or a hard drive issue. Follow these suggestions, not necessarily in order, to help deal with this problem.

- Power down the Mac and all attached devices.

- If the drive is internal, disconnect the SCSI cable from your Mac and power up again. If the drive is external, follow the suggestions under the SCSI voodoo section to diagnose the problem.

- If you have an internal drive, and the other steps don't work, it could be your drive has a bad partition map, which is used by a SCSI driver and your Mac to find the location of drive partitions. If (and only if) you have a second internal drive or an external drive with which to boot your Mac, there's a way to deal with this (at least sometimes). But you need to handle this carefully. Don't be afraid to seek outside help if you have any qualms about any of this:

1. Power down and open your Mac's case.

2. Locate the SCSI cable attached to the offending device and remove it. Leave the power cable inserted.

3. Boot your Mac. It should start up normally.

4. Being careful not to touch any metal parts inside your Mac (I said you had to be cautious about this), quickly push the SCSI cable into the drive's jack. This may get the drive to mount.

5. Now this is important. If you're running Mac OS X, launch System Preferences, open the Startup Disk panel, then restart with your Classic (Mac OS 9.x) System Folder.

6. Locate your hard drive software (such as the Classic version of Drive Setup in the Utilities Folder), and launch it.

7. Select the drive in the application window and use the "update" function (available in the Functions menu) to update the hard drive with the problem.

NOTE   *Why not the Drive Setup feature in the Mac OS X Disk Utility application? Simple. No driver update function. All you can do is reformat the drive with that application.*

8. Reboot your Mac. If it works, power down and close the case.

9. If you have a successful result, feel free to return to Mac OS X, courtesy of the Classic Mac OS's Startup Disk Control Panel.

10. Now go ahead and check the offending drive with the First Aid component of Apple's Disk Utility (see Figure 15-2), Alsoft's Disk Warrior, or Norton Utilities for possible directory damage.

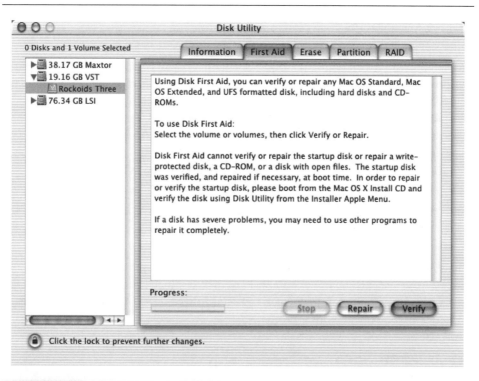

FIGURE 15-2   Use this program to diagnose and repair possible hard drive
directory damage.

CAUTION   *Disk Utility cannot examine a startup drive (this is done automatically at startup anyway), only other volumes, either on the same drive or an external device. In addition, do not use a non-Apple disk repair program on your Mac until you make certain you're using a version that is compatible with Mac OS X. Recent versions of all the major programs ought to work, although you may have to reboot your Mac from the Classic Mac OS version you're using first.*

11. Even if the drive checks out all right, consider backing up your data and reformatting the drive at the earliest opportunity.

12. If the preceding steps don't help you solve the problem, consider replacing the internal SCSI ribbon cable. A bad cable can also produce similar symptoms.

The End of SCSI?

Until recently, all Apple computers had standardized on SCSI for both internal and external hard drives and other peripherals. But that began to change with the advent of Apple's Performa series, when Apple decided to move to a lower-cost peripheral bus, ATA (short for AT Attachment), for internal drives and CD drives. The advantage is that such hard drives are cheaper to buy, and hence Apple lowered the cost of their Macs as well, the better to compete with the rapidly dropping costs of Windows-based computers.

From this humble beginning, the presence of ATA drives on Macs spread rapidly. Soon all PowerBooks had them, then regular desktop Macs (including the iMac) and, of course, the iBook.

What's ATAPI?

This variation on the ATA protocol stands for AT Attachment Packet Interface, and it's used to describe so-called non-hard disk products, such as removable drives. These include such items as a CD-ROM drive, DVD-ROM drive, Iomega Jaz and Zip drives, and similar products.

Master and Slave

Unlike SCSI, you cannot daisy-chain a number of devices. If your Mac supports the feature, you can, however, install a second ATA device in what is called "slave" mode.

If the hard drive's ATA bus doesn't have "slave" support (and this covers pretty much all Macs prior to the Blue & White G3 series), you may find it on your CD drive's ATA bus. A quick look at your Mac's manual will explain how to add extra drives.

CAUTION   *If you don't see an extra set of cable and connectors, there may be no obvious evidence to show whether or not your Mac can support ATA "slave" mode. If it's not mentioned in your manual, contact Apple or consult their technical information library (http://til.info.apple.com) for the details. In addition, due to motherboard revisions, some Macs may support ATA "slave" mode and some not. A savvy drive vendor may also have the answers for you.*

Once you've determined whether you can install a "slave" drive, the process is not much different from installing an internal SCSI drive. First, you need to check if you need a special bracket for the drive and a special faceplate. Then just follow these steps:

1. If your Mac doesn't have one, get an ATA ribbon cable from your dealer.

2. If your "slave" device requires a special driver to be installed (which is usually the case with a removable drive), run the installation now (so you don't have to be faced with the prospect of the drive not working later).

> **NOTE** *Mac OS X includes built-in drivers for Iomega Jaz and Zip drives, FireWire drives, and a number of USB devices, but don't expect to find drivers for any other removable device (such as an Orb or SyQuest drive).*

3. After installation, shut down your Mac.

4. Open your Mac following the instructions provided in your manual. Be sure to ground yourself to the power supply (or use a wrist strap, if available) before you poke around in there.

5. Check your second drive to make sure it has the proper jumper setting to enable "slave" mode. On an Iomega Zip drive, the jumper block has to be removed. Since this setting may vary from product to product, the best resource is the manufacturer or your dealer.

> **NOTE** *Our ever-alert technical editor, Greg Titus, tells us that he's encountered drives with separate jumper settings for master, slave, and alone (intended for a drive to run all by itself), with the "alone" position activated. After adding a second drive to the channel, it was necessary to move the jumper on the master drive from "alone" to "master" to allow the second drive to be recognized.*

6. Install your second drive in an available drive bay. I won't detail the steps here, as they vary from model to model. Your owner's manual should explain how this is done. If you cannot locate the instructions, check with your dealer or visit Apple's Knowledge Base Web site and do a search for your specific type of Mac.

7. Plug in the cable at your "master" drive (if it doesn't already have it there), and run it to the "slave" drive. You may have to fiddle and move and duck and bob and weave around metal fittings to get this to work. There are too

The End of SCSI?

many models to detail the procedure or the best way to make it function. The key is to make sure you are not tearing the ribbon cable (it's delicate) and that you are not bending it sharply.

8. Once installation is complete, close up your Mac, restore all cables, and boot up. Your "slave" drive should be recognized.

Doesn't Work?

If the new drive or removable isn't recognized, make sure that any needed drivers are installed. If they are, shut down, open the Mac, and recheck your installation. If you still have problems, contact Apple or the drive's manufacturer.

Case History

And the Cause of Those Crashes Is . . .

What do you do if your Mac, which has run stably and reliably, suddenly can't stay on for more than a couple of hours before everything locks up tight? This is a question I encountered on a Mac that I use for product testing, a dual-processor G4/500.

The symptom was always the same. Regardless of which program I was using, the computer would just stop running, usually in the Classic mode, although the mouse cursor could be moved. Force quitting yielded no result, and I had to hit the restart button on the G4.

Unfortunately, the problems were not frequent enough to pinpoint a suspect, unless I was willing to stretch the process over a period of days, which I was not about to do. I rebooted under Mac OS 9.1 and ran MicroMat's Tech Tool Pro, which analyzes hardware, and it said everything was in perfect shape. The crashes hadn't even caused any disk directory damage.

Neither clean system installs nor reformatting the G4's 40GB drive improved the situation. There had been no hardware upgrades on this computer, and all it had was a single 256MB RAM module, so there were none to remove.

Then I decided to look at the things I took for granted. As soon as I installed this computer, I placed an Adaptec 2930 Ultra SCSI card inside. It had been installed there for a tape backup drive, and a Jaz 2, and had always run reliably. Removing those devices failed to change the situation. Adaptec's PowerDomain Control software—used to change the settings of the card, such as automatic termination—showed that everything was set to default. In addition, I had installed Adaptec's Mac OS X–compatible drivers prior to moving to Mac OS X, so I should have been in good shape, right?

However, after I removed the card, the system freezes stopped dead in their tracks. Ah, sweet relief....

Adaptec has a great technical support staff, and they agreed with me that I had a defective card and arranged for fast replacement. They even followed up with an email confirmation that it had been sent to me via overnight carrier. The replacement card runs fine, thank you. It just shows that sometimes a solution sits right before your eyes, but you don't see it until you experience a lot of pain and agony.

FireWire: The End of SCSI Hassles?

Sometimes it's known by its official name, IEEE 1394, and sometimes (if you have a Sony product) i.LINK. But the original name is FireWire, and it's an Apple technology that promises to rid the computing universe of SCSI hassles forever. What's more, FireWire is rapidly spreading across Apple's product line, and more and more FireWire products are coming to market.

NOTE   *FireWire is also going to spread rapidly for the "other" computing platform, too, especially in light of Microsoft's endorsement of the technology for Windows XP.*

The first thing you'll notice with a FireWire peripheral is that there's no SCSI ID number to be set, no jumpers or DIP switches to push and pull. Nowhere, no how. And there's no worry about termination, because a FireWire bus doesn't have to be terminated.

What's more, it's hot-pluggable, which simply means that you can connect or disconnect any FireWire peripheral, be it a CD, camcorder, hard drive, printer, scanner, or whatever, without having to turn anything off. If it's a drive, you just have to remember to eject the drive icon from your desktop before you disconnect the device.

Yes, it's true plug-and-play. You finish using your FireWire device, and you unplug it and take it over to another Mac user. Or even a PC user, if they have a computer with a FireWire connection and reformat the drive to the PC disk format.

With a smaller drive, you can even use the FireWire port for power, so you don't even have to worry about finding a convenient AC outlet.

What's more, you can daisy-chain up to 63 devices and use cable lengths of up to 14 feet. There are a few considerations, such as the need for a FireWire repeater hub on a large chain; but compared to SCSI, it's a revelation.

The first time I used a FireWire hard drive, I made sure I tested it in the worst way possible. It was a big 14GB device from MacTell (a company that has since departed to dot.com heaven), part of their FirePower product line. I simply plugged it into my power strip, and then deliberately powered up the drive. Then I connected a cable from the drive to a Power Mac G3 with FireWire port (after installing a driver for the drive, of course). Within seconds, the drive's icon was on my Mac's desktop. Then I dismounted the drive icon, disconnected the drive, and installed it on another Mac with the same result.

Working with one of VST Technology's FireWire drives was also enlightening. Their lower-capacity models don't need AC power; they draw the current from the FireWire port. VST is now a division of Smart Disk, but has retained much of its product line. You can learn about VST's product line at http://www.vsttech.com.

FireWire Limitations

Though it stands head and shoulders above SCSI in convenience and ease of setup, I don't mean to tell you that FireWire is perfect. For example, the first Apple computers to ship with FireWire ports couldn't boot from the drives. In addition, the initial releases of Mac OS X won't support bootable FireWire devices, even from later Macs that can boot from such a drive.

In addition, despite the high performance capabilities of FireWire, many of the early drives barely match SCSI speeds. This is also a short-term phenomenon, being addressed by speedier device driver software and improvements to drive technology.

NOTE *One of the prime reasons for the performance hit is the fact that FireWire drives are usually just ATA devices with electronics to adapt to the FireWire standard.*

But one thing is sure: the arrival of FireWire promises freedom from SCSI chain hassles. And that means one less book chapter to write.

NOTE   *If you want to learn more about FireWire technology, visit the Apple Web site devoted to the subject at http://www.apple.com/firewire.*

Summing Up

The world of SCSI remains a source of headaches and inconsistencies, even under Mac OS X. But with Apple's move to other drive standards, the situation is quickly sorting itself out.

In the next chapter, I'll cover another Mac peripheral category in which problems sometimes arise, scanners.

The End of SCSI?

Chapter 16

Making Your New Scanner Work Better

S o much of the work you do on your Mac amounts to receiving data from disk drives and the Internet. But there is another significant player in delivering data to your Mac: the scanner.

A scanner is, in effect, your Mac's eyes to see the outside world. You use it to digitize artwork and text documents so you can edit them on your computer or send them for someone else to see.

In the not-so-distant past, a scanner was an expensive luxury. Any decent model would retail at well over a grand. By the time you added an option or two, such as an automatic document feeder (for multipage documents) and a slide adapter, for example, you were approaching the two grand level. But, as with computers, the pricing has gone down a lot.

Today, you can buy some very nice scanners for not much more than $100, although the dollars add up if you want to get that slide attachment or an automatic document feeder (if they're available). Either option can fully double or triple the original cost of the product.

NOTE *An automatic document feeder is similar to the paper bay on a printer, because it lets you scan more than one document at a time. This is quite useful if you intend to use your scanner to convert printed documents to text (OCR). I'll cover the subject of OCR in more detail later in this chapter.*

At the same time, professional-grade scanners, the ones beginning at around $750 or so, provide features and image capturing capabilities that approach those of scanners costing many times that figure just a few years ago.

In fact, many graphic artists manage to do some very professional work on scanners that would be quite affordable to any consumer.

The Right Way to Install a Scanner

Although scanning speed, quality, and some features may differ, scanners are usually more alike than different, so you can often follow a basic set of installation instructions to cover most models.

1. Shut down your Mac and all peripherals (this isn't critical if you have a FireWire or USB scanner).

2. Unpack the scanner and remove packing materials.

3. Check the directions for unlocking the scanner's optical assembly (this is important!). The process is discussed later in this chapter.

4. If you have a SCSI scanner, verify the ID and termination settings, and configure as required. SCSI ID adjustments on a scanner may be done by pushbuttons or a little wheel that you turn with a small screwdriver (a very small screwdriver, sometimes). For more information about SCSI chain issues, see Chapter 15.

5. Attach all cables and make sure they are firmly seated.

6. Turn on the scanner and other peripherals, and make sure the scanner's "ready" light is on. If it isn't, check the section entitled "What If the Scanner Freezes?" for advice on how to cope with the situation.

7. If your scanner works all right, boot your Mac.

8. Once the startup process is complete, install your scanning software.

9. After your scanning software is installed, perform a few test scans on photos or printed artwork and make sure everything works as you want. If you are not satisfied with the results of your scans, consult the section entitled "Quick Routes to Better Quality Scans" for further advice.

Scanning Software: The "X" Factor

There's little doubt that Mac OS X shipped without a lot of support for third-party peripherals, particularly scanners. In fact, there wasn't a single scanning or OCR software package supporting Mac OS X available when this book was written, with the exception of a shareware utility, VueScan, which supports a limited number of mechanisms.

As a result, you aren't seeing any illustrations of such software in this chapter. More to the point, if you want to use a scanner, you have to hope and pray that the Classic Mac OS version will function under Mac OS X (and it might for some USB scanners) or restart under the older Mac OS.

By the time you read this book, this situation will probably be remedied. The initial batch of Mac OS X–savvy scanning software should deliver support for the new operating system's spiffy Aqua interface and industrial-strength reliability, but don't expect any great new features.

Later in this chapter, I also mention some popular scanning and OCR applications, but it is not at all certain which of these programs, except for the core applications from the major scanner makers, will be redone for Mac OS X.

The Right Way to Install a Scanner

Checking SCSI Settings and Hardware Locking Switches

The theory goes that you can place a SCSI device anywhere on the SCSI chain, and as long as you make sure there are no ID conflicts, all devices are switched on, and the last physical device is properly terminated, everything should work as advertised. However, scanners tend to be rather more sensitive to SCSI chain positioning than some other products.

Before you try out your scanner, you might want to look at the manufacturer's setup instructions to see if they recommend any particular placement. For example, several Epson scanners I checked before writing this chapter were configured for SCSI ID 2. The documentation only suggested this setting as a precaution, because ID 0 is commonly used for an internal SCSI drive and ID 1 for a second internal drive.

But I have also seen documentation for Microtek scanners suggesting placement at the beginning of the external SCSI chain, and some users report best results if a scanner is located at the very end of the chain.

If the manufacturer doesn't give you guidance, follow the usual guidelines, and check out Chapter 15 for more suggestions on configuring a SCSI chain.

A Warning about Hardware Locking Switches

There's one thing most of the cheapest and just about all of the most expensive scanners have in common. They both contain delicate optical mechanisms that can be damaged if allowed to slide back and forth during shipment. As a result, manufacturers install a special locking switch or screw of some sort to tighten the optical mechanism down.

If you try to use your scanner without unlocking the optical components first, you risk damaging the unit, not to mention the system freeze that may happen when the scanner locks up.

So before you try out that new scanner, look over the installation instructions to find out where the locking assembly is located (if present). I have seen them underneath a scanner, at the rear, or beneath the cover. Whether or not the documentation is clear, such a mechanism will usually have a Lock and Unlock label on it, or little icons that represent the locked or unlocked position.

If you receive a new scanner that hasn't been locked in this fashion, you should contact the manufacturer or dealer right away and arrange for a replacement. If the scanner had a smooth trip to your office, it may work just fine. I had just such a situation with a new high-cost scanner I had received as a review sample for my "Mac Reality Check" column (see http://www.azcentral.com/computing/steinberg for the latest edition). Despite being shipped unlocked, the scanner worked just fine, and it continued to function like a champ throughout the review process (where I subjected it to a lot more abuse than most users might under similar situations).

But the manufacturer said I was lucky. They were apologetic and assured me they would have replaced the unit on the spot if necessary.

However, it's also fair to say that not all scanners have hardware switches. Shortly before writing this chapter, I installed a Umax FireWire scanner for a client, and there was no sign of a hardware lock, nor any mention of such a requirement in the spare setup booklet. The scanner, in fact, worked fine when it was hooked up, so it appears that manufacturers may be moving away from the need to unlock the optical mechanism before use.

What If the Scanner Freezes?

Scanners are complex devices and work by a clever interaction between hardware and software. Among these variations, there is plenty of room for conflicts, and scanners often generate quite a few support telephone calls as a result.

There are several areas where your scanner may suddenly stop working or cause your scanning software or photo-editing program to freeze up. One is due to the regular range of SCSI chain problems, such as improper termination and SCSI ID conflicts, but that's not the only source of trouble.

NOTE   *Just because Mac OS X is designed to handle application freezes gracefully doesn't mean the applications themselves won't behave badly. If the application is native to Mac OS X, you can launch it again or continue to run without it and not have to restart. But if the application runs from the Classic environment, you will want to restart Classic, courtesy of the Classic panel in the System Preferences application. Otherwise, other applications you run from that environment may run badly, just as they did in the old days on a Mac.*

Here are a few other issues that might make your scanning experience less than pleasant. I'm dividing them into SCSI and USB categories, although some of the solutions may overlap.

SCSI Scanner Problems and Solutions

If you run into one of these situations, use the following ideas to help you out:

■ **Scanner freezes when you activate software.** This may be a SCSI chain problem. As soon as the software driver communicates with the scanner, if there's a problem in your SCSI setup, that's where the freeze may occur. But don't overlook the software. Scanning software is frequently updated by manufacturers to address possible conflicts, offer improved features, or just fix bugs. A quick check at the publisher's Web site or the VersionTracker Web site (at http://www.versiontracker.com) can bring forth this information.

■ **Scanner freezes during its startup process.** When you turn on a scanner, it goes through a little self-diagnostic process. If your scanner appears to seize, and an error light or flickering light shows, it may indicate one of two things. You may have a problem on the Mac's SCSI chain that's preventing the scanner from operating (consult Chapter 15 for more information), or the scanner itself may not be working properly. As a test, power down, remove everything from the SCSI chain but the scanner, and make sure it's terminated. Then turn it on. If it still fails to run, contact the dealer or manufacturer to arrange for service.

NOTE *You may also want to verify that the scanner's optical assembly was properly unlocked when you first set it up (assuming a hardware locking mechanism is present on that model). Turn off your Mac and unplug the scanner before you check this out.*

Case History

Getting SCSI Scanners to Work on SCSI-less Macs

When Apple ditched standard SCSI on Macs, they left a whole lot of products without something to connect to. In addition to external hard drives and removable devices, and even some special printers used in the publishing industry, millions of scanners no longer had a place to plug into.

One of my clients, a busy graphic studio, relied heavily on the office scanner, a mid-priced Umax, to capture photos for various brochures and package labels.

The promise of new, ultra-fast Macs finally got the better of the owner, and he ordered his first new Mac in a couple of years, one of the first Blue and White Power Mac G3s. He also selected a SCSI card from a mail order catalog, and within a few days his new computer arrived at his office.

The installation went just fine until I hooked up the scanner. The SCSI chain was fine with just an attached Iomega Zip drive and SyQuest SyJet. But as soon as the scanner was hooked into the chain, SCSI voodoo reared its ugly head. The client used the very same cabling and SCSI settings as he did with his previous computer. The cables were short and had been recently purchased. They were top-quality cables, from one of the large manufacturers.

As soon as the scanner was activated to capture a photo, the computer froze.

The usual range of system diagnosis didn't change the situation (see Chapter 18 for more information on checking for system-related conflicts). A quick visit to the Umax Web site revealed a somewhat later version. We downloaded and installed the new version, but it didn't help.

On the next restart, I went to the SCSI card manufacturer's Web site and found a newer firmware update. The update modified the card's flash ROM with code that was supposed to make it more compatible with the new generation Macs.

Sure enough, after the ROM update, my client restarted his Mac and, with crossed fingers, proceeded to scan a photo as a test. The scanner worked like a charm.

What If the Scanner Freezes?

Getting a SCSI Device to Run on a FireWire Port

Buying a SCSI card isn't your only option in using a SCSI peripheral on a newer Mac. Another alternative is a FireWire SCSI adapter, a little interface module that contains one or two FireWire ports and attaches to the rear of a SCSI device. Such adapters are particularly useful if you have a Mac without a PCI slot, or where the slots are already filled.

The technology has a downside, however. Such devices are usually (but not always) designed for a single SCSI device, and they typically cost more than a basic SCSI card. More to the point, you need a separate adapter for each SCSI device, and this cost can begin to add up.

What's more, not all such devices will work with all SCSI devices. For example, I was never able to mate a vintage Umax PowerLook scanner with a Microtech FireSCSI Xpress adapter for a client's system, despite going through endless bouts of SCSI voodoo. In the end, the client ended up with a simple SCSI card for his Power Mac G4's PCI slot.

USB Scanner Problems and Solutions

The perennial problems that afflict scanners on a SCSI chain are pretty much gone if you get one of these scanners, since the USB ports are free of ID and termination conflicts. You can even hot plug your scanner if you so choose (just remember to install your scanning software first).

However, there are some potential pitfalls you'll want to consider with such a scanner:

- **USB is much slower than SCSI.**   While the bandwidth requirement of a scanner isn't as much as a big, fast hard drive, you should expect it to take longer to capture artwork, particularly a large color picture. If you have "one-slot loading" iMacs or later model or the Power Mac G4, you can benefit from their twin USB buses (only a single USB bus is available via the two USB ports on the older iMacs and Blue & White Power Mac G3). Just plug the scanner into one USB port and the other devices into the other USB port to get the best possible performance. However, if optimum speed is paramount, and you have a Mac with a SCSI port or a SCSI card, consider getting a SCSI scanner, or consider a FireWire scanner if your Mac or iMac has FireWire ports.

NOTE   *FireWire capability can be added to any Mac with PCI slots, so even if your model came without this feature, you can buy an expansion card to add this capability. I cover the subject of adding expansion cards to your Mac in Chapter 3.*

- **Scanning drivers are susceptible to conflicts.**   As with SCSI scanners, there are apt to be occasional conflicts with the software. As Apple continues to update Mac OS X, you'll want to keep tabs on the manufacturer's Web site (or VersionTracker) for news of new versions that may address the specific problems you encounter.

■ **Scanner is not recognized.**   Follow the usual steps, making sure the unit is plugged in and turned on. If you've connected the scanner to a USB hub, you may want to check with the hub's manufacturer about a revised version. For example, some older Macally USB hubs do not open their USB ports until after your Mac has begun the startup process. As a result, they may have trouble recognizing some devices for which software was loaded early in the Mac's startup process. Should you encounter a problem of this sort, contact your dealer or the manufacturer about replacing the hub.

How to Do That First Scan with Confidence

Most lower-cost scanners are designed with software that's supposed to be user friendly. While many people use scanners for work, scanners are also popular simply for capturing family photos and making digitized copies to email to family or friends.

In the past, the manuals that came with a scanner were much like the ones that came with your Mac: big and impressive, well illustrated and with plenty of tips and tricks to get you going, even if you're not a professional computer artist.

With low-cost scanners, printed manuals are strictly bare bones. You get some basic setup instructions and maybe a few pages about capturing an image, but that's about all. The rest of the documentation usually lies on the software CD, in electronic form. Not having to print a large book saves plenty in production costs.

Before you go through the process of learning the intricacies of the software, however, you'll want to get a good basic scan of a color photograph, just as a starting point.

The best way to get started is simply to let the scanning software do its job. Check for an Auto or automatic exposure mode. That way the scanning software will act in the same fashion as the automatic adjustments available on your camera or camcorder. While it may not be perfect for all types of artwork, such a setting ought to be enough to give you an idea how the scanner performs.

Just follow these steps:

1. Open your scanning software. If you're using Photoshop, there will be an Import or Acquire function you'll use to launch your scanning software. PhotoDeluxe has a Scanner option that you use for the same purpose.

2. Once the scanning software launches and appears on the screen, click the Preview or Prescan mode (or whatever it's labeled) to capture the image. When you activate this feature, the scanner's optical assembly will begin

to travel across the length of the scanner, digitizing your artwork. Depending on the speed of the scanner, within a short time you'll see a preview of the image you captured on the left or right of your scanning software's control palettes.

NOTE *Some scanner assemblies work in the opposite fashion. Rather than moving the optical assembly, the paper is transported across stationary optics. One example of this sort of product is the multifunction printer, which offers copying, faxing (not all models include this feature), printing, and scanning all in one unit.*

3. From here, your scanning software will have several options to touch up the photo, but for the purpose of this test, locate the automatic exposure mode (it may not be obvious). You'll need to look over the scanning window for a check box or button that engages this feature.

4. When you're satisfied with whatever adjustments you've made, or you've selected the automatic mode, go ahead and click the Scan button (it's Scan RGB for LaserSoft's SilverFast, a popular high-end scanning application).

5. Within a short time (depending on the size of the image), you'll see the scanned photo appear in a document window in your photo-editing software.

6. If you want to save the file, do it now. Or just discard it and try another photo or piece of artwork in order to get used to the program.

NOTE *Some scanning software includes a direct save option, where you can save your image within the scanning software rather than with your photo-editing program.*

Quick Routes to Better Quality Scans

Once you have put your scanner through its paces and had a little time to get used to the software, you'll want to begin to take advantage of your scanner's features.

You may find, unfortunately, that the scans you've made aren't satisfactory. You try to print them or just view them on the screen, and they're blurry or the color is off, way off. Each scanning program has a set of adjustments you can use to fine-tune your image. If the scanning program is bare bones, the actual image-editing software (be it Photoshop, Photoshop Elements, or something else) can do the task.

There are a few things to consider as you learn the route to top-quality scans:

- **Crop your image.**   For several years, I ran an area on AOL called The Gallery, where members posted photos of themselves. You'd be surprised how many files came in showing a small picture surrounded by the huge scanner bed. Of course, we couldn't accept the photos, since they didn't meet the size requirements we set up. All scanner programs have a cropping tool of some sort, usually an adjustable rectangle that you move back and forth to cover just the part of the artwork you want to capture.

- **Watch your target resolution.**   It's normal to scan at roughly twice the resolution (measured in dots per inch) that you actually need. That leaves enough room for quality loss due to editing the artwork or if you want to enlarge it somewhat. For example, if you're scanning a photo to view on your Mac, use 72 dots per inch as your guidepost, then scan at twice that, 144 dots per inch (or the closest option available in the scanning software). If you plan to print photos at a typical resolution of 120 lines per inch, scan at 240 dpi. If you scan at too high a resolution, file size goes up tremendously, and all you'll end up doing is using excess storage space on your hard drive unnecessarily.

NOTE *The file size also affects the memory required by your image-editing software. The bigger the file, the more likely the software will have to swap file data from your hard drive, thus slowing up performance. Even though Mac OS X has an advanced virtual memory system with optimized performance, there is no substitute for lots of RAM, and image-editing programs need lots of it.*

- **Try the automatic mode first.**   The scanner software will attempt to color-correct the original artwork. But if the preview image doesn't look right, try the scanner's color adjustments to see if you can bring it in more accurately. If the adjustments don't seem to help, go back to automatic mode, and do a final scan. Then try to adjust the image with your photo-editing software. Don't forget that the color quality you see on the screen may not quite match the quality of the color in your printout. In Chapter 10, I cover the subject of using Apple's ColorSync to calibrate your monitor. Many scanners also come with color profiles and software that help you get more accurate color reproduction.

■ **Save in the correct file format.**   If you're scanning artwork for printing, the usual format is TIFF, which provides maximum image quality. If it's for your Web site or to exchange with family and friends, choose GIF or JPEG instead. If you're transferring files to Windows users, you'll also want to read Chapters 7 and 11 for information on how to live in harmony with that other computing platform.

■ **Don't make it too large.**   Scan at a higher resolution if you want to make the image very large. An example is a slide. If you need to enlarge the picture 8 or 10 times or more, you'll want to increase scanning resolution proportionately, so the quality is retained. Otherwise, the little dots that make up bitmap artwork will just get very large, too, and quality will suffer.

OCR Trials and Tribulations

Back in the 1970s, when you wanted to convert a document to text for editing on a typesetting system, you either had to go through the tedious process of retyping everything or have it sent to a firm who handled optical character recognition (OCR).

OCR technology uses various forms of computer logic to recognize and convert printed text to a file you can edit. In those days, equipment that performed this task was very expensive, far beyond the budget of the average user.

Today, the technology has advanced to the point where many scanner makers give you OCR software as part of the package, for no extra cost. As stated in "Stuck with Bundled Software?" you can buy an OCR package if your scanner didn't come with one or you don't like the accuracy level of the one you have.

One thing I'll say at the outset: no OCR program is letter-perfect. No matter how good the program or the source document, you will almost always have to go back and fix something in the translated file. Worse, such errors are unpredictable, not the typical ones a human typist will make. So it may take spell checking or proofreading to find the mistakes.

But here are some things you can do to get the maximum possible OCR accuracy:

■ **Use a clean document with large, readable type.**   Small type, unfamiliar or artistic typefaces, smudges, and pen and pencil marks will confound the OCR program and will make accurate recognition difficult. Material in 10- or 12-point type in a common typeface such as Helvetica or Times will be easiest to handle. If you must edit the text, try doing it on your Mac after you've recognized the material.

■ **Avoid faxed originals if possible.**   In the past, some fax software packages actually came with OCR components, but not anymore. The reason is that a fax provides poor text resolution. It may be fine for reading, but not so fine for OCR software to recognize accurately. If you must work with a fax, insist the person who sends you the material use the "fine" resolution mode where available. Also, large type and easy-to-read faces (such as Helvetica and Courier) tend to offer the best chance of accurate performance.

■ **Keep the scanner bed clean and orient the paper properly.**   Smudges on the glass or paper tilted one way or the other will also give the scanning software fits. Although such programs as Caere's OmniPage Professional are designed with techniques to straighten tilted copy, the results never seem to be quite as accurate.

■ **Watch out for thin paper or newsprint.**   If text is visible on the back of the document you're copying, the OCR software will capture that text, too, resulting in gibberish. If you must use this sort of document, try backing it up with a few sheets of paper to make it more opaque. If your OCR software has a brightness control, turn it down slightly and see if you can get better quality; it may just work if the actual text you want to scan is clear and dark.

NOTE   *Some OCR programs simply launch your scanning software to capture the image, before they extract text from it. If you have this sort of program, the actual brightness setting will be made in the scanning software.*

■ **Dot matrix is a hassle.**   The small dots that make up the characters can also confuse the OCR's built-in logic. If the OCR program has a dot matrix option, try that (although in my experience it only does a little bit better that way). Another trick is to make a photocopy of the document, which will tend to smooth out the little dots and make recognition more accurate.

■ **Use the training feature.**   Some programs are trainable, which means you can flag common errors and save the corrected characters in a special preference or dictionary file. These files tend to have a limited capacity, but they can help you resolve the common mistakes and save wear and tear on your blood pressure.

■ **Try the OCR software's spell check feature.**   You can usually spell check your recognized document before you save it in its final format. This will help you flag many of the mistakes on the scanner's preview screen, and it may also help you adjust its training feature to recognize those mistakes (assuming the scanning software has a training mode).

How to Do That First Scan with Confidence

Twain vs. Plug-In: Any Difference?

Scanner software comes in several forms. You may get a simple standalone application that you can launch just like any program and do your scanning chores. More often, though, the software comes as a plug-in (add-on) for an image-editing program such as Adobe Photoshop Elements or Adobe Photoshop. To activate the software, you'd need to use the Import or Acquire function.

Another type of scanner driver uses something called TWAIN, which, strangely enough, stands for Technology Without An Interesting Name. With a single TWAIN scanning driver, you should be able to work with any program that supports the technology, without having to install extra copies or get special versions for those programs.

In practice, there aren't a whole lot of programs that support TWAIN these days. Adobe's Photoshop Elements and Photoshop recognize TWAIN drivers, but two of their other major programs, Illustrator and InDesign, do not, nor does another desktop publishing heavyweight, QuarkXPress.

NOTE   *On the other hand, the latest version of Microsoft Office has full support for TWAIN and many scanners work just fine with this great business software suite. In addition, the current version of Word has a few image-editing tools (such as eliminating the red-eye effect that's caused by some camera flash attachments).*

In practice, this is not anything to be concerned over. Whether the scanning software comes as a program plug-in, a TWAIN driver, or both, if it works to your expectations, that is all you need be concerned about.

Stuck with Bundled Software?

Your new scanner comes with a CD filled with bundled software, beginning with the scanner drivers, and usually including an image-editing program and possibly an OCR program. You could very well be perfectly happy with the programs you get.

But you are not forced to use those programs. For example, if you receive Adobe's entry-level image-editing package, PhotoDeluxe (since replaced by Photoshop Elements), you can choose to install a much more powerful alternative, Photoshop, instead.

As far as the basic scanning software is concerned, if you feel the one provided with your scanner is, well, a little too basic for you, perhaps you'd like to try something more powerful. You can consider such programs as LaserSoft Imaging's SilverFast (which is bundled with some Epson scanners) or Second Glance Software's ScanTastic (which is also used to make some HP scanners compatible with Macs).

Summing Up

Whether you just want to capture a family photo, or edit a complicated legal document, a scanner can be an almost indispensable option for your Macintosh. In this chapter, I gave you some tips and troubleshooting techniques to help you get your scanner and software to work at top efficiency.

In Chapter 17, you'll learn the secrets of getting the best possible networking performance from your Mac, from sharing files with a family member's iMac to sharing files with users of that other platform (a subject also covered in Chapter 11).

How to Do That First Scan with Confidence

Chapter 17

Overcoming the Network Hassle

Apple often says that education is in its DNA, which explains its sharp focus on that market. But, if we're looking at the company's DNA, networking is also pretty high on the list. From the very first day the Mac was unleashed on the world, it was set up for networking. At first, it was just with Macs and laser printers. You could share the office printer among all Macs. But the ability to print a file was only half the battle. What if you had to make a copy for another user on another Mac? In the old days, you just took out a floppy disk or media from a removable hard drive, and walked over to the other user. Sneaker net is good exercise, of course—it keeps you healthy if you get enough of it, but it's time consuming if you have to send and receive files on a regular basis from one or more coworkers.

That's where computer networks became important. In the days of System 6, you could either use Apple's AppleShare software and establish one computer as a central repository of files (a server), or use one or more unsupported programs that would make it possible for you to share files directly with other users. But the personal file sharing feature we take for granted today wasn't available.

File Sharing Basics

Throughout this chapter, I'll offer hints and tips to get the best possible network performance on your Mac. But first let's pause for a few basics on file sharing with a Mac.

The Fast Way to Share Files

If you just want to open up the contents of your drive to a family member or coworker without any limitations to access, here's what to do:

1. On the Mac from which you want to share files, launch the System Preferences application and choose the Sharing panel (see Figure 17-1).

2. Click the Sharing button. Within a few seconds, it'll be on. Once sharing is activated, anyone on the network can access the contents of your drive (which is why you will want to consider specifying access privileges, as explained later).

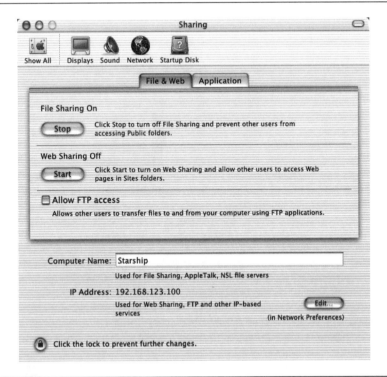

FIGURE 17-1   Engage File Sharing from this preference panel.

3. To access the shared Mac, click on the Go menu in the Finder and choose Connect to Server. You'll see the dialog box displayed in Figure 17-2.

NOTE   *If you are accessing a shared Mac while running in an older Mac OS version, just open the Chooser, select AppleShare, and choose the shared computer from among those listed. The rest of the access process is quite similar.*

4. If you don't see a separate listing with the IP number or name of the Mac you want to access, click on AppleTalk for an AppleTalk network or Local Network, and you'll see a list of available computers on the network. When you see the name of the computer, click on that name; the IP number will appear in the Address field.

FIGURE 17-2 Select a computer from this list.

NOTE *Mac OS X is not only capable of checking Macs on the network, but servers running Windows NT and Windows 2000 (and no doubt Windows XP, but I didn't have a chance to test it out when this book was written) and Unix servers running SAMBA. If all is configured properly on those computers, network access should be transparent. You'll see the correct name of the computer and can access it using the same process I'm describing here.*

5. Click Connect to bring up the login prompt for that computer. If the computer is on the network, you'll see the standard login prompt where you need to enter the name of the administrator of that computer and the password (see Figure 17-3). As an alternative, you could just enter the name of another user of that Mac, but you're access would be limited to that user's files.

TIP *If the computer's name isn't listed, type the IP number in the address field (using the prefix to represent the type of network, such as afp:// for a standard Mac network and smb:// for a Windows or Unix server).*

FIGURE 17-3   Log into the other computer here.

> **NOTE**   *Keychain is a feature that first debuted in Mac OS 9. It lets you store many of your passwords in a single file (itself password protected) for simple access.*

6. If you want to add the login to your Mac's keychain, click the Options button. In the next dialog box (see Figure 17-4), check Add Password to Keychain, and click the Save Preferences button to store the settings.

7. Once you've logged into the other computer, you'll see a dialog box where you can select the volumes you want to access on your Mac. In a moment, perhaps after a short bout with a spinning cursor, the shared volume will appear as an item with a network icon on it.

> **NOTE**   *By "volume," I'm referring to the items that are being shared. They are not necessarily entire drives. They may also be one or more folders or one partition of a drive. The "volume" containing a user name, for example, is that user's folder on the shared Mac. Turning on file sharing on a Mac without customizing access will, in essence, share whatever drives are connected to that Mac.*

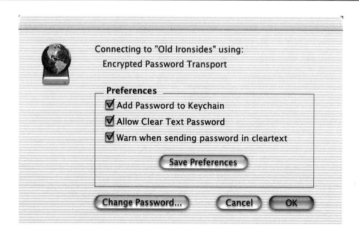

FIGURE 17-4   Add your login to your Mac's keychain here.

8. When you're ready to turn off file sharing on the other Mac, return to the System Preferences application, choose the Sharing panel, and click Stop. You'll see a warning prompt where you can specify a delay for actually turning sharing off and send a message warning that it's going to occur (see Figure 17-5).

This technique is basically the easiest possible method to use file sharing. It makes the entire contents of the shared Mac available to anyone who logs in on the network.

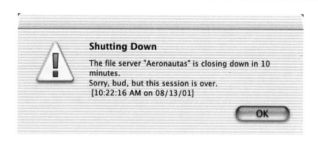

FIGURE 17-5   This is your final warning. So get ready.

Setting Access Privileges

By default, a "guest" user gets read-only access to the contents of the Public folder for each user on your Mac. Inside the Public folder is a Drop Box folder, to which a guest can write but not read files. This is probably the file sharing method least fraught with danger or configuration problems, because it requires no special setups, and there's no need to give out a password to access a share.

But if you want to fine-tune the access of other users to a networked Mac to allow differing access levels, you need to set up access privileges. This will let you control which users can log on and read and write certain files and which cannot.

The settings are made by selecting the item you are sharing, whether it's a folder, file, or drive, and then choosing Show Info from the Finder's File menu. True, the Users and Groups feature of Mac OS 9 is history, but the substitute method should work just fine in most situations.

There are three levels of access privileges to set. For the Owner or administrator (you), for the Group (which is the default group that Mac OS X establishes), and for Everyone, meaning all the others who might access your Mac.

Granting Access Privileges to Shared Macs

There are several levels of access that you can configure, depending on which access category you select (only Everyone has all four available), as shown in Figure 17-6.

FIGURE 17-6 Choose the appropriate access privilege for your situation.

File Sharing Basics

Here's the list:

- **Read & Write**   Anyone can access and modify the item.

- **Read Only**   Items can be opened but not changed.

- **Write Only (Drop Box)**   You can set aside a Drop Box (not shown) in your Shared directory, where files can be placed but not modified.

- **None**   Need I say more?

Here's how you set access privileges under Mac OS X:

1. Activate file sharing via the Sharing panel of the System Preferences application.

2. Select a folder or file that you want to share.

NOTE *Why didn't I mention a disk? The way Mac OS X is set up, only the administrator or owner of a Mac can access an entire volume, by logging in remotely with your user name and password. If you want to give out this information to family or trusted employees, they will be able to access everything on your Mac across the network or via the Internet, using your Mac's IP number.*

3. Go to the Finder's File menu, and choose Show Info, which brings up the window shown in Figure 17-7.

4. Click the pop-up menu next to each category to choose options. By default, the Owner has Read & Write access. If you want to limit this to Read Only (but why?), click on the pop-up menu and choose that option.

NOTE *Grayed out options do not apply to that specific category.*

5. After making your selections, click Apply to activate the settings.

6. Repeat the preceding steps for each file or folder you want to share.

FIGURE 17-7   This is Mac OS X's way of setting file and folder access privileges.

> TIP
>
> *Got access privileges problems? The various Mac OS X versions can sometimes foul up access privileges on your Mac, so you can no longer modify a file or folder. One useful way to sort things out is a shareware program from Gideon Softworks, Get Info. This handy utility also sports a batch mode, to handle multiple access changes, plus a way to change type/creator information on a document. You can find this and other handy Mac OS X utilities at the VersionTracker Web site (http://www.versiontracker.com/macosx/).*

Once your settings are complete, only those who are granted proper access rights can read or write the files on your shared Mac.

Fixing AppleTalk Network Troubles

Your Mac networks via AppleTalk (especially older Macs) or TCP/IP (the native language for Mac OS X). This networking capability is part of your standard Mac OS installation, so you don't have to do a thing to get it. Using AppleTalk, files are transferred, however, via Ethernet, which first coexisted with LocalTalk, but now has replaced it entirely on all recent Apple computers.

NOTE   *The initial release of Mac OS X had no support for AppleTalk networking, which meant Macs using system versions prior to 8.6 wouldn't appear on a Mac OS X desktop as a share. Beginning with Mac OS X 10.1, however, this shortcoming was remedied by the addition of AppleTalk networking support.*

While being supplanted under Mac OS X with TCP/IP networking, AppleTalk is basically a very robust network protocol. But from time to time, you will find that it no longer works as it should. When trying to figure out why you are having troubles with your AppleTalk network, here are a few simple troubleshooting techniques to help you solve the problem:

■ **Is it just one Mac or all of them?**   The first thing you should do when troubleshooting your AppleTalk connection is to find out if the problem affects only your Mac or if it is a group problem. If it is just one Mac, make sure the cables are connected and that AppleTalk is turned on. Check the AppleTalk Network panel of Mac OS X's System Preferences application or the Chooser on a Mac running an older Mac OS. On an older Mac, check to see that the right network connection (LocalTalk or Ethernet) is selected in the AppleTalk Control Panel; this is understandably confusing if you have a LocalTalk printer and an Ethernet network for sharing your Macs, but you need to use Ethernet for Mac OS X. If the settings are correct, move the Mac to another location on the network. If it now works, it could be your cabling or, if it applies, your network hub or switch.

NOTE   *You should not have to put up with a split network setup. You can easily get a LocalTalk-to-Ethernet adapter module, available from such companies as Asante and Farallon, so your LocalTalk Macs or printers mate with your Ethernet network. No more network switching! This is a must for Mac OS X, where there's no support for LocalTalk networking.*

Mac OS X includes a program that you can use to "ping" a network. You'll find Network Utility in your Utilities folder. When the application is launched, just click the Ping tab to use the feature, which works in a fashion similar to sonar or radar. It will send a signal across the network, and wait for an echo from the devices on the network. Using this information, you can look for dropped packets, which would indicate a problem on a specific device.

■ **If the hardware is at fault**   Look at the cables. If there's no obvious physical damage, swap the cables with the ones on another Mac, or use a spare. If the cable checks out, look at your network hub or switch. Check to see that the link and activity lights for the port you are looking at are lit and show activity. If the lights are on but there seems to be no activity, try moving the network connection to another port on the hub or switch and see if both lights become active on the new port. If the port is functioning properly, you should see the link light come on, provided that the Mac is plugged into the network on this connection. You should also see a small amount of activity, indicated by the flickering of the activity light. Another good test is to look at the port you disconnected the cable from. If the link lights do not go out once you remove the cable, you can assume the port is probably defective. If the Mac still does not work on a new port, you need to try either a different network hub or switch to see if that works.

■ **Serial printer issues**   When Apple removed serial ports on Macs and went to USB, many of the headaches of working with a network yet using a personal printer went away as well. But if you have an older Mac with a standard serial port, you'll face the old bugaboo about having to turn off AppleTalk when the printer is hooked up to the printer port. And that, of course, conflicts with use of your network, where AppleTalk must be on. One possible solution is to see if the printer's manufacturer has a network card. For example, Epson and HP supply Ethernet and LocalTalk network modules for some of their products. Another solution is to attach the printer to the modem port, then use a switch or port switching software, if you need to work with several serial devices (such as a modem or another serial printer).

CAUTION *Just because you can get a network card for your printer doesn't mean it'll work with Mac OS X. While writing this book, I struggled with the JetDirect 300X card to which my HP DeskJet 990c printer was attached; it never showed up in the Print Center application and a solution wasn't immediately forthcoming.*

■ **More than one Mac has the problem.**   If your Mac is one of many that cannot access the network, check the components they have in common. Normally, this is the network hub or switch where all your network connections are brought together. When a large number of computers all have network trouble, you should first look at the hub or switch to make sure it is still alive. In almost every case, you will discover either that the hub or switch has failed, or that someone has misconfigured the switch. If the hub or switch has failed, you will need to replace it with a good one. If the programming on the switch has been changed, you will need to get the original programming restored so that all your Macs can once again access the network; consult the manual that came with your networking hardware on how to check and change the setup.

■ **Check Ethernet drivers for Ethernet cards.**   When your Mac has an Ethernet card installed to provide support for a faster standard, make sure the software provided by the manufacturer is installed. Such products generally require custom drivers and will not run with the standard networking stacks provided under Mac OS X. You will probably need to check the company's Web site to see whether updated software is required for Apple's industrial-strength operating system.

File Sharing Headaches

Even when the network is working just fine, hardly a day goes by when I don't receive a call from someone who has a problem getting file sharing to work properly. For the most part, the solutions are simple. Setups aren't correct; preference files are damaged. Some of the problems are more obscure and take some troubleshooting to resolve.

Here's a mixture of both—problems and solutions to help you understand the file sharing hassle.

Can't Turn on File Sharing

You switch file sharing on, and, whoops—it won't activate. You get the dreaded message that file sharing can't be enabled. Here are some ways to resolve the problem:

■ **Enter or reenter your Network Identity information.**   In order for you to share files, your Mac has to have an owner's name. When you configure your Mac with the Mac OS X Setup Assistant, your computer will bear the name of its owner, such as "Gene Steinberg's Computer." While this won't be a problem if you're networking via TCP/IP, where the numbers rather than the name are considered for access, a naming conflict can foul up your AppleTalk network. You'll want to make sure that the name you give your computer is not the same as another on the network. I ran into a situation of this sort once, where there were four Macs named "Don's Computer" on the network, and he wondered why he couldn't access any of those computers. After I turned off file sharing and renamed each Mac, when file sharing was switched on, the problem was history.

NOTE   *In theory, the network should have been polled during the setup process to check for a conflict, but these computers were moved around a bit, so the safeguards might not have come into play.*

■ **Zap (reset) the PRAM.**   Hold down the COMMAND-OPTION-P-R keys at startup, and wait for two or three startup tones to sound before releasing them. This step will clear network and serial ports. I've seen it, on rare occasions, clear up network problems.

■ **Check for extension-related conflicts.**   In Chapter 18, I cover the process of figuring out if a particular control panel or extension is causing a performance problem for the Classic environment. While this shouldn't affect anything in your Mac OS X environment, you'll want to keep Classic lean and mean for the most reliable performance. You'll want to review that chapter before you do anything more drastic (such as the next suggestion).

■ **Reinstall the Mac OS.**   This seems a drastic step, but if all else fails, it may be your next approach. Since I cover the subject fully in Chapter 2, I'll refer you to that chapter for information on the best way to reinstall your system software for both the Classic and Mac OS X environments.

Fixing AppleTalk Network Troubles

Can't Connect to a Networked Computer

If your problems are at the other end—you cannot connect to the networked computers—you'll find that some of the previous suggestions, such as checking for extension conflicts, resetting the PRAM, and reinstalling system software, are things to consider. But first you'll want to look over these problems and solutions:

- **AppleTalk is off.** As mentioned in the earlier section entitled "Fixing AppleTalk Network Troubles," AppleTalk has to be on the network (unless you're networking via TCP/IP, the standard protocol for Mac OS X). Make sure it's on in the Network panel of the System Preferences application and in the Chooser on Macs running an older Mac OS version. If you must use a serial printer on an older Mac, check the item concerning serial printer issues in the section "Fixing AppleTalk Network Troubles" for more advice.

- **Wrong username and password.** Quite often when you access a shared Mac, the Registered User dialog will display *your* name and password, not the information from your networked computer. You'll need to reenter the correct information. You may also want to verify the information first, especially if the password is complicated.

- **Recheck your access privileges.** Make sure the owner of the shared Mac has granted you access privileges. If not, you won't be able to access the shared disk or disks. Even if you can network with that Mac, you'll still want to double-check that you can see the files you need to work on and read or write to them, as necessary.

SyJets and File Sharing

Although SyQuest has gone belly up, a successor company (SYQT, Inc.) still sells the products and arranges for repair. While the SyJet drive, a 1.5GB removable device, still performs well for many users, it seems to have a conflict with file sharing, at least on some older Macs. If you have a SyJet cartridge in the drive when you turn on file sharing on one of those older Macs, you'll get a message that it cannot be enabled. The solution is to eject the cartridge, switch file sharing on, and when it's activated, reinsert the disk.

Getting Started with Ethernet

Ethernet has become the standard method of networking Macs these days. The older, slower LocalTalk connections have been removed, along with serial ports and ADB ports.

Before I explain how you work with Ethernet, it is useful to discuss the background of this high-speed networking standard that has come to dominate the Macintosh universe (yes, even the new AirPort wireless networking system has an Ethernet link).

A Brief Ethernet History

Ethernet was developed at Xerox PARC laboratories in the mid-1970s by Bob Metcalfe, who later was one of the founders of 3Com—the manufacturer of modems, networking hardware, and (until the company was spun off) the Palm Organizer.

NOTE   *As you no doubt recall, this is the very same place where Apple founders Steve Jobs and Steve Wozniak were inspired to develop what later became the Mac operating system. Where's Metcalfe these days? Well, as a Vice President for International Data Group (IDG), he used to write an excellent, sometimes humorous, commentary for InfoWorld, a magazine designed for PC network managers, and he also loves Macs. Unfortunately, Metcalfe's column has since been retired.*

At the start, Ethernet was designed as a high-speed network standard for large network-based printers. I remember, in fact, when I would add Ethernet cards to various Macs to communicate on a network with color printers and imagesetters. Over the years, Ethernet developed from being used in sophisticated network setups to being the most common network format around.

Ethernet has supplanted LocalTalk for Mac networks in recent years. In fact, every Apple computer you buy has Ethernet as standard equipment; LocalTalk isn't even supported for Mac OS X. And a number of Windows-based computers also include Ethernet either as part of the original installation or as a low-cost upgrade.

Today's Ethernet Standards

The most common types of Ethernet you will encounter in your home or office are 10BaseT and Fast Ethernet, also known as 100BaseTX. Fast Ethernet was first approved in 1996. Newer Power Mac G4s support 1000BaseTX, or Gigabit Ethernet.

All Mac computers, even the iMac and iBook, support the two slower standards and will automatically switch from one to the other, depending on what's supported on the network. These types of Ethernet use low-cost, twisted-pair network cabling, which simply looks like thick modular phone cable.

Getting Started with Ethernet

The 10BaseT Ethernet standard supports transmission speeds up to 10 megabits per second, 100BaseTX at 100 megabits per second. Compare this to LocalTalk speeds, which run about 230,000 bits per second. This begins to add up, especially when you want to transfer large files, or send large, graphic-heavy documents to a printer.

A Realistic Look at Speeds

This business about being able to transfer data at 10 or 100 megabits per second has to be qualified. Obviously, you cannot send any files faster than your Mac's hard drive can read them, nor receive files any faster than your drive can copy them. If the network is busy transferring data among different computers and printers, there will be a slowdown, as capacity isn't unlimited (call them packet collisions), and processing overhead from your computer's system software will also add a performance bottleneck.

At the very least, you can expect real-world Ethernet data transfer rates to be several times that of LocalTalk on a 10BaseT connection, and quite higher (though not 10 times higher) for the Fast Ethernet setup. Gigabit Ethernet is expensive, and it is sensitive to quality of cabling and equipment. So it will not, in turn, be 10 times faster than 100BaseTX, but it's still plenty fast if you are willing to pay the price for a hub or switch and need to transmit huge files on a regular basis.

The Quadra Had It First

While Macs until very recently had LocalTalk connections as regular issue, Ethernet came later. The first Mac to have an Ethernet port right on the logic board was the Quadra 700, released in 1991. Since then, most Quadras and all subsequent desktop Macs, with the exception of some of the Performa models, have offered Ethernet. When the iMac was unleashed on the personal computing world in August 1998, it was the beginning of the end for LocalTalk. The iMac didn't have it, and, instead, supported both 10BaseT and 100BaseTX.

NOTE *Just for general information: older Macs had nonstandard Ethernet ports, called AAUI (short for Apple Attachment Unit Interface, though it was used on some Windows-based computers, as well). In order to connect to an Ethernet network, you need a special interface module, called a transceiver. Beginning with the so-called PCI generation of Power Macs (7500, 8500, 9500, and so on), Apple has incorporated RJ-45 Ethernet jacks, which don't require a special interface module.*

The Future of Ethernet

As with CPU processing speeds, Ethernet technology isn't standing still. The newest technology, Gigabit Ethernet, made its debut on the Power Mac G4 desktops in the summer of 2000, and may, one day, appear on other models in Apple's product line. As the name implies, it's theoretically capable of data transfers that are 10 times faster than Fast Ethernet, although speeds may be much lower in the real world.

The Gigabit Ethernet standard was first set up by a task force in 1996 and is slowly impacting large corporate networks and educational institutions that require the fastest possible networking.

It's not something, however, that will turn up on a large number of consumer personal computers any time soon. For one thing, Gigabit Ethernet cards still can cost upward of $250 each (assuming you have a Mac without the feature), with switches and hubs reaching the low four figures (I hesitate to be specific on pricing, as it changes often).

It'll probably be a while before the technology becomes more prevalent, and pricing reaches a point where the products are cheap enough to be incorporated on the motherboard of the iMac, the iBook, and the PowerBook. And that assumes you'd be able to use the tremendous level of performance.

NOTE   *In the last edition of this book, I had suggested that Gigabit Ethernet would eventually show up on a Mac. That happened six months after I wrote the comment. I wonder how long it'll take for the rest of the line to gain this feature.*

Common Sense Ethernet Advice

If you have an older Mac and were used to networking with LocalTalk, I'm sure Ethernet may seem somewhat intimidating to you, with all the complex buzzwords about BaseT and so on.

However, actually setting up an Ethernet network is quite simple—it's no more difficult than connecting a cable here, a cable there, and making a couple of settings; and since LocalTalk isn't supported under Mac OS X, there is, as they say, no choice other than to join the program.

Ethernet: The Fast-and-Dirty Method

If you have only two computers or just want to connect your Mac to a printer, you don't need anything more than a single Ethernet cable. But not just any old

Ethernet cable (unless you are going to get ahold of a hub (a central connection module). Instead, you need to purchase an Ethernet crossover cable. A crossover cable is, as the name implies, different from a regular Ethernet cable because the first two wires (typically black and yellow) are swapped with the last two (typically red and green) at one end of the cable.

> **NOTE**
> *Sad to say, not all computer dealers understand what a crossover cable is, so be certain you are getting what you asked for (prepackaged cables will have the proper label). If the cable isn't covered with a rubberized fitting, and has a clear plug, you can also visually inspect the cables at both ends, to make sure that the proper cable is being provided. The clever folks at Apple, by the way, designed the PowerBook G4 with a "smart" Ethernet port, which can work just fine with either cable; perhaps this feature will eventually spread to all Macs.*

Ethernet: The Regular Way

If you intend to connect more than two computers or combinations of computers and printers together, you will need either an Ethernet hub or an Ethernet switch. Both the hub and switch are designed to connect all your Ethernet devices together so they can communicate with each other. What's more, they don't depend on having all devices on at the same time. All you need to turn on are the actual devices that will be networking and file sharing on the Macs that will be making files available to other computers. This means you can turn on a single Mac and a single printer to get some output, and any two Macs to share files, without regard to whether anything else on the network is running.

> **NOTE**
> *The big difference between a switch and a standard hub is that the switch creates virtual circuits between the two Ethernet devices that are talking. A hub creates a single circuit that is shared by all the various Ethernet devices.*

Activating Ethernet

For Macs running Mac OS X, there's nothing to configure. Ethernet is active by default. If a networked computer is running an older Mac OS version, however, you'll need to make sure that the proper network port is set up in the AppleTalk Control Panel. LocalTalk is the default for older Macs, and even on Macs where

LocalTalk isn't present, a network setting could have been left on AirPort, for example, by mistake.

NOTE

One of the great features of Mac OS X is multihoming. This means all network ports are always active, and the computer can switch, as needed, from one to the other without having to change a setting.

The main thing you need to do is make sure that the speed and duplex options are set correctly for your network and that the Ethernet frame type is also set correctly. On Macs with only 10BaseT connections, you cannot change the speed or duplex options on the Mac. However, if you are accessing your network via the TCP/IP Control Panel on a Mac running a Classic system, you can choose between using the 802.2 Ethernet frame type, the default, and the 802.3 frame type, known also as Ethernet II, the frame type frequently used on Novell networks.

AirPort Networking Basics

Apple's AirPort wireless networking system ushers in a new area of connectivity, especially for home and small office users. Rather than having to go through a complex process of wiring nooks and crannies of an office, under the carpets or inside the walls, you can situate your Power Macintosh G4, Cube, iBook PowerBook, or iMac (second-generation model) wherever it is convenient for you.

You do not even have to be near a telephone line, as the AirPort Base Station can serve as a network router for your Internet connections, too. AirPort's maximum range is 150 feet, but that's far more than you'd need for most setups, unless you place computers on another floor or at different ends of a larger office. You can also wire up banks of AirPort Base Stations in a "roaming" configuration, somewhat similar to a cell phone network.

NOTE

The ability to log on to the Internet and share a connection doesn't work with AOL's dial-up numbers. However, you can access AOL if you connect first through a regular ISP.

In addition, the Base Station has a regular RJ-45 Ethernet jack, so you can attach it to a regular wired network. That keeps your wireless installation connected with a regular Ethernet network.

Getting Started with Ethernet

Setups Are Easy

Once you have installed an AirPort card on a Mac that supports the feature, and set up a Base Station (if needed), you just install Apple's AirPort software, if it's not already present on your Mac (and it usually is on new models). The AirPort Setup Assistant (see Figure 17-8) can be used to configure your network setup. While you're connected, a handy system menu icon (activated in the Network preference panel of the System Preferences application)—or a Control Strip module for the Classic Mac OS—will report on signal strength, so you'll know if you're close enough to get solid networking performance. The display is not unlike what you see on your cell phone's display.

In use, AirPort networking is no different from a regular wired network. You can share files, surf the Internet, and play games, as you prefer. About the only area where it may fall down is in speed. Apple rates AirPort at 11 megabits per second, somewhat faster than a traditional 10BaseT Ethernet connection (but, as you'll see shortly, only if you network via TCP/IP). If you're using Fast Ethernet, you may see an impact, but otherwise you'll never see any particular difference. The possible exception is when you're at the extremes of its operating range, where it's always possible AirPort will step down to a lower speed to maintain signal integrity as signals degrade.

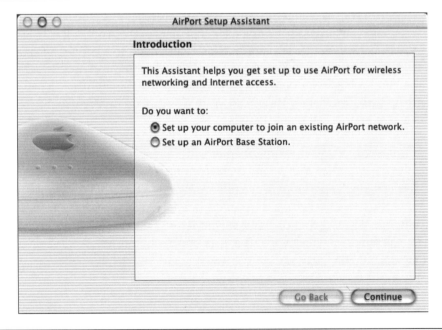

FIGURE 17-8   The AirPort Setup Assistant lets you go wireless in seconds.

NOTE
The AirPort Base Station is designed to support up to 10 users with good performance. If you plan a larger network, you'll want to fit it with extra Base Stations and set up extra access points for them. These are the equivalent roughly to zones on a regular computer network. As explained preceding, you can also have AirPort Base Stations sharing a wired connection run in "roaming" mode, so the signal is shared across all units, in the fashion of a cellular phone network.

Is AirPort Exclusive to Apple?

True, Apple Computer has been known to embrace unique standards that create hurdles when third-party companies try to be compatible.

But AirPort is based on a worldwide standard, IEEE 802.11b, more commonly known as Wi-Fi. In theory, any company that makes a product that's compatible with the standard could make it work with an AirPort network. An example would be Asante's AeroLAN and Farallon's SkyLINE.

A PC that has wireless networking ports that support Wi-Fi ought to be able to network with AirPort, though the considerations of cross-platform network connections would still have to be followed. There's no free ride in this sort of setup.

On the other hand, having an international standard also means you don't need an AirPort Base Station at the center of your wireless network. You can go computer to computer on Macs with AirPort cards, and you can even access wireless routers from such companies as Asante and Farallon. In fact, while writing this book, I was accessing my wireless network courtesy of an Asante FriendlyNET Wireless Cable/DSL Router.

NOTE
Since Microsoft's Windows XP operating system has built-in support for Wi-Fi, you can expect an explosion of devices to exploit the standard, perhaps even extending it to handheld devices, such as Palm OS products.

Networking via TCP/IP

While AppleTalk networking isn't going to disappear just yet, it's not the only option available for you to network your Macs. Mac OS X has native support for TCP/IP, the same protocol you use to talk to the Internet after you've established a connection to your Internet service provider. In fact, Mac OS X shares many attributes with servers used by ISPs and Web hosting services, by virtue of the fact that it includes the Unix-based application, Apache, for one-click Web sharing.

Networking via TCP/IP

TCP/IP, short for Transmission Control Protocol/Internet Protocol, is set up via the Network preference panel of Mac OS X's System Preferences application or your TCP/IP Control Panel in the Classic Mac OS. It lets you access another computer or printer on your network, using its IP address (the unique information that identifies the specific device to which you want to connect).

If your Mac is part of a large network, this information will be established by your systems administrator and you'll want to consult that person about proper setups. In such installations, the network server, for example, would typically assign the IP address dynamically.

But you can also use TCP/IP networking on a regular peer-to-peer Mac network, even if you don't have a predefined TCP/IP setup. You'll find your Mac's IP number conveniently displayed in the Network and Sharing preference panels under Mac OS X, or the File Sharing Control Panel for the older Mac OS.

NOTE   *If you can't find the IP number, don't despair. It's also displayed in the Apple System Profiler application, available in Mac OS X's Utilities folder. When you launch the application, click on the Network Overview arrow to see the list.*

Once your network information is available, you just enter the IP number of the Mac you want to access when you bring up the Connect to Server window under Mac OS X; typically you'd enter it as a URL, such as afp://<put number here>. Under the Classic Mac OS, when you click on the Chooser and select AppleShare, you'll see a button labeled IP number, where you can conveniently enter this number.

Is It Faster?

Your mileage may vary. Apple won't officially say whether changing your network setup will provide any greater level of performance. Their technical information document on the subject fits in the "maybe yes, maybe no" category.

When it comes to an AirPort network, however, TCP/IP is the hands-down winner. Wi-Fi works much more efficiently this way, and you're apt to find serious slowdowns if you choose to network via AppleTalk instead. The same thing applies for Macs using the Classic Mac OS; this shortcoming isn't well documented, but I ran into it when I reviewed an AirPort system once, and talked with Apple executives about slow file sharing performance. When I went the TCP/IP route, performance was much better.

How to Protect Your Files on a Network

Just as your access to the Internet requires a username and password, similar protections are available when you share files from your Mac. However, the concept of personal file sharing also means that security measures with some added controls are, at best, skimpy.

Here are a few suggestions for maximum security (within the limitations of the process):

- **Give yourself a hard-to-guess password.**   The principles that apply to creating a password with your ISP apply here as well. Use a combination of letters and numbers, random if possible (write it down, of course). Don't use birth dates or your lucky number, or any other password someone is likely to guess.

- **Configure Mac OS X's Multiple Users feature.**   Set up a separate user account for each person who will be using your Mac, or password protect your Mac OS X screen saver. Once everything's set up, you can use the Log Out command from the Apple menu or let the screen saver activate to block access to your Mac (making sure that the Use My User Account Password option is selected under Activation in the Screen Saver preference panel). Otherwise, someone can get to your Mac and delete or change the password in the Users preference panel.

- **Get security software.**   At the time this book was being written, Intego's FileGuard and DiskGuard, and Power On's DiskLock and OnGuard, were both being developed to support Mac OS X. These programs will all, with various degrees of security, let you prevent unauthorized users from gaining control of any Mac system, from disk to file level (depending on the settings). That way, someone cannot simply go to the computer directly and mess with the file sharing configuration.

- **Set access privileges.**   Assuming you have your Mac under control, customize access to the various files and folders on your Mac, as I explained in more detail in the next section, "Setting Access Privileges on Dedicated File Servers."

- **Consider a file server and server software.**   Apple's AppleShare software and Mac OS X Server give you centralized control of user access and privileges. A server computer puts needed files for the network in one place, for convenient access by everyone and the maximum possible level of protection. A server setup is probably best suited for the larger Mac networks, though I've seen such programs used in installations with as few as 10 or 15 computers and a handful of printers.

Setting Access Privileges on Dedicated File Servers

You want to know how your files can best be protected from tampering. With the peer-to-peer file sharing setups described earlier, you can set a file for read and write access, read access only, write access only, or no access at all. You can grant these rights to the owner of the file—the person who creates the file—a group of users, or everyone. In limiting the number of users and groups to which you can apply permissions, the Macintosh OS significantly limits your ability to lock down your files—that is, unless you help it along.

There are other options that will provide that help. Two are direct from Apple: AppleShare IP and Mac OS X Server (the advanced version of Mac OS X, sporting the same Aqua user interface). Both are client-server programs that provide robust tools to administer a network.

Another option requires that you explore that other computing platform, and this option is especially applicable if you are in a mixed-platform environment. It involves setting up a server using Windows NT, Windows 2000 Server, or Windows XP. These setups don't suffer from the limitations of personal file sharing if you set privileges using the network administrative tools they provide.

With AppleShare IP, Mac OS X, or the Windows-based server options, you can set the file permissions right from the server, so that one group of users has write access to your files while another has read access only. These are especially valuable options to consider if you need to assign large numbers of users various types of file and networked volume access.

If you are using one of these solutions, you need to spend the time to set up your file permissions so that they give you the maximum amount of flexibility in how you access your files, and still limit the ability of other users on the network to make changes. As explained earlier in this chapter, Mac OS X's built-in SMB networking support makes the process of accessing those servers (and Unix-based SAMBA servers) no harder than sharing with another Mac.

However, setting up a Windows NT, Windows 2000, or Unix server is no cakewalk. It requires a lot of attention to detail and a lengthy process—more so if setting up an email server (such as an Exchange server for Windows) is part of the process. You'll find yourself wandering through many complicated dialogs and configuration setups. But if you do follow basic setup instructions carefully, you'll find it an alternative that is at least worth consideration, particularly on a large computer network.

NOTE   *Still another option is the networked hard drive, such as the Quantum Snap. If simple file storage is all you need, and you don't want to tackle complicated setup and maintenance, this might be an option to consider.*

Summing Up

Networking on your Mac, whether under Mac OS X or the Classic Mac OS, is usually just a matter of turning on file sharing, but as you see from this chapter, sometimes you need to do more to protect your files or ensure best possible performance.

While Mac OS X frees Mac users from many of the problems caused by adding a system utility of one sort or another, such problems can still occur when software behaves badly. Living in two operating system environments makes things all the more complicated. I'll tell you more in the next chapter.

How to Protect Your Files on a Network

Chapter 18

Adding System Utilities and Overcoming System Conflicts

Talk about reliability—no, make that lack of reliability. My first Macintosh froze up within two hours after I turned it on. For a second, I thought the message was kind of cute: a "bomb" icon within a white, rectangular screen.

But the result wasn't quite as cute. The keyboard froze, the mouse froze, and I was left without the ability to get any work done. I tried clicking on the convenient Restart button on the screen, but it did absolutely nothing. So I had to force a restart (I cover this topic later in this chapter, in the section "Forcing a Restart").

It was my first encounter with the realities of personal computing. Computers are not appliances, no matter what the advertising copywriters tell you. They can and will crash at unexpected, inconvenient moments.

This chapter is designed to focus on a number of areas that can make your Mac look better and work better. That, in itself, will be useful. But the arrival of Mac OS X has made the situation all the more complex, because you will be living with two operating systems, and you will encounter two ways of configuring things and two areas where problems may arise.

Before you reach for the aspirin, read on.

The Classic Appearance Control Panel and Mac OS X

Apple did wonders for the look and feel of your Mac desktop when they introduced the Appearance Control Panel (see Figure 18-1), beginning with Mac OS 8. Many of the features for which you formerly had to use third-party system extensions are now comfortably handled with Apple's software.

However, the arrival of Mac OS X has given Classic Mac OS Control Panels a sort of limited functionality, with most features disabled (even though they clearly show up when the Control Panel is launched).

Before I explain how you can set up the Appearance Control Panel for good performance, let me tell you what it can't do:

> **NOTE**   *Remember that whatever settings you make here can only work within the Classic environment. They don't show up in the Mac OS X Finder or in a native application.*

■ **Themes**   Sorry, no can do. While the themes you select will show up if you reboot under Mac OS 9.1 or 9.2, under Mac OS X, the desktop pattern

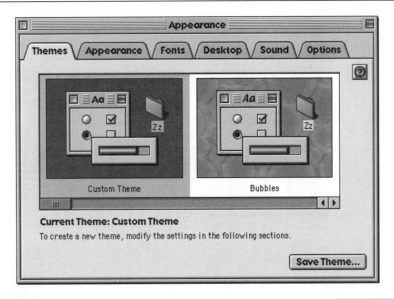

FIGURE 18-1   Some of the features of the Mac OS 9.1 Appearance Control Panel still work in Classic under Mac OS X.

selected in the Desktop panel of the System Preferences application is the one used. So scratch this option.

■ **Appearance**   Yes, you can use an add-on that changes the look of menus and titles, and you can continue to alter highlight color within the Classic environment.

■ **Fonts**   The fonts used to display such things as menus and the ability to switch off anti-aliasing within the Classic environment can still be controlled as before. It's still a good idea to switch off the Smooth All Fonts On Screen option (see Figure 18-2), because anti-aliasing will never be as good as it is under Mac OS X.

NOTE   *Even if you turn off font smoothing, you may find it turns on again when you do a clean system software installation or switch themes. If it returns, revisit the Fonts tab in the Appearance Control Panel and turn the feature off again.*

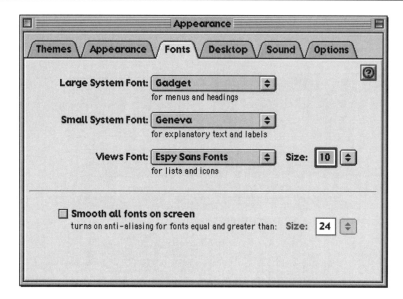

FIGURE 18-2 Turn off font anti-aliasing to avoid a smeared look of text in Classic.

- **Desktop** What you do here only becomes visible when you reboot under Mac OS 9.x. You needn't be concerned about such settings unless you need to run in your older Mac OS from time to time.

- **Sounds** Yes it works for Classic applications, but I've always found the feature annoying rather than entertaining.

- **Options** Both scroll bar modification and the window shade feature (double-clicking on a title to minimize a window to the title bar) still work in the Classic environment.

Desktop Makeovers and Mac OS X

It seems as if each operating system upgrade provides fewer and fewer options to beautify the Mac desktop. However, it doesn't mean there are no opportunities for third-party software developers to get in the game.

Here's what Mac OS X 10.1 offers, in its own limited way.

■ **Desktop preference panel**   To alter the standard Mac OS X backdrop, just open the System Preferences application and click on Desktop (see Figure 18-3). Either drag an image to the well or choose from among the ones supplied by Apple. In a few seconds, your desktop pattern will change to the picture you've added.

■ **General preference panel**   The remaining appearance changes are done via the General preference panel (see Figure 18-4). You can change between Blue and Graphite themes, and alter highlight color. The font anti-aliasing threshold can be varied from 8 point to 12 point, but it can't be turned off.

Desktop Decoration Programs: Good or Bad?

Does such a limited array of choices with which to alter the appearance of your Mac OS X backdrop mean that you have to settle for less? Not necessarily.

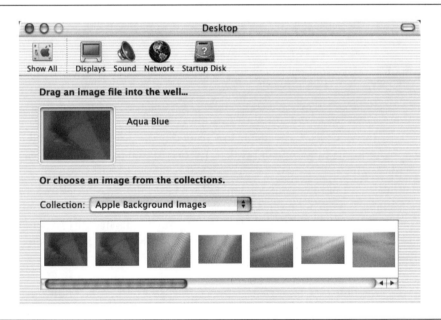

FIGURE 18-3   Change Mac OS X's desktop picture here.

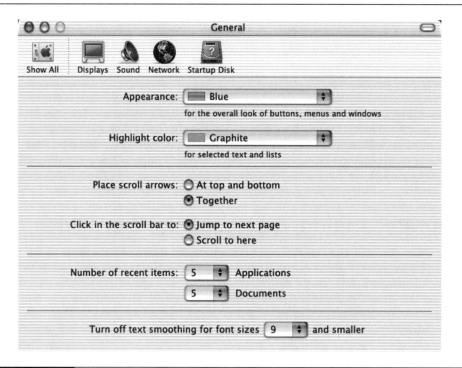

FIGURE 18-4   Make your remaining appearance adjustments here.

There are a number of enterprising third-party software developers who were busy working on Mac OS X enhancements from day one. Some just looked to the Darwin core, to locate hidden features that, for one reason or another, weren't activated by Apple.

One utility that I have examined, TinkerTool (see Figure 18-5), allows you to change system and application fonts and turn font smoothing on or off, or configure the threshold. There are limits to this clever utility, such as its inability to control the standard Mac OS X Lucinda Grande font and the fact that some applications will ignore the settings.

NOTE   *As of the time this book went to press, it wasn't certain just how the changes to the Dock under Mac OS X 10.1, which allow it to be moved to the left and right of the screen, and the ability to change the threshold for font smoothing, will affect TinkerTool and other utilities. More than likely, they'll just adapt and add a different set of options.*

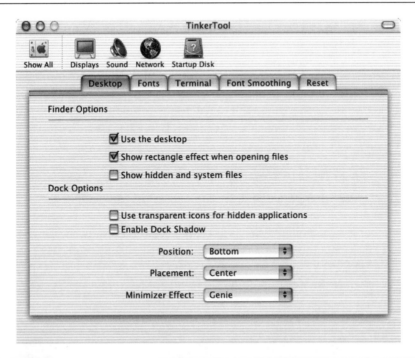

FIGURE 18-5   TinkerTool can configure some of the hidden features of Mac OS X.

Another Mac OS X product category is the theme switcher, which can morph your Mac OS X desktop with a new look. Similar to what Kaleidoscope did for the Classic Mac OS, such programs as the MetaMorphX and Xmorph are designed to take you away from Aqua and into totally new territory.

NOTE   *The authors of Kaleidoscope have, alas, decideJump Table Head too many obstacles to developing Section Titlesion. Unless they change their minds Warning Body B this particular utility will remaiNote Headc-only option.*

NOTE   *As with ClaCross Table Body Aterface makeovers, changes to MCross Table Body Bake theme utilities incompatible. I cannot, for example, show you how MetaMorphX and Xmorph look, because Mac OS X 10.1 made existing themes for these applications incompatible. However, that was expected to be addressed by the time you read this book. In the end, recheck compatibility with the publisher's Web site before you try an appearance-changing utility.*

Desktop Decoration Programs:
Good or Bad?

Use Classic System Enhancements with Few Problems

Even if your visits to the old Mac OS are limited to the Classic environment, you don't have to settle for the look and feel of Apple's Open and Save dialog box. There are programs out there that will make it look different, wider, and more robust, with extra added features. Consider ACTION Files (see Figure 18-6), Default Folder, or DialogView.

NOTE *What about Mac OS X's Open and Save dialog boxes? Why mess up a good thing? But no doubt there will be ways to change this, too, over time.*

What about the font menus? Wouldn't it be nice if they showed you the font in WYSIWYG fashion, grouping fonts by families in submenus? And what about telling you what sort of font you have, PostScript or TrueType? Try ACTION WYSIWYG Menus, Adobe Type Reunion Deluxe, MenuFonts, or TypeTamer.

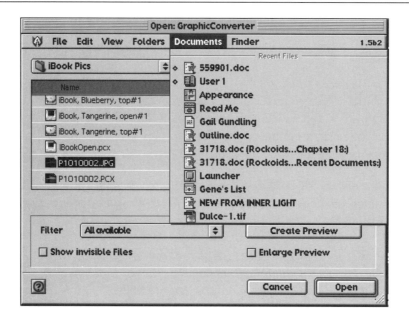

FIGURE 18-6   ACTION Files owes a lot to the original SuperBoomerang in its methods and appearance.

NOTE   *Unfortunately, none of the font menu modifiers appeared destined for Mac OS X. For one thing, there are two font menus, the Carbon version, which looks the same as the one you see in Classic, and the Font Panel, for Cocoa-based applications. Maybe Apple will eventually sort out this confusion.*

Don't like Apple Menu Options (the program that puts up those submenus in the Classic Apple menu)? Would you like similar submenus to appear anywhere on your Mac's desktop with a click here or there, or maybe by pressing one keyboard combination or another? More full-featured solutions include ACTION Menus, BeHierarchic, and MenuChoice.

NOTE   *None of the things that these utilities do will have any impact on the Mac OS X environment.*

Almost anything you can imagine, some enterprising programmer has probably found a way to perform the task. However, if you are going to be using your Classic Mac OS strictly within Mac OS X, it's best to be cautious. You may end up finding out that the system utilities you used to cherish are now more trouble than they're worth. But don't despair. Every day, more and more handy Mac OS X utilities appear that not only fill in the gaps in the core operating system but present possibilities never dreamed of in the Classic Mac OS.

TIP   *If you need to capture screen images for documentation, consider SnapZ Pro X, an all-new version of my favorite screen shot utility and the program I used to gather all the illustrations for this book. The Mac OS X edition of this shareware utility comes in two forms; the high-end version adds the ability to capture QuickTime movies. It's shareware, from Ambrosia Software, and don't forget to pay the fee if you like it.*

A Guide to Using System Enhancements

This little guide can serve well for both the Mac OS X and Classic environments. With thousands of possibilities for mischief here, I won't even try to list the conflicts of any particular program. More to the point, the authors of these programs are usually dedicated and responsible and responsive to handling problems when they occur.

Use Classic System Enhancements with Few Problems

If you take a few precautions, you'll find some wonderful ways to enhance your Mac computing experience:

- **Don't install two or more enhancements that do the same thing.** Whether it's a dialog box enhancer or font menu modifier for Classic, or a theme enhancer for Mac OS X, pick only one. If you choose any two programs that have the same function, they will quite possibly prevent one another from working properly. At worst, they'll just crash. If you're not sure whether you like one program or another, try each separately (making sure the other has been disabled, if it becomes a Login application), then make your decision.

- **Watch diligently for updates.** Any time Apple updates its system software, the very same system tools that allow such enhancements to work may be changed. Programs that enhance Finder or basic system functions are especially vulnerable. It's not a bad idea to check such Web sites as VersionTracker to look for a new version. Some authors or publishers may even have mailing lists, and they'll let you know about a new version and what is fixed or changed.

- **Be careful about using older system enhancements with new system versions.** That program that may have worked perfectly fine on your Mac five or ten years ago may fail miserably with your Classic Mac environment. Even under Mac OS X, a once-handy utility may suddenly stop working due to the rapid and sometimes unexpected changes in the new operating system. If you cannot find a newer version out there, consider removing it. Perhaps there's something newer that'll work just as well.

NOTE   *A very notable example was ApplWindows, a utility from the early 1990s that, among other things, allowed you to instantly switch to an open document window and hide all applications other than the current one. Mac OS X's Dock can, with native software, let you go right to an open window. A freeware utility, ASM, can handle the other chore, application hiding (a COMMAND-OPTION click on a Dock icon does it, too); ASM even puts up an old-fashioned, Classic Mac OS application menu at the right end of the Mac OS X menu bar.*

- **Pay your shareware fees.** Many of the best system enhancements are shareware. You don't pay for them in advance, but the authors expect you'll send them the small fees if you continue to use the program after a 15- or 30-day trial. If you want these programs to be updated and enhanced, so you can continue to use them as Apple upgrades its operating system, you'll want to make sure you reward them for their work.

> NOTE   *It's a sad, sad fact that only a small fraction of those using shareware programs ever pay for them. While some publishers, such as Ambrosia Software, manage to keep going under these conditions, others simply stop writing software or join commercial publishers and produce the same programs at much higher prices.*

How to Check for System Conflicts

When your Mac crashes, it can be a frustrating experience. It usually happens when you're in the midst of doing a complex job, which taxes your Mac's capabilities, and you're minutes away from having to deliver the document to someone in your office or a business contact.

With so many thousands of system and software and hardware combinations, it's inevitable that problems will arise from time to time. There is no possible way for me to list every conceivable possibility of a conflict. No book can be that large. Instead, I'll cover the ways you can isolate the cause. Once you do that, you can stop using the offending program or seek out help or updates from the publisher.

Since Mac OS X often forces you to live in two operating system environments at the same time—at least as long as you need to use Classic software—I'm going to separate the two in this section of the book. So even if some procedures are the same, it'll be perfectly clear what steps apply to which operating system.

Classic Mac OS System Crashes: Finding the Cause

The most vexing sort of system problem is the one that isn't consistent. One day everything is fine, the next day, your Mac crashes at an unexpected moment, in a program that never gave you a lick of trouble before.

This sort of problem is part and parcel of the personal computing experience. Software has bugs, the operating system has bugs, and until computers are truly as elegant as your basic toaster oven (although even a toaster oven may, at times, burn your toast), you can expect such happenings as a normal part of your computing experience.

Even the arrival of Mac OS X didn't deliver perfect software/system harmony, although things are much better. But I'm getting ahead of myself.

While your older software can, with some exceptions, work just dandy in Classic (sometimes even faster), in other areas you are going to have to find alternatives. Such programs that talk to hardware, such as CD burner and scanning software, won't run. You have to seek Mac OS X alternatives.

NOTE   *While Apple has included CD burning software in Mac OS X, the version I checked for this book couldn't make a disk-for-disk copy or a bootable CD. That job is left to the Mac OS X versions of such applications as Roxio's Toast.*

But even if you avoid the hardware pitfalls, what do you do if your Classic environment continues to freeze? The best solution is simply to run lean and mean.

Making Classic Run Faster and More Reliably

Without doubt, the Classic environment of Mac OS X is its Achilles heel. Forget about Mac OS X's industrial-strength stability. Any application that runs under Classic is no better behaved than it was if you booted your Mac under an older OS, although sometimes (except for 3-D games) it may run faster.

Worse, the first time you run a Classic application, you have to endure a wait of up to a minute or more for Classic to start. The first step in optimizing Classic performance is to make it a startup application so it boots whenever you start or log into your Mac, and then I'll show you how to configure the environment to run as reliably as possible.

But first things first.

1. To configure Classic to boot whenever you boot your Mac, first launch the System Preferences icon.

2. Click on the Classic preference panel (see Figure 18-7).

3. In the list, select the startup volume that contains the Mac OS 9.x System Folder that you want to use.

4. To make Classic boot at the end of the startup process, click the check box that is labeled Start Up Classic On Login To This Computer. From here on, at about the same time the Mac OS X Finder loads, so will Classic.

5. If you prefer to get Classic going right away, click the Start button.

6. When you're finished, quit System Preferences.

NOTE   *Did I miss anything? All right, you got me. There's also an Advanced tab in the Classic preference panel, but I'll get to that shortly.*

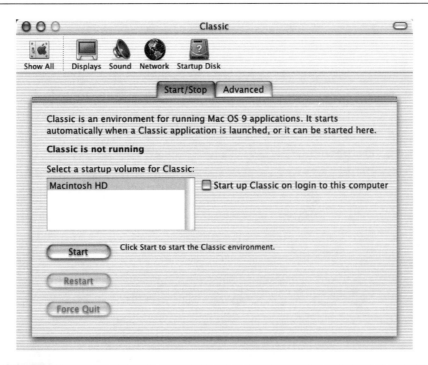

FIGURE 18-7   Configure Classic for optimum performance here.

Now that Classic has become, in essence, a startup application or process under Mac OS X, the next step is to make it run as reliably as possible. And that takes us to that Advanced feature:

1. When you're ready to fine-tune Classic, launch the System Preferences application from the Dock or the Applications folder.

2. With System Preferences up and running, click on the Classic preference panel (again take a look at Figure 18-7).

3. Now here's what you've been waiting for. Click on the Advanced tab (shown in Figure 18-8) to fine-tune your Classic setups. The Advanced tab offers three choices to consider in the Startup Items pop-up menu.

   ■ **Turn Off Extensions**   This is the equivalent of holding down the SHIFT key when starting up in the Classic Mac OS. When you choose

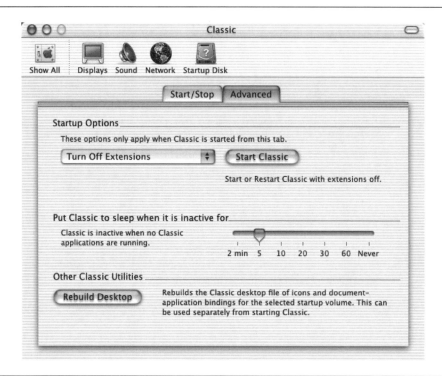

FIGURE 18-8   You can make Classic behave well (or at least better) with a little fine-tuning.

this option and click Start Classic, your Mac OS 9.x system software will start with extensions off. This isn't the most efficient way to run Classic, particularly since it also turns off video acceleration and will make window drawing much slower. But if chronic crashes greet your efforts to use Classic, this is a way to see whether it's an extension conflict, or you simply need to reinstall your Classic system.

■ **Open Extensions Manager**   When you choose this option and click Start Classic, it'll be the equivalent of holding down the spacebar if you boot normally from Mac OS 9.x. At the startup of the boot process, Extensions Manager will appear. This gives you a chance to change startup sets or turn off extensions that might be causing you trouble.

■ **Use Key Combination**   This is an awesome command, if you compare it to the usual brand of keyboard combos. Rather than the standard two-letter shortcut, you can type up to five keys, in succession, to trigger a launch of Classic. But there's no reason to go beyond the obvious—COMMAND-C-L. If you make a mistake, you have to click the Clear Keys button that appears to make a new decision.

4. So what choice should you make? I'll choose Option B, Open Extensions Manager. Once Extensions Manager appears (see Figure 18-9), pick the Mac OS 9.x Base set from the Selected Setup pop-up menu.

5. Once selected, go to Extension Manager's File menu and choose Duplicate Set. You'll see a dialog box where you can give the set a new name.

NOTE *Why am I putting you through all this if the Base set is enough? Well, you can't modify a Base or All extensions set, so if you want to add new extensions to the list, you have to have a new set in which to list them.*

6. You can call it whatever you like (even "Hassle-Free Set"), but Classic Set might be easiest. This new set is nothing more than a copy of the Base set you selected. Consider it a building block for stability.

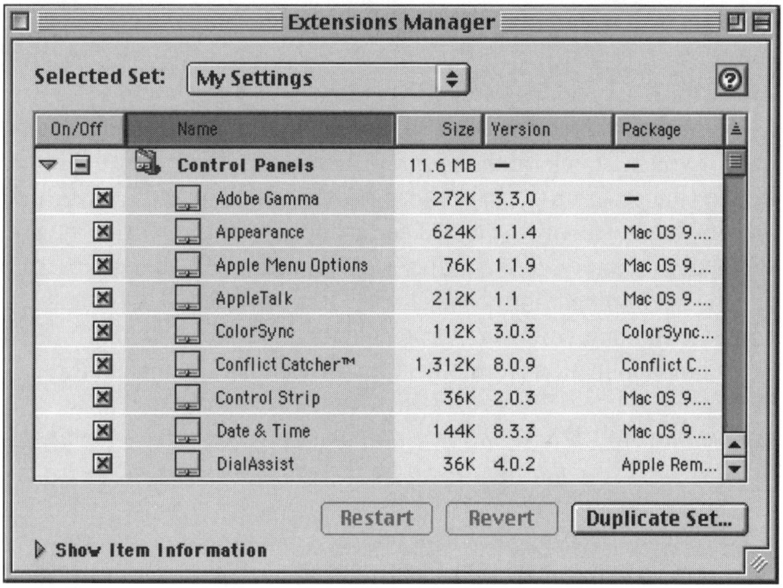

How to Check for System Conflicts

Extensions Manager

| Selected Set: | My Settings | ⬥ | ? |

On/Off	Name	Size	Version	Package	⬥
▽ ⊟	**Control Panels**	11.6 MB	—	—	
☒	Adobe Gamma	272K	3.3.0	—	
☒	Appearance	624K	1.1.4	Mac OS 9....	
☒	Apple Menu Options	76K	1.1.9	Mac OS 9....	
☒	AppleTalk	212K	1.1	Mac OS 9....	
☒	ColorSync	112K	3.0.3	ColorSync...	
☒	Conflict Catcher™	1,312K	8.0.9	Conflict C...	
☒	Control Strip	36K	2.0.3	Mac OS 9....	
☒	Date & Time	144K	8.3.3	Mac OS 9....	
☒	DialAssist	36K	4.0.2	Apple Rem...	

Restart   Revert   **Duplicate Set...**

▷ Show Item Information

FIGURE 18-9   Change startup sets here.

7. Click Extension Manager's close box to dismiss it and continue the Classic startup process. From here on, you'll be running the Classic environment as reliably as possible.

> **NOTE** *Can you do the same with Casady & Greene's Conflict Catcher? Absolutely. But you'll have to hold down the spacebar at startup, or just click the Conflict Catcher menu bar icon in a Classic application to bring it up. Also, remember to use version 8.0.9 or later for maximum compatibility with Mac OS 9.1 and 9.2. Earlier versions produce a serial number prompt every time you boot Classic.*

Is this the end of the process? No, as soon as you run a Classic Microsoft application, such as Office 2001, your Classic Mac OS System Folder will be populated with a handful of extensions from Microsoft. You can, if you want, also restore other extensions with fingers crossed, to see if they operate under Classic. But the best approach is just to take it easy on the extras for the most reliable performance. In the end, if all or most of your favorite Mac applications migrate to Mac OS X, you won't have to fret over Classic.

Forcing a Restart   If your Mac freezes up, there are several ways to get out of the situation and make it restart. Here are the common methods:

- **Force quit**   Press COMMAND-CONTROL-ESC. You should see a window asking if you want to force one of the listed programs (see Figure 18-10) to quit. If you do, click on the program to select it, then click the Force Quit button (the program you were using when you accessed Force Quit is usually, but not always, selected automatically). If this works, the program will quit gracefully. If it's a Classic program, you'll have to restart the Classic environment for good stability. If it's a Mac OS X program, just continue running your Mac. Protected memory has walled off the offending application from others, to provide maximum stability.

> **NOTE** *Sometimes, you'll have to force quit an application twice for the process to "take." If you quit the Finder, it'll relaunch shortly all by itself.*

- **Force quitting the Dock**   If the Dock is misbehaving—showing applications that aren't supposed to be present, or as launched when they're not launched, or just freezing up entirely—here's the solution: Process Viewer. Just locate this handy utility in the Mac OS X Utilities folder and

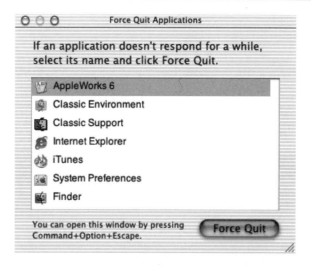

FIGURE 18-10   Choose an application, and then click Force Quit to dismiss it.

launch it. From the list of running processes, select Dock (see Figure 18-11), and then choose Quit Process from the Processes menu. The Dock will vanish for a moment, then relaunch, all safe and sound.

■ **The "Three-Fingered Salute"**   This is a tried-and-true method to restart many (but not all) Macs. If your Mac hangs at the Force Quit attempt, or freezes entirely, this is a way to make it restart. How do you do it? Depends on the Mac. For the iBook, PowerBook, and older Macs with ADB keyboards, press COMMAND-CONTROL-POWER ON. If your Mac supports the feature, it'll restart. This command sequence won't work on later generations of Macs using USB keyboards and mice, or on some PowerBooks and older Macs. What's more, the famous Apple Pro Keyboard doesn't even have a power switch. So you have to resort to the next method.

■ **Press the Reset switch**   Where is it? Depends on which model you have. On older Macs, there was actually a small switch with a little left-pointing triangle that you used to force the restart process. Even the newest generation of PowerMac G4s have this feature. But on some PowerBooks and the first-generation iMac models, the actual reset switch is recessed, located below this little triangle. In order to access the switch, you have to straighten the end of a paper clip, then insert it gently into the hole, and press the button and release.

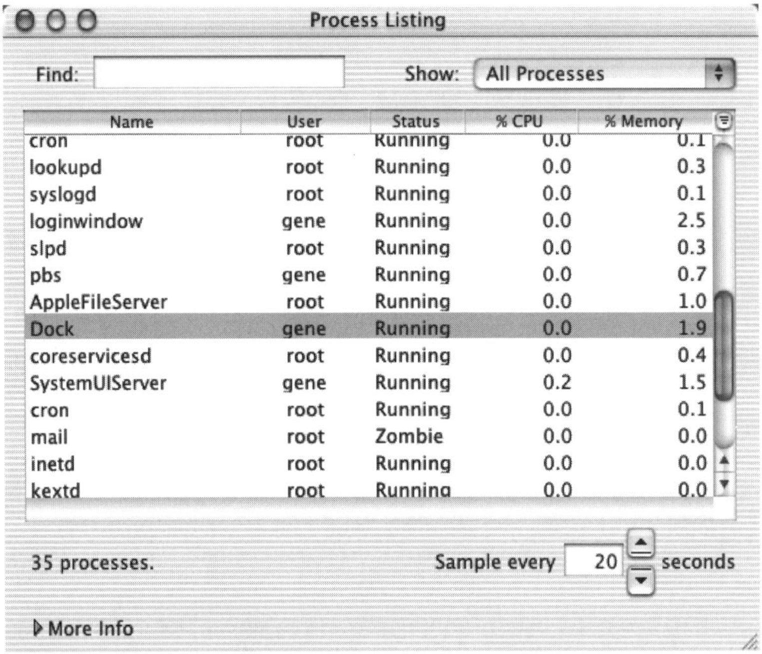
Process Listing
Find:
Show: All Processes
Name
User
Status
% CPU
% Memory
cron root Running 0.0 0.1
lookupd root Running 0.0 0.3
syslogd root Running 0.0 0.1
loginwindow gene Running 0.0 2.5
slpd root Running 0.0 0.3
pbs gene Running 0.0 0.7
AppleFileServer root Running 0.0 1.0
Dock gene Running 0.0 1.9
coreservicesd root Running 0.0 0.4
SystemUIServer gene Running 0.2 1.5
cron root Running 0.0 0.1
mail root Zombie 0.0 0.0
inetd root Running 0.0 0.0
kextd root Running 0.0 0.0
35 processes.
Sample every 20 seconds
More Info

FIGURE 18-11 Process Viewer lets you see what's hogging your Mac's resources.

NOTE *For first-generation iMacs, there is a solution to the paper clip dilemma. It's called the iMacButton, and it costs $9.95 (last I checked) from this Web site: http://www.imacbutton.com. The product consists of a large button with adhesive backing that you install by inserting into the little hole located behind the removable door on the right side of the computer and hold tightly for a few seconds (until it sticks).*

How to Handle Mac OS X System Problems

One of the great advantages of Mac OS X is that all those system extensions are history, and with them the attendant conflicts. It doesn't mean, however, that Apple's "world's greatest operating system" is trouble-free. In fact, as you see later in this section, there is indeed another brand of extensions, called kernel extensions; they provide added capabilities and are sometimes installed by third-party developers.

I will show you how, in some rare situations, you may find the need to disable one or more of those extensions in case that particular program is giving you trouble.

About Super User Access

Some of the steps I'm going to invoke require that you use the Terminal application (located in the Utilities folder) to log into your system and issue a few commands to get things straightened out.

Although using the Terminal isn't hard to do, as long as you follow the instructions exactly, it's best used as a last resort, unless you have had experience with Unix. In the normal course of events, the System Preferences application and the various other settings' features, such as the Privileges option in the Show Info Window, ought to be sufficient to configure the system the way you want. But there are circumstances where the tried and the true won't work, which is why I wrote this section.

If you follow these commands exactly, you'll be able to get out of harm's way on occasion.

The commands all have a single thing in common, which is that they involve authenticating yourself as administrator by using the "sudo" command, which, in Unix parlance, is short for "super user do." The super user isn't the fellow with the red cape, but the administrator of your Mac, the person who has full access to all its functions.

NOTE   *When you issue a sudo command in the Terminal, you will enter your password as administrator, after which access will be granted for a total of five minutes, which means you can issue additional commands for that period without having to give the password again.*

CAUTION   *Although easy to use, once you know the commands, there is no opt-out prompt when you use the Terminal. You can issue a command to delete a critical system file, and the action will proceed without further ado, which means you'd end up having to reinstall Mac OS X. Don't say I didn't warn you.*

Fixing File Permission and Ownership Problems

Mac OS X is a multiple-user operating system, which means that each user can have their own set of preferences and fonts, and even their own personal desktop.

You, as owner of the Mac, are the administrator of the system, so in theory you should have the authority to move and delete your files when you want. On occasion, it doesn't work, and the problems seem to be more prevalent if you have been moving files around from one drive or network share to another, or you have used earlier versions of Mac OS X, some of which mangled file permissions from time to time.

In this section, I'll show you how you can easily deal with common file permission difficulties.

■ **You can't trash a file.** You try to delete a file, and you get the dreaded message that you don't have permission to perform that action. The solution is to launch the Terminal application (see Figure 18-12), type the following command, then press RETURN, which will delete everything in the Trash:

```
sudo rm -rf .Trash
```

NOTE   *Remember that the first time you call up "sudo," you'll have to enter your administrator's password at a password prompt followed by the RETURN key. Also, you may have to click on the Trash icon on the Dock, to bring up a window of its contents, before the Dock shows the contents as empty.*

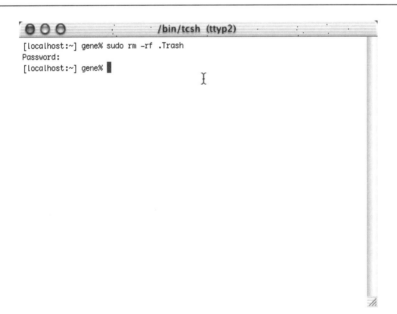

FIGURE 18-12   This command empties the trash.

■ **You don't have permission to open or edit a file you own.**   Once again, the result is confounding. It's your Mac, yet whenever you try to move a file or modify it, the dreaded message about lacking permission to do so rears its ugly head. Is there a solution? Again, let's take a trip to the Terminal application. The command you'll use is "chmod," which is short for change mode. It's essentially the command-line equivalent of the Privileges feature of the Show Info window, but it is more effective. To change permissions via the command line, and give read and write access to the file, open Terminal and type

```
sudo chmod -R u+rw filename
```

■ **You want to change permissions for a file you don't own.**   All right, this is more critical. In order for you to change the privileges, you first have to change the ownership. To do that, type the following:

```
sudo chown -R gene filename
```

Disabling a Kernel Extension

Did I contradict myself? First, I write that the traditional way of handling system extensions is history under Mac OS X. However, some applications do indeed install what are called kernel extensions, which add capabilities to the core of Mac OS X, as part of the setup process. One particular example is Norton Personal Firewall.

Under normal circumstances, this shouldn't be an issue, as such extensions aren't going to cause the grief you had experienced under the Classic Mac OS. In addition, Norton Personal Firewall comes with an uninstall feature, so you can rid yourself of the program in just a minute or two, if you want.

Kernel extensions are files that have a "kext" file extension and are stored in Mac OS X via the following path: System>Library>Extensions. They are loaded either at startup, or in the case of extensions for handling particular hardware devices, when the associated hardware is attached.

Unfortunately, you cannot just remove items from the Mac OS X System folder. When you drag a file out of that folder, it's copied, not moved. This is the ounce of protection Mac OS X puts up to keep you from removing the actual file or the wrong file—which, in effect, "hoses" the system, since you can't start from it anymore. However, there's a way around this. Using the sudo command in the

Terminal application, you can easily disable kernel extensions. To disable an extension with the file name X.kext, use the following command:

```
sudo mv /System/Library/Extensions/X.kext
/System/Library/Extensions/X.disabled
```

TIP
Don't want to bother with Terminal? Restart under Mac OS 9.x. Now you can manually locate and delete the kernel extension without having to wrestle with permissions problems.

The next time you boot your Mac, Mac OS X will not see "X" as a valid or active kernel extension, and it won't be loaded.

NOTE
I don't want to tell programmers what to do, but if the kernel extension issue becomes important, I can well imagine an enterprising developer coming out with an extension manager to deal with the issue. At this early stage in the life of Mac OS X, though, it hasn't been shown to be necessary.

Common Mac OS X System Problems and Solutions

For this section, I've assembled some of the most common (and vexing) Mac OS X troubles you're apt to encounter, along with some simple solutions:

■ **You can't log in to Mac OS X.**   Are you sure your password is entered correctly? If it's not, the login panel will "shake" to indicate it wasn't entered correctly. If this happens, try again. Remember, you have to enter the *exact* password, complete with proper upper- and lowercase letters and the right numbers (make sure the CAPS LOCK key wasn't engaged by error). Did it fail again? Maybe you just want to reset the password. To do that, restart with your Mac OS X installer CD in place, by holding down the C key at startup. Wait for the Installer to launch, and then choose Password Reset from the application menu. Click on the drive on which your Mac OS X installation is located, then select the password you want to reset from the pop-up menu. When you're finished, choose Save to store the changes, and quit Password Reset. Once you're back in the Installer application, choose quit from the application menu. Confirm the "Are you sure?" dialog box by pressing Restart. When your Mac reboots, the new password should be active.

■ **System preferences don't "take."**   Do you find that your mouse tracking speed resets itself on the next restart, or your ColorSync calibration has been undone? The best solution here is usually to restart your Mac, and then do all the settings again. To test the settings, restart yet again. The second time, they should usually take.

■ **Where's my network printer?**   Network printers can be configured either by AppleTalk or by LPR. If Print Center reports that it can't find your printer, make sure that AppleTalk is turned on in the Network panel of the System Preferences application. Also be sure that the setting is engaged for the network you use. For example, if you use AirPort, the setting you made under Built-in Ethernet doesn't apply. It has to be made again. Once you've changed the setting, click Apply Now to make sure the setting "takes" (you'll be reminded by a dialog box if you don't save the change). If the setting still doesn't seem to work, try restarting your Mac. One way or the other, it should work next time out.

■ **Screen is darkened when booting from Mac OS X.**   Apple's support for graphic cards is strictly limited to products from ATI, NVIDIA, and the now-departed iX Micro, which shipped graphic cards for some older Macs. What about the infamous Voodoo cards from 3dfx Interactive, which is now out of business, or from Formac or ProMax? Well, in the first case, there's no hope, unless someone wants to try to produce a modified driver. As far as other companies making Mac OS graphic cards, it's up to them to offer driver updates to make their products work under Mac OS X.

■ **Your CD burner won't operate.**   Mac OS X's burn CD feature (whether from the Finder or iTunes) is limited to Apple's own CD writers, plus a select line of recent third-party products. This should cover most recent mechanisms. If your CD burner won't operate under Mac OS X, contact the company that made your CD software to see if a Mac OS X version is out. At the time this book was written, Roxio, publisher of Toast, was publicly testing a Mac OS X version of Toast 5.

■ **Why won't my digital camera work?**   Do you remember the demonstration of Mac OS X 10.1 at the July 2001 Macworld Expo? Apple CEO Steve Jobs tossed a digital camera to a waiting aid in the audience when it wouldn't sync with his test computer. In that case, it was strictly a matter of the settings on the camera itself, not a bug in the operating system. Most popular digital cameras should work fine with Mac OS X 10.1 and later. If yours doesn't, contact the manufacturer about Mac OS X support.

■ **Where's that cursor?**   A chronic bug in the Classic environment is the disappearance of the cursor. I've seen this on occasion in writing this book (which was done in Word 2001). The best solution, until a more reliable fix comes, is just to click on the desktop, which usually restores the cursor. Then go back to work.

NOTE   *Actually, the Mac OS 9.2.1 and Mac OS X 10.1 updates have reduced the symptom, but it still rears its ugly head on occasion.*

■ **Why can't I install that Classic application?**   Many Classic applications install fine from Mac OS X. Classic is launched, and the installation proceeds without a blip. If it doesn't work for you, restart under Mac OS 9.x and try again. It should work that way (as long as the installer is compatible with that system version, of course).

Case History   Why Did That Command Line Appear?

Someone once said to be careful what you wish for; you might get it. I was thinking about that while researching this book. The very week when Steve Jobs first demonstrated the Aqua user interface at the Macworld Expo in San Francisco in January 2000, I joined a group of longtime friends for dinner. On the way back to the hotel, we happened to get involved in a discussion with another Mac enthusiast, who confessed his fears about the new operating system.

"What if I'm doing something, and the command line suddenly appears?" At the time, we all tried to reassure him that Apple would surely do its best to bury all vestiges of the command line except for folks who really wanted to use it. We didn't know then just how real his concerns were.

Shortly after I first installed the Mac OS X Public Beta, I discovered the kernel panic. One second there was the shimmering Aqua interface, and the next, a black screen with white text. Ouch! I thought back to the first time I installed a new Mac in my home back in the 1980s, when, within a few minutes, a bomb message suddenly appeared. The sudden onslaught of text across the bright, crisp LCD display I use on my Mac was far more jarring.

A kernel panic, which is actually a system error that can occur in an operating system based on Unix, can result from some of the same causes that trigger system errors on the original Mac OS. According to Apple, "A kernel panic is a type of error that occurs when the core (kernel) of an operating system receives an instruction in an unexpected format or that it fails to handle properly." Does anyone remember those so-called "illegal instruction" errors?

Other possible causes include software incompatibilities, damaged programs, or even a hardware problem. The contents of the kernel panic messages, however, are usually only useful for programmers to help isolate the cause. So what do you do if it appears? Well, Apple asks that you log the information on a kernel panic and send it on to Apple for review. They can use this information to trace the causes of such problems and perhaps find a solution.

Whether or not you record the information for posterity, what's the next step? Run for the reset button? Most times, it's not necessary. Just type **r** to reboot. If all goes well, your Mac will restart normally. If you get repeated kernel panics, you may want to consider reinstalling Mac OS X. Usually, however, the problem is triggered by performing some specific action and not because your Mac has a hardware problem. For example, the symptom sometimes occurred on multiprocessor Macs during a dial-up (PPP) connection. This problem was resolved by the 10.0.2 and 10.0.3 updates to Mac OS X, and is, for the most part, long gone with the Mac OS X 10.1 upgrade.

But I think back to that little discussion back in San Francisco about the sudden appearance of a command line. I just wonder if that dude will now just tell me, "See, I told you so."

Where to Learn About Software Updates

How can it be? Apple Computer seems to release one software update or another every couple of weeks. And your regular software publishers are no different. Just keeping up with this confusion can be a challenge that no single person (or two or three) can overcome.

Fortunately, there are folks who have devoted a great part of their time to checking for software updates, and as I'll explain at the end of this chapter, Apple has a neat way of dealing with it. They check for updates from far-flung places, and they make the information available to you on the World Wide Web.

Here are some of these Internet-based resources with their addresses and some information on what additional material they offer:

- **MacCentral (http://www.maccentral.com)**   MacCentral, now a part of the same publishing combine that brings you *Macworld* magazine, is a highly trafficked Web site that has news and views and product update information. With a full-time staff of writers combing the computing universe for news and views, you can expect a surprising range of information about your Mac and keeping it healthy and happy.

■ **MacFixit (http://www.macfixit.com)**   Ted Landau, a *Macworld* contributing editor, heads up this site. The focus is on problems and their solutions, and it's usually updated five times a week. They also have active message boards, and a band of visiting experts who can provide answers and feedback on specific issues.

■ **Macintouch (http://www.macintouch.com)**   Ric Ford, former *MacWeek* columnist, tracks the latest reports and rumors about doings in the Mac universe and offers new product listings. The site is updated daily, and you will find a lot of exclusives. The focus, though, is on problems, and when bugs or complications arise with a new Mac or software, you may learn about it here.

■ **Macsurfer's Headline News (http://www.macsurfers.com)**   This site is a digest listing, containing links to Mac news from popular Web sites and the mainstream press. You'll be surprised at the scope of the coverage. I've seen reports here from Mac Web sites in Italy and online business sites in the United Kingdom.

■ **The Mac Night Owl (http://www.macnightowl.com)**   Well, this is a little self-serving, perhaps, but I have set up my own Web site to be more than just a place to hawk my books. I have designed it from the ground up to be an information center, and I will be presenting regular tips and tricks and daily news commentaries for my readers there. (Notice I didn't list my site first.)

■ **VersionTracker (http://www.versiontracker.com)**   The title says it all. The site keeps day-to-day tabs on just about all the hardware and software publishers known to produce PC-related products. Click a Tab and move from the Mac OS, Mac OS X, and Windows to the Palm OS. They offer you direct links to upgrades, updates, and new product information. The site is updated as often as once an hour. If you mark this one as a "favorite" in your Web browser (bookmark it), you'll become an expert on what updates are available and when.

And Now, Apple's Solution

Beginning with Mac OS 9, and continuing with Mac OS X, Apple finally realized that it's not easy to keep track of system updates you might need. So they will do the walking for you, to paraphrase that old line used for Yellow Pages advertising.

One great feature of Mac OS X, like its predecessor, is the ability to receive software updates from Apple automatically. All you need to set this up is an Internet connection and maybe a minute of your time. The feature, called Software Update, can be set to automatically connect to Apple's Web site and retrieve the updates you need.

This is a brief description of how to set it up:

1. Launch the System Preferences application from the Dock or from the Applications folder.

2. Click on the Software Update preference panel (see Figure 18-13).

3. You have two ways to get your updates. One is on demand, by clicking Update Now. Once you activate that feature, your Internet service will be dialed, and Apple's Web site will be checked for any updates that apply to your version of the Mac OS.

FIGURE 18-13   Choose your update method here.

Where to Learn About Software Updates

NOTE
To automatically dial out, you need to choose the option to automatically connect when a TCP/IP application launches, which is available under PPP Options in the Network panel of the System Preferences application (it's usually checked by default). If you're a member of AOL or CompuServe, and you use their regular dial-up access numbers, you need to connect to the service first before you can use the Software Updates feature.

4. If Apple has updated software for you, you'll see an onscreen dialog listing the updates that are available. To retrieve them, simply check the box next to the item, then OK the download. After the download finishes, each software installer will run, in turn, until all updates are made. Then you'll just have to restart your Mac to put the new software into action.

TIP
If you want to save a copy of the downloaded installer to your hard drive so you don't have to retrieve it again, choose Save As from Software Update's File menu, and specify a location to store the file. This feature only appears if an actual update is available.

5. The other way to use the Software Updates preference is to schedule regular visits to Apple's Web site to search for such updates. To activate that feature, click the check box labeled Automatically, as I have done.

6. Then click on the pop-up menu next to Check For Updates and choose Daily, Weekly, or Monthly. At the appointed time, whenever you're logged onto your ISP, Software Update will go into action and scan Apple's Web site for updates. If one is available, Software Update will appear as an icon in the Dock and the dialog box showing the updates will be presented to you.

7. All done? Quit System Preferences to finish the process.

TIP
If you want to see a list of the software you've previously downloaded, click Show Log in the Software Updates preference panel.

Summing Up

In this chapter, you discovered the world of system enhancements and system headaches, and you learned some techniques to rescue your Mac from constant crashes and optimize performance both in Classic and Mac OS X. In Chapter 19, we'll take a look at the wide world of desktop video editing.

Chapter 19

How to Make Video Capture Hardware Work

How things have changed. In the old days—and when you reach my age, just about all days are old—when you wanted to edit a movie, you had to physically splice the film. That meant you had to cut the film apart, and move a section to its new location or remove it altogether. In the days of reel-to-reel tapes, you did pretty much the same thing with radio plays (yes, I do remember radio also). You'd cut the tape apart physically, take out passages and move scenes around, and then reattach it with a special type of splicing tape.

In my teens, I did this many times at home, creating my own little plays and variety shows, and I especially enjoyed taking out words and phrases to fix a bad "take" as they say in show business. I finally exercised the skills for a paycheck when I became a radio broadcaster.

NOTE   *All right, so I'm not that old. Yes, there was such a thing as television back then, too—there just weren't any low-cost VCRs to play around with.*

Another way to edit required having two decks. You used one to build your master tape, the other to pick segments. For video, you even had little editing computers that would, once you had marked your edits, do your work on automatic pilot. The editing computer would go back and shuttle the tapes to their marked locations and play them back as you continued to record the finished production.

Even though computers do most of the movie and video editing chores these days, the basic principles are the same. You create a project (your production) and piece it together with scenes from one source or another; then add titles, music, audio, and special effects; and now you have your number one movie or TV show—well, not quite, but you get the idea.

Are You Ready to Capture Video?

Apple Computer pioneered in delivering easy-to-use computers, and even though our favorite platform remains the minority platform by a great margin, the company's influence is significant.

Apple also has dominance in the entertainment industry. The majority of computers you see on your movie or TV screen are Macs. Yes, it's product placement and Apple works hard to get it, but their models are also distinctive-looking enough to stand out from a great percentage of the computing pack.

Macs are also used behind the scenes for editing and special effects. In fact, it's not uncommon for a video production house to have a bank of Mac systems handling commercials, TV shows, and other productions.

The biggest development, though, was to bring this great technology down to the consumer level. Today, with an iMac DV, a digital camcorder, and Apple's wonderful iMovie2 software, you can easily create productions that, at least in terms of picture quality, rival professional productions.

> **NOTE**   *If you're lucky enough to have a PowerMac G4 with a built-in Pioneer SuperDrive, you can even take those edited videos (and still pictures) and make your own DVDs with them. The discs will play on just about all but the very oldest-generation DVD players.*

A Brief Look at Video Editing Techniques

When you edit a video, you take the basic production, called raw footage, and you can add transitions (special effects, such as dissolves, that smooth the transfer from one scene to another), titles, narration, music—the limit is your imagination. Once you've done your editing, you transfer the finished product to the final master tape.

There are two different ways to edit videos: nonlinear and linear (the old-fashioned way).

Linear editing is still used today, though less often than it used to be. The process consists of taking video clips and adding them one at a time in order onto a final tape. However, this sort of work can be very time-consuming and tedious, and it doesn't allow for much in the way of creativity.

On the other hand, nonlinear editing can give you the ability to take a collection of totally separate clips from different tapes, transitions, and sound tracks—whatever raw material you have—and add them in any sequence you wish. Once you're done, you "print" the project to tape in one, smooth sequence.

> **NOTE**   *iMovie2 is a nonlinear video editing application, allowing you to mix and match and come up with your own production, complete with sound, titles, and a limited number of special effects.*

Putting Together Your Video System

Video editing can be a fun and exciting process. You can go wild making your own movies and transferring them onto tape to show to the whole family, or shoot weddings, birthdays, and special events.

Depending on the level of quality you wish to achieve, there's some very specific equipment you need to create your original videos, transfer them to your Mac's hard drive, and edit the final production.

If you're just setting up a system for family or friends or a small business, a regular Power Macintosh G3 or G4, or iMac with FireWire port, is probably sufficient; even a FireWire-equipped iBook or PowerBook will do the job. All you need to add is a digital camcorder (these can be had for prices beginning at less than $750 these days) and the software. However, since all new Macs come with iMovie preinstalled, you need go no further unless you have professional aspirations.

> **NOTE**   *If you have a Beige G3, a model without a built-in FireWire port, that's not a problem, either. Belkin, Maxtor, Orange Micro, and other companies make low-cost FireWire interface cards for many of these models.*

If you have an analog camcorder, you're not left out. A lower-cost video capture board can work with almost any Mac with a PCI slot. A video capture board is a device that will convert the analog video signal to digital when it's transferred to your Mac's hard drive, and, when edited, let you "print" it on your camcorder or VCR after converting the signal back to analog.

If you intend to deliver your videos to a commercial marketplace, prepare to spend thousands for a suitable system (the success of *The Blair Witch Project*, which essentially originated on home video equipment, notwithstanding).

Regardless of your budget, if you have the will and the imagination, there are incredible things you can do at the editing screen once you get involved in a project.

Selecting and Installing the Right Video System

To start making your mere video into a masterpiece, you need a variety of hardware and software. I'll cover some of those needs in more detail in this section.

The Camcorder

You'll need some sort of video recording device to film your movie. If you have a Beige G3 (or one of those models officially unsupported as far as a Mac OS X installation is concerned) and you don't need the best quality possible, an analog camcorder will do you just fine. If you have a camcorder with one of the so-called "high-band" video technologies, such as Hi8 and SVHS, you can create master tapes that will look simply superb on a regular VHS VCR when you make a regular copy of the finished project.

Of course, if you have a recent Mac, such as the iMac, PowerMac G4, the famous (or infamous) Cube, or a FireWire-equipped Apple laptop—or even an older Mac with a FireWire card—you may want to opt for a new, low-cost digital camcorder. Once very costly, the DV camcorder now costs essentially what a Hi8 analog model did just a few years ago.

Just about all the major consumer electronics companies have gotten into the act. You can get digital camcorders from such companies as Canon, JVC, and Sony. Most of them have a FireWire port, though it's not always called FireWire. Sony calls their FireWire ports i.Link. Other companies identify the feature by its technical name, IEEE 1394.

When you connect your camcorder to an open FireWire port on your Mac, you can use a video editing program to transfer video directly from your camcorder to your computer, eliminating the need for sometimes expensive video capture boards and devices.

Video Capture Cards

If your computer is not equipped with FireWire, you will need some sort of video capture device to transfer the video from your camcorder to your computer.

There are video capture cards that can be placed in an available PCI slot in your computer. An exceptionally low-cost option is ATI's Xclaim VR 128, which was still available at the time this book was written for $239 (based on the most recent suggested retail price taken from the company's Web site).

Can You Hook Up an Older Camcorder to a FireWire Port?

If you happen to have an analog camcorder with a regular composite audio/video port lying around the house and a computer outfitted with a speedy FireWire port, don't feel left out. You can probably buy an A/V-to-FireWire converter, so you can use the camcorder with your computer. Or just consider a regular video capture board. Check your local camcorder or electronics dealer to see what they have. If the dealer doesn't have what you want, check with the manufacturer's Web site or contact their customer service department to see if this is possible.

One useful solution is the Formac Studio, a $429 module with all sorts of connectors that handle composite video and S-video, and allow you to interface with almost any standalone video device (from analog camcorder to DVD) and capture video courtesy of your Mac's FireWire port.

Selecting and Installing the Right Video System

The card features ATI's Rage 128 graphic accelerator chip, similar to the one that used to be featured on Apple's Power Macs before the company switched to NVIDIA graphic cards, so you can go ahead and use it with your regular display. In addition to providing accelerated 2-D and 3-D display, it doubles as a video capture board. The card has video inputs and a TV output, and claims to be able to perform real-time video capture at resolutions of up to 640 x 480, at 30 frames per second. This ought to be enough to look good on an SVHS VCR.

Farther up the line is the MiroMOTION DC-30plus, from Pinnacle Systems. This card can slide into the PCI slot of most Macs. It uses Motion-JPEG, an industry standard compression method, to reduce file size, yet maximize picture quality. In addition, a copy of Adobe Premiere is included, so you can begin to edit videos right out of the box. The DC-30plus has an onboard digital audio chip, so it doesn't have to use your Mac's onboard sound capability. This will help ensure synchronization of sound and video, especially on longer projects.

If you're looking for something that can produce near-professional caliber videos, consider the TARGA 1000 and the TARGA 2000 in the Pinnacle Line. Professionals also work with systems from such firms as Avid and Media 100.

All right, now let's talk about the "Mac OS X" factor. Will any of these products ever be updated? Pinnacle Systems had no plans, unfortunately, which would mean that you'd have to run the card after rebooting under Mac OS 9.x. However both Avid and Media 100 confirmed full Mac OS X support was in progress for many of the current products (unfortunately, not for the MiroMOTION card, which, therefore would have to be run under Mac OS 9.x); you'll want to confirm this, however, before buying a system.

If you want to explore any of these systems in more detail, please check the following Web sites:

- **ATI** http://www.atitech.ca
- **Avid** http://www.avid.com
- **Media 100** http://www.media100.com
- **Pinnacle Systems (MiroMOTION and TARGA)** http://www.pinnacle.com

Can You Capture Video with USB?

If you have a regular iMac or first-generation iBook, you shouldn't feel completely left out when it comes to doing home video editing. A case in point is the Interview

USB by XLR8, a division of Interex. Considering the limitations of USB speed (up to a maximum of 12Mbps), don't expect miracles.

However, the low-cost video capture device promises full motion video at 320 x 240 pixels, which is sufficient to deliver quality that should approximate that of a regular VHS tape deck. This sort of picture ought to work fine for home use, so don't sell it short. More information can be had at the company's Web site, http://www.xlr8.com.

ATI also has an entry in this area, the Xclaim TV USB Edition. It's essentially a TV tuner and video capture pod in one unit that connects through a Mac's USB port. It features a standard 125-channel, cable-ready tuner and full-screen TV playback, plus the ability to capture video at 320 x 240.

Don't feel you're losing out with either product, however. Quality is probably not going to differ much from regular VHS, so if you're satisfied with your regular video tape deck, you won't be disappointed with what a USB video capture device might offer.

Video Capture Software

All right, you've got yourself a video editing station in the making. There's a camcorder to capture the picture, and some way to transfer it to your Mac's hard drive, such as a FireWire port or video capture card. There's one more variable in the video editing equation, and that's the editing software, which brings to your screen the capability to capture the video scenes and make a finished project.

Many of the video capture boards are outfitted with Adobe Premiere, which can provide professional-quality editing. The learning curve isn't so difficult (see Figure 19-1) that you will have to wait long to capture and edit your first production.

NOTE   *The version of Premiere being shown in Figure 19-1 is for information only. A Mac OS X version wasn't available to examine.*

However, having said that, it doesn't mean it's especially easy to do sophisticated work. You will want to take some time poring over the manual and Help screens to get the maximum possible performance from this program.

Apple's entry into the video editing business is Final Cut Pro (shown in Figure 19-2), which is priced and designed toward a professional audience. Its system requirements are prodigious. You need a Mac with a 266MHz G3 CPU or faster, 128MB of built-in RAM, a 6GB A/V-capable hard drive.

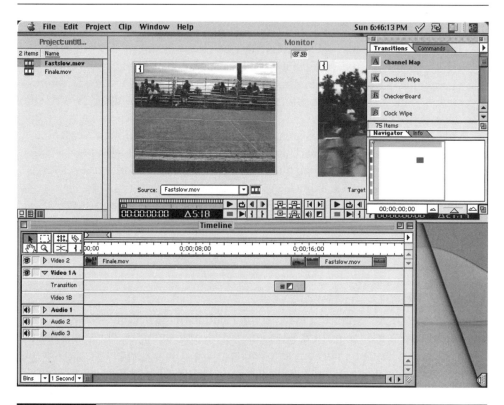

FIGURE 19-1 Premiere has yet to make the transition to Mac OS X.

NOTE
Final Cut Pro 2 for Mac OS X was not available when this book was written, but it was under development.

You don't need to spend an arm and a leg to capture video on your Mac, however. All new Macs come with an ultra-simple, smooth-as-silk video editing program for home movies and small corporate videos, called iMovie2. This application was designed so the average consumer user can master it in minutes, but it has enough power to handle some corporate and agency projects, too. All you have to do is hook up your DV camcorder to your iMac DV (shown in Figure 19-3), and you have a complete video editing workstation.

NOTE
iMovie2 is tailor-made for any Mac with a FireWire port, so check Apple's Web site to download a copy of the latest Mac OS X version if it didn't come with your Mac.

FIGURE 19-2 Final Cut Pro is Apple's entry into the video capture arena.

FIGURE 19-3   Slick and simple. No wonder so many Mac users love iMovie2.

Where Do I Store It?

Before transferring your video to your computer, be prepared to have a huge amount of space available on your hard drive. A typical video can take up as little as 100 megabytes of space and up to two gigabytes or more. Changes in Apple's File Manager for Mac OS 9 make it possible to handle even larger video clips, and Mac OS X has no such limits, but you'll want to make sure your video editing software can handle files that size.

You should also have a fast SCSI or FireWire drive and lots of RAM available (128MB or more). However, the high-speed IDE drives Apple uses in its current products are quite capable of handling video capture chores. If you have an older

Mac G3 (or something you upgraded to Mac OS X "unofficially"), make sure your hard drive is A/V capable, meaning it can sustain long file transfers without having to recalibrate, which results in dropped frames as the drive briefly pauses while capturing or printing your video. The stock drives on older Macs aren't always capable of delivering this level of performance (and Apple's specs don't mention any such limitations). Fortunately, just about any of the large hard drives available from dealers these days will suit, but if you have concerns, check the drive maker's Web site for information as to whether the product is suitable for A/V projects.

NOTE *While it is possible to use such removable media as a Jaz 2 drive as your source drive, don't expect to capture videos of the highest possible quality. You'll need to slow down the capture rate, which will result in lower quality. More to the point, removable drives are not apt to be as reliable as fixed hard drives for prolonged use. Products of this sort are better suited for archival purposes.*

Consider RAID for Serious Video Work

A RAID (redundant array of inexpensive disks) installation uses two or more drives that can be accessed as a single drive. This can provide ultra-fast video transfer performance. You can also use RAID to mirror your drives, so that the same data is copied to two or more drives at the same time. This is insurance against the possibility that one drive may go down during an important editing session, resulting in loss of data. To deliver good performance with a RAID system, you also want to get a high-performance SCSI card.

NOTE *As of the time this book was written, several FireWire RAID systems had come to market. One such product comes from the VST Technologies division of SmartDisk (http://www.vsttech.com), who also supplies standalone FireWire devices.*

TIP *Another possibility for setting up a RAID system is Apple's Disk Utility. The version that shipped beginning with Mac OS X 10.1 has a RAID option that lets you set up multiple drives for various RAID options such as striping (using two or more drives as one) or mirroring (which feeds identical drives to a pair of separate drives for automatic backups).*

Where Do I Store It?

How to Handle Video Capture Problems

As easy as it is to edit your videos, it's nevertheless true that video editing on a Mac requires attention to proper setup, to avoid operating system quirks that'll cause lost frames and inferior quality.

In this section, I've collected a list of common setup issues and some application-specific problems that you might encounter, along with their solutions.

Preparing for Your Editing Session

Before you begin to capture and edit your project, you'll want to take some precautions to make your Mac into a reliable video editing workstation:

- **Use a high-quality video source.** Old-fashioned VHS camcorders are cheap these days, but their quality level is not going to please you once you copy the tape back to the camcorder, then begin to make copies of your finished production. Each generation on an analog tape deck results in further loss of quality. The better the quality of your camcorder or tape deck, the better the finished movie. Even if you don't go for a DV camcorder, a Hi8 model, which can be had for several hundred dollars, is perfectly capable of near-broadcast quality.

- **Capture your videos onto a speedy hard drive.** This is a must! At the very least, you need a speedy drive, capable of sustained reading and writing of over 3.5 megabytes per second (the minimum capture rate for high-quality video capture from a capture board). The rule of thumb is that the drive must be capable of handling at least twice that speed to sustain long transfers. Otherwise, you will lose frames or be forced to lower the capture rate, which will, in turn, provide inferior quality pictures.

- **Prepare to optimize the drive regularly.** In Chapter 13, I suggested that having to regularly optimize your hard drive wasn't all that essential. When it comes to video editing, ignore that statement. When you do this sort of work, you'll be transferring huge files on a regular basis, and the drive is bound to become fragmented quickly. You'll want to get hold of a copy of one of the hard drive optimizing programs, such as Alsoft's Plus Optimizer, MicroMat's TechTool Pro, or Symantec's Norton Utilities.

Can You Use a Classic Video Capture Application with Mac OS X?

Although the Classic environment is a clever, robust piece of work, don't expect miracles. You can definitely run many high-energy Mac programs in Classic, including Adobe Photoshop, Microsoft Word, and QuarkXPress. But functions that access the hardware are different. Scanners generally won't run without a Mac OS X version, and don't expect to capture video, either.

On the other hand, editing video already present on your hard drive is another story entirely. Since the process only involves opening a file, rather than interfacing with an external video device, you may be able to create movie projects and edit them. When it comes time to export, or print to video, however, you'll be limited to making QuickTime movies rather than sending the finished project back to your video hardware—at least until a native version of the application appears.

NOTE   *Some old video capture boards came with Alsoft's Disk Express Pro, which optimizes in the background, when your drive is idle. It's a brilliant piece of work from programmer Al Whipple and his clever crew, because you don't have to monitor your drive's fragmentation situation. As of the time this book went to press, Alsoft was hard at work on Disk Express Pro 4, which will provide full compatibility with HFS+, Mac OS 9, and Mac OS X.*

- ■ **Put media in removable drives.**   When you have a removable device, the driver software polls the port regularly, again affecting capture speed. You'll also want to put floppies and CDs in their respective drives.

Capturing Live Video from a Camera

Most of the time, you'll simply be copying an existing videotape to your Mac. But it is quite possible to capture a live event. Here's what to do:

1. Connect your camcorder to your Mac's video input or FireWire port.

2. Switch the camcorder to Camera mode and set the Lock/Standby switch on the camcorder to Standby.

How to Handle Video Capture Problems

NOTE *Check your camcorder's documentation on how to use specific features and how the features are labeled on your particular unit.*

3. Remove any tape cassettes that are in the camcorder. If any tapes are left in there, the camcorder could time out and go into sleep mode. If you need to have a tape in the camcorder, make sure the write-protection tab is locked, so you don't accidentally copy the image to it.

4. Be sure the camcorder's demo mode is not active. Some camcorders will automatically switch to demo mode when left on standby without a tape inside. Check for any demo function in your camcorder's settings menu and disable it.

Common Video Editing Problems with iMovie

Apple's iMovie2 software is so easy to use, it's easy to forget that it is doing a tremendously complex set of tasks when you capture and edit your projects.

Here are some common problems and solutions when capturing and playing back video in iMovie2:

- **Missing audio or audio dropouts in videos exported to tape** If there's no audio when you play back the production on your DV camcorder, open up your project file, then lower the volume level of the affected clip with the volume slider in the audio viewer. Once you've done this, export the movie again.

- **No video when in capture mode** If you can control your DV camcorder with iMovie, try this: disconnect the FireWire cable while the device is still on, then reconnect it and try again. This usually fixes the problem.

- **Device Too Slow Alert when using FireWire storage device** If you are capturing video to a FireWire drive, check the manufacturer's Web site for an updated version of their driver software that's compatible with Mac OS X. While Apple has included support for hundreds of third-party peripherals, it's always possible the one you have isn't recognized. Once you retrieve the software, install it and restart. See if the problem is solved.

NOTE *All of the FireWire hard drives I've used, from such companies as Evergreen, LaCie, Maxtor, and VST (Smart Disk) work fine under Mac OS X.*

Common Video Editing Problems with Final Cut Pro

Final Cut Pro is a serious, robust video editing tool that provides superb performance. But there are problems that will arise on occasion that you'll have to address.

Here are some of those common problems and some solutions:

- **Camcorder or video deck not recognized**   First, check to be sure your device control or FireWire cable is properly connected, and also that your camcorder is set to VCR mode (check the product's manual if in doubt of the proper setting). Once you've made sure you have the proper configuration, quit Final Cut Pro. Then turn on the camcorder, and launch the program again. Make sure that the proper protocol for your camcorder is selected in the Device Control tab, located in the Preferences window.

- **Video doesn't show up on external NTSC display**   The first thing to check is the cables. Make sure they are properly connected, and that one hasn't slipped out. It is easy, for example, for S-video cables to just pop off. You'll also want to make sure that your camcorder is in VCR mode. Return to Final Cut Pro, look at your General Preferences tab, and make sure the proper hardware is chosen from the View External Video Using pop-up menu. You need to select Rendered Frames from this menu in order to display those frames before they are output to an NTSC video source. One more thing: you need to choose the External Video submenu from the program's View menu, and select All frames or Single frames.

- **Dropped frames on NTSC display during DV playback from Timeline**   In order to address this issue, try reducing the project's Canvas or Viewer display size to 50 percent. Go to the General Preferences tab, and turn off Mirror On Desktop During Playback. Your next step is to disable the View As Sq. Pixel feature in the View pop-up menu. As a final step, try reducing the display's bit depth from millions of colors (24-bit) to thousands of colors (16-bit). You probably won't notice much, if any, difference.

- **Video doesn't appear on display**   First thing to do is make sure your cables are properly connected (you didn't disconnect one end when you moved things around, right?). You'll also want to consult Final Cut Pro's Capture preferences tab and make sure that your QuickTime video settings are correct.

■ **Poor quality playback or stuttering video**   If you see these symptoms during your editing session, make sure you aren't using such keyframe compression options as Cinepak or Sorenson when working with your media.

■ **No sound from computer when playing footage from camcorder or deck**   Once again, check your cables. Make sure the audio cables haven't come loose somehow. You'll also want to revisit the Capture preferences tab and make sure your QuickTime audio configuration is correct.

■ **No audio from camcorder speakers or headphones**   First, check the Sound (or Monitor & Sound) Control Panel (or the Sound preference panel for Mac OS X) and make sure the proper audio inputs are selected. Then try the cables. Be sure they are properly seated. If you are scrubbing (scanning) audio using the program's Audio tab in the Viewers menu, increase the output volume.

■ **Some camcorder or desk functions don't work**   The first thing to check is the cables. Be sure the connections are good and tight. Also check the Device Control tab in the program's Preferences window and make sure the protocol needed to control that device is selected. If your video device uses FireWire, try switching from Apple FireWire to Apple FireWire Basic and see if it fixes the problem.

Common Video Editing Problems with Adobe Premiere

You'll find that many of the difficulties that afflict the other programs are there in equal form with Adobe Premiere, plus a few others specific to this program. There will be different solutions, but most come to the same result.

Here's a list of common problems and solutions:

■ **File doesn't appear in Import dialog box**   First thing to do is check to be sure the file format is supported by Premiere. If you have a Windows file, check to be sure it has the proper filename extension. You may also try opening that file in another program that recognizes the format. If the file can't be opened in a program that supports the file, it may be the file itself is damaged (in which case try to get another copy). If the file opens in another program but not in Premiere, it may be one of Premiere's plug-in modules is damaged. In this case, reinstall the program.

■ **Only first frame of still image series imported**   This is usually a configuration issue. Check to see that the first file in the sequence and the Numbered Stills option are selected in Premiere's Import dialog box.

■ **Low image quality during playback of previewed or exported image**   The typical symptom is a pixilated, blurred, or distorted picture. The usual cause is failure to specify a correct data rate when you are using Motion-JPEG as your codec. Check the setting of the Quality slider and enter a specific data rate (check your capture medium's instructions for the best settings).

■ **Audio and video not in sync during export or playback**   Go to Premiere's Project Settings dialog box, and set the timebase to 29.97 fps and the frame rate to 30 fps. If you set the timebase to 30 fps (which would seem a logical assumption), it'll throw the audio out of sync with the video, making your project look like a badly dubbed movie.

■ **Tracks not in sync**   Check your project window to see if there are red triangles displayed at the In locations of the audio and video clips that fail to sync. Click on each of these red triangles and select the timecode that appears on the screen. This action will resynchronize the audio and video.

■ **Export, playback, or preview operation seems slow**   The first thing you'll want to do is make sure the size of the frame is correctly set. Consult your Export Settings or Project Settings and make sure they match up closely. You may also want to check your audio and video filter selections. Look for the Keyframe or Rendering Options from the Export Settings or Project Settings dialog box. Choose Ignore Audio Filters and Ignore Video Filters and see if that helps.

■ **Flickering during playback**   Check your source clip and see if it flickers. If the flickering only turns up in an exported clip, select In. Then apply Premiere's Flicker Removal option. If these steps do not help solve your problem, consult your hardware and software setups to make sure they are correct.

■ **Can't drag an audio or video clip in the timeline**   You have to check to be certain the track you want to drag isn't next to another audio or video track. If this is the case, there will be no place to drag the clip. Also check to see if the track has been locked by mistake.

■ **Exported or previewed video runs too short or too long or is the wrong clip**   When you export video in Premiere, first check the Export Settings dialog box. Look for the Range option in the General Settings panel. Make sure that your project work area is properly specified. When you select Work Area under the Range option, Premiere will dutifully export the work area as part of your project.

How to Handle Video Capture Problems

Summing Up

Some of the issues in running video editing software are complex and arcane, but most of the basic steps, such as dragging clips and extras into your project window, are very intuitive. If you pay attention to detail and setups, you'll do fine with your Mac video workstation, even if that workstation is an easy-to-use iMac DV with iMovie2.

In the next chapter, we'll move from videos to the analog world of modems.

Chapter 20

Making the Modem Connection

Ever since the iMac appeared on the landscape in the summer of 1998, Apple has touted the Mac platform as Internet ready. More to the point, there are few Mac users who don't surf the Internet at one time or another. Although so-called high-speed Internet connections are continuing to spread across the landscape, most of you are still using a regular analog modem to get connected to the Net.

In this chapter, I'll focus on the ways to set up your modem for best performance, and why you may not be getting the top-quality connections you expect. Since the modem is just one leg of your Internet hookup, you'll want to read the next two chapters as well, which focus on Internet performance and what you can do to make your Web browser work faster for you.

Making 56K Work

At one time it was thought that the fastest regular modem would be V.34, with a top speed (*if* everything was working smoothly) of 33,600 bps. However, the modem manufacturers managed to find a clever way around that limitation, using digital technology.

Basically, Internet services use digital lines to connect to phone companies. They employ a digital-based technology to encode the information so they can pump it faster through the phone lines. The theoretical maximum speed is 56K. Forgetting for the moment that the FCC limits top speeds (explained in the next section), you will still have trouble realizing the potential, as you'll see shortly.

However, this marvelous technology only works downstream. That means you can receive data at these higher speeds, but sending data is limited to no more than 33,600 bps. That's because your connection to your local phone company is still analog.

For most purposes, this limit doesn't really matter. Graphic-heavy Web pages, streaming audio and video, and file downloads will get to you faster, and on average, you're not as apt to send as much content in the reverse direction. Well, at least that's how the theory goes.

NOTE   *A later modem standard, V.92, promises upload speeds of up to 48,000 bps; however, this newer standard only works if your ISP supports those speeds (and few do, as of the time this book was written).*

The Cold, Hard Facts about Modem Connection Speeds

You've read the ads for all those V.90 or V.92 modems. And 56,000 bps connection: sounds great, right? This is especially true if you're migrating from a much slower modem, say with 14,400 bps performance. The reality, however, is not always what it's cracked up to be. First off, no 56K modem can connect at 56,000 bps. The FCC mandates a top limit of 53K. The technical reasons aren't important, but the fact of the matter is that your modem has that handicap from the get go.

The second problem: High-speed modems take phone lines to their technological limits. Unfortunately, phone lines are generally rated strictly for voice transmission, and your local phone company is not apt to guarantee that you'll ever be able to achieve high connection speeds.

In the real world, if you're right up close to the phone company's switching center and have brand-new phone lines at your home or in your neighborhood, maybe you'll get speeds from 50K to the maximum 53K. For the rest of you, you should realistically expect actual connection speeds of 34,000 bps to 48,000 bps.

> NOTE   *I live in a relatively new neighborhood, and the latter is what I usually get, but some folks down the street don't do as well, so it's not altogether consistent.*

If you are far from your telephone company's switching center, and perhaps the lines in your neighborhood are old, you would be extremely lucky to see anything approaching 56K-class speeds. You'll be lucky to get 26,400 bps or 28,800 bps.

> NOTE   *To make matters more confusing, before the original V.90 56K standard was approved, modem manufacturers competed with two preliminary standards. One was K56flex, the other x2. If your modem hasn't been upgraded from the preliminary standard to V.90, you'll want to contact the manufacturer about getting a V.90 update. Usually the update files (which update the modem's firmware) can be downloaded directly from the company's Web site.*

The Right Way to Hook Up a Modem

All new Macs come with a built-in modem, and most older Macs that can support Mac OS X have internal modems, as well. But what if your modem fails, and you don't want to bother with a new internal modem—or you have an older Mac that, for whatever reason, didn't ship with an internal modem? Fortunately, there are still a few external modems available, designed either for a Mac's serial (modem) port or the USB port.

Once you've brought home your new modem (or your smiling delivery person brings it), it's time to make it work. All you do is plug it in and turn it on, right?

When it comes to setting up a modem, such simple processes aren't always successful. The modem lights are blinking nicely (of course, the blinking lights only apply if you have an external modem), but you cannot connect to your online service. Or you connect all right, but you're disconnected unceremoniously within just a few seconds or minutes.

Is it you or the modem or your Mac? In this section, I'll cover some of the basics of modem installation. Then I'll get on to the business of helping you deal with common setup and connection problems.

Before You Install Your Modem

When you set up your modem, it's a good idea to consider first whether or not you intend to also use it for faxing. Every new modem you buy comes with fax software, and it would seem a great convenience to be able to prepare documents and fax them without having to resort to printing them first. In practice, this doesn't always work as well as you might hope. While fax software these days is flexible, here are a few of the reasons why you might prefer to stick with a separate fax machine:

■ **The bundled fax software may not be compatible with Mac OS X.** As of the time this book was written, SmithMicro, publishers of FaxSTF, was promising a Mac OS X version, but the versions included with your Mac will only work if you reboot from your Classic Mac OS. This is apt to be awkward, but it's the only answer until you upgrade your software.

■ **Fax software is buggy.** Whether the Classic Mac OS or Mac OS X, every time Apple has updated its system software, one class of products that tended to have problems is fax software. Fax software is heavily tied to various system functions to send and receive faxes immediately or at a preset time, and to notify you that the fax was received. If your Mac crashes regularly when trying to, for example, send a fax, check with the software publisher to see if they have a newer, better version. The one that comes with the modem may not be the latest, or it may be a "lite" version lacking some features that may be useful to you. In addition, some popular programs, such as Microsoft Word and QuarkXPress, have traditionally had conflicts with fax software. You may want to check with your application software publisher as well when troubles arise.

■ **Fax software doesn't handle vector graphics.** If you do desktop publishing and you work with EPS documents, fax software will have a problem transmitting those files, since such software doesn't support the

PostScript page description language. When you fax such documents, your illustrations will be no better than bitmapped pictures on your screen. They'll be usable, but jagged, and grayscale shadings will lack distinction. You may wonder why nobody has come up with a fax-based PostScript feature to deal with this. Actually, a long-gone company once tried to offer a PostScript interpreter for fax software, but it never worked as advertised. I have also asked the publishers of the existing fax programs about this limitation. In general, they feel it would either be too expensive to develop, or the market wouldn't be sufficient for them to make a profit from the venture. So that's where it stands.

NOTE *Despite the inability to handle EPS files, fax software tends to be superior to many standalone fax machines in rendering regular photos and other graphic images.*

■ **Your Mac must be on all the time to receive faxes.** Well, let me amend that. Your Mac could be in Sleep mode, and awake when a fax is coming. But the unit is still on nonetheless. If your Mac is off, the fax can't be received. Consider this issue if you expect your business contacts to send you faxes after hours.

■ **You must scan printed documents.** If you have a printed document you want to fax, you must first scan it (which means you must buy a scanner if you don't already have one), save it as a file, then fax that file. This may be fine for an occasional printed piece, but if you intend to fax a lot of material this way, it can become a time-consuming process. You may end up needing a separate fax machine anyway.

NOTE *A clever alternative to the need for separate devices is the multifunction printer. Such products come from Brother, Canon, Epson, HP, and Lexmark. Since the basic image scanning engines are the same, these manufacturers build in scanning, faxing, copying, and printing features. But then again, you still end up with a standalone fax machine here. None of the preceding shortcomings should necessarily mean you should not use your modem's faxing feature, however. I know of one client who uses a fax modem for the convenience of sending letters and desktop publishing documents directly from his Mac. But the very same client keeps a regular fax machine on hand for faxing printed pieces or documents with EPS graphics. It gives you the best of both worlds.*

The Right Way to Hook Up a Modem

Installing Your New External Modem

Before you install the modem, check the manual or setup brochure to see if you need to install any special software. If you intend to use the modem as a fax machine, you'll need to use an installation disk. If you just want to use the modem, it depends. Some installation disks will include modem scripts for the Classic Mac OS, but you'll probably have to rely on the built-in modem scripts for Mac OS X, unless you can somehow separate those scripts from the installer.

From there, follow these basic steps:

1. For an external modem, make sure it's plugged into the electrical outlet, your phone lines, and, of course, your Mac.

NOTE   *USB modems are actually bus powered, meaning they draw their current right from a connection directly to your Mac. You may, however, need a powered USB hub if you have several devices connected to your Mac's USB ports. The modem's manual should explain all this.*

2. Take the installation disk or CD and insert it into your Mac's drive.

CAUTION   *Don't bother installing software for a new modem if the box doesn't specifically state it's Mac OS X compatible. Otherwise, you'll be left with software that will probably run only when you reboot under the Classic Mac OS.*

3. Locate an installer icon and double-click on it. If there's no installer icon, check the manual or setup instructions for information. You may simply have to manually drag some files to the Classic Mac OS System Folder or elsewhere on your Mac's drive and restart.

4. As soon as your modem's software is installed, try logging on to your Internet or online service and test the fax capability, if it applies, to see if the modem is performing as you expect. If anything's wrong, read the next section for help.

TIP   *If you don't already have an Internet connection, you may find some possibilities in the box in which your new modem was shipped. Look for special offers from AOL, EarthLink, and other services. The great thing about these offers is the free trial period. If you don't like one service, you can switch to another without having to pay an extra fee.*

How to Manually Install and Set Up a Modem Driver Under Mac OS X

The vast majority of modems you're apt to buy will probably not be aware of the special locations for modem scripts under Mac OS X. Fortunately, the very same scripts that worked under the older versions of the Mac OS should function perfectly fine under Mac OS X.

Here's how to install them.

1. Make sure you're logged on under the owner or administrator's account on your Mac.

2. Locate the Library folder at the top level of your Mac's hard drive.

3. Now locate the Modem Scripts folder located inside the Library folder.

4. Drag the modem script into the Library folder. That's all there is to it. I'll show you how to set Mac OS X to use that modem script a bit later in this chapter.

NOTE *Before trying to install a modem file, see if the ones provided with Mac OS X will do the deed. Mac OS X 10.1 includes modem scripts from over three dozen manufacturers.*

How to Connect with a Modem Under Mac OS X

With the most recent versions of the Classic Mac OS, you could dial up your ISP in two ways. One was by launching the Internet program you wanted to use. If you selected "Connect Automatically When Starting TCP/IP Applications," an Apple Remote Access option, the act of launching the program would trigger a login attempt.

If you wanted a straight connection before you launched the software, you would click on the Remote Access Control Strip, and click Connect or click the very same button in the Remote Access Control Panel.

Under Mac OS X, the actual connect functions are rolled into the Internet Connect application (see Figure 20-1), which is found in your Applications folder.

Click Connect to log in; click Disconnect to log out. That's all there is to it. The display will show connection speed and the progress bars will show modem upload and download activity.

To change any other setting, however, you have to visit the Network panel of the System Preferences application. With your modem connection port selected in the Configure pop-up menu, click the PPP tab, then the PPP Options button to

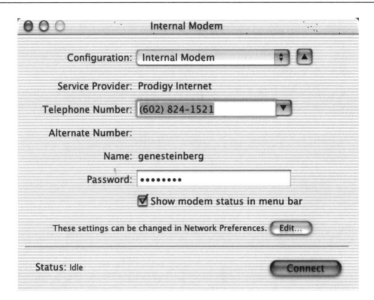

FIGURE 20-1   This application incorporates the actual connection functions of Remote Access.

find the automatic login feature. The other options available are very much what you had with Remote Access; the more things change, the more they stay the same, someone once said.

An Overview of Internal Modems

It was once just the province of Apple's consumer products and laptops, but now all new Apple computers are now fitted with internal modems (or come with provisions for them).

While this may not sit well with the folks who make Mac modems, it's a great convenience for you, because you don't have to fret over installing a new hardware device and finding the right connection scripts (see the next section) or software.

But as with other products, Apple hasn't made the internal modem equation as simple as it should be. Good examples are Apple's desktop line. If it comes standard equipment, fine. But if you want to add an internal modem to any of Apple's desktop models beginning with the original Beige G3, you'll find that each product generation requires a different modem. So you cannot, for example, transfer the modem you pull from the communications slot of a beige G3 into the Blue and White G4 or G4, and vice versa. And it's not that each of these products has a better internal modem than the previous generation, either.

When you buy a brand new Power Macintosh, you'll get a modem built in, but don't expect that it'll serve duty for anything but that specific model line.

Setting Up the Network Preference Panel to Recognize Your Modem

If your modem doesn't come with a special software installer, check the supplied disk or CD for a modem script (CCL file) for your new modem. While Apple supplies modem scripts for a variety of models for Mac OS X, the ones prepared by the manufacturer are often optimized for better connections. Once you find the modem script, install it as described in the previous section. (I'm assuming the modem's software installer may not recognize Mac OS X's special needs.)

Now it's time to follow these steps:

1. Launch System Preferences from the Dock or the Applications folder.

2. Click on the Network preference panel.

NOTE *Mac OS X consolidates the Modem and TCP/IP Control Panel functions in a single preference panel; having it separate was an eternal source of confusion in previous system versions. Way to go, Apple!*

3. Choose Internal Modem from the Configure pop-up menu and click on the PPP tab, which brings up the dialog box shown in Figure 20-2.

4. Click on the Modem tab.

5. Click on the Modem pop-up menu, and choose the make and model of your modem from the list (see Figure 20-3).

NOTE *If you have an external modem, it'll be listed as to type in the Configure menu. Just choose the connection port to which it's attached.*

The Right Way to Hook Up a Modem

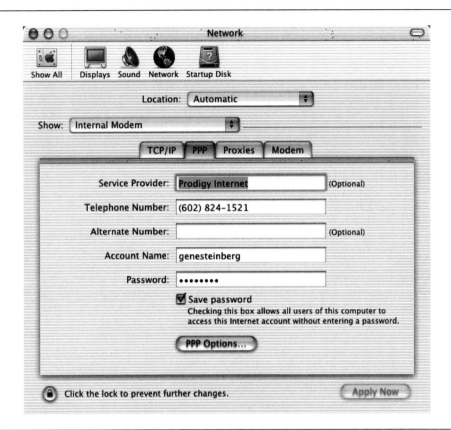

FIGURE 20-2   Configure Mac OS X to dial up your ISP from this preference panel.

NOTE

If the exact make and model isn't listed, choose one from the same manufacturer. Many companies design modems to work in a similar fashion. If several scripts are listed, try the one that most closely matches the product you have. You can easily change it later on if performance doesn't meet your expectations.

6. Leave the Sound and Dialing radio buttons as they are unless you want to turn off the modem's dial-out sound or you're using a phone service without touch-tone capability.

7. Choose Quit from the application menu or press COMMAND-Q.

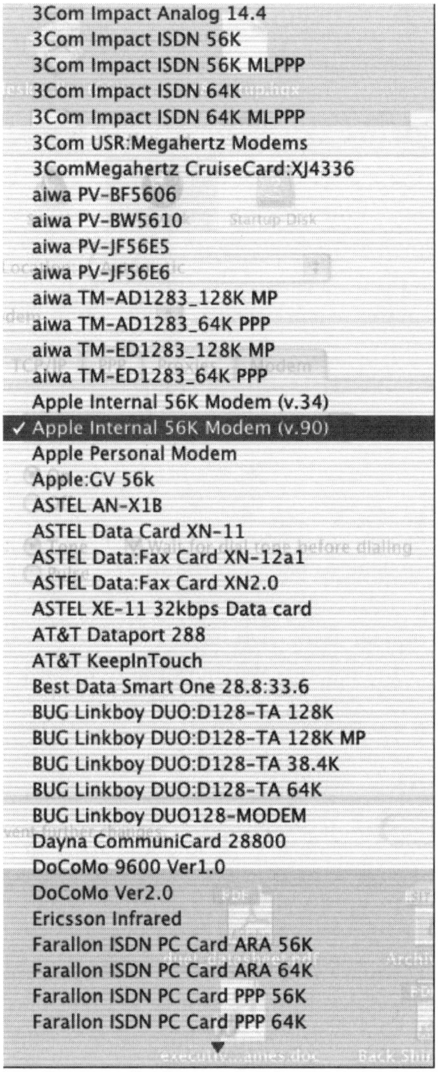

3Com Impact Analog 14.4
3Com Impact ISDN 56K
3Com Impact ISDN 56K MLPPP
3Com Impact ISDN 64K
3Com Impact ISDN 64K MLPPP
3Com USR:Megahertz Modems
3ComMegahertz CruiseCard:XJ4336
aiwa PV-BF5606
aiwa PV-BW5610
aiwa PV-JF56E5
aiwa PV-JF56E6
aiwa TM-AD1283_128K MP
aiwa TM-AD1283_64K PPP
aiwa TM-ED1283_128K MP
aiwa TM-ED1283_64K PPP
Apple Internal 56K Modem (v.34)
✓ Apple Internal 56K Modem (v.90)
Apple Personal Modem
Apple:GV 56k
ASTEL AN-X1B
ASTEL Data Card XN-11
ASTEL Data:Fax Card XN-12a1
ASTEL Data:Fax Card XN2.0
ASTEL XE-11 32kbps Data card
AT&T Dataport 288
AT&T KeepInTouch
Best Data Smart One 28.8:33.6
BUG Linkboy DUO:D128-TA 128K
BUG Linkboy DUO:D128-TA 128K MP
BUG Linkboy DUO:D128-TA 38.4K
BUG Linkboy DUO:D128-TA 64K
BUG Linkboy DUO128-MODEM
Dayna CommuniCard 28800
DoCoMo 9600 Ver1.0
DoCoMo Ver2.0
Ericsson Infrared
Farallon ISDN PC Card ARA 56K
Farallon ISDN PC Card ARA 64K
Farallon ISDN PC Card PPP 56K
Farallon ISDN PC Card PPP 64K
▼

FIGURE 20-3   Choose your modem from the list.

8. You will be asked whether you want to save your settings. Click the Save button to retain your new settings, or Cancel to keep the ones that are already there.

If you change the Network preference panel while logged on to an Internet service, the settings won't be used until you've disconnected from your service, then logged on again.

It's True! Most Modems Are Basically the Same Inside

Despite the fancy advertising, variety of bundled software, and markedly different case designs, at heart many of the modems you buy are made from some of the very same stuff. The digital signal processing (DSP) chips these modems use are commonly made by Conexant or its predecessor in the modem chip market, Rockwell. There may be some variations in the way a modem manufacturer uses this core technology, but in the end, basic performance ought to be similar.

There are some exceptions to this rule, notably U.S. Robotics, a former division of 3Com, which uses modems incorporating chips from Texas Instruments.

Why It Won't Connect

You have followed my instructions or the manufacturer's to the letter. You have checked every single step, yet your modem just won't give you a reliable connection, or maybe it just won't connect at all. Is it time to toss it out and try another modem?

Let's explore some of the reasons why a modem doesn't work and go over some quick solutions.

Defective Modem

Even if the modem appears to dial out, and, with an external modem, the lights flash on and off in the appropriate fashion, the modem may be defective. If it's brand new, you should return it to your dealer; otherwise, most manufacturers have product warranties of from five to seven years and should be able to handle your request for a replacement promptly. Some manufacturers may offer an overnight exchange, for which you have to give a credit card number as a deposit to guarantee return of the defective unit. Others require that you ship the defective product back first for repair or replacement.

Bad or Incorrect Serial Cable

When higher-speed modems came out, beginning with the 9,600 bps models, they used a special cable known as a "hardware handshake" cable. You can't immediately tell this cable from the older one, but the performance difference is glaring. The new cable will work just fine with high-speed modems; the older ones won't support the connections. New modems come with the right cable. If you plan on hooking up an older cable to a newer modem, my advice is don't! You can buy a brand new cable from your Mac dealer for $10–$20, and you'll avoid the aggravation.

If you're sure the cable is correct (it came with your new modem, for example), it still could be defective. Try another cable if all the following connection solutions don't help you.

NOTE   *This cable problem, fortunately, doesn't afflict USB modems. A USB cable is, well, a USB cable.*

Slow Connection Speeds

First of all, you'll want to take a realistic view of what speeds you can achieve (see "The Cold, Hard Facts about Modem Connection Speeds" earlier in the chapter). But even if you're near a phone company switch and in a newly developed area, it's quite possible you'll encounter troubles getting good performance. Here are a few possible solutions to consider:

■ **Try another connection number.**   If you live in a city of reasonable size, you will probably find several access numbers for your online service. If you're an AOL member, you can use the Setup feature to locate another access number for a given area code or country. Other services will usually have a list of access numbers at their Web site, or you can telephone their technical support people for help. If there's no other access number in your area, try one in a nearby city as a test to be sure there's not another cause for this problem.

NOTE   *If you're using AOL, try their software's auto-detect feature. If the software picks the wrong modem, you'll have a chance to pick the right one from the scrolling list after the setup process is complete.*

■ **Modem needs firmware update.**   Nearly all current modems have Flash ROMs, which means the code that operates the modem (a modem's equivalent of an operating system) can be upgraded to fix bugs and improve performance. You can usually get the latest updates (called "firmware") from a manufacturer's Web site. A great source of information about new and updated software is the Mac VersionTracker Web site (http://www.versiontracker.com).

Why It Won't Connect

■ **Remove other phone devices on your line.**   Each item you have on your phone line, from phones to fax machines to modems, uses a small amount of current from the line. If you have too many devices connected, it could impair performance. The best way to check for this problem is to remove everything except your modem, and make sure it is plugged directly into the wall jack (and not to just another phone device). If it seems as if another phone device is contributing to the problem, it'll be up to you to decide whether to keep the other device disconnected or have it checked for a possible hardware problem.

NOTE   *If you need to have your modem working regularly throughout the day, without interruption, it's probably a good idea to give it its own dedicated phone line. That will free up your other line for regular phone calls.*

■ **Have the phone lines checked.**   If you hear static on the line (even light static), be assured your modem's performance will be impaired. Contact your local phone company to deal with this problem. Bear in mind that their primary concern is voice quality, not modem quality. But since phone companies are now actively promoting business or small business use, you might actually find a sympathetic ear from a customer service representative.

■ **Try another modem.**   If all else fails, it could be that your modem is defective. It may not matter that it dials out and makes a connection. Sometimes problems with a modem are more subtle than working or not working. If you have another modem or access to one, try it and see if performance is better. If it is, contact the manufacturer's technical support people for assistance.

Busy Signals

An Internet service's access number is basically just a network of modems, with a finite capacity. When that capacity is reached, you get a busy signal, same as when you call a regular private phone line that's being used.

The easiest solution is just to try again. The PPP settings in the Network preference panel include a dialog box under PPP options, in which you can set your modem to automatically redial a number after a small delay (see Figure 20-4). If you continue to get busy signals, try logging on at a different hour. Internet services tend to be busiest during the so-called primetime hours in the evenings or on weekends.

If you get persistent busy signals, try another telephone access number for your service, if available in your city. If you cannot get satisfactory performance from

Session Options:
- ☐ Connect automatically when starting TCP/IP applications
- ☑ Prompt to stay connected if idle for [15] minutes
- ☑ Disconnect if idle for [15] minutes
- ☑ Disconnect when user logs out
- ☑ Redial if busy
  - Redial [1] times
  - Wait [30] seconds before redialing

Advanced Options:
- ☑ Send PPP echo packets
- ☐ Use TCP header compression
- ☐ Connect using a terminal window (command line)
- ☐ Use verbose logging

[Cancel] [OK]

FIGURE 20-4	Choose how often your modem redials and when from this preference dialog box.

your Internet service, you may want to consider another provider. Check the ads in your newspaper or favorite computing magazine, or use one of those free online service offers you get in the mail.

TIP *When you first install Mac OS X or a new Mac, Apple runs you through a setup assistant where you can let your favorite fruit company set you up with an EarthLink account. The benefit is that you usually get a 30-day free trial, so if the service doesn't appeal to you, you can choose another option. In addition, all of the critical setup information is done behind the scenes, so you don't have to mess with inserting the right TCP/IP numbers and other access information.*

Sudden Disconnects

Sometimes your modem will appear to connect just fine, but after a few minutes, you're logged off, apparently for no reason. First and foremost, check the earlier section entitled "Slow Connection Speeds." The same solutions may apply to either problem. Then check out these possible causes:

- **Your online service logged you off.**   America Online and some Internet services may log you off if you're inactive for a period of time. For AOL, it's usually 45 or 46 minutes, and other services will usually specify in their instructions or online information how long they wait before disconnecting you. This problem is doubly difficult on AOL because you may be downloading a file using a separate Web browser, such as Internet Explorer or Netscape. AOL won't sense the modem activity because they only recognize it with their built-in browser, or at least that's how the theory goes. Otherwise, their idle-time feature seems to only function when you access features that are strictly on AOL. Even writing email or a message for a message board isn't counted as being active, because the modem isn't sending or receiving any information.

- **Your Internet dialer disconnected you.**   The PPP Options dialog box, in the Network preference panel, has a setting that will disconnect you if you're idle for 15 minutes. This preference can be unchecked, or the idle time interval changed.

> **TIP**   *If you have a habit of forgetting to log off your Internet service when you finish your session, you may want to leave the automatic log-off option checked. This may be especially helpful if you have a low-cost ISP plan that adds hourly fees if you exceed a maximum number of hours online.*

- **Call waiting interrupted your line.**   Call waiting is a great feature. It lets you literally have two phone lines in one and to switch between two calls (if you like juggling acts). Unfortunately, the little noise a call waiting announcement makes can also drop your Internet connection. If you have this feature, be sure to insert a ***70,** (including that comma) as part of the number that's being dialed. It will disable call waiting for that call. AOL's software setup also includes a provision for inserting this number string.

How to Test Your Modem's Real Connection Potential

Here's a fast way to see how well your modem can handle a high-speed connection. It involves calling up U.S. Robotics' LineTest center. Although this test was designed with users of its own products in mind, this test should work with any V.34 or V.90 model.

To run this test, you'll need a terminal program such as Zterm, which is available in a Mac OS X–compatible edition. You can download the latter from http://www.versiontracker.com. Now just follow these steps:

1. Dial up U.S. Robotics' test number, using this command: **ATDT1-847-330-2680**. Your modem will go through its usual dialing connecting routine, and then you'll see a series of text prompts.

> NOTE *Don't be intimidated by a text-based interface. Just follow the instructions you see carefully, as they may change from time to time from the ones I list here.*

2. Once you're connected, type the words **LINE TEST**.

3. Press the ENTER key.

4. Follow the prompts in the text interface to enter a first name or user name.

5. Over the next minute or so, U.S. Robotics' LineTest feature will run some diagnostics on the connection you've made. If your 56K modem is really connecting at a 56K speed, you'll see, "This connection supports 56K technology!" For each stage of the test, follow the prompts in the terminal screen to progress through the test process. Since the interface changes from time to time, I'm not describing each test exactly as provided.

6. To end your LineTest session, type the letter **g**, then press ENTER. You'll be disconnected within a few seconds.

If your modem fails to connect at a 56K speed, you'll see this message: "56K is not currently possible on this connection, or is likely to be highly impaired." This is no problem if you don't have a 56K modem, but if you do, it may indicate other problems you'll need to address, some of which, as I explain in this chapter, may simply be beyond your ability to control.

> NOTE *This line test feature can, itself, be a little flaky and can be busy for hours on end. If you cannot make a connection to run the test, just try again at a later time (early morning may be best).*

How to Test Your Modem's Real Connection Potential

The Case of the Modem That Wouldn't Reset

This really happened to me.

I had installed a brand new Global Village 56K internal modem in my Blue and White Power Macintosh G3. Everything worked just great. Apple's clever industrial design team has done wonders to prevent headaches when putting things inside your Mac (although the first-generation iMac remains a distinct exception).

> **NOTE** *What happened to Global Village? After changing ownership twice, it's now in the hands of Zoom Telephonics, a long-time modem maker who also owns Hayes, one of the original manufacturers of consumer modems. Profits are tight, and, with just about all Macs and Windows computers shipping with built-in modems, the replacement market is diminishing.*

The modem worked just dandy until it locked up when connecting to the Internet. I tried connecting with the Internet Connect application over and over again, and it wouldn't work. I restarted my Mac, and still the modem wasn't recognized. On a hunch, I shut down the Mac (through the normal procedure), waited a few seconds, and restarted. The modem was recognized again and it worked like a charm!

I telephoned Global Village's technical support folks and asked just what went wrong. The response was simple: with an external modem, if it locks up, you just turn the unit off and then on again. With an internal modem, your Mac is the on/off switch, powering all internal devices, so your Mac has to be shut down and restarted to accomplish the same result.

What's a Modem String and How Do I Use It?

As I said earlier in this chapter, modems are analog devices that convert your computer language to little beeps and squawks that your phone system can handle. But in order to talk with your modem and get good performance, the Mac has to give it a set of commands, called a modem initialization string. The string is designed to activate specific features of your modem, so you get the best possible performance.

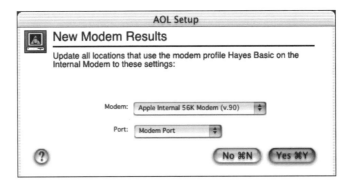

FIGURE 20-5   AOL marches to the beat of a different drummer with its own modem setup routine.

For the most part, you shouldn't have to bother with a modem string. When you set up your modem, configuring the Network panel of the System Preferences application should take care of it.

If you're using AOL for Mac OS X, you'll need to use its own dial-up and modem configuration features. For example, AOL has an auto-detect feature (see Figure 20-5), which is used to check your modem's hardware and pick a profile optimized for best performance.

> NOTE *U.S. Robotics modems usually have a separate volume control that handles sound functions, so the sound-related strings are not needed.*

> NOTE *I have deliberately left out higher-speed protocols, such as cable modems or DSL (Digital Subscriber Line), in this chapter. They involve new technologies that provide performance way beyond what a regular modem can handle. I'll cover these so-called "broadband" features in the next chapter.*

Summing Up

The world of modems can sometimes seem daunting, especially since they don't always work as seamlessly or as predictably as you think they should. But usually, with a little adjustment here and there, you'll find you get the level of Internet performance you expect.

In the next chapter we'll move the discussion to the Internet. You'll learn how to cope with Internet performance problems and how to make your surfing go more swiftly.

What's a Modem String and How Do I Use It?

Chapter 21

Dealing with
Internet Access Problems

The dot.com meltdown has affected many aspects of society. As companies with flawed business plans or overambitious visions of profitability have failed, it has become more and more evident how the Internet has taken on a huge presence in our daily lives.

The Internet has advanced from its humble origins at the government and university levels to encompass a multibillion dollar industry that affects most everyone who uses a computer. For example, an Apple Computer survey of new iMac users reported that fully 90 percent use their computers to surf the Internet. More to the point, Mac OS X actually depends on Internet access for delivery of the latest updates to the operating system and even for updated help text.

You use the Internet to send and receive email, visit Web sites, download software, post messages, chat, join online communities, and buy lots and lots of merchandise, from books to cars, and a lot more in between.

Getting good Internet performance should be a given. New Macs have high-speed modems, and Internet services have spent untold amounts of money to improve their services. Alas, the reality is something else altogether.

As you saw in the previous chapter, there are ways to spruce up your modem's performance to get the best possible connection speed. But even after you have done all that to tune up your connections, you may find that getting reasonable speed from the Internet is a challenge. And that's what this chapter is all about.

Solving Internet Connection Problems

Many of the issues I discuss in the previous chapter can be responsible for the problems you may have in getting on the Net. Check that chapter for information on problems that may be caused by your modem rather than the service to which you're trying to connect.

Bad or Lost Internet Connections

If your modem is set up properly, there are some other causes of problems getting on the Internet:

- **Improper TCP/IP settings**   In order to connect to a regular Internet service provider (ISP), you need to specify the correct connection protocol and correct IP numbers in your Network panel of the System Preferences application (see Figure 21-1). If you specify the wrong information in either category, you either won't connect at all, or you'll connect but be unable to access one or more of the service's features. Each ISP will have its own unique settings. In addition, if you use a cable modem or access the Internet at your company (which may have a special connection to the Internet, such as a secured firewall), other settings may be required. If your modem seems to be set up properly, you will need to verify your Internet settings using whatever information you received from the ISP or system administrator. If there's no documentation around as to what the settings are, contact your ISP directly for the details.

- **Missing TCP/IP settings**   If you recently reinstalled Mac OS X or you've set up a new Mac, you may have to reenter these settings (unless you use the following tip).

TIP   *Before you install a new Mac or install Mac OS X, be sure to write down all of the settings needed to access your ISP (AOL will perform the setups behind the scenes when you set up its software). If you're transitioning from a Classic Mac OS, you'll find them in the Modem, Remote Access, and TCP/IP Control Panels. Having this information will greatly simplify your setup process.*

- **Corrupted TCP/IP settings**   Hard drive directory damage or a system crash can destroy your Internet settings if it happens when you're trying to access your ISP. You should be ready to replace them when necessary with a backup.

NOTE   *To make matters all the more confusing, I have seen situations where ISPs have sent out installer CDs that place the wrong setup on your Mac. More to the point, make sure the installation CD, if there is one, specifically states that it's compatible with Mac OS X. Otherwise, don't use it. Contact your ISP directly for assistance.*

- **User authentication failed**   When you set up your Internet access, you not only have to enter the proper phone numbers in the PPP tab of the Network preference panel, but the proper username and password as well. If one or the other is missing or incorrect, you may connect, but you won't be able to log in. The same setups will apply if you're using AOL, except that the setups are done with AOL's own software.

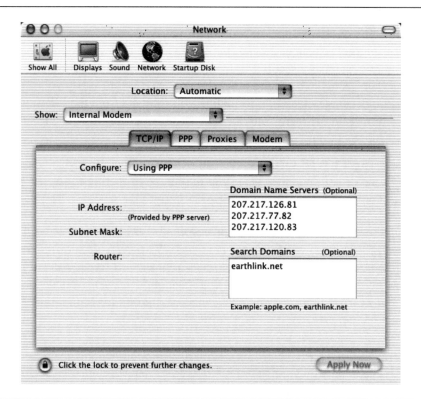

FIGURE 21-1   The settings you make here are crucial for proper access to your ISP.

NOTE   *When you enter your password, be sure you're not confusing a zero with the letter "O." You need to enter the letters and/or numbers correctly, upper- and lowercase included.*

NOTE   *ISPs use something referred to as "authentication servers" to verify a member's username and password. If the system is not working for some reason, you may find that you cannot connect to your Internet service even if your Mac's settings are 100 percent correct. If you encounter this problem, try connecting again later. If that doesn't work, I suggest you contact your ISP about it.*

The Magic and Mystery of the Internet Preference Panel

Aside from your modem and TCP/IP settings, there's one more key player in the great drama of getting connected to the Internet, and that's the Internet preference panel, part of the System Preferences application.

This preference panel is, you'll note, very similar to the one that first appeared in Mac OS 8.5. Prior to that, handling Internet preferences was a mess, supported by a little application called Internet Config, one of the major sources of confusion for earlier Mac OS versions. Internet Config was an application that let you configure such things as your email address, preferred email software, default home page and browser, and so on and so forth. Finally, Apple incorporated all the functions in the Internet Control Panel, which forms the basis of the Internet preference panel under Mac OS X.

During the era of Internet Config (which still hasn't ended, because some applications continue to install the software), I cannot tell you how many times I've fielded questions from troubled clients on how to make the proper settings. I would have to take them through the tiresome process of figuring out where the Internet Config application was located, and then how to use it.

Having all these settings consolidated in one place, easy to locate and use, will ease the process of setting up your Internet preferences under Mac OS X.

The Internet Preference Panel by the Numbers

When you install and set up AOL, it does what it needs to do to your Internet configuration behind the scenes. In addition, if you opt to allow Apple's Mac OS X Setup Assistant to establish your account, via EarthLink, you won't have to concern yourself about what to set and where. It'll all be done automatically for you.

But if you have an existing account (even with EarthLink) that you simply want to continue to use, you'll probably need to make the settings manually. As you'll see, this isn't a difficult process.

Following is a brief tutorial on the proper Internet preference panel settings. To change settings, just click on an icon that represents the category you want to change and enter the information in the text entry fields. If you're familiar with the Classic Mac OS's Internet Control Panel or Internet Config, this will be familiar territory.

NOTE   *When you install Classic Internet programs such as Netscape, you'll find a proliferation of copies of Internet Config, one for each installation. It's not much different from all those copies of SimpleText and its predecessor, TeachText, that used to turn up all over your hard drive. Best advice is to trash them all. You don't need them anymore.*

NOTE
None of the settings I'm describing in this section will have any effect on AOL's software. Some of the settings, such as a default Web home page and the location for downloaded files, can be set by opening AOL for Mac OS X and choosing Preferences from the Applications menu.

1. Launch System Preferences from the Dock or the Applications menu.

2. Click on the Internet icon. This brings up the screen shown in Figure 21-2.

NOTE
No sets? No, none at all in Mac OS X. You can establish a set of Internet preferences for each user, however. Apple must assume you have just one email address (plus the one for iTools, of course); however, individual email applications and browsers can store multiple account settings.

FIGURE 21-2   The Internet preference panel is simplified compared to the Classic Mac OS version.

3. If you have an iTools account, enter your member name and password. If you don't, feel free to click on the Free Sign Up button; your Web browser will open, and you'll be able to sign up for your own mac.com email account.

4. Click on the Email tab to move to the next section (see Figure 21-3).

5. First, pick your Default Email Reader from the pop-up menu.

6. Specify whether you want to use your iTools account as your default address. If you do, the rest of the information will be entered automatically.

7. Otherwise, specify your account information, clicking on the appropriate text box. As with all text fields in a dialog box, the TAB key can move you to the next one, and the SHIFT-TAB shortcut can move you to the previous field.

FIGURE 21-3   Put your default email information here.

NOTE *The information you enter here has to be obtained directly from your ISP (if it wasn't already copied from a previous Mac OS installation).*

8. Click the Web tab to change or check your browser preferences (see Figure 21-4.) You can specify whatever home and search page you prefer; you needn't stick with the ones placed there by Apple's Mac OS X installer or your ISP.

NOTE *Although Internet Explorer is Apple's default browser, there's nothing to prevent you from running any compatible Web browser. When you change the setting, applications with Web links or email with Web links will launch the default browser to call up the chosen Web site.*

9. The final setting in this window would normally place downloaded files on your Mac OS X desktop (this is the easiest location to use, for you don't have to think about which folder you put them in). If you prefer to have

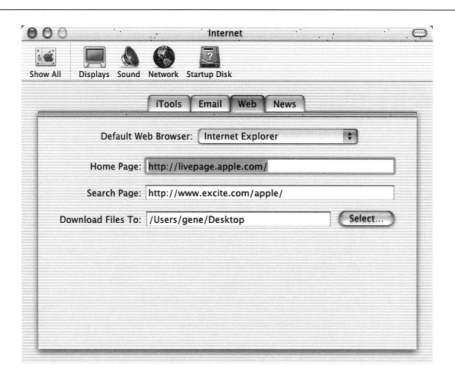

FIGURE 21-4   Choose your favorite browser here.

downloaded files placed elsewhere, click Select and choose a different location. Either way, you can put the files in a different location after the download is done.

NOTE

The settings you're making strictly apply to your user account. Each user account on your Mac can be configured with a different set of user preferences (except for those requiring administrator or owner access).

10. Once your Web preferences are complete, click the News tab (see Figure 21-5) to enter information about your ISP's newsgroup server settings. If you don't intend to access any newsgroups, you need not be concerned over this screen. Otherwise, you'll want to choose a news reader application, if none are shown. Mac OS X doesn't include such an application, but you'll be able to find a selection at VersionTracker.com. My personal preference, as of the time this book was written, was Thoth, a shareware entry from Brian Clark, author of YA-NewsWatcher, a popular Classic Mac OS news reader.

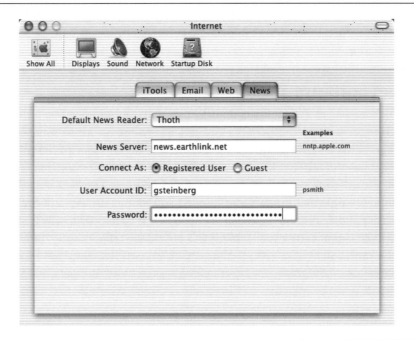

FIGURE 21-5   Configure your newsgroup settings from this window.

NOTE
Some ISPs, such as EarthLink, insist that you set your newsgroup software to log into the service to retrieve messages. This is done as a backlash to problems with some unsavory folks forging newsgroup messages on another service's facilities to get away with posting spam announcements.

No Advanced Internet Preferences? Something missing? Yes indeed. In the Internet Control Panel under the Classic Mac OS, you had another tab, Advanced, in which you could select helper applications, programs that would open automatically if you downloaded a specific document, such as Adobe Acrobat for PDF files. You can still set these so-called "helpers" in Microsoft's Internet Explorer, as a preference, but similar settings weren't available in the versions of OmniWeb and Opera I checked while writing this book.

NOTE
Our technical editor reminds us that Mac OS X has built-in settings to recognize files based on type and extension, and automatically selects the application with which to open them. However, you will still see a dialog box asking you to select the proper application if the one used to create a document isn't available.

NOTE
The loss of the Advanced setting isn't critical. Some application installers will configure themselves to become a "helper." This is true, for example, with Adobe Acrobat.

Internet Software Problems

Internet software has been implicated as the cause of a number of Macintosh ills—mysterious crashes while you're online or sudden slowdowns in performance. Why this happens is beyond the scope of this book. Even the presence of the robust Mac OS X kernel hasn't entirely eliminated the well-known flakiness of some of these programs, even though many of them have made the transition to Mac OS X.

It's quite possible that the fact that Internet software is usually free may mean that software publishers are not quite as inclined to test such products as thoroughly as retail products that earn a profit, but that's not necessarily a fair comment (and the publishers will deny it anyway). The climate for conflicts may just be the result of the fact that such programs are being asked to do a lot of complex tasks at the same time.

Whatever the cause, when a program unexpectedly quits or freezes, or suddenly runs slow as molasses, you're probably more concerned with finding an answer than worrying how the program got that way. In Chapter 18, I describe easy techniques to help you diagnose system-related crashes; I'll separate Classic from Mac OS X, even though the end result may be quite as annoying either way. If none of the solutions I provide here or in the next two chapters help you solve your Internet software crashes, you'll want to read that chapter as well.

> NOTE   *While you rarely have to restart Mac OS X in the event of a crash, you should always restart Classic if a Classic application quits, or you must force quit an application that's misbehaving. This can be done in the Classic preference panel of the System Preferences application. Otherwise, Classic behavior can get mighty flaky.*

Here are some common causes of crashes and other problems while surfing the Net, and their solutions:

- **ObjectSupportLib in Classic System Folder**   This system extension (which goes in the Extensions folder) was required for AppleScript and other functions before the arrival of Mac OS 8 and later system versions. Apple thoughtfully merged the program into the System file to reduce System Folder clutter, but some older software installers (from AOL, Netscape, and others) dutifully placed it in the Extensions folder anyway. In theory, its presence isn't supposed to matter. The System file overrides the function. In practice, removing this file has made some mysterious system crashes disappear. So be on the lookout for it if you're using Mac OS 8 or later.

- **Corrupted Web cache**   Follow the instructions in Chapter 22 to delete your Web cache. Such steps are among the first things you should do when you experience a crash when running your browser.

- **Corrupted preferences files**   This is a major cause of crashes when using a specific program. These files are in use all the time. Every single change you make to how a program runs will end up in that preferences file, and if it becomes corrupted, you may experience frequent, unexplained crashes when opening an application or just doing one function or another. Unfortunately, it's not always easy to find the preferences files, as each Internet program puts them in another location—not necessarily the Preferences folder inside the Library folder in your Mac OS X's user directory or the one inside the System Folder for Classic applications. My suggestion is that you use Apple's search application, Sherlock, to locate all files with the name of your Internet program in it, then pay attention to the one with the word "preferences." That's the one you should remove and place on the desktop. Then start the program again and see if the problems still occur. You'll have to redo your program settings, of course, but this step could also stop the problems you're having.

NOTE *You should not attempt to remove a program's preferences files while the program is running. Quit the program first. Otherwise, the program may crash.*

NOTE *If you launch some Internet software, such Netscape, after removing the regular preferences file, you will probably have to endure a brief questionnaire or setup routine to restore your basic program settings.*

- **Buggy Internet software**   Internet software gets frequent updates to fix one problem or another. You might want to check the publisher's Web site for information about problems and solutions. Another great source of information is the VersionTracker Web site at http://www.versiontracker.com.

- **Classic Mac OS extension conflicts**   This is the usual bugaboo with any Mac running the Classic environment. I suggest you read Chapter 18 for a no-frills strategy to isolate extension conflicts.

- **Kernel extension conflicts**   Believe it or not, Mac OS X also has its own brand of extensions, though the impact isn't as severe as in the Classic Mac OS. I will show you how to remove a kernel extension in Chapter 18.

- **Java**   Java makes it possible for Web sites to embed fancy graphics and animation. Unfortunately, there are different versions of Java used for these sites and different versions used by Apple or with your Web browser. Sometimes your browser may freeze when you access a Java-capable site. If this happens, there's not much you can try other than (after restarting, of course) trying a different browser or looking for an update to your browser or to Apple's Java software. If you can get on the problem Web site at all, contact the webmaster or the company running the site and alert them as to your problem. In the meantime, you may just want to switch off the browser's Java feature (it'll be a program preference) until the problem is resolved.

NOTE

The decision of Microsoft to remove Java as a standard component of the forthcoming Windows XP might cause webmasters to scurry for other means to provide special content. Only time will tell how Java will fare in this new climate.

Mysterious Extensions Appear in Classic System Folder

When you install new software, sometimes you just cannot predict what files a program needs to run. In the old days, the application's folder contained everything. You tossed out that folder, and all elements of the application went with it.

As programs and system software become more and more complex, however, various and sundry files began show up in different parts of the System Folder. There are extensions that contain various files, settings files in the Preferences folder, and perhaps a module or two for the Control Strip and Contextual Menus Items folder.

And that isn't all.

If you install Netscape Communicator, you'll find a mysterious item appearing on your Classic menu bar that accesses the Netscape-branded version of AOL Instant Messenger (whether or not you even care about using that program).

Solution? Go to your Extensions folder and look for two extensions, AIM Menu and Idle Time. Remove them and restart.

Presto! No more menu bar link to Instant Messenger.

Another AOL-related extension is OpenOT, which was designed to address an AppleTalk conflict with Macs using Apple's Open Transport networking software. Apple fixed the problem in Mac OS 8 and later, but this wayward extension has been implicated as the potential cause of some system crashes.

Fortunately, such ills don't afflict Mac OS X, but as long as you need to run Classic applications, those mysterious extensions can still do enough damage to make your Mac experience less than stable.

Solving Internet
Connection Problems

How to Speed Downloads and Uploads

It would be nice to be able to tell you that once your Internet and modem settings are correct, everything will run the way you want it to. But what if the performance is still not what you expect? You try to retrieve a needed software update or send an important document file to a business colleague, and it seems to take a very long time for the process to end.

Here are a few tips to get the best possible download and upload performance:

- **Check for faster dial-up access numbers.**   Make sure the number you use to dial your ISP supports the fastest speed of which your modem is capable. While most services have upgraded their numbers for 56K access, some numbers still support slower speeds. You should double-check this, or just try another number when connection speeds aren't what you expect. Chapter 20 has more information on this subject.

- **Don't log on during evening prime time.**   It doesn't matter how many access numbers your ISP has in your city or how big their network is. When you log on during the hours when most other folks are trying to access the Internet as well, performance may suffer. You'll get the best possible performance from your Net connection during the early morning hours. This is important if you want to download a big file, which can tie up your Mac for quite a long time.

- **Use the latest Internet software.**   This is especially true for Web browsers, as the publishers try to find ways to make them run faster and retrieve Web pages and files more efficiently. I'll cover this subject in more detail in the next chapter.

Getting Top Performance from Your Internet Connection

The Internet is getting more and more graphic heavy every day. Attractive artwork, animation, sound, and video help bring people to a Web site. But they also make it take a lot longer for you to access a site.

Consider these possibilities if you want top-flight Internet performance:

- **Get a faster modem.**   At the time this book went to press, 56K modems for Macs were less than $100, give or take a few dollars and the manufacturer's rebate of the week. Read Chapter 20 for information on optimizing modem performance.

■ **Upgrade to a "broadband" Internet service protocol.**   Both cable modems and DSL (and a few related options) are touted as the next great thing for high-speed Internet access. I'll cover these subjects in more detail at the very end of this chapter.

■ **Get a RAM upgrade.**   Internet software works best with a healthy dose of RAM (especially a Web browser). While Mac OS X has a highly efficient virtual memory system, performance can still bog down if you have just the minimum of 128MB of RAM available. With RAM prices still quite cheap, it wouldn't hurt to stock up. Chapter 4 covers the topic of RAM upgrades.

NOTE   *A personal experience: I installed Mac OS X on a grape iMac/266 (commonly known as Rev. C). At 128MB, performance was perfectly awful; upgraded to 256MB, it was quite decent, thank you. 256MB appears to be a "sweet spot" for Mac OS X.*

■ **Get a faster Mac or a processor upgrade card.**   Processor upgrades are readily available for G3 desktops, and they get cheaper all the time. You can choose from a speedier G3 or even go for a G4, which better exploits Mac OS X's speed potential. But before you spend a few hundred dollars on such an upgrade path, you'll want to check pricing on an all-new or more recent Mac. You may be able to get a newer, faster Mac for a similar amount of money (assuming you can get a reasonable sum for selling your old Mac). This subject is covered in more detail in Chapter 3.

NOTE   *Yes, I know the makers of G3 and G4 upgrade cards can deliver unsupported Mac OS X installation solutions for older Macs. While performance appears to be quite decent and reasonably reliable in such systems, you should seriously consider an approved option first before going this route.*

The Low-Down on Broadband Access

How times have changed! It wasn't so long ago when a 28,800 bps or 56,000 bps modem seemed to speed along at a blazing rate. Web pages appeared much faster, and it didn't take quite as long to retrieve software from an FTP or Web site.

But as files get bigger and the Web offers more and more multimedia content (including streaming audio and video), performance seems to drag. And ongoing network problems in the evening hours contribute to this mess.

Getting Top Performance from Your Internet Connection

Fortunately, there are ways afoot to speed up your Internet access to do the same things Apple's G3 and G4 microprocessors did to speed up your Mac computing experience. But it means the days for the conventional analog modem are probably numbered.

Here's a fast look at the newest methods out there to speed up delivery of Internet content to your Mac.

Cable Modems

If you have cable TV, it's quite possible your cable provider is offering Internet service, too. A cable modem attaches direct to your Mac's Ethernet port or your hub, using settings you make with your Network preference panel, in the System Preferences application. The result? Ultrafast Internet access, using the cable provider's own high-speed network. Depending on a firm's promotional literature, they are advertising speeds of over 1,000,000 bits per second (sometimes much higher). Awesome! In addition, pricing may not be all that high, especially when the service is first offered and the cable provider wants to build a customer network fast.

The reality is something else altogether, however:

- ■ **Speed depends on traffic load.**   You are sharing your cable with others, and if there's a lot of traffic on the network (especially during the primetime evening hours), your speed will suffer, so take promises of any particular performance level with a grain of salt. But even at their worst, cable modems perform a whole lot faster than your 56K modem.

- ■ **Upload speed may be throttled.**   To limit excess traffic on their network, cable services may throttle back the potential speed for uploading. This may not be very important to you, unless you intend to send large files via email or FTP to an Internet site on a regular basis. The usual upload rates range from 128 Kbps to 256 Kbps, but may be less when traffic is heavy.

NOTE   *Even worse, some cable ISPs use an analog modem for uploads, which means that performance may be no better than a 33.6K modem, frequently worse. Sometimes this is a preliminary measure, until the neighborhood wiring process is finished, but that's not always the case. My sole experience with such a service, something called Cox@home Express (a interim service that was provided until full two-way service was instituted in a neighborhood), offered upload speeds no better than a 14.4K modem.*

■ **You may have to change your email address.**   When you hook up to a cable modem, you may have to sign up with the cable provider's own Internet service, not the one you have now. This may be an inconvenience if you're used to a specific ISP, or perhaps if you have lots of online contacts you'd have to notify if you go to another company. If this represents a problem, see if your ISP is offering or plans to offer DSL access (which is described in the next section).

NOTE   *In the wake of the huge AOL Time Warner merger, cable companies are beginning to allow other ISPs to use their networks. So it may very well be that you won't have to switch providers. You'll need to check with your ISP or your cable service for more information.*

■ **Availability may be limited.**   This is the real kicker. You just may not be able to get a cable modem, period. Your cable provider not only has to have the facilities to offer this service, they need to wire your area for digital service. That can take a while, a long while (figure months or even years).

■ **There may be security issues.**   When you are using a cable modem, you are, in effect, part of a large Ethernet network. If you must use file sharing, make sure you limit file access in the Show Info window to registered users. This is done by choosing None in the pop-up menu in the Everyone Else category under Privileges. You may want to turn off file sharing altogether, except during the actual file exchange process. And don't be surprised if you see someone else's LaserWriter in the Print Center application, if AppleTalk is activated. If you have concerns about network security, contact your cable provider and see what protection they offer. If you don't get a satisfactory answer, consider setting up a firewall to protect your Mac from outside intruders. This subject is covered in the final section of this chapter.

DSL

Another fast-rising high-speed Internet feature is DSL, short for Digital Subscriber Line. DSL takes your existing copper phone lines and uses digital technology to pump data through at a much higher rate.

Speeds depend on the sort of DSL service that's available in your city, from 256K to 1500K! A similar service, ADSL (Asymmetric DSL), offers top speed on file and Web downloads, but limits uplink speed (how much depends on the service). ADSL has been approved by the International Telecommunications

Getting Top Performance from Your Internet Connection

Union (ITU), the agency that handles such standards, and it was designed with the hope of delivering high-speed access to a greater number of users at lower cost.

Unfortunately, not everyone can get this service, be it regular DSL or ADSL. For one thing, you have to be within three miles of your phone company's switching center. In addition, your phone company may need to install new switching equipment to accommodate this feature.

However, if you live in a large metropolitan area or a newly developed neighborhood, it is quite likely that you do meet these basic requirements. Contact your local phone company or Internet service for specifics about availability.

If you are able to receive DSL service, you will still have to pay for a special modem (or routing device), costing as much as $300 or more, and pay an extra installation charge. When you factor in monthly rates of $30 to $60 plus the cost of your Internet service, it begins to add up. However, as the service is deployed in more areas, competition heats up, and the costs per installation go down, you may expect prices to fall to more respectable levels.

NOTE *To be perfectly fair, some DSL services do have special sign-up offers that may include free installation or low-cost or no-cost DSL modems. However, the well-publicized failure of some third-party DSL providers has lessened the incentive to offer such deals. However, that doesn't mean you still won't have to wait weeks for installation. A* Time *magazine writer wrote once of his 6-month odyssey to obtain DSL at his California home.*

As with cable modems, DSL is always on, and uses your Ethernet network and your Network preference panel for access, so setup isn't terribly difficult.

Other Broadband Alternatives

Cable modems and DSL aren't the only ways to join the fast lane. There are other alternatives, one of which is only barely available on a Mac at this point in time. Here's a brief description:

- **Fixed wireless** If the wired alternatives aren't available in your neighborhood, there may be yet another alternative. A fixed wireless service, typified by Sprint Broadband Direct, uses a small antenna installed on the roof of your home or office. Uploads and downloads are sent over the air to the service's transmission towers at a distance of up to 35 miles.

The advantage is that capacity can be increased at the tower or "head end" without having to do rewiring. However, it's also a line-of-sight service, and large obstacles, such as trees or hills, may eliminate this as an option. When it works, performance can be stunning. In my particular home office setup, I can routinely see downloads of 1-1/2 to 4 megabits per second, but uploads usually range from 25 to 128 Kbps (this area of the service was still a work in progress).

■ **Satellite**   The very same services that deliver digital TV via satellite may also be able to give you broadband Internet. However, such services tend to be more costly than cable or DSL, performance is usually much slower and, as of the time this book was written, Mac support was still a promise rather than a reality. But in a small community where wired or fixed wireless options aren't feasible, this may be the only way to go.

It remains to be seen which broadband access protocol, cable, DSL, or one of the less used options, emerges triumphant. But if 56K is getting you down, and you'd like to harness the real power of the Internet, these technologies are definitely worth more than a second look.

A Fast Look at Firewalls

One of the best security measures to keep intruders from vandalizing your Mac is the firewall. A *firewall* is software that, in effect, puts up a wall of protection around your Mac, preventing unwanted network traffic from getting in, and, in some cases, preventing information from getting out.

There are a number of firewall options for you, one of which actually uses the built-in Unix tools of Mac OS X. I'll describe them next:

■ **Firewalk X**   You needn't concern yourself with Mac OS X's command-line interface to configure a firewall. This shareware program puts all the settings in a pretty Aqua interface for you. The heart of Firewalk X is a convenient setup assistant that walks you through all the settings you need to provide the maximum level of protection. That way you don't have to concern yourself over user settings, just the results.

- **Norton Personal Firewall**   Symantec's solution is a user-friendly application (see Figure 21-6) that automatically establishes the settings you need to deliver robust protection. In case the setup interface looks familiar, Symantec's application is based on DoorStop Personal Edition from Open Door Networks.

- **Intego NetBarrier**   Intego is becoming a utility alternative to Symantec. NetBarrier (which was expected to appear in Mac OS X trim when this book goes to press) offers a simplified tabbed user interface that lets you customize a number of settings, including blocking passwords from leaving your Mac.

- **Hardware firewall**   If you want to share your broadband Internet connection across a Mac network, you'll want to consider a sharing router. Such products, which come from a number of network hardware makers, such as Asante, Farallon, and Linksys, serve as a DHCP server. They distribute the net connection to a number of computers, whether they use the Mac OS, Windows, or Linux operating systems. Some of these products also include Ethernet hubs or switches, and can even function as a print server. That lets you run a small network with a single product. A few products also offer a wireless connection, compatible with the 802.11b standard used by Apple's AirPort products. The actual firewall protection is provided using a feature called NAT (short for Network Address Translation), which, in effect, hides the IP numbers of computers connected to the router (so they cannot be seen).

TIP   *Is your Mac safe from Net vandals? One way to check is to access Gibson Research's Web site (http://www.grc.com). The site offers several tests to determine whether outsiders can break in. While they are primarily designed for Windows computers, the folks at Gibson tell me they work on Macs, too.*

CAUTION   *Remember that when you share an Internet connection, you are also sharing the bandwidth, so each computer on the network will get slower performance if several are accessing the Internet at the very same time.*

| FIGURE 21-6 | This application eases the process of setting up a firewall on your Mac. |

Summing Up

In this chapter, you discovered how to get the most reliable performance from your ISP and explored some of the options that can deliver ultrafast net surfing to your home or office.

In the next chapter, you'll learn how get the highest level of performance and reliability from your Web browser.

Chapter 22

Making Your
Web Browser Browse

A large part of your Internet experience is confined to a single piece of software, the Web browser. The browser is the easiest Internet software to use and without doubt the most aggravating.

When you connect to your ISP, your Web browser is putting a face on your Internet access (well, except for such services as AOL, which has its own unique interface and considers the browser just one part of the service).

What to Do When You Cannot Access a Site

There's not much you can do to get better browser performance if you cannot first access the sites you want. I cover connection problems in Chapters 20 and 21. But once you tackle those issues, there's more you can do if a site still won't show up.

You may have accessed the very same site just an hour earlier. Now you try again and get a message that it's not available, or your Web browser just chugs along and nothing happens. Here are some common causes and solutions:

- **Sorry, wrong address.**   If you even mess up one letter in the URL, you'll get either the wrong site or a message (see Figure 22-1) that the server can't be found. All you can do is recheck the address and make sure it's entered correctly.

- **DNS server can't be found.**   This is another typical message you'll get if you try to access a site that, for some reason, isn't available (it's Netscape's version). Check, and maybe reenter, the URL. You should also verify that you haven't been disconnected from your ISP.

- **Computer cannot establish a network socket connection.**   You see this message if you try to access a site via Netscape, but you didn't make a proper connection to your Internet service. If you see it, verify that you really logged on, and if not, try logging on again (you may have to actually use the Disconnect button in the Internet Connect application, then press Connect again to get online).

NOTE   *In theory, you should see a warning prompt if a connection to your ISP isn't achieved, but that doesn't always happen. So manually logging off and then on again is the best solution.*

■ **Site is down for maintenance.**   This can happen early in the morning, when Web hosting servers and Internet services schedule maintenance on their equipment. Your best solution is to try at a later hour and see if the problem is still there.

■ **Site has closed.**   It happens. A business goes under—and many have during the so-called dot.com meltdown—or they choose to cancel a Web site for one reason or another. Or maybe they changed the name. Usually in that case, at least for a while, a big site will set up a way to redirect the user from the old name to the new one, but after a period of time, the older address may no longer point to the new one. Your best solution here is to try to contact the business directly.

■ **Your Internet provider has a problem.**   Whether it's AOL or a regular Internet service provider (ISP), they will have scheduled maintenance from time to time. If you succeed in logging on, check the service's site for system status. On AOL, you use the keyword **AOL Update** to access this information feature. EarthLink subscribers can check the System Status page at their Web site (http://help.mindspring.com/netstatus/).

NOTE   *Don't be misled by the MindSpring link to access EarthLink's network status page. The two companies are now one, and I don't want to guess why the network status link is set up this way, even though the combined company is still called EarthLink.*

■ **User identification failed (a dilemma for AOL users).**   This has nothing whatever to do with the user identification and password you use when you access your ISP. It's an error message that shows up on occasion with AOL's browser. You can try logging off and logging on again, or even deleting the Web cache of your AOL browser (see "Removing Web Caches," later in the chapter). Sometimes, one of these solutions will work. But just as often it's an AOL problem, and until they fix it at their end, you're out of luck.

■ **Attempt to load failed.**   If you cannot access a site, make sure you're really logged on. It's possible you're disconnected. If you don't have some visual indication that you are online (a modem light on an external modem or a light on your regular phone, for example), just close your Internet connection and log on again. If you still experience this problem, try the same site or another Web site to be certain that the problem isn't just a one-time thing.

■ **128-bit browser needed.**   There are two types of security with Web browsers today. The standard 40-bit is secure enough for most purposes, but experienced computer hackers can usually break through given enough time. The second option is 128-bit, which, the theory goes, would take years and years and years to overcome. The browsers you get on your new Mac or via an online service are now all 128-bit, but if you're using an older browser in the Classic mode, it may still be 40-bit. But such places as banks and brokerage houses will not let you access your accounts from their Web sites without 128-bit. While all current Web browsers are supposedly 128-bit capable, some Web sites may not recognize the browser, in which case you may have to contact the site's support link or webmaster to address this problem.

NOTE   *It's a sad fact that some sites do not know there is such a thing as a Mac, and test their sites and online security systems only on Windows browsers. However, if you make it clear to the company that it will not get your business if they don't change—and enough Mac users do the same— they will probably mend their ways. Proper coding of a Web site should make it platform neutral.*

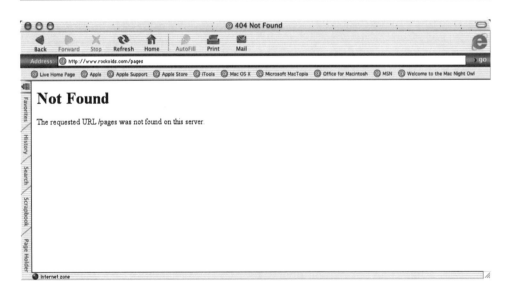

FIGURE 22-1   Where's that site? Your browser can't find it.

Making Your Browser Run Faster

Even if you've followed the suggestions I made in Chapters 20 and 21 to make sure your modem and Internet connection are running at top efficiency, it's possible your browser isn't quite delivering the performance you expect. Fortunately, there are still more things you can do to get things up to speed.

Tips on Speeding Up a Web Browser Cache

There are caches and there are caches. It seems that Macs are filled with caches of one sort or another. Under the Classic Mac OS, you had the Memory Control Panel, used to set aside a portion of RAM to speed up drive access by storing frequently used data. Your hard drive has a cache used to make it work a bit faster. In addition, the G3 and G4 processors your Mac uses have their own cache memories to decrease "wait states" and get data to the CPU faster.

Your Web browser uses a cache, too. But it's not a piece of RAM. It's a set of files (or one file if you're using the latest versions of Internet Explorer and AOL's bundled browser) that contain the Web files you've retrieved.

Every time you access a Web site, your browser consults the cached files to see if the artwork is already there, and if not, retrieves it directly from the Web site. Of course, the process is not quite that simple. The browser is using its own internal logic to locate cached files and purge the older, less used ones.

When you set up your browser, a fixed size for the cache is established. As you'll see from the following problems and solutions, you can change that size, or purge the cache and start over for improved performance.

Removing Web Caches

As the cache gets filled with older artwork, sometimes the browser doesn't work as efficiently, and the benefits of having the files on your Mac are lost. The best thing to do is just start over.

NOTE
There is a separate Web cache for every user who has a login account on your Mac. You'll need to follow these steps for each user, or log in as administrator and manually locate the cache files for each Web browser in the Library>Preferences folder for each user and trash them (after quitting the browsers, of course).

Here's how to do it with AOL and other popular Web browsers:

NOTE *Even though a Mac OS X–savvy version of Netscape 6.1 was being previewed when this book was written, I am including another version in this section because many users still prefer the previous generation of Netscape, and it actually works quite well in Classic mode.*

Netscape Navigator (or Communicator) 4.7x

1. Choose Preferences from the Edit menu.

2. Look for the Advanced category, and click on the arrow to expand the view (if the view isn't already expanded).

3. Click on the item labeled Cache (see Figure 22-2).

4. Click on the button labeled Clear Disk Cache Now.

5. OK the confirmation message you see next. Now you just have to be patient. If you have a big cache, it'll take a few seconds for the purging process to complete.

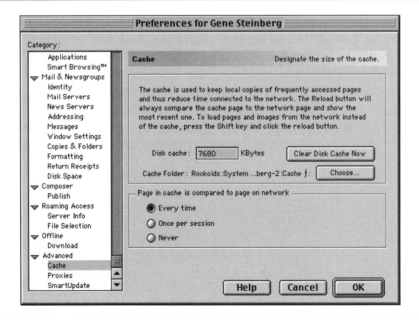

FIGURE 22-2   The Classic version of Netscape is still preferred by many Mac users to the Mac OS X–savvy alternatives.

Netscape 6.1 for Mac OS X

1. Choose Preferences from the Edit menu.

> NOTE
>
> *Yes, I know the Preferences dialog box should be in the Applications menu, but this was an early version of Netscape for Mac OS X; I expect the folks at AOL's Netscape division will get the message and put it in the right place by the time you read this book.*

2. Look for the Advanced category, and click on the arrow to expand the view (if the view isn't already expanded).

3. Click on the item labeled Cache (see Figure 22-3).

4. Click on the button labeled Clear Disk Cache.

5. OK the confirmation message you see next. Now you just have to be patient. If you have a big cache, it'll take a few seconds for the purging process to complete.

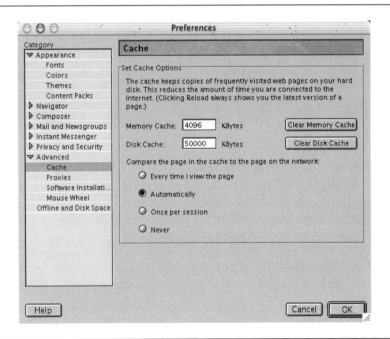

FIGURE 22-3 Netscape 6.1 had not been fully developed when this book was written, so what you see here may change slightly.

Tips on Speeding Up a Web Browser Cache

Microsoft Internet Explorer

1. Choose Preferences from the Application menu.

2. Click on the arrow to the left of the Web Browser category to expand the view (if it's not already done).

3. Click on the Advanced category, which brings up the screen shown in Figure 22-4.

4. Click the Empty Now button to clear the cache. The purging process is done in the blink of an eye.

NOTE   *Internet Explorer's cached artwork is placed in a single file, called IE cache.waf. This is done to speed access of the artwork. When you empty the cache, the file itself isn't actually deleted, just the cached information inside the file.*

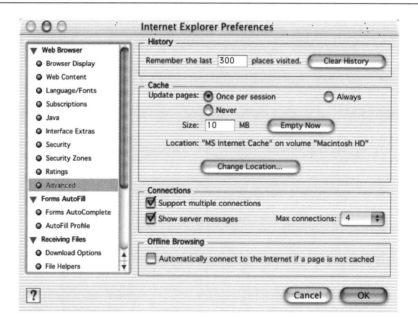

FIGURE 22-4   Internet Explorer for Mac OS X's Web cache is removed this way.

AOL for Mac OS X

1. Choose Preferences from the Application menu.

2. Scroll to the WWW option.

3. On the screen that appears (see Figure 22-5), click the Empty Cache Now button. AOL shares the cache file allocated to Internet Explorer once it's set up, and purging its contents is nearly instantaneous.

4. Click OK to close the Preferences window.

NOTE *Are you using CompuServe 200 for Mac OS X? If so, you'll find that the preceding steps apply in exactly the same fashion to that application, which is just a redesigned version of AOL's regular client software.*

FIGURE 22-5 Killing two birds with one stone. Clearing AOL's Web cache has the same effect on Internet Explorer for Mac OS X.

Tips on Speeding Up a Web Browser Cache

iCab for Mac OS X

1. Choose Preferences from the Application menu.

2. Click on the arrow to the left of the Caches category to expand the view (if it's not already done).

3. Click on the Web Page Cache category, which brings up the screen shown in Figure 22-6.

4. Click on Clear Cache Now to clear the page cache.

5. Now choose the Images/History category (see Figure 22-7), and click Clear Cache Now to purge downloaded images from RAM.

> **NOTE** *As the setting implies, the image cache is strictly loaded into RAM for fast retrieval; the contents are not placed on disk.*

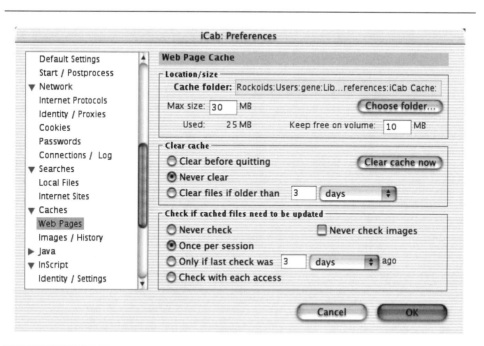

FIGURE 22-6   Clear iCab's Web Page Cache from this dialog box.

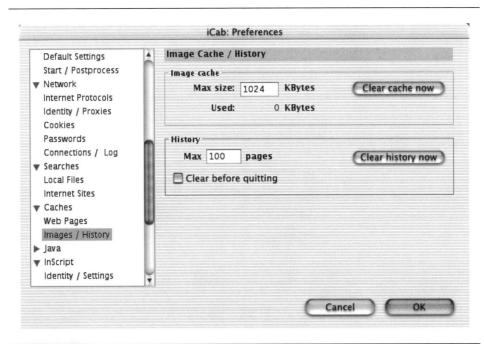

FIGURE 22-7   The second part of iCab's cache removal process is shown here.

OmniWeb

This is the easiest of all. Just choose Flush Cache from the Tools menu and the process is complete. While there are preferences to establish the timeout settings for cache files, the default configuration should be fine for good performance.

Opera for Mac OS X

1. Choose Preferences from the Application menu.

NOTE *Yes, I know the first preview version of Opera stubbornly insists on putting the Preferences dialog box in the Edit menu, but this is likely to change as the software matures, since the Application menu is the preferred location for Mac OS X programs.*

2. Click on History and Cache, which brings up the dialog box shown in Figure 22-8.

3. Click Empty Now to zap the cache.

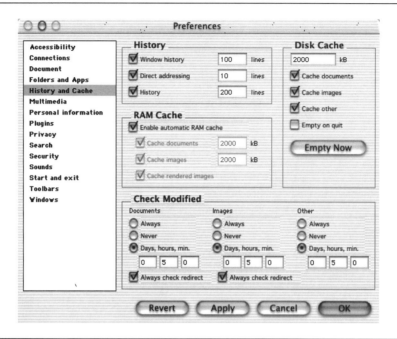

FIGURE 22-8   As with other browsers, a single press of a button will empty
Opera's cache.

Deleting Cache Files

If emptying a browser cache doesn't solve your problem, you may just want to trash
the actual files. First quit your browser, so you can actually empty the Trash can.

For Internet Explorer, do a Sherlock search for the IE cache.waf file
(depending on whether you use AOL, it may be in different locations), drag it to
the Trash, then empty the trash.

Netscape's Cache folder is generally located in a folder labeled Cache *f*, which
is usually in a folder with your Netscape username on it, inside the Netscape Users
folder (it was called Netscape *f* with older versions of the program) that is placed
in your System Folder's Preferences folder (complex, but that's how it goes).
When you find it, take the whole Cache *f* folder, drag it to the Trash, and then
empty the trash.

NOTE   *Don't delete the Netscape Users folder itself, because it contains other
files you need, such as your email address book, stored email, and
bookmarks (used to display your favorite Web sites).*

The other files and folders you'll want to seek out are called iCab Cache, a folder, and Opera Disk Cache, a single file.

> NOTE *Also remember that there will be a separate disk cache file or folder for each user of your Mac having a login account, which means the process can be repeated multiple times, unless, of course, you do it all via Sherlock.*

Boosting Web Cache Size

If you do a lot of Web surfing, the Web cache you set may fill up much too quickly, so the browser has to return to the site for updated artwork. This can slow down performance. By default, the publisher may assign from 2MB to 30MB for its Web cache. If you are unhappy with these settings, use the instructions in the following sections to locate and change your cache settings. Increasing the size of a Web cache in 5MB increments is best.

> NOTE *Too high a Web cache may be as harmful as too small. If you increase the cache by 10MB or more above its default setting, your browser may end up spending too much time checking the cache before retrieving an updated version of the site, which can slow things down. It's a balancing act; for the most part, I've stuck with default settings and managed to achieve good performance on all the Web browsers.*

As they say in the automobile business, your mileage may vary, so don't hesitate to do a little experimentation. If you reduce your cache size, first delete the existing cache, so you can start with a clean slate.

Netscape for the Classic Mac OS and Mac OS X

1. Choose Preferences from the Edit menu.

> NOTE *As stated previously, the Preference dialog box for the Mac OS X version of Netscape is apt to be found in the Application menu by the time you read this book.*

2. Look for the Advanced category, and click on the arrow to expand the view (if the view isn't already expanded).

Tips on Speeding Up a Web Browser Cache

3.   Click on the item labeled Cache, which brings up the screen that was shown back in Figure 22-2 (for the Classic version) and Figure 22-3 (for the Mac OS X version).

4.   Enter the cache figure in kilobytes.

5.   Click the OK button to store your settings.

Microsoft Internet Explorer for Mac OS X

1.   Choose Preferences from the Application menu.

2.   Click on the arrow to the left of the Web Browser category to expand the view (if it's not already done).

3.   Then click on the Advanced category, which brings up the screen shown back in Figure 22-4.

4.   Enter your Web cache setting in the Size text box, using MB.

5.   Click OK to save your settings.

AOL and CompuServe 2000 for Mac OS X

1.   Choose Preferences from the Application menu.

2.   Scroll to the WWW option.

3.   On the screen that appears (again see Figure 22-5), go to the Cache column at the bottom and choose a Web cache size from the pop-up menu.

4.   Click OK to close the Preferences window and store your settings.

> **NOTE**   *As mentioned earlier, AOL (or CompuServe 2000) and Internet Explorer share cache settings, so the change you make to one will, ultimately, affect the other.*

iCab for Mac OS X

1.   Choose Preferences from the Application menu.

2.   Click on the arrow to the left of the Caches category to expand the view (if it's not already done).

3. Click on the Web Page Cache category, which brings up the screen shown back in Figure 22-6.

4. Enter the new Web Page cache setting in the Max Size text box.

5. Click OK to save the settings.

OmniWeb

The cache size wasn't adjustable in the versions available when this book was written. You can, however, as explained earlier, adjust the Cache Timeout setting in the browser's preferences, under Cache. But this setting is confined to just a few minutes, normally.

Opera for Mac OS X

1. Choose Preferences from the Application menu.

2. Click on History and Cache, which brings up the dialog box shown back in Figure 22-8.

3. Enter the size in KB in the Disk Cache text field.

4. Click the Apply and then OK buttons to store your settings.

Case History

Hundreds of Thousands of Macs Ship with Beta Online Software

It is becoming more and more common for software publishers to post preview or beta versions of new software. There's an undeniable marketing advantage to such practices. It helps introduce potential customers to the new product, maybe even get them hooked on using it before the actual release.

Sometimes there's an advantage from the programming standpoint as well. The publisher is able to deliver the software to a wide range of potential users and get some feedback about potential problems or shortcomings that can be addressed before the software is released in its final form.

There's no shortage of such products that have come out. Apple, AOL, Microsoft, Netscape, Quark, Symantec, and other companies have put out these public betas or previews from time to time. What makes it confusing, however, is when the preview shows up already installed on your new Mac or on your new system software disks. A case in point is the preview version of AOL 4.0 that came out in 1998.

The final version of AOL 4.0 wasn't finished in time for the arrival of the iMac, or for Mac OS Systems 8.1 through 8.5.1. So Apple included the preview edition instead. This version didn't even have the same Web browser as the final release.

On the other hand, users of Windows 98 didn't fare any better. The version of AOL software that came with the original Windows 98 installation was also a preview.

For Mac OS X, the situation hasn't changed all that much. The version of Microsoft Internet Explorer that shipped with the original release of Apple's new operating system was also a preview edition. Only with the arrival of Mac OS X 10.1 did a final version of Internet Explorer ship.

Coping with Web Slowdowns

A corrupted or clogged cache file isn't the only cause for slow Web performance, though it's a common one. If clearing the cache (or dumping the files) doesn't do the trick, here are some additional things you may want to consider:

- **Problems at the Web site**   Some Web sites are actually run by a single computer, possibly a regular Mac or PC desktop computer. When capacity is filled, everyone's access slows down. Even larger sites have a finite capacity. All you can do is try again at a different hour.

- **Heavy Web traffic**   Whenever a popular Web site has a huge amount of activity, such as when a new movie trailer (such as the one for *Lara Croft: Tomb Raider)* is posted, or a new software update is offered, things may slow to a crawl. Your best bet is just to try again at a later time (early in the morning is best; set your alarm clock).

- **Heavy traffic at your ISP**   Whether you use AOL, CompuServe, or a regular ISP, there are times when the service's network will be clogged. Evening hours, equivalent to a prime time on a TV network, will tax their servers. If you intend to do heavy-duty Web surfing, you may want to avoid those hours.

Internet Software Crashes

Internet software has been implicated as the cause of a number of Macintosh ills—mysterious application freezes or quits while you're online—even when the crashes occur with software that isn't Internet related. This is beyond the scope of this book and a matter that would probably be more interesting to a computer programmer. In addition, it's not important whether the problems are caused by the fact that Internet programs are usually free, so a publisher may not be as inclined to test them thoroughly. There doesn't seem to be a lot of evidence for that theory. The most important thing here is the solution to the problem.

NOTE *Even though Mac OS X's Unix underpinnings are supposed to be virtually bullet proof, applications can still freeze or quit. The advantage to the Mac user is that you do not normally have to restart if you run into an application-specific problem. If the application freezes, just invoke Force Quit (COMMAND-OPTION-ESCAPE), pick the application you want to close, and move on.*

Chapter 21 covers a number of problems with Web software and solutions. In addition, you'll want to read Chapter 18, which covers fast techniques to find troubleshooting Mac OS X and Classic environment problems. Along with those suggestions, I have two more problems and their solutions to offer here:

- **Corrupted Web cache** In addition to slowing down your Web access, the cache files may contribute to other problems. For example, you access a site, your browser calls up the cache file, and the application quits or freezes up. It's hardly likely you'll be able to pick exactly which cache file has caused the problem (doubly so with AOL and Internet Explorer, which use a single cache file). One fast way out of this dilemma is simply to follow the steps I outlined earlier in the section called "Removing Web Caches."

- **Upgrade from the Preview version** For Internet Explorer, you can always depend on the Software Update preference panel to yield information about available updates. But for the other browsers, you'll want to check the publishers' Web sites, or VersionTracker.com for news. While OmniWeb was in a final release version, both iCab and Opera were in public preview mode when this book was written, and you should expect ongoing updates for either or both.

NOTE   *Truth to tell, iCab has been in public preview form for at least two years, as of the time this book was written, still with no certain date as to when the final version would be out. However, the previews have been pretty stable, with features expanding for each new release.*

Case History

Shimmering Pool of Water Causes Crash

As an audio and home theater buff, I enjoy visiting Web sites devoted to these subjects. One of those sites, which belongs to a popular American audio component manufacturer (one of the few remaining in an industry where much of the design and production is done outside the USA), used to feature a fancy home page, in which the faceplate for one of their top-selling products is reflected in a shimmering pool of water. At least that's how it is supposed to work, but every time I'd access the site from Internet Explorer, my Mac would crash.

I went through the usual routine of trashing the Web cache, isolating questionable system extensions—the whole nine yards.

Everything worked just fine with Netscape.

The webmaster for the site had no solution. The site looked fine to him and it worked fine, he said; he didn't seem upset that a potential visitor to the site had to endure such grief.

Finally, I decided to switch Internet Explorer's Java option to the Microsoft Virtual Machine. The site no longer crashed. On the other hand, I never saw the shimmering pool of water either, but at least I could examine the site safely for other treasures.

Since then, Microsoft has switched to Apple's own Java implementation, as standard issue. And, when the site's designers decided to use a different design motif, I no longer had to concern myself about missing pools of water.

How to Make Online Graphics Look Sharper

First and foremost, your Web experience is governed by the graphical display. There's almost no limit to what a Web site may provide, ranging from a simple picture to a full-blown video.

Naturally, you have no control over how the folks who created the Web site set up their graphics. Some will opt for high quality at the expense of it taking longer for you to receive the artwork. Others value speed above everything, since it's been shown that Web sites that deliver their artwork faster may get a greater number of visitors.

NOTE   *If you run a site with extremely high visibility, however, it may not matter what bag of tricks you use. The evidence of that is the vast number of downloads of movie trailers, some of which exceed 25MB in size. However, unless you are a major company with high pent-up demand for your products and services, lean and mean is always best. My science fiction Web site, http://www.rockoids.com, has a musical stinger on the front page, but we set it up so that visitors can just click the image or a navigation button to move on to the content and save time, especially with a slow dial-up connection.*

For AOL Users Only

AOL has a feature in its Web browser that compresses Web artwork into a special format (called .ART if you want to be technical). The advantage is that you see the pages faster, but quality may suffer (a lot in some cases). In some situations, you may find that those cute animated GIFs don't always animate as they should. And if you try to save the artwork to your hard drive, it will be in a format you can only read with AOL's software. Since the speedup really isn't all that much, here's how to rid yourself of this feature with for Mac OS X:

1. Launch AOL (don't bother signing on).

2. Choose Preferences from the Application menu.

3. Scroll to the WWW option.

4. On the screen that appears (refer back to Figure 22-5), uncheck the Use Compressed Images option.

5. Click OK to store your settings.

NOTE   *CompuServe 2000 for Mac OS X has the very same option, and it causes the very same damage to GIF artwork. So you'll want to turn it off, too, following the above instructions.*

Breathe a sigh of relief that your artwork will look better and you won't have to endure headaches trying to open any of the artwork in another program.

Web Artwork Advice for All Users

Whether you're on AOL or not, there are ways to make Web-based artwork look nicer. Try these suggestions:

- **Delete the Web cache to fix poor quality artwork.** If artwork previously retrieved by your browser gets damaged, it may crash your Mac, or the artwork will just not display properly. Consider deleting the Web cache if the quality of artwork deteriorates.

- **Refresh the page.** For whatever reason, maybe heavy network traffic, there's a problem in delivering the Web artwork to your Mac. The pages look grainy, or parts are missing. When you click the Refresh or Reload button on your browser, the page is retrieved from scratch from the Web site and often this fixes the problem (but not always).

TIP   *The Classic version of Netscape has a Super Refresh feature, where you hold down the OPTION key when you choose Reload from the View menu. It's supposed to provide a more efficient retrieval of the Web page. I've not seen any difference, but it doesn't hurt to try.*

- **Try another browser.** Not all browsers interpret the same artwork in the same fashion. Mac OS X comes with Internet Explorer as part of the package. There's no problem in using that program, plus iCab, Netscape, OmniWeb, and Opera at the same time. Mac OS X's superior memory-handling feature will allocate RAM as needed for best performance to the application you're using at the time. In addition, you'll want to check the publisher's Web sites for updates that might address a specific problem or improve performance. And, by the way, you can even run separate Internet software if you're an AOL member, as part of your AOL connection. While AOL uses Internet Explorer 5.1x for Mac OS X as its embedded browser, you can run the standalone version or one of the others, too, to see if you get better performance and improved or more accurate display of a Web site.

CAUTION   *AOL and CompuServe have many built-in Web links throughout the service. When you access those links, they will launch the service's built-in browser, not a separate browser. There is no way to change this setting (or at least not the version reviewed for this book), and switching default browsers in the Internet preference panel will have no impact.*

■ **Check your monitor settings.**   Web artwork is usually optimized to look good on both Mac and Windows computers, which means there's a compromise. But if you set up your Mac at the highest possible color depth (millions of colors if possible), you'll benefit from being able to see all the color your Mac is capable of delivering. You can also calibrate your monitor with ColorSync (see Chapter 10 for the specifics) to get the best possible color balance on your Mac.

Summing Up

If you follow through on the information in this chapter, you'll be able to resolve many of the problems you might encounter surfing the Web, and you'll be able to get better performance.

In the next and final chapter, I'll cover another, and perhaps the most important, element of your Internet experience—email.

How to Make Online Graphics Look Sharper

Chapter 23

Making Email Work for You

The U.S. Postal Service may not like it, but email has come to dominate our lives. Whether it's within the office or on the Internet, you just open your email program, write a message, and send it. Next to cell phones, it's *the* way to communicate.

In theory, email ought to be one of the simplest things you can do on your Mac. In practice, there are complexities. Sometimes the mail doesn't get through; sometimes your email program can't manage more than a few sessions without a crash. And then there are all those side issues, such as how to handle email attachments and the threat of virus infections, that make the process even more involved.

This chapter focuses on how to harness the power of email without having to put up with the nasty side effects.

When Email Doesn't Reach Its Destination

More often than not, email doesn't get to the right place because you made a simple mistake. You left out a letter, a number, or an underscore, or entered the domain (service) name incorrectly. Usually you'll get some kind of message explaining what happened and why. Then all you do is send the message again.

But getting a notice isn't a given. Some services won't "bounce" email with any sort of notice, so you may want to consider these possible solutions.

- **Send it again.**   Sometimes the message just, well, gets lost. Internet traffic is a gigantic relay race. Data is passed from computer to computer, from service to service. That it works most of the time is a miracle, and sometimes it doesn't.

- **Recheck the address.**   Yes, even a single incorrect character in the username or domain name (the name of the service) can make the email go astray. You may not even get a message indicating it went to the wrong place, especially if the incorrect address is real (just not the person you wanted to contact).

- **Try a different address.**   If your recipient has another email address, use it. See if it works.

- **Remove file attachments.**   As I will explain later, services often impose restrictions on the size of email attachments, so if the email isn't getting there, try it without the attachment and see if it works any better.

■ **Try another email program.**   If you're not on AOL, you have a choice of some really terrific programs, and some of the major ones are free. If, for example, Mail, Apple's Cocoa-built email client, isn't doing the job, try Netscape Communicator (or vice versa). If you want a different range of features, consider such commercial options as Eudora from Qualcomm (the very same folks who used to make cell phones before selling off the product line to Kyocera) or Entourage, the email and personal information manager component of Microsoft Office.

NOTE   *When it comes to Internet email, there is no guarantee it'll get there right away. Sometimes it seems to arrive in an instant; at other times, it takes hours. You may just have to be patient.*

Case History   There Is Only One Gene

Having a single-name screen name (email address) on AOL is supposed to be a sign of distinction (or at least it means you've been there a long time). But sometimes it can be a curse.

A case in point: On AOL, I'm known simply as Gene (it's gene@aol.com for nonmembers). It's not that I got there first; in fact, there was another Gene on AOL, but that fellow left the service, and I was able to create the screen name before anyone else got there (thanks to the help of a long-gone AOL producer, who alerted me in time to grab the name ahead of anyone else).

Unfortunately, it creates the climate for mistakes.

As I have said in this chapter, there is no room for an incorrect email address, just as there is no room for an incorrect phone number. One wrong letter, an incorrect domain, and you get the "wrong number."

Hardly a day passes when I don't receive email or an instant message on AOL from someone thinking I am somebody else. Folks mistake me for their long-lost brother, father, or schoolmate. I have received emails congratulating me on my birthday, my recovery from an illness, plus personal documents that include financial statements and tax returns.

One of the biggest sources of confusion is the relationship between the online or screen name and someone's real name. The real name might be different, or it might be the same, but novice users don't always understand the distinction.

When Email Doesn't Reach Its Destination

Naturally, I correct these folks about their mistakes, and no, I don't look into their private files to see what's what. Most folks are glad I caught them in a serious mistake; some get, shall we say, huffy that I'd dare tell them they made a mistake.

But the upshot is that you should be absolutely, completely sure that you have your recipient's email address correctly entered before you send your messages.

How to Handle Email Attachments

You have just finished a project on your Mac, and your client needs the files right away. So you open your email software, click the Attach button, and speed it on its way. Two hours later, your client calls, frantically worrying over the fact that the email never arrived. You assure your client the files were sent and to just be patient.

But another hour passes, and your email is bounced back to you, with some arcane message or other that doesn't make any sense, since you know the email address is correct. What went wrong?

Here are some things you might want to consider when sending attachments with your email messages:

- **Avoid large attachments.** An ISP may have limitations as to how big a file attachment can be, and that information isn't always readily available. With the exception of messages from one AOL member to another (see also the section entitled "AOL Email Quirks and Solutions"), I'd recommend you try to restrict your email attachments to 2MB in size. You can use StuffIt to compress your files to the smallest possible size. If the file ends up larger than 2MB, you may want to break up the file into segments and send it as separate pieces or consider another way to transfer the file. Some Internet providers give you free FTP or Web space (it's 2MB on AOL, 10MB for Excite@Home, 6MB on EarthLink, 10MB for Prodigy Internet). You can use that space to contain files. Or you may just want to place the files on a disk and send it in the traditional fashion to your recipient.

NOTE   *If you plan on handling large file attachments, you might want to contact a Web hosting service and see if they can set you up with some FTP space for file transfers. The price is often cheaper than what it would cost to store a regular Web site. (For example, pair Networks, at http://www.pair.com, which hosts some of the larger Mac Web sites, charges a mere $5.95 a month for FTP-only service.)*

■ **Try again.**   Maybe you didn't address the email properly or there was a network-related problem that prevented the message from going to its proper destination. If the file is mission critical, it doesn't hurt to try a second time to be sure. If your recipient has more than one email address, try sending to another address, or just send the email to all the addresses at once (if the recipient doesn't mind getting multiple copies, of course).

Is There a Danger from Email Viruses?

You read the email warnings. Don't open this, that, or the other email, or your files will be destroyed, your hard drive wrecked, your life made miserable. Is there any reason to worry?

Absolutely not (but with just one condition).

First and foremost, the only way a virus can be activated or transferred is for you to download and launch an infected file. While email programs (other than AOL) do download the file as part of the process of retrieving the messages, you'd still have to launch an infected file for it to do some damage. Just reading an email message is not going to cause your Mac to go haywire because of a virus.

But that doesn't stop folks from sending bogus warnings about such things. A big example dates back to 1994. Tens of thousands of folks received email warnings about something called the Good Times virus. This is the myth, the progenitor of many of those phony email virus warnings, and many of you no doubt got email about it way back then if you were active on the Internet:

The FCC has discovered a virus which infects your computer if you read a message with "Good Times" or some other evil phrase in the subject line. Simply reading the message with your eyeballs will destroy your computer's processor by setting it into an "nth complexity infinite binary loop."

An "nth complexity infinite binary loop" sounds like something even a science fiction writer like me, used to technobabble, would worry about.

The fact of the matter is that there never was such a virus, and the statement that just opening email can infect you happens to be false. If you receive a warning of this sort, don't pass it on. Just delete it, or let the sender know it's a fake (probably they were taken in as well).

A Real Email-Driven Virus

Even though opening a message won't pass a virus on to your Mac, it doesn't mean that a virus-infected file can't be attached to your email. That is where the real threat may exist.

In March 1999, there was a real virus threat and it caught even experienced system administrators unaware. Fortunately, users of the other platform were most vulnerable to this problem (Mac users would only suffer a side effect if they used Microsoft Word 98 for the Mac).

One day, email by the ton reached recipients around the world with the words "Important message from…" in the subject line, and giving the name of someone these recipients knew. The body of the message included such lines as "Here is that document you asked for…" and sure enough a Microsoft Word document was included.

As I said, this particular virus was most destructive if you used Windows or worked in a cross-platform installation that used Microsoft Office for Windows (and most do). If a Windows user actually downloaded and launched that document it would invoke a macro virus, called Melissa, which would replicate itself and send the very same message on to the first 50 email addresses in your address book. Worse, Melissa would disable the virus alerts that Word puts up to warn about macro viruses.

Since Microsoft Word macros work on both Macs and PCs, the threat was everywhere. The damage to Mac users was basically to the Normal template under Word 98 or Word 2001, which in itself would be enough to cause trouble when you tried to create and edit documents. For Windows users, the virus was potentially a complete and devastating way to mess up your email system.

Fortunately, the publishers of virus software worked overtime to produce updates that would detect and eradicate Melissa (and the new strains of a similar nature that emerged shortly thereafter).

AppleScript Virus Causes Havoc

Although email viruses have done the worst damage on the Windows platform, the situation underwent a change in the spring of 2001. The disheartening news came from Symantec's AntiVirus Research Center about a virus created in AppleScript, which does its dirty work with Microsoft's free email client, Outlook Express, or in Entourage, the email and personal information manager application that comes with Office 2001 and Office for Mac OS X. Outlook Express is installed on all Macs as part of a standard Classic Mac OS installation.

The modus operandi of the so-called "Mac.Simpsons@mm" virus, bearing the title "Simpsons Episodes," is similar to the PC "worms" that afflict email software. When the AppleScript is run, it launches these email applications, and then it proceeds to send a copy of itself to everyone in your contact list, accompanied by the following message:

Hundreds of Simpsons episodes were just secretly produced and sent out on the Internet, if this message gets to you, the episodes are enclosed on the attachment program, which will only run on a Macintosh. You must have system 9.0 or 9.1 to watch the hilarious episodes, in high quality. Just download and open it. From, <your name> — To get random signatures put text files into a folder called "Random Signatures" into your Preferences folder.

As part of its trickery, the virus made a copy of itself that was placed within the Startup Items folder inside the Classic Mac OS System Folder. Even if you quit your Microsoft email application, it would relaunch itself on the next restart. Aside from propagating itself via your address book, it will also apparently delete the contents of the Sent Items folder and put them in the Deleted folder (from where they can be retrieved until the folder is emptied, of course). If you are infected, this is the worst symptom of all, especially if you want to keep tabs of the mail you've sent to your various contacts.

Fortunately, Entourage is designed to put up a warning before it executes a script, which gives you the chance to stop it in its tracks (Outlook Express doesn't offer this advantage). In addition, if you disable the actions of the Startup Items folder by holding down the SHIFT key just as soon as extensions load, but before startup applications launch, you can apparently keep the worm from running (and then delete the file itself manually).

New virus definitions that target the AppleScript virus were posted by Symantec and Intego for their virus software within days of the discovery. While constant vigilance kept this virus from spreading too far and wide, its presence should warn Mac users that even worse AppleScript-related viruses may be on the horizon.

Regardless of the kind of virus, the plain truth is the same: your Mac cannot get infected by a virus sent via email unless you actually launch an infected file; the normal process of downloading isn't enough to trigger the virus.

The moral of the story is this: When you get a file attachment you're not expecting, even if you know who sent it, it never hurts to write back and verify the recipient really sent it to you. If you're sending a file, include a message in the body of your email explaining specifically what the file is and what it is to be used for, so the recipient knows it's nothing suspicious.

How to Avoid Email Problems

Even if you address your email correctly, put in a proper subject line, and prepare your message in the normal fashion, there are no guarantees that the message will get to the recipient in the same form—or at all. Some of the problems are due to factors you can't control, such as your software or the service you and the recipient are using.

NOTE   *I try to practice what I preach. When I send files to my publisher via email, I always put something in the subject line that clearly identifies the contents of the attachment, plus something in the message that also makes it clear that it's part of the project I'm working on.*

But there are precautions you can take to make sure that your email comes through reasonably untarnished, especially if there are attachments added.

AOL Email Quirks and Solutions

With more than 30 million members around the world, a great percentage of the Internet's email traffic goes to and from members of the world's largest online service. But because of the inconsistent way in which AOL handles email, problems may arise if you don't observe a few simple precautions:

- **Don't send multiple attachments from the Internet to AOL members.**   AOL doesn't fully support the MIME (Multipurpose Internet Mail Extension) protocol. What that means is that you cannot attach more than a single item to AOL's email without it using its built-in compression software to make an archive. The archive will be StuffIt on the Mac and WinZip on the Windows platform. When you receive a file with multiple attachments from the Internet, it'll come as a single attachment, which you must then run through a decoding program. Fortunately, the latest versions of StuffIt Expander and such shareware programs as Decoder can extract the contents of the MIME file, but sometimes it just won't work as advertised. If you must send more than a single file via your Internet service to an AOL member, use StuffIt first to compress them all into a single archive (use Aladdin's DropZip to send files to Windows users).

- **Avoid large files outside of AOL.**   As of the time this book was published, AOL's limit was approximately 2MB for files sent to and from the Internet. For email from one AOL member to another, it's a more practical 16MB. If you must send large files regularly to anyone on AOL, having a membership there may be a good idea.

NOTE

If you use a regular ISP to log on to AOL (rather than their dial-up network), you'll benefit by paying a much lower monthly fee for the service (less than half the regular monthly rate). This way you can enjoy what you like of AOL, yet get a second route of Internet access.

■ **Be careful addressing email from AOL to the Internet.**   AOL doesn't handle email addresses quite the same as the rest of the world. For one thing, their variation of an email address, a screen name, allows for a space between words, something that's a no-no in most of the rest of the online world. If you're on the Internet and want to send email to someone with a space in his or her name (such as bear bear@aol.com), don't forget to put an underscore between the words: bear_bear@aol.com. Otherwise, the space will likely be ignored and someone with the name of bear@aol.com will mistakenly get your email. The reverse situation can also occur. You can address a message that should be bear_bear@<anyisp.com>. If the word space is mistakenly used, the first name, bear, will be assumed to be on AOL, and thus a bear@aol.com will get a message, and the second name will be recognized as a name meant for the other service (right or wrong).

NOTE

This oddity in AOL's mail handling is one of the root causes behind that "wrong Gene" phenomenon I described earlier.

■ **AOL mailbox sizes are limited.**   AOL allows you to have only 550 messages in a member's incoming mailbox at any one time. The older ones are purged automatically, seven days for received email, 30 days for sent email. But if you get a lot of email in a short time, the sender may just get a "mailbox is full" message. If you're on AOL, you'd best be advised to read your email promptly, and use the service's Personal Filing Cabinet feature to store email you want to save beyond the time limit.

■ **Don't be alarmed about messages from MAILER-DAEMON@ aol.com.**   Such messages are not viruses or anything threatening. They are just notices that your email couldn't be delivered, and the body of the message will contain information as to why (well, usually).

■ **Don't use special formatting for email sent to non-AOL members.**   AOL has a number of formatting features, such as typeface, style, size, and color. In general, these formatting features don't pass through to the Internet, or if they do, formatting may not be completely retained. So the best thing to do is just to leave the standard text formatting if your email is being sent to folks outside the service.

How to Avoid Email Problems

■ **Don't embed a photo in your AOL message to the Internet.**   This feature, which was first introduced in AOL 4.0, is not something that will translate to Internet email. If you want to send a photo to someone outside the service, make it an email attachment instead.

Internet Email Quirks and Solutions

AOL isn't the only source of email quirks. Some of the very same problems and solutions apply when you use a regular ISP. I'll cover them here:

NOTE   *In case you're wondering, I consider AOL to be a perfectly valid way to get on the Internet. But because the service doesn't always follow standard Internet protocols, confusion can occur. Unfortunately, this seems to work heavily against AOL's promise of being easier to learn for novice PC users.*

■ **Crashes when you open Netscape Messenger email**   Netscape's Messenger module, a component of the Classic version of this application, has a feature that lets you compact a message folder. This removes deleted data and optimizes the file. To use it, just select the email folder you want to compact, and choose Compact This Folder from Netscape's File menu (it's only there if you have the Messenger module open). You'll probably also want to use the Empty Trash Folder function every so often, as a lot of trashed email will just bloat your email files.

■ **Mysterious, unexplained program quits**   Even though Mac OS X offers unparalleled stability, individual programs can quit, and you can safely continue to compute without need of a restart. The lone exception is the Classic environment. Should any Classic application freeze or quit, be sure to restart the Classic environment, because it will behave in a less than stable fashion.

CAUTION   *Watch out for the dreaded ObjectSupportLib file, which sometimes turns up in the Classic Mac OS Extensions folder. Older software installers may put the extension in there. ObjectSupportLib is not needed, because the functions are present in the Mac OS 9.x System file, and it may cause Classic environment crashes or sudden application quits if the file is present. If you find this file has been left by mistake in the Extensions folder, trash it right away and restart Classic via the Classic panel in the System Preferences application.*

- ■ **Mailbox full messages**   AOL isn't the only service that puts restrictions on the size of an email box. If your recipient has an interoffice email system and has gone on vacation, or has not checked the email in a while, the mailbox may really be filled. The only solutions are to wait and try sending the email again at a later time, see if the recipient has another email address, or try a telephone call (see, telephones aren't obsolete—yet).

Try an Email Forwarding Service

It's not uncommon to have several email accounts, or even to switch from one service to another as you experiment to see which provides the best performance and service. You may work as a contractor and switch from one office to another, hence changing email addresses more than you like. Or you might travel and use one service at home or the office, and another for the road.

Whatever the case, you may want to consider an email forwarding service. Such firms will give you a single, convenient email address, and you can designate where email will be automatically sent at any point in time.

Two well-known firms that provide this service are Pobox (http://www.pobox.com) and Bigfoot (http://www.bigfoot.com). Another useful alternative is Apple's iTools feature, where you can sign up for your free mac.com email address; it's part of the initial setup process for Mac OS X and also used if you establish an EarthLink account via any new Mac. You can access your mac.com email via most any email application (other than AOL) and the rest are available via any Web browser.

NOTE   *In the previous edition of this book, I also mentioned iFORWARD, but this firm appears to have gone to dot.com heaven.*

Other Web-based email services include Excite, Yahoo!, and Microsoft's Hotmail. The advantage of Hotmail is that Microsoft's Entourage, Outlook Express, and Outlook applications can also handle the account, so you aren't forced to use a sometimes clumsy, slow browser interface to manage huge numbers of messages.

Getting a Handle on Email Spam

On the Internet, spam is not a form of lunchmeat of mixed content from Hormel. It's downright annoying, sometimes worse than the mail you get in a physical mailbox, because you can't just rip it up (though you can delete such messages if the titles are obvious, and that's not always the case). It fills your mailbox and you are forced to wade through annoying announcements about pornography or one questionable promotion or another.

TIP

If you want to learn about the original (or the real) SPAM, the lunchmeat concoction from Hormel, feel free to visit the official Web site for this product, http://www.spam.com/. You can even join The Official SPAM Fan Club and examine the SPAM Gift Catalog at the site. This is serious business.

NOTE

As enticing as some junk email might seem, I have never seen any evidence that any of the work-at-home or pyramid promotion schemes advertised actually work. The reason junk email is so widely sent is because it's very cheap to do, costing just a fraction of what it would cost to mount a regular direct mail campaign to one's physical mailbox. The purveyors of these schemes probably figure that even a handful of orders will produce more than sufficient income to cover the cost of sending those messages.

Fortunately, email programs do deliver ways to help you filter out this junk, though, for the most part (except for Microsoft's Entourage and Outlook Express 5), it has to be done on a case-by-case basis. As you receive email, you simply create filters that apply to the specific domains or that have a keyword in the subject line that is common.

Here's how you do it with some of the popular email programs:

America Online

The unfortunate side effect of being the number one online service on Earth is that AOL is a target for junk mail, far beyond that of other services. AOL's legal eagles, however, have gone to court to fight junk mailers and have won a few legal victories, so the problem is not as bad as it used to be.

In addition, AOL has in place a Mail Controls feature that you can use to filter out the most offensive email you receive (and even block mail from folks you don't want to hear from for any reason). Here's how it works:

1. Log on to AOL, using your master account name (this is the one you used when you joined AOL, which appears first on your list of screen names).

TIP

As an option, you can give "master" status to your other AOL screen names. This feature lets you set Mail and Parental Controls while using those names.

2. Type the AOL keyword **Mail Controls**. This will bring up a screen similar to the one shown in Figure 23-1.

3. Click on the Next button, which will bring up the screen shown in Figure 23-2.

4. Choose the screen name to which you want to apply Mail Controls. Choose the basic criteria listed, or click Customize, and then the Next button to proceed. This will bring up the actual editing screen, shown in Figure 23-3.

5. Enter the email address or domain from which you want to block email in the text entry field, and click Add to include them, or choose a setting to apply to all email.

TIP

If you only want to receive AOL email from a small number of recipients, use the fourth option shown in Figure 23-3, to block all email except from specified recipients. Then enter the email addresses of your recipients, one by one, in the text field.

6. When you click Next, you'll have the option to restrict email with pictures and files. The final setup screen will produce a summary of the changes made to the selected account. Once your Mail Controls are set, click the Save button to store your settings.

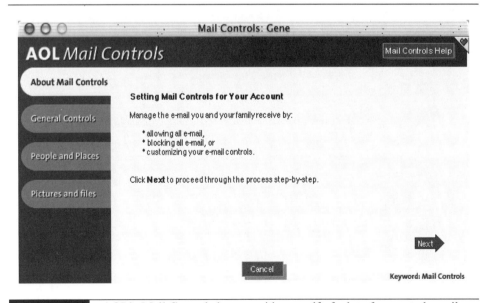

FIGURE 23-1   AOL's Mail Controls lets you rid yourself of a lot of unwanted email.

How to Avoid Email Problems

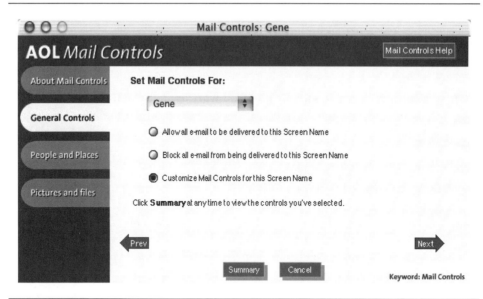

FIGURE 23-2   The Mail Controls setup screen is your starting point.

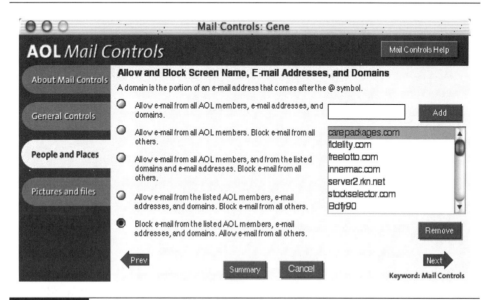

FIGURE 23-3   Select your email blocking options here.

7. Click Return to Mail Controls to make settings on other names in your account, or click Close to leave the Mail Controls feature.

The filtering features I'm describing in the next few sections can be used not just to remove junk email, but also to sort email into different categories, forward the messages to another account, automatically download attachments, and so on. With a little practice, you can apply a host of powerful filters to your favorite email program. Our fearless technical editor, Greg Titus, does the reverse. He filters the email he normally expects into separate mailboxes, so the Inbox contains just the leftovers (usually the junk mail).

Claris Emailer

Apple is no longer updating this excellent email program. It only runs in the Classic environment in Mac OS X, and the chances that anyone will take it over are zilch. But it has some great features that are still useful, and it's the only non-AOL program (other than Netscape 6 or the Web-based AOL Anywhere) that you can use to retrieve your AOL email.

NOTE *I still love Claris Emailer and will continue to use the program as long as it remains compatible with Apple's fast-changing system software. To quote the technical editor of the first edition of this book, "Emailer rules!"*

Here's how to set up an email filter with Emailer:

1. Choose Mail Actions from the Setup menu, which brings up the screen shown in Figure 23-4.

2. Click the New button, which brings up the screen shown in Figure 23-5.

3. Enter a name for your mail action. "Junk Mail" is perfectly fine.

4. Enter the Criteria in the appropriate field. It's best to include one or more keywords that appear in a typical piece of email.

5. Under actions, click the Define Actions button.

6. On the next screen, select an option to apply to messages that meet your Criteria. The option I suggest is to place it in the Deleted Mail folder (which means, of course, that the email will be removed automatically).

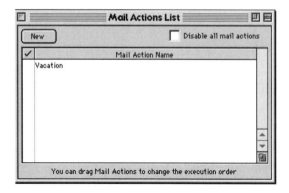

FIGURE 23-4 Mail Actions is used to set up your Claris Emailer filtering.

Eudora for Mac OS X

Despite the fact that there are great free email programs, Qualcomm's Eudora remains popular because of its powerful mail-handling features. Actually it comes in several formats, depending on your tolerance for advertising—paid, sponsored, and light. If you can tolerate banner ads in the various application windows, you

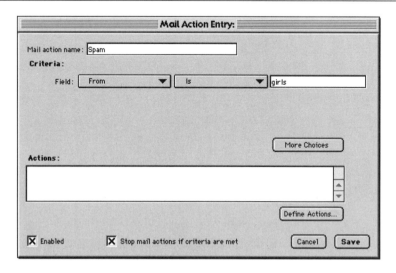

FIGURE 23-5 Start your junk mail filtering here.

can get the full feature set for free; otherwise, you pay the publisher's licensing fee. A reduced feature version, replacing Eudora Lite, gives up the ads.

> **NOTE** *In case you're wondering, the "light" mode deprives you of such nifty features as Secure Sockets Layer (SSL) for added security, MoodWatch to block offensive text, and the ability to insert photos in your Address Book.*

And as with the other email applications, it has a flexible Filters feature that lets you block email from selected sources.

> **NOTE** *The description I'm providing here is based on Eudora Pro 5.1. The filtering function is substantially changed from earlier versions of the program.*

1. Launch Eudora.

2. Choose Filters from the Window menu, which will bring up a setup screen similar to the one shown in Figure 23-6 (which I've already completed).

3. Under Match, click the email category to which your filter applies.

4. Choose the words that will trigger the filter and enter them under Header. Click on the pop-up menu adjacent to the keyword and pick a category. I chose "contains" for this example in both Header fields.

5. Under actions, pick a function from the pop-up menu. I picked Redirect To and then entered Trash in the text field, which is where I want all my junk email to go.

6. Click the close box to store your settings.

Netscape Communicator 4.7x

Netscape Communicator remains the choice of many dedicated users. What's more, it's no slouch when it comes to providing powerful email filter capability. By setting up a reasonable set of email actions you should be able to block a reasonable amount of junk email.

> **NOTE** *I'll cover Netscape 6 in the next section.*

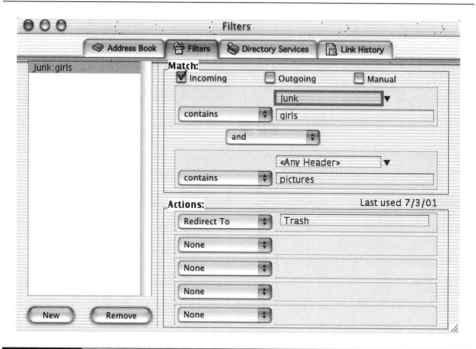

FIGURE 23-6   Set up filters with Eudora beginning with this dialog box.

The following list shows you how to use the Message Filters feature of Netscape's Messenger email module:

1. Launch Netscape.

2. Choose Message Filters from the Edit menu, which brings up a screen similar to the one shown in Figure 23-7 (this one has my Junk Mail filter already applied).

3. At the top of the screen, select the location where your rules will apply from the pop-up menu. I chose Inbox, which is where your newly received email will show up.

4. Give the rule a name in the text field, and then click the Enabled check box to activate it.

5. Under Description, type a short description of the purpose of the filter.

6. Click the arrow at the left of the Filter Action label (if it's collapsed).

7. Choose the various matching categories from the pop-up menus.

8. Under Then, choose an action from the pop-up menu. I picked Delete for this example.

9. Click the close box to activate your settings.

Netscape Communicator 6

To say Netscape 6 is controversial is a vast understatement. Like it or hate it, you will not pass on its strange interface without forming an opinion.

NOTE *The following description applies equally to both the Mac OS X and Classic versions of Netscape 6.*

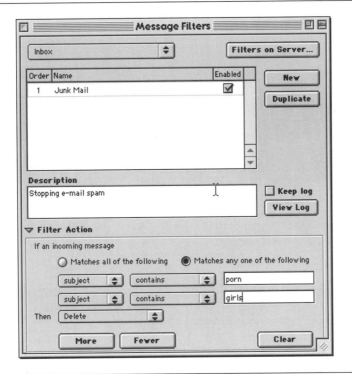

FIGURE 23-7   The author's Junk Mail filter is already set up.

Here's how to use the Message Filters feature of Netscape's Messenger email module:

1. Launch Netscape.

2. Choose Mail from the Tasks menu to deliver the Mail screen.

3. Now select Message Filters from the Edit menu, which brings up the dialog box shown in Figure 23-8.

4. To create a new filter, click the New button, which produces the dialog box displayed in Figure 23-9.

5. Give the rule a name in the Filter Name text field.

6. To create a match statement, click on the two pop-up menus to specify the circumstances under which a message is filtered. In the example shown, I've asked Netscape 6 to look at messages with "Work at Home" in the subject line.

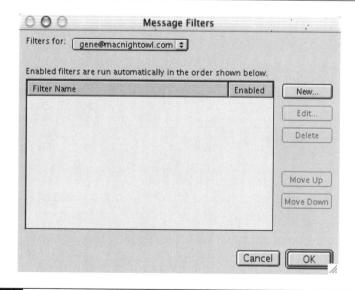

FIGURE 23-8   Set up your message filtering here.

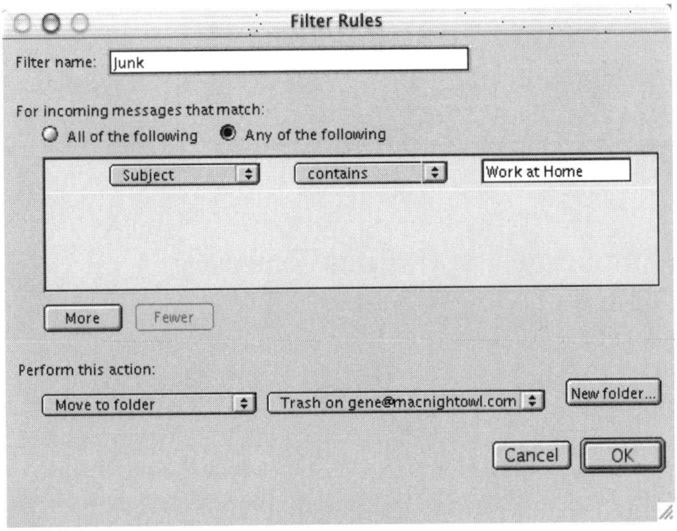

FIGURE 23-9   Name and configure the Netscape 6's message filtering feature from this dialog box.

> **NOTE**   *I have been very specific about filters here to show you how it's done. You'll probably want to watch for the typical junk email subject lines you receive to get a sense of what to use.*

7. If you need to create additional conditions, such as additional subject lines, click the More button to produce additional sets of conditions for you to configure.

8. Click on the Action pop-up menu (see Figure 23-10) to specify what to do with a message if it meets your criteria. If you choose to move the messages to another folder, specify the folder from the pop-up list at the right of the Action menu.

> **NOTE**   *I'd recommend Delete if you're absolutely certain all messages that meet your criteria are junk mail. If you have doubts, move the messages to a folder and check them all later on. Over time, you'll be able to finetune the process as more and more messages are processed by the filter.*

9. Click OK to activate your settings.

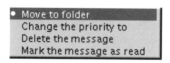

| FIGURE 23-10 | Choose an action to apply from this menu. |

Microsoft Entourage and Outlook Express

Although based on the same core components, Entourage differs from Outlook Express in two key ways. One is that it's a commercial product, available with Microsoft Office 2001 or Office for Mac OS X; the other is that it offers a personal information manager that helps you organize contacts and events. However, the core filtering components of the two programs are similar enough to allow me to explain both with the very same steps.

The key weapon in the arsenal of Entourage and Outlook Express to combat spam is the Junk Mail Filter. This feature uses either application's internal logic to figure out whether the email you're getting fits into the junk category. One of those criteria is a forged email address, a common occurrence in junk mail.

NOTE   *While Entourage was being updated for Mac OS X when this book was written, Microsoft had not as yet committed to delivering an OS X version of Outlook Express. But the Classic version runs fine.*

Here's how to use the Junk Mail Filter:

1. Launch Entourage of Outlook Express.

2. Choose Junk Mail Filter from the Tools menu, which brings up the screen shown in Figure 23-11.

3. Click the Enable Junk Mail Filter check box to activate the feature.

4. Drag the Sensitivity slider to control how carefully the program checks email for evidence that it fits into the junk category. If you subscribe to Internet mailing lists, you'll probably want to try a setting between Low and Average so legitimate email isn't flagged as junk by mistake. Otherwise, you can experiment with a higher setting.

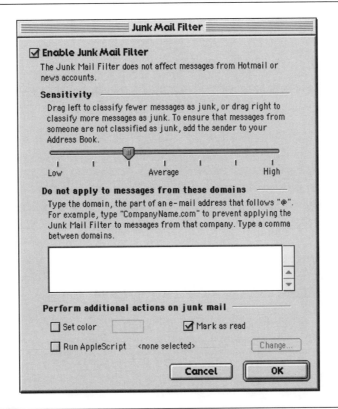

FIGURE 23-11   Activate and configure the filter from this dialog box.

5. If you want to make sure the filter isn't applied to email from a specific domain, enter that domain in the text field at the bottom of the Junk Mail Filter setup screen.

6. Choose the actions to be applied to your junk mail from the bottom of the screen.

7. Click OK to store your settings.

If you find your Junk Mail Filter settings aren't strong enough, or are too strong, it's easy to go back and change the settings.

You can also apply powerful filters to specific types of email from Entourage and Outlook Express. Here's how:

1. Launch Entourage or Outlook Express.

2. Choose Rules from the Tools menu, which brings up the screen shown in Figure 23-12.

3. Click the tab that applies to the Rule you want to apply. For regular Internet email accounts, for example, you'd probably choose Mail (POP). The other email categories will depend on the sort of service you have (the program also supports office email systems). This will bring up the screen shown in Figure 23-13 (which has already been filled out).

4. Enter a Rule name in the text field at the top.

5. From the If category (which applies to the conditions under which a filter is applied), choose the criterion from the pop-up menu, which includes a number of categories, including From and Subject lines.

6. Enter the keyword or words you want to use in the text field.

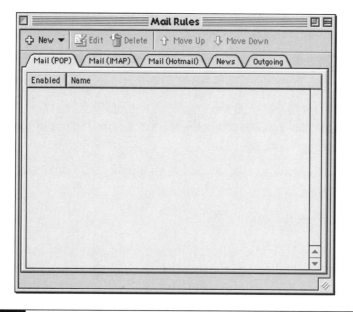

FIGURE 23-12   Specify your Rules choices here.

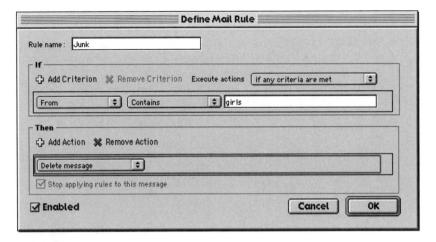

Just to show you how it's done, the author has already made up a junk mail Rule.

7. Under the Then category (which covers what will be done if the conditions are met), pick the action from the pop-up menu. I chose the Delete message option, but there are other choices, such as automatically moving a message to a specific folder.

8. Click the Enabled check box to be sure the rule is active.

9. Click OK to store your settings.

Mail

Apple's Mac OS X email program is a showpiece of the advantages of programming in the Cocoa environment. It sports a built-in spell checker, and it allows you to use the Font Panel to spruce up your messages. You can also configure multiple mailboxes, multiple signatures, and even, with some limits, import your mailboxes from other programs.

There's even a powerful range of filter options that will help you fight the spam menace, or just process your messages for easier handling. Here's how they work:

1. Launch Mail, and select Preferences from the program's application menu.

2. In the Preferences window, click on Rules, and then Create Rule in the Setup dialog box. This will produce the dialog box displayed in Figure 23-14.

How to Avoid Email Problems

FIGURE 23-14
Mail gives you some simple but powerful mail filtering options.

> **NOTE**   *What are those rules for? Apple put them there to help manage its own mailings, but feel free to uncheck Active for each rule to put them to sleep.*

3. Name your email sorting routine in the Description category. The usual name is Rule #1, etc.—not too clever, but easily changed.

4. Click on the Criteria pop-up menu, and choose the message field to which a rule will apply, such as From, To, etc.

5. Select the criteria that activates the email rule in the second pop-up menu. You can specify whether the message Contains, Not Contain, Includes, and so on and so forth.

6. Now type a phrase or even a single word that is used to activate a rule. Specifically, say you want to move all messages from grayson@rockoids.com to a different location; you'll specify the message Contains that information.

7. Now you need to decide how the rule is applied in the Action category.

NOTE *The top two Actions, Set the Color To and Play Sound, simply give you a way to make the messages stand out from the crowd.*

8. So what do you do next? Click on the pop-up menu and choose the Transfer To Mailbox option to specify a mailbox in which to place the message.

NOTE *Don't have a mailbox that fits? No problem. Just go to the program's Mail menu, choose Create Mailbox, and name it. Now you'll be able to have all messages that meet the rule you've created go to this folder.*

TIP *You can use a Mail Rule to automatically forward messages to a different address. Just select the Forward Message To check box and enter the address to which the messages are to be sent. Nifty! Another option allows you to actually delete messages that come from a specific junk mailer or bearing a certain subject line.*

9. All done? Click OK to save your email rules.

How to Complain about Junk Email

If filters of one sort or another don't stop the flood of junk mail, there's another possible remedy: complain to the Internet provider from whom the email seems to have originated. I say "seems" because quite often the address you see in the "From" line is a forgery, someone hiding their tracks and blaming someone else for their annoying behavior. But if you use the option in your email software to show Internet headers (that's automatic with AOL), the folks who investigate may likely be able to track it down to the real offender.

Just use your email program's Forward feature to send the actual email message, along with your comment or complaint, to either of these addresses: abuse@<domainname> or postmaster@<domainname>. Insert the actual domain from which the junk email seems to originate in the space for the domain name, such as aol.com, earthlink.net, and so on.

Most of the major Internet and online services have tough rules against members sending such material, and they will definitely investigate the problem.

How to Avoid Email Problems

> **NOTE**   *It really doesn't help to send an email complaint to the source from which the junk mail originated. Even if the address is real and not a forgery (in other words, an innocent party may get your complaint), when you send your email to the sender of such material, you're just confirming that your address is correct. And all that does is make you eligible to get more junk email.*

Summing Up

Are we there already? Yes, this is the final chapter of this book.

I hope you enjoyed our little trip into the world of Mac OS X troubleshooting and upgrading. If you have questions or suggestions for future editions, feel free to write me: gene@macnightowl.com. I look forward to hearing from you.

Appendix

QuickStart Upgrade and Troubleshooting Guide

A re you ready to upgrade your Mac, or have you encountered some unexpected problem using the Mac OS? This appendix is designed to help you on your new installation or on your hardware or operating system upgrade.

To help get you started, I've assembled some important tips and troubleshooting information to alert you to potential trouble spots. If you need more information, feel free to review the chapters in this book that cover these subjects in more detail.

Installing a New Mac

- Check each system separately. Make sure your new Mac, keyboard, mouse, and display are working first before checking the rest of the system.

- Don't copy system software. Forgetting software license restrictions, the system software that works on an old Mac is not likely to support the new one. Stick with what's on your new Mac.

- Be careful when copying applications. Some application installers put various and sundry things in different locations beyond the basic application folder. Reinstallation is usually best. Also check with the publisher to make sure the old program is compatible with your new Mac, particularly if you plan on spending lots of time in Mac OS X.

Reinstalling System Software

- The most effective way to install your Mac OS system software is a clean installation. Under the Classic Mac OS, it means that your existing folder is renamed Previous System Folder and a new System Folder is created. The clean install option is available on the first Mac OS 9.x installation when you click Options.

- Under Mac OS X, you actually need to delete all the system files or erase the drive partition to make it clean. Since some system files are invisible (you cannot see them on your Mac's drive), you need a program that can read such files, such as File Buddy, a popular shareware application.

- If you want to keep your user settings and documents and your Applications folder, leave it in place. If you plan on erasing the drive, back up both folders and restore them after the new Mac OS X installation.

Adding Peripheral Cards

■ Make sure that any software required for such products (particularly SCSI cards and video capture cards) is compatible with Mac OS X.

■ Turn off the Mac and ground yourself to the Mac's chassis before installation. Use a wrist strap if one is provided.

■ If you plan on installing a processor upgrade card, be careful about settings of jumper switches to speed up the card. Don't try to run the card too fast; the slight speed gain may be outweighed by increased system hang-ups. Also, make sure that any required software work with Mac OS X, or such features as a processor's cache may not work.

CAUTION *Remember that Mac OS X is only supported on Apple computers that shipped with a G3 or G4 processor (except for the original PowerBook G3 in a 3400 case). While it may be possible to get Mac OS X to work on an older Mac with a processor upgrade card and special software, Apple won't provide help. You have to depend on the manufacturer of the upgrade card or software in case you run into difficulty.*

Adding RAM

■ Make sure the RAM is compatible with your Mac. RAM modules may look the same, but they can have different electrical characteristics. For example, the Power Mac G4 models shipped since the beginning of 2001 require PC133 RAM, while older models work fine with PC100 RAM. You can use the former chips on older models, but not the reverse, because the computer may run slowly or not at all.

■ Be careful about installing a RAM module, because plastic hinges on the Mac are delicate and may break easily. If the Mac refuses to boot after a RAM upgrade, shut down, reseat the RAM, and try again. If it still fails to run, remove the upgrade, confirm that the Mac works, and contact the dealer for replacement.

■ If system crashes suddenly increase after a RAM installation, the RAM is often at fault. To test, remove the RAM and see if the problems vanish. If they do, have the RAM replaced.

Adding RAM

Advice for Road Warriors

- iBooks and PowerBooks are theft magnets. Hang on to them tightly at public places, including airports. Also, be sure to get insurance coverage in case the worst happens. Some companies offer special riders for home policies to cover computers and software, including notebooks.

- Before traveling with your iBook or PowerBook, make sure the battery is fully charged and take a spare if you can. Also, consider taking backup drives and media, connection cables and special plug adapters (if you travel abroad).

- Use Mac OS X's multihoming feature to let you connect to networks and dial-up Internet access on the road. Use the Location feature to create custom setups for different cities.

Mac OS X Font Management

- Under Mac OS X, you get not one, but four Fonts folders. Three are in the Library folders in your user's folder, on the top level of your hard drive and under Network. A fourth Fonts folder is found inside the Mac OS X System Folder, but you cannot remove or add items to that Fonts folder without gaining root access or by rebooting under Mac OS 9.x.

- To add to the confusion, Classic applications only see fonts in the Classic operating system's Fonts folder, but native Mac OS X applications see Classic fonts, too.

- Mac OS X applications that are created in Apple's Cocoa environment have a feature called Font Panel for font management. Other Mac OS X applications have a font menu similar to the one in the Classic environment.

Graphics Files

- When sending graphics files to a Windows or Unix user, be sure the file is named with the three-letter extension that identifies its file type. So a file named myphoto.jpg would be a JPEG file, and a file named myphoto.gif would be a GIF file.

- Remember that changing the name of a file isn't enough. The actual format of the file must be correct also.

- Windows users can read files in GIF, JPEG, and TIFF, usually without any problems. Mac users can read those files and such Windows files as .BMP in Mac OS X's Preview application (which also reads PDF).

Printing Under Mac OS X

- When you use Mac OS X, you must print from different environments, depending on whether you are using a native application or a Classic application. Classic applications use the Chooser to select printers, the original Mac way, and PrintMonitor to check a job's progress. All these functions are reserved for Print Center under Mac OS X.

- Mac OS X will automatically recognize a USB printer, as long as proper drivers are installed. Most laser printers are recognized, too, but you may need a custom PPD (PostScript Printer Description) file to recognize special features, such as extra paper trays or custom paper sizes.

- Under Mac OS X, PPD files are placed in the en.lproj folder in the following folder hierarchy. From the top level of the hard drive: Library>Printers> PPD>Contents>Resources>en.lproj (there's a separate folder for each language system supported by Mac OS X).

Using Input Devices

- New Macs support USB; older Macs still support ADB. You can convert ADB to USB with a special converter module. To do the reverse, you need to install a USB card on your older Mac.

- An input device with special buttons and features requires special software to run. Although Mac OS X includes native support for the second or right button on some devices and the scroll wheel on others, you may have to install special drivers to make everything work right.

Installing a New Monitor

- You can use a so-called PC monitor on a Mac, but some displays (usually LCD) require a digital video output to run. New Macs include a feature called ADC (Apple Display Connector) that works with any recent Apple monitor. You need a special ADC-to-DVI adapter to use a different digital display.

- CRT displays usually have a set of buttons used to access onscreen menus for adjustments. You can usually set image size and width and sometimes fix geometry (such as rounding at the edges) or rotation (in case the image is tilted one side or the other). All displays have brightness, and many (mostly CRT) have contrast. Few displays are perfectly adjusted at the factory and so may need further tweaking.

- Apple's ColorSync, available from the Displays preference panel of the System Preferences application, lets you fine-tune color and white balance settings on your monitor. On current Apple displays, you may be limited to brightness and white balance, because of the native support for ColorSync on these products.

- If a monitor shows color artifacts or severe distortion, turn off your Mac and reseat the graphic card (assuming it doesn't use onboard video on the motherboard). If that doesn't work, reseat the connectors. Failing that, contact the manufacturer for service.

Living in the Windows World

- Macs are able to read HD floppies (if you have a floppy drive), and such removable media as Zip disks and CDs, even if made on a Windows computer.

- To share files from your Mac on other computing platforms, make sure the file name includes the proper file extension (such as .doc for a Microsoft Word document) and that the file format is correct.

- Mac OS X, beginning with version 10.1, can share files with Windows NT, Windows 2000, and Windows XP file servers using the Connect To Server feature in the Finder's Go menu. You can also use Thursby Systems' DAVE to share files with regular Windows computers.

■ If you need to run Windows applications occasionally, applications that have no Mac equivalent, consider getting a Windows emulator, Connectix Virtual PC. While this program won't give you hot gaming performance, it runs fast enough for business and simple graphic applications.

Computer Viruses and Mac OS X

■ The Classic environment is still vulnerable to infection by computer viruses. Unix-based viruses are always a possible danger. In addition, both Classic and Mac OS X are vulnerable to AppleScript and macro viruses.

■ To check for viruses under Mac OS X, you need a Mac OS X–compatible virus application, such as the latest versions of Norton Anti-Virus or Virex.

■ Use a personal firewall to protect yourself against Internet intruders if you spend a lot of time online (whether with a high-speed connection or modem). Mac OS X includes a simple firewall that can be configured via shareware utilities, but you can also use Symantec's Norton Personal Firewall (which supports Mac OS X) or Intego's NetBarrier (a Mac OS X version should ship by the time this book is in the stores).

Hard Drive Diagnostic Tips

■ Hard drives are vulnerable to directory damage that might cause loss of data. While Mac OS X performs a basic drive check every time you boot your Mac, it's a good idea to run a Mac OS X–compatible disk-checking program on a regular basis to be sure the drive is healthy.

■ If you leave hard drive directory damage unfixed, the drive could crash, which means files may no longer be available. If disk diagnostic programs fail to fix a problem (or it just keeps on happening), consider backing up your files and reformatting your drive.

■ Before partitioning your drive (dividing it into smaller segments), check the documentation for Mac OS X about where the operating system should be placed.

Don't Forget Backups

■ A no-frills method: Make daily backups of your document files on another drive, removable device, or CD.

■ If you need to back up large numbers of files, consider dedicated backup software to handle the job for you. Use the program's scripting capability to automate the process.

■ Make sure the backup software is Mac OS X savvy, because many of the "invisible" files installed by Mac OS X are not seen by older programs.

Take Care with SCSI Chains

■ If you plan to continue to use SCSI devices on your Mac, make sure that devices are not connected or disconnected until you turn off the Mac and all devices first.

■ Make sure last physical device is terminated, and that there are no SCSI ID conflicts.

■ All SCSI devices must be left on while your Mac is running.

■ Make sure that SCSI adapter cards are Mac OS X compatible before using them with the new operating system.

Take Care Setting Up a Scanner

■ When installing a new scanner, make sure that you unlatch the optical locking mechanism before use. Check instructions for its location (some low-cost scanners don't use a lock).

■ Make sure scanning software is Mac OS X compatible before attempting to use. Running scanning software from the Classic environment has little chance of working.

■ If you are using OCR software, try to work with clean originals. Originals with ink notations and faxes will yield poor accuracy.

Network in Confidence

■ When networking your Mac with other Macs or in a multiplatform installation, take care in selecting user passwords. Use a random combination of upper- and lowercase letters and numbers for best security.

■ Under Mac OS X, use the Finder's Show Info feature to customize access privileges for disks, folders, and files.

■ If a file share can't be found, make sure that file sharing is activated on the computer in question. Also make sure network connections are working. Check lights on the Ethernet hub, if one is being used.

Add System Enhancements with Care

■ Make sure your fancy new utility is compatible with Mac OS X or that it will run safely in Classic environment.

■ To speed Classic environment performance and reliability, make a special set in Extensions Manager using the Mac OS 9.x Base set as the basis (just duplicate the set). Use caution in adding extra system components.

■ If an application freezes, use the Force Quit command from the Apple menu or press COMMAND-SHIFT-ESC to bring up Force Quit window. For Classic applications that freeze or quit, restart Classic. For Mac OS X applications, you can continue without a restart.

■ If you forget your login password, restart from the Mac OS X installer CD. Use the Password Reset application, in the application menu, to reset a password.

■ If you see a kernel panic, a sudden appearance of white on black text filling part of your screen, press R to restart. If that doesn't work, press the reset button on your Mac to force a restart. After restart, recheck new programs you may have added for Mac OS X–compatibility issues.

Add System Enhancements with Care

Make Video Editing Work Better

- To avoid dropped frames, keep Mac computing activities to the minimum when capturing video. Try not to download or transfer files, or do processor-intensive work.

- Using Mac OS X's RAID feature, in the Disk Utility application, to set up two or more drives for maximum performance for video editing.

- Consider a special breakout box, such as the Formac Studio, to use an old camcorder with a new Mac's FireWire port.

Make Your Modem Connect Faster

- Don't expect a 56K modem to connect at 56K. The FCC limits maximum speed to 53K, and usually connection speeds are much lower.

- If you get frequent disconnects or slow speed connections, try another access number for your ISP, if one is available.

- If connection quality remains poor, disconnect other phone devices on the line to see if performance improves. Some multifunction devices with fax capability may cause problems on a phone line.

- Check with the manufacturer to see if there's a firmware upgrade for your modem.

Broadband Access Concerns

- High-speed Internet access setups, such as cable modem, DSL, or wireless (fixed and satellite), are always on, increasing risk of access to your network by outsiders. Be sure not to use file sharing unless necessary, or get firewall software to protect your Mac.

- Before considering a broadband alternative, check with other users about a company's support and about connection performance.

Improving Web Access

■ Clear your browser's Web cache if performance slows or images don't show properly.

■ Keep on the lookout for updates to your Web browser and other software if you encounter performance problems or frequent application freezes or quitting.

■ AOL or CompuServe 2000 members: turn off the "Use Compressed Graphics" option in the Client's preference dialog box to improve the quality of Web graphics.

Make Email Work Better

■ To protect yourself from email viruses, use current virus protection software and do not open file attachments you didn't expect, whether you know the sender or not.

■ Before sending a large file attachment, check with your ISP and recipient's ISP about file size limits. Files that are too big will not go through or will be bounced (returned) by ISP.

■ Use the email application's filters or rules features to protect yourself from junk mail or to organize the mail you do receive.

Make Email Work Better

Glossary

10BaseT   The standard form of Ethernet networking, using twisted-pair wires that resemble regular telephone wires. Ethernet capability has been offered in all Apple computers for several years. *See also* **Fast Ethernet**.

A

ADB (Apple Desktop Bus)   Apple's original implementation of a bus standard for input devices, such as a keyboard, mouse, or trackball. *See also* **USB**.

access privileges   Used for file sharing, the act of allowing other users different levels of access to your shared drive.

active application   The application you are currently using, the one you are working in.

active matrix screen   Typically used on a laptop computer, a form of LCD display that uses a separate circuit for each pixel. By activating each pixel separately, it provides clearer, faster display than the other type of LCD display, passive matrix. All current PowerBooks and the iBook have active matrix displays. *See also* **passive matrix display**.

AGP (accelerated graphics port)   An expansion bus used for high-performance graphic cards. All current Mac desktops incorporate either 2x or 4x AGP slots.

AirPort   Apple's wireless networking product line, which provides networking services at approximately 10BaseT Ethernet speeds among devices for distances of up to 150 feet. The technology uses the 802.11b standard, also known as Wi-Fi.

alias   A Mac OS feature, which creates a file that links or points to the original file, folder, or disk. You can activate an alias by double-clicking it; the original item is opened. You can use an alias to help organize your Mac desktop, by keeping the original items in their original folders.

AltiVec   The original name for the Velocity Engine, a vector processing engine used in the G4 CPU to provide noticeably speedier performance for programs designed to support the feature. Mac OS X is optimized to work better on a G4 Mac.

Anonymous FTP   A method to access files from an FTP resource by logging in as a guest. *See also* **FTP**.

AOL (America Online)   The world's largest online service with, as of the time this book went to press, almost 31 million members around the world. Part of AOL Time Warner, it owns a number of other companies, including Netscape and the former number-one online service, CompuServe.

AppleScript   A scripting language that is a part of the Macintosh operating system. It allows a user to automate repetitive functions by writing little scripts that function as mini-applications.

AppleShare   The server and client software that comes standard with the Classic Mac operating system. You use AppleShare to exchange files with other networked Macs.

AppleTalk   The network standard protocol Apple Computer uses. There are two types of AppleTalk. The original protocol, AppleTalk Phase 1, was introduced with the first Mac in 1984. A later version, AppleTalk Phase 2, is designed to address the networking limitations of the original version. All Macs (including the iMac and the iBook) support AppleTalk, but Mac OS X is designed to network via TCP/IP (although AppleTalk support was added in Mac OS X 10.1).

application   Software that provides a specific productivity function, such as a word processor, illustration program, or Web browser. Examples of applications include Adobe PhotoDeluxe, AppleWorks, Microsoft Word, and QuarkXPress.

Aqua   The name of the splashy user interface for Mac OS X that features 3-D effects, drop shadows, and live movement of objects.

arrow keys   The keys used for navigation on a computer. The arrow keys are designed to move the cursor in four directions.

ASCII (American Standard Code for Information Interchange)   The ASCII character set includes the basic 128 characters, including letters, numbers, and basic symbols.

ASCII text file   A file that includes ASCII characters, without the special formatting that identifies paragraph and text formats.

archive   When you compress a file to make it smaller, the file you create is called an archive. An archive may contain one or more compressed files.

attach   A feature of email, in which you connect or link one or more files to your message. When you send your message, the file or files you attach go with it.

B

back up   The process of making extra copies of your files, in the event the originals are corrupted or destroyed. Backups may be made of individual files, folders, or an entire disk.

BBS (bulletin board system)   Essentially, the original online service. A BBS consists of one or more computers that store information, such as files, messages, news, and email. Online services, providing a nationwide network of local access phone numbers, grew out of the concept of a BBS.

beta   The common word for prerelease software. Beta software usually contains all or most of the features of the finished product, but it will have bugs that may cause performance anomalies or system crashes. *See also* **preview software**.

BinHex   A file format commonly used for encoding Mac binary files. The process converts the files to a text format, usually bearing the file suffix .hqx for easy identification. It's designed to allow for transfer of files among multiple computer operating systems, yet retain the two elements of the Mac file format, the resource fork and the data fork.

bit   The smallest unit of computer data. Eight or more bits make a byte. *See also* **byte**.

bitmap   A standard for storing and generating computer-based images, which are made up of single dots (or pixels).

bitmap fonts   A font designed for display in a single point size. Compare with scalable fonts, in OpenType, PostScript, and TrueType formats. Bitmap fonts designed to be used with scalable fonts are called screen fonts. All of these font formats are supported by Mac OS X.

bits per second (bps)   Typically the speed at which a modem transfers data. Normal speeds range from 28,000 bps to 56,000 bps. Higher speeds can be achieved via so-called "broadband" connection methods. *See also* **cable modem, DSL**.

boot   Refers to the process of starting your computer (it comes from the word "bootstrap").

browser   A program designed to download Web pages, and reproduce the text, images, animations, and sound that comprise the original page.

byte   A byte represents a single piece of computer data. It contains eight or more bits, which are represented by the binary numbers 1 and 0. *See also* **bit**.

C

cable modem   A technology that lets you access the Internet through your regular cable TV connection. The cable modem is close in function to a router, which directs the signal to your Mac using its Ethernet port. Cable modem service may require expensive rewiring by your cable provider, and it's not available in all areas.

cache   A portion of memory or storage space set aside to hold frequently used data. By using an onboard cache, performance is boosted on such processors as the G3 and G4. *See also* **disk cache**.

Carbon   A set of application programming interfaces (APIs) that can be used by programmers to speed development of software that is native to Mac OS X. A Carbon program inherits Mac OS X's Aqua user interface and robust system features. Many (but not all) Carbon applications can run in both Mac OS X and the Classic Mac OS. See also **Cocoa**.

card   A printed circuit board that provides expanded capabilities for your Mac, such as the ability to add an extra display, high-speed networking, and high-speed disk access.

CCD (charge-coupled display)   CCDs are typically used in camcorders and scanners to deliver high-quality images.

CD-ROM (compact disc read-only memory)   A standard based on the audio CD, it lets you store computer data on a CD, and is commonly used today for games and as a carrier for software installers and backup files.

character set   The content of a font. It contains letters, numbers, and special symbols, such as a copyright symbol or a number sign. *See also* **ASCII**.

check box   A feature of the Mac operating system and other graphical computer interfaces. It consists of a small square box in a dialog box. It's used to turn certain program features on or off. You click on a check box and a check appears inside, which activates a specific program feature. When you click again on the check box, the checkmark is removed, and the feature is turned off.

Chooser   A Classic Mac program used to select AppleTalk network and printer connections. Under Mac OS X, it has been replaced by the Print Center application for printer and print queue management and the Connect to Server feature in the Go menu for accessing networked volumes.

click   The process of pressing and releasing the button on a mouse or other pointing device.

client   A computer that receives services from another computer, which is known as a server. Internet software, for example, is considered client software, since it receives content from the servers.

clip art   Boilerplate or canned images used for enhancing a document one creates. Some firms and Web sites provide clip art collections for you to install or download.

Clipboard   In the Mac operating system, a temporary location in which an item is stored, so you can transfer it to another place in the document you are working on or in another document.

close button   A feature of the Mac operating system, in which you click a small red circle in the upper-right side of a title bar to close that window.

Cocoa   A set of application programming interfaces for Mac OS X that provides extensive tools for simplified development of Mac OS X applications. However, such applications cannot run in the Classic Mac OS environment.

Command key   The main keyboard modifier key found on a Macintosh. It's used, along with one or more keystrokes, to activate a specific function. It is identified on a keyboard by an apple or cloverleaf symbol (usually both). Some simply call it the "Apple" key.

command line   An older-style computer interface, in which you type in commands rather than click on an object to perform a specific function. Mac OS X includes the Terminal application, which allows you to access the Unix command line for various functions.

commands   A set of instructions you give to your computer to tell it to carry out a specific function or set of functions.

compression   A technique used to make a file smaller, by providing pointers to or removing redundant data. Compression protocols such as StuffIt and Zip are said to be *lossless*, because the compressed files can be restored to their original form. Another compression type is *lossy*, which actually removes portions of a file that may not be audible or visible. JPEG, the popular image format, is lossy in nature, as is the compression protocol used to pack a complete motion picture onto a 5.25-inch DVD.

CompuServe   Today AOL has gained ascendancy as the world's largest online service, but CompuServe was there first. Now, CompuServe is an affiliate of AOL and offers services to a more professional audience, using a modified version of AOL's software. *See also* **AOL**.

configuration   The term used to describe the settings you make to such things as your Internet and network setup.

control panel   Under the Classic Mac OS, a program used to direct system-related functions or the functions offered by a system extension. Many control panel functions under Mac OS X are performed by the System Preferences application.

CPU (central processing unit)   The brain of a computer. It refers either to the principal microchip the computer is built around (such as the Pentium or PowerPC chip) or the box that houses the main components of the computer.

CRT (cathode ray tube)   The picture tube that is the main component of most computer displays and regular TVs. *See also* **active matrix**, **LCD**, **passive matrix**.

D

daisy chain   The way many computer devices are connected when using such topologies as ADB, LocalTalk, SCSI, and USB. You hook up one device, attach a second device to the first, and so on.

Darwin   The open source core components of Mac OS X that provide its industrial-strength operating system features.

database   On a computer, a file that contains structured data that can be accessed and manipulated in a variety of ways. Databases are used for business records, address books, and so on.

DAVE   A program from Thursby Software Systems, Inc., that you use to network Macs and Windows computers. It is especially useful in smaller networks, because you don't have to go through the fuss and bother of working with the complexities of setting up a Windows NT or Windows 2000 network server. Also see **DoubleTalk**.

debugger   A program or a component of a program used to locate and help fix programming errors.

default button   You will find a default button in many dialog boxes. It is the one that pulsates, under Mac OS X, which you activate automatically with the ENTER or RETURN key.

desktop   Also known as the Finder Desktop, the graphical background of the Mac operating system in which disk, file, and folder icons are displayed against a background pattern of one sort or another.

desktop publishing   A program designed to create and design completely formatted documents useful for printing or display. Word processing programs can be used for some desktop publishing tasks, but for professional-caliber work, such programs as Adobe InDesign, Adobe PageMaker, or QuarkXPress, are used.

device   A component that is part of a computer system. It may consist of a disk drive, keyboard, mouse, modem, printer, removable drive, or scanner.

device driver   The software that allows your Mac to communicate with a device, such as a printer or scanner. Examples of a device driver include the laser printing software that comes with all Mac OS computers.

DHCP (Dynamic Host Configuration Protocol)   This network protocol is used to automatically assign an IP address to a networked computer. The IP addresses are considered "leased," because they can be reused if they are not accessed for a period of time (usually specified by the network administrator).

dialog box   A window in which you must OK an alert, check a box, or enter information in order to provide a result, such as naming and saving a file, or starting or canceling an operation. *See also* **sheet**.

DIMM (dual inline memory module)   A type of RAM module, typically used on many recent Macs. Compared to a SIMM (single inline memory module), a DIMM has a wider data path, which allows for speedier memory access.

dimmed   *See* **grayed out**.

DIP (dual inline package) switch   The small on or off switches you find on a hard drive, modem, or other device. They are used to configure the product to support specific features or, in the case of a drive, to set SCSI ID or termination.

directory   A list of files or folders found on your Mac.

disk   The common storage medium for computer files. Such storage mediums come in the form of floppy disks for a floppy drive or media (such as Jaz or Zip disks) used for removable drives. A hard drive consists of one or more disks in an airtight enclosure.

disk cache   This sort of cache allocates part of RAM to store frequently used information from a disk. The end result is faster retrieval, which speeds up performance.

disk drive   A device that contains one or more disks used to store computer data.

display   A device used to display the visual representation of a computer's output. Displays can use either CRT tubes or LCDs.

display adapter   Typically, a plug used to convert the signals from your Mac or graphic card so they can be seen on your display.

Dock   A picturesque taskbar, at the bottom or side of your Mac's screen, which displays icons for active applications and documents, and also can be used to store icons for items you want to easily access.

document   A file you create with an application. Documents may contain words, images, or animated matter. They are stored on a disk for later viewing, editing, or printing.

document window   A window that appears within an application in which a document you created in that application is displayed.

domain   A portion of an Internet address that identifies the name of the organization, network being accessed, or the designated address of a computer server—for example, apple.com, which is Apple Computer's domain, or rockoids.com, which is the author's site devoted to a science fiction adventure series. In email, the information after the "@" symbol represents the domain, such as earthlink.net or aol.com.

double-click   The act of clicking a mouse button twice in fairly rapid succession. It is done to open an icon (which will, in turn, open a file, launch a program, or bring up a directory).

double-click speed   An adjustment you make, in the Mouse preference panel, to determine how fast you must click the mouse button to activate a function, such as opening an icon.

DoubleTalk   Software from Connectix that allows Macs to share files with Windows-based computers. *See also* **DAVE**.

download   The act of transferring a file from one computer to another. When you download something, you receive it. In contrast, you upload something to send it to another computer.

downloadable font   A scalable font sent to a printer to allow a document containing that font to be printed. Two downloadable font formats are PostScript fonts and TrueType fonts.

DPI (dots per inch)   Measures the sharpness of a display or printer output.

drag   An action performed with a mouse or other pointing device. It is done by clicking the mouse button, dragging the cursor (and whatever it selects) to another portion of the screen, and then releasing the button.

drag-and-drop   The process of selecting an item and moving it to another location.

drawer   A feature of some Mac OS X applications, in which a panel opens from the right or left corner of a window. An example of how the feature is implemented is Apple's Mail application.

DSL (digital subscriber line)   A technology that uses your regular telephone line to offer very fast Internet service, with speeds typically ranging from 256 Kbps to 1.5 Mbps. The ability to hook up to DSL depends on whether you are close to a phone company switch (usually three miles or less) and whether your ISP offers the service.

DVD-ROM (digital versatile disc read-only memory)   Based on the popular DVD format used for video movies, DVD-ROM stores computer data, up to 5.2GB worth. A variation of the format, DVD-RAM, can be used to store data. The latter medium is suitable for backup purposes, but as of the time this book was written, a final standard hadn't been set. Another standard, DVD-R, is used to make DVDs that can be played in most DVD video players. The DVD-R format is supported by Apple's SuperDrive, a Pioneer-built device that is included on some Power Mac G4s.

E

Email   The abbreviation for electronic mail. It's the method used to transfer messages from one computer or network to another.

emulation   The method used to imitate another computer CPU or operating system. When Apple switched to PowerPC CPUs, they used an emulator to work with older software that supported the 680x0 CPU family. The programs that let you create a Windows environment on a Mac, such as Connectix Virtual PC and FWB's SoftWindows (now discontinued), are emulators.

Ethernet   The standard for high-speed networking. It's available on all currently produced Apple computers. The standard version offers performance of up to 10 Mbps. The high-speed version, called Fast Ethernet, transfers speeds at up to 100 Mbps. The newest Ethernet variation, Gigabit Ethernet, is capable of speeds of up to one billion bps, which is supported by the current generation of Power Mac G4 desktop computers.

EtherTalk   Apple's method of supporting its AppleTalk networking protocol over Ethernet (though it's not been used since Apple introduced Open Transport).

extension   For Macs using the Classic Mac OS, a special program that adds or extends functions of the operating system. Such programs are placed in the Extensions folder within the System Folder. (2) For file naming. DOS and Windows files, for example, have three-letter extensions that identify a specific type of file, such as .doc for Microsoft Word files.

F

Fast Ethernet   This variation of the Ethernet network standard offers speeds that are up to 10 times faster than regular Ethernet, up to 100 Mbps.

FAT   A term with two definitions. For Macs, it is a program compiled with computer code that supports both 680x0 and PowerPC Macs. For DOS and Windows users, it stands for File Allocation Table, and it's the disk file system.

Fax/data modem   The kind of modem that has taken over the market since the early 1990s. It functions as a modem to transmit and receive data, and can also support sending and receiving faxes, when used with software that supports the feature.

file   In the computer world, an item (such as a document or a program) stored on a disk or opened, using a computer's memory.

file extensions   The DOS and Windows operating systems identify a file's type via a three-letter extension or suffix. A typical example is using .jpg for a JPEG file, or .doc for a Microsoft Word file.

file server   A computer that serves as a repository for files shared across a network (including the Internet). File servers may be dedicated, performing just file-handling tasks, or nondedicated, in which the computer may also function as a regular workstation.

file sharing   A feature of the Mac operating system in which users may share files across a network.

Sharing Preference Panel   A component of the System Preferences application that is used to configure and activate the file sharing feature.

file system   The technology used on a storage medium that handles files stored on a disk.

Finder   The application that provides the unique look and feel of Mac OS X's spiffy Aqua interface. It is used to provide both a desktop display and file-handling features.

FireWire   Also known as IEEE 1394 or (by Sony) i.LINK, a high-speed peripheral standard that's capable of speeds of up to 400 Mbps. It allows you to daisy-chain up to 63 devices, including digital camcorders, hard drives, removable devices, and scanners, without having to set special ID numbers or termination.

firmware   Software stored in a ROM chip, used by computer hardware to provide specific operating functions.

fixed disk   *See* **hard disk**.

fixed-width font   More often called a "monospace" font, a font in which all characters have equal-width spacing. Examples include Courier and Monaco. Fonts in which width values vary are called proportional fonts. *See also* **proportional font**.

fixed wireless   A technology used to provide high-speed Internet access, which includes the installation of an antenna, similar to a satellite disk, on the roof of the home or office, which in turn accesses the service over the airwaves from a transmission tower. An example of such a broadband ISP is Sprint Broadband Direct.

floppy disk   Although it's been phased out of new Apple computer products, the floppy disk is one of the earliest storage mediums. The word "floppy" refers to the flexible material inside the disks, used to store the data. *See also* **hard disk**.

flow control   The phrase generally applies to modems or networking functions. It's a method where one device communicates with another, indicating when information can be transferred. It's also known as a "handshake."

folder   A directory on Mac and Windows computers (and other graphical operating systems). A folder is a container that may contain files or other folders.

font   A collection of letters, numbers, punctuation, and symbols all fitting a specific design or size. Fonts that are of fixed size are typically bitmap fonts. Outline font formats, such as OpenType, PostScript, and TrueType fonts, are scalable fonts, meaning they can be specified in any size supported by the program in which they're used. *See also* **OpenType fonts**, **PostScript fonts**, **TrueType fonts**.

font family   A label for a group of fonts of similar style, such as the various forms of Helvetica or Times. It also refers to a class of fonts, such as serif or sans serif.

format   (1) Preparing a disk to receive files by clearing out all existing data and setting it up to support a specific computer operating system. A related process, initializing, wipes out a drive's directory. (2) The way in which the text in a document is set up, such as the type style, the size, paragraph indents, and so on. (3) The file type, such as an Adobe Photoshop document, or a Microsoft Word document.

FPU (floating-point unit)   This is a coprocessor that supports mathematical calculations. The original 680x0 Mac CPUs required separate FPU chips. The PowerPC chips have integrated FPU functions and don't require separate chips.

fragmented   Usually a description of a condition in which the pieces of a file are spread around widely separated parts of a disk.

freeware   Software offered without charge, but the author or publisher retains rights to the product. Contrast this with the term shareware.

FTP (File Transfer Protocol)   The Internet protocol for file transfers among Macintosh, Windows, and Unix. *See also* **Anonymous FTP**.

full backup   The process of making a complete copy of the disk you wish to back up.

G

G3   The popular label for the PowerPC 750 CPU, developed by IBM and Motorola and used in a number of Apple Computers.

G4   The newest family of PowerPC CPUs that also incorporate a vector processing unit called AltiVec or Velocity Engine, which can speed up performance on software, such as Mac OS X, that's designed to exploit the features.

GB (gigabyte)   The equivalent of 1,000,024 megabytes.

GIF (Graphic Interchange Format)   A popular file format for compressed graphic images, developed by CompuServe. GIF files are commonly exchanged on the Internet, and are used for images on Web sites because of their ability to provide animation and other effects.

grayed out   A phrase used to indicate that a specific command is not available or accessible or has been disabled.

H

Handshake   *See* **flow control**.

hard disk   A type of disk drive that contains one or more rigid platters used for data storage, sealed in an airtight enclosure. Hard drives can typically support as little as 10MB (obviously these are just the very old hard drives) to capacities exceeding 80GB (based on capacities available as of the time this book was written).

hardware   Various components of a computer system, which include the core component, consisting of CPU and disk drives, as well as displays, printers, and scanners. Contrast with software.

hardware handshaking   A special type of modem cable that supports automatic handshaking or flow control. All external high-speed modems require a hardware handshaking cable.

hierarchical menu   Also known as a submenu, identifies an extra menu that appears when you drag and hold the mouse cursor over an item.

highlighted   When you select an object or text, it is shaded in a dark color or reverse video to indicate it has been chosen.

home page   On a Web site, the opening page, typically used to offer a description or introduction of a site and provide links to other content on the site and elsewhere.

HTML (Hypertext Markup Language)   The language of the Web, consisting of text documents with tags or formatting keys that describe how the text will look in a Web browser. A Web site contains one or more HTML documents.

HTTP (Hypertext Transfer Protocol)   The protocol used for the transfer of HTML and similar files, generally from sites on the World Wide Web.

hub   A device that serves as a central connection point for hooking up network or serial devices. Hubs are used for such things as Ethernet networking and to expand FireWire and USB ports.

hyperlink   A text or graphic that, when you click on it, takes you to another page in a document or a Web site.

I

icon   A picture that provides a graphical representation of an item on a Mac or Windows computer (or a Unix computer with graphical interface). Icons can represent such things as an application, a file, a folder, or disk drive.

IDE (Integrated Drive Electronics)   A type of hard drive used on both Macs and PCs. Compare with FireWire and SCSI.

IEEE 1394   *See* **FireWire**.

i.LINK   *See* **FireWire**.

incremental backup   A backup that consists strictly of the files that have been added or changed since your last full backup.

infrared port   A feature on some Macs and other computers that allows for wireless networking. It has since been largely replaced by Apple's AirPort wireless networking products.

initialization files   Also known as INITs, the original designation for system startup programs that are known as extensions or system extensions under the Classic Mac OS.

initialize   Usually, the process of resetting a hardware device or recreating a disk directory. *See also* **format**.

insertion point   The flickering vertical bar you see in a text area, indicating where text is to be entered.

Intel   The world's largest manufacturer of CPUs, maker of the 80x86 and Pentium chips used in DOS and Windows-based computers.

interface   (1) The process of communicating with another component in a computer system. (2) The face that a program puts forth to the user. Also known as user interface. An example is the Aqua user interface of Mac OS X.

Internet   The worldwide collection of computer networks that provides a variety of services, such as email, FTP, and the World Wide Web.

intranet   A system of networking using Internet technologies within a single organization.

ISP (Internet service provider)   A company that offers a connection to the Internet. Such services include large national operations, including AT&T WorldNet, EarthLink, Prodigy Internet, and smaller companies that offer connections in one or two cities. These include FastQ and Teleport.com. *See also* **AOL**, **CompuServe**.

J

Java   Developed by Sun Microsystems, a platform-independent programming language often used to display special visual effects on the World Wide Web. When you access a Web site using Java, a small program, called an applet, is downloaded to your browser (if it supports Java, and all recent browsers do) and run to display the appropriate content.

JPEG (Joint Photographic Experts Group)   A format for compressed images, which makes files that are typically smaller than a GIF. It's best for handling images rather than text, and is capable of extremely high quality, sometimes indistinguishable from the original.

K

kilobyte   Equivalent to 1,024 bytes. It is usually abbreviated as K, and is used to describe such things as file size, memory, and hard drive storage. *See also* **megabyte**.

L

L2 cache   A special type of cache memory that resides between the CPU and the main memory or on the processor chip and is used to store frequently used instruction data, allowing the CPU to process those instructions faster. The primary memory cache, on the CPU chip, is called the L1 cache.

L3 cache   Another level of cache memory designed to provide an even greater range of performance improvement. Newer generations of the G4 processor incorporate an L3 cache.

LAN (local area network)   The common type of network that includes computers and printers, and is used to share data, programs, and messages.

laptop   A small personal computer, equipped with one or more batteries for power, designed for convenient transportation. Apple's laptops include the iBook and the PowerBook.

laser printer   A printer that works in a fashion similar to a copy machine, using a laser beam to generate high-quality output.

LCD (liquid crystal display)   LCD is the display technology used in laptop computers and a growing number of standalone computer displays. The most common types of LCD displays are active matrix and passive matrix.

LED (light-emitting diode)   LEDs are employed for display purposes in some electronic products.

link   *See* **hyperlink**.

list box   Typically found in a dialog box, offers a listing of items, such as files and folders, that you can select.

LocalTalk   The network hardware that, until recently, was built into all Macintosh computers. It uses the AppleTalk protocol to offer network services. Current Apple computers and Mac OS X only support Ethernet as a network standard.

M

MacBinary   The file format used for transferring Macintosh files between different computer platforms. It places the data and resource folks of a Mac file in the data fork, so it can be easily transferred over the Internet and to other computing platforms. MacBinary files are usually saved in BinHex format.

Macintosh HD   The typical name of a Mac's hard drive when it leaves the factory.

Mac OS   The popular abbreviation and Apple's official trademark for the Macintosh operating system, for example, Mac OS X. Contrast to the former use of the word System to identify operating system version, such as System 7.

macro   An automated sequence of functions designed for simple repetition of complex tasks. The Microsoft Office program suite offers macro functions, as do other programs. Some programs, such as Adobe Photoshop, refer to macros as "actions." *See also* **AppleScript**.

math coprocessor   *See* **FPU**.

maximize   When you click on a window's green button to expand it to its optimum size, you've maximized it.

MB   *See* **megabyte**.

Mbps (megabits per second)   Refers to data transfer of 1,048,576 bits per second. Hopefully, as modems and serial transmissions become faster, Mbps will be used to discuss their speed.

media   Typically, the name for items that carry data, such as floppy disks, hard drives, CD-ROMs, hard disks, removable drives, and tape drives. It can also refer to items that carry data for network transfer, such as cables and wireless technology.

megabyte   1,024 kilobytes of computer data.

MegaFLOPS   Short for a Million Floating Point Operations Per Second, representing computer power.

memory   The temporary storage area for computer data. Memory products include RAM and ROM. Sometimes hard drives and other storage mediums are referred to incorrectly as memory.

memory protection   The ability of a computer operating system to allocate a dedicated portion of memory to a program, which is designed to enhance stability. Mac OS X, for example, is designed to offer protected memory.

menu   In a graphical operating system, such as Mac OS X, a small screen in which a series of commands are available for the user to select.

menu bar   A single-line, horizontal bar, which appears at the top of the screen on a Mac, containing menus.

MHz (megahertz)   Each hertz being one cycle, the speed at which a computer's CPU runs. Since many factors govern CPU performance, the MHz rating isn't the only factor to use in comparing speeds of different CPU families.

MIDI (Musical Instrument Digital Interface)   A protocol that allows for communication between musical instruments and computers.

MIME (Multipurpose Internet Mail Extension)   A method in which binary files (such as images, sound, and word processing documents) can be transferred via email.

MIPS (millions of instructions per second)   The speed at which a computer handles data. Supercomputers are said to handle billions of instructions per second, which is why the G4 CPU was promoted by Apple Computer as a "supercomputer on a chip," because if its capability of achieving such levels of performance.

minimize button   A yellow button at the upper-right end of a window's title bar, which you click to reduce a window to its icon, which is placed in the Dock.

modem   A device used to convert a computer's digital language to analog signals to allow for data to be exchanged, typically over a telephone line.

monitor   *See* **display**.

monochrome   A type of computer display (no longer being made) that is capable of displaying just a single color.

motherboard   Also known as a logic board, the printed circuit board that stores the main components of a computer.

mouse   Invented in the 1960s, a small pointing device with a ball on the bottom and one or more switches at the top. As you move the mouse, the cursor on a computer's screen moves as well. A so-called upside-down mouse, with the ball at the top, is known as a trackball. A newer version of this device, the optical mouse, such as the Apple Pro Mouse, doesn't use a ball or mechanical component for movement.

MPEG (Moving Pictures Experts Group)   The standard for compressed audio and video. It is *lossy*, meaning that data is lost as part of the compression process, but it is designed so the lost data has minimal impact on what you see and hear.

MS-DOS (Microsoft Disk Operating System)   A text-based computer operating system, also known as DOS.

multimedia   A combination of various components of a computer experience, such as animation, audio, graphics, text, and video.

multiprocessor   A computer that has more than one CPU running at the same time for faster processing speeds.

multisync   A type of display that can run at different scan rates, providing a selection of different resolutions. All current displays are multisync.

multitasking   A technique that allows a computer to perform more than one task at a time. Under the Classic Mac OS, multitasking is cooperative, meaning the programs themselves do the task management, as opposed to preemptive, a feature of Mac OS X, in which the operating system does the task management.

multithreading   The capability of a program to perform more than a single function at the same time. Compare to multitasking.

N

Netscape   The company who made the original commercial Web browser for the Macintosh, Windows, and Unix operating systems, now part of AOL Time Warner. Although the program is known by the name of the company, its full name, at least for versions prior to 6, is either Netscape Navigator or Netscape Communicator.

network   The process of linking two or more computers and other devices, such as printers, so they can exchange data.

newsgroup   An Internet-based discussion group, also known as Usenet.

notebook   *See* **laptop**.

O

object-oriented graphics   Graphic objects that are represented by mathematical shapes rather than pixels. This allows for the objects to be scaled to any size without loss of quality.

open   An operation in which you display the contents of a file, folder, or disk, or launch an application.

OpenGL   An industry-standard 3-D imaging technology used for computer games and 3-D software. This technology is used in the imaging layer of Mac OS X.

Open Transport   The Classic Mac OS's networking technology, used for local networking and Internet networking.

OpenType fonts   A type font technology that can incorporate PostScript and/or TrueType in a single font file. Mac OS X supports OpenType. *See also* **fonts**, **PostScript fonts**, **TrueType fonts**.

operating system   The software that provides the core functionality of a computer, also known as system software. Operating systems include the Mac OS in its various forms (including Mac OS X), MS-DOS, Windows in its various forms, Unix, and others.

P

passive matrix display   A type of LCD display used on laptop computers. The display is accomplished with parallel wires running horizontally and vertically across the screen, which power the screen pixels. Current laptops, with the exception of entry-level Windows-based models, do not use this type of display. Compare to active matrix.

password   A combination of letters, numbers, or both, used to control access to a computer, the contents of a computer's drive, or a network or Internet service.

PC (personal computer)   Although the name usually applies to small IBM and compatible desktop and portable computers, Apple's computers are also, strictly speaking, personal computers.

PC100   A high-speed RAM module that's used on a number of recent Apple computers. It supports 100 MHz logic board speeds.

PC133   A higher-speed RAM module that's used on the latest generation of Power Mac G4 desktops. It supports 133 MHz logic board speeds. PC133 RAM is often backward compatible with PC100 systems.

PCI (peripheral component interconnect)   An expansion bus standard used on both Macs and PCs. It allows for installation of printed circuit boards (cards) that provide enhanced graphic display, faster networking, faster SCSI, video capture, and other capabilities.

PCMCIA (Personal Computer Memory Card International Association)   A standard for hardware expansion cards, about the size of credit cards, used mostly on laptop computers. Commonly known as a PC card.

PDF (portable document format)   A standard for creating and viewing electronic documents, created by Adobe Systems. PDF is a component of the Quartz imaging technology used in Mac OS X.

peripheral   A device, added to a computer, that provides enhanced functions, such as a display, printer, or removable drive.

pixel   A single dot, the smallest graphic unit of display.

plug-and-play   Various hardware standards designed to allow you to easily hook up a device without having to go through special configuration steps. The ideal method of plug-and-play allows you to hook up a device without needing to turn off the device or the computer to which it's connected or having to do a special configuration to recognize the device (other than, perhaps, installation of a software driver). Both FireWire and USB are plug-and-play standards. Also known as PnP.

plug-in   An add-on program that will enhance an application's capabilities. For a Web browser, plug-ins are typically added to provide multimedia features (such as QuickTime and RealAudio). Some program plug-ins are also referred to as XTensions (for QuarkXPress add-ons) and XTras (used in some Macromedia products).

point   The act of placing the mouse cursor over a specific object on your screen.

pointing device   The name of an input device used to point to objects on a screen. A mouse and trackball are both common pointing devices.

POP (Post Office Protocol)   The standard that allows a user to receive email from a mail server. It's used by most ISPs.

pop-up window   A window that will pop up on your screen when selected.

port   A jack into which you plug a cable from a device to make it work with your Mac.

post   The act of placing a message on a message board, either a newsgroup or a message board on an online service.

PostScript   Developed by Adobe Systems, a page description language that uses mathematics to describe the contents of a page. It is device independent, meaning that output devices, such as laser printers, can reproduce the page at their maximum possible resolution. The PDF technology used for generating 2-D images in Mac OS X is based on PostScript.

PostScript fonts   The original scalable font technology based on PostScript, which allows a font to be used in all available sizes with maximum quality. PostScript fonts are considered industry standards in the publishing and printing industries. Compare with OpenType and TrueType, other scalable font formats.

PowerPC   The generic name of a family of CPU chips designed by Apple, IBM, and Motorola. The current crop of PowerPC chips are the G3 and G4.

PPD (PostScript printer description)   Usually consists of a text file that provides information to a printer about the device's unique features, such as extra paper trays or special paper size handling capabilities.

PPP (Point to Point Protocol)   A TCP/IP standard that allows a modem to access the Internet or an online service.

PRAM (parameter RAM)   A small amount of RAM on a Macintosh used to store basic system settings, such as display, networking, serial port, and startup disk. Zapping the PRAM is the act of clearing this portion of RAM to eliminate erratic system problems.

preview software   A version of software designed to promote interest in a new product. The software is usually in beta form, meaning it probably has bugs that may cause performance anomalies or system crashes.

Print Center   An application that ships with Mac OS X, which is used to select and configure printers and monitor the progress of a print queue.

printer driver   A program that works with a computer and printer, allowing the two devices to communicate with each other.

printer fonts   Sometimes called outline fonts, the PostScript fonts files that are downloaded to a printer and used to output your actual text. Sometimes also known as soft fonts. Compare with bitmap fonts.

print queue   A list of files sent to the printer that are waiting to be printed.

print server   A device, computer, or software designed to host and manage a print queue.

program   *See* **application**.

proportional font   A font in which each character has a different space or width value, with a letter such as "i" having a narrow width and the letter "m" having a much wider width. Contrast with fixed-width or monospace font.

pull-down menu   When you click on a menu bar, the pull-down menu provides the list of available commands. On the Windows platform, it's referred to as a drop-down menu.

Q

queue   A list of files destined for printing or processing of some sort.

QuickDraw 3D   An older Apple technology for creation and display of three-dimensional objects. Apple uses OpenGL for 3-D graphics under Mac OS X.

QuickTime   A multimedia technology from Apple Computer that provides support for dozens of audio and video standards. QuickTime technology is used for video editing, and to create online audio and video presentations. The software is available in both Mac and Windows versions.

QuickTime TV   A standard from Apple Computer designed to compete with RealAudio and RealVideo. It lets you view streaming audio and video productions on the Internet. Apple has entered the competition with big guns, by making the source code freely available and not charging a license fee for use of its server software (the software that sends the streaming productions).

R

radio button   A small circular button that appears in a dialog box. Clicking on it will activate a specific function.

RAM (random access memory)   The memory used as a temporary storage location for computer data.

read-only file   The name for a file that you can read but cannot change, either because it's password protected or it's on a storage medium you cannot write to (such as a CD-ROM).

RealAudio   The most popular protocol for streaming audio and video productions. RealAudio and its companion program, RealVideo, are available free, but users of the streaming software pay a license fee for its use.

reset switch   A button on a Mac that forces the computer to restart. Used to get the Mac working again when it crashes.

resolution   A measurement of the number of pixels in a document or display screen.

RISC (reduced instruction set computer)   A type of CPU, such as the PowerPC chip, which uses a smaller set of instructions to process data. The speed with which the instructions are processed accounts for the high performance of RISC-based CPUs.

ROM (read-only memory)   A computer chip onto which data is written that cannot be changed and does not disappear when the computer is switched off. A special type of ROM, called Flash ROM, allows for the data to be changed with a special software program. Compare with RAM.

router   Software or a hardware device that directs data to different segments of a computer network.

S

scalable font   A font designed to work in all sizes available to an application. Scalable fonts usually are provided in the OpenType, PostScript, and TrueType formats.

screen fonts   *See* **bitmap fonts**.

screen saver   A program that darkens the screen or provides a moving picture when your computer is idle for a specified period of time. With CRT-based monitors, it is designed to prevent a so-called "burn-in" effect, in which areas displayed for long periods of time are permanently etched onto the display. The jury is out about whether screen savers really work or not with modern computer displays, and they do nothing for an LCD display. Mac OS X includes a built-in screen saver.

scroll   The act of moving through a display or document window.

scroll arrow   The arrow located at each end of a scroll bar that's used to navigate through the contents of a window or list box.

scroll bar   The little bar that appears at the right and bottom of a window or list box when it's too small to show all of its contents.

SCSI (Small Computer Systems Interface)   A standard used for storage devices. SCSI capability has been removed from Apple computers, in favor of FireWire and USB.

SDRAM   A type of memory used on first-generation iMacs and some Apple laptop computers.

select   The act of marking or choosing an item so you can perform an action on it. With a mouse or other pointing device, you select the item by clicking on it.

serial port   A port provided on older Macs for use by modems and non-network printers. *See also* **USB**.

shareware   Software that is freely distributed, for which the author or publisher requests payment if you like using it after a brief trial.

Sheet   A Mac OS X–style dialog box, that drops down from a document's title bar, commonly used for Open and Save functions.

SMTP (Simple Mail Transfer Protocol)   A counterpart to POP, used for sending email. SMTP transfers email to server computers across the Internet, using TCP/IP.

software   Files that contain instructions that tell a computer how to perform specific tasks. These include Mac OS X, the applications you run, device drivers, and so forth.

source code   A text file that contains the information from which a computer program is compiled. Apple has released source code for some elements of Mac OS X, under the collective name Darwin, and for its QuickTime streaming software.

spool   The act of transferring data to a device, usually a printer. A spool file is a file that contains the instructions needed to perform an action, such as printing a document. *See also* **print queue**.

spring-loaded folders   A feature of the Classic Mac OS (beginning with Mac OS 8) in which a folder expands to reveal its contents when you click and drag your input device over the folder.

startup disk   The disk used to start your Mac, containing a usable Mac OS version. Startup disk settings can be made with the Startup Disk Control Panel under the Classic Mac OS and the Startup Disk panel of the System Preferences application under Mac OS X.

StuffIt   The industry-standard compression program for the Mac. StuffIt uses a special algorithm to make files smaller by using pointers to redundant data. StuffIt archives (a file containing files compressed with StuffIt) are routinely transferred via disk, networks, or the Internet. This is the Mac counterpart of the Zip format, which dominates the DOS and Windows computing platforms. *See also* **compression**, **Zip**.

submenu   A secondary menu that displays when you click a pointing device and hold it over the main menu's name. Also known as a hierarchical menu.

SuperDisk   A removable disk standard that supports 1.4MB floppies and a special floppy-like high-capacity format. It's become popular since Apple removed floppy drives as standard issue on their computers. SuperDisk media can hold up to 240MB of data.

SuperDrive   A floppy disk drive installed on many older Macintosh computers, that supports 400K, 800K, and 1.4MB floppies. With proper translation software, such as File Exchange under the Classic Mac OS and built into Mac OS X, a SuperDrive can also read MS-DOS floppies.

surf   The act of exploring the Internet, typically the World Wide Web.

surge suppressor   A device designed to provide protection of electronics from power surges from a power line or due to a lightning strike. Surge suppressors typically have several outputs for connection of computer equipment and other electronic components (such as a TV or VCR).

swap file Used with virtual memory, a portion of your hard disk set aside to handle data that doesn't fit within the available amount of RAM.

system The basic file that provides core functionality of the Mac OS, also known as a system file. It can also refer to the operating system itself, such as System 7, an older generation of the Mac OS.

system disk *See* **startup disk**.

system software *See* **operating system**.

T

TCP/IP (Transmission Control Protocol/Internet Protocol) The networking standard used for Internet networking and connections.

text box An enclosure on a document, icon, or dialog box window in which you insert text.

title bar The top area of a window in which its name is displayed.

toolbar A row of buttons in an application that you click to activate a specific function.

trackball A pointing device that resembles an upside-down mouse, in which you move the ball rather than the device itself to point to objects on your computer's screen.

tracking speed An adjustment in the Mouse or Trackpad Control Panel that sets how fast a mouse pointer moves across the screen.

trackpad Used on laptop computers, a pointing device consisting of a little square or rectangular pad on which you use your finger to move the cursor across the screen.

TrueType fonts A scalable technology first released in 1990 by Apple Computer, in part as a way to avoid paying the then-high licensing fees for PostScript fonts. Beginning with Mac OS System 7, built-in support was provided for display of TrueType fonts. Both Mac and Windows computers come with a small selection of TrueType fonts.

twisted-pair cable The type of wiring used for both telephone and network connections. Twisted-pair cable is made up of two pairs of wires. One pair is used for receiving data, the other for transmitting.

type style　An attribute of a typeface, such as regular (or normal), bold, italic, shadow, strikeout, or underline.

typeface　A collection of characters, numbers, and symbols in a distinct form or design.

U

Unix　A popular operating system first developed by AT&T in 1972. It provides all the features considered critical to a modern operating system, such as preemptive multitasking and protected memory. There are many Unix-based systems, including Linux and Mac OS X.

UPS (uninterruptible power supply)　A device that provides backup power in the event of a power failure. UPS devices available for personal computers commonly have a large battery that's used to provide power for a brief period to give the user time to shut down the computer safely without risk to the files or disk drives.

URL (uniform resource locator)　The address of a specific site on the Internet.

USB (universal serial bus)　A high-speed serial port standard used on current Apple computers, beginning with the iMac. It is used for input devices, digital cameras, storage devices, and other products.

Usenet　*See* **newsgroup**.

user interface　*See* **interface**.

utility　A program designed to help a computer function better. A utility may include a hard disk diagnostic program or something that enhances computer performance, such as Adobe Type Manager, which offers clear rendering of PostScript fonts for the Classic Mac OS.

V

virtual memory　A method of extending available memory on a computer by setting aside a portion of the hard drive to store and swap data that exceeds the size of available RAM.

W

Web   *See* **World Wide Web**.

Web browser   *See* **browser**.

window   The rectangular screen in which the contents of a disk, folder, or document are displayed.

Windows 95 and 98   The consumer versions of Microsoft's 32-bit graphical operating system, which offers preemptive multitasking, as long as the application is also 32-bit.

Windows NT and 2000   The so-called high-end versions of Windows, used for content creation and for networked servers.

Windows XP   The newest version of the Windows operating system that incorporates an advanced user interface, Luna, running atop the core of Windows 2000.

word processor   A program that allows you to create, edit, and format text. Examples of word processors include one of the components of AppleWorks and Microsoft Word. Such programs also offer graphic-editing capabilities of one sort or another.

World Wide Web (WWW)   A collection of Internet sites that offer a variety of content, ranging from text to pictures to animation and sound. You view a Web site with a browser, software designed to interpret Web documents, which are coded in HTML. *See also* **browser**, **HTML**.

WYSIWYG (What You See Is What You Get)   Pronounced "wizzywig," describes the ability to display a close representation of the look and feel of a document on your Mac's display.

Z

Zip   The DOS, Windows, and Unix counterpart to StuffIt. It's a protocol that uses a special algorithm to reduce file size by using pointers for redundant data. Files compressed with Zip (which are said to be "zipped") are commonly used for file transfers. There are also Mac versions of Zip, used to provide cross-platform compatibility, and all current versions of StuffIt also can expand Zip files. *See also* **compression**, **StuffIt**.

Zip drive   A storage device developed by Iomega Corporation, using a small disk, resembling a thick floppy. Zip drives store either 100MB or 250MB of data.

Index

INTERNATIONAL CONTACT INFORMATION

AUSTRALIA
McGraw-Hill Book Company Australia Pty. Ltd.
TEL +61-2-9417-9899
FAX +61-2-9417-5687
http://www.mcgraw-hill.com.au
books-it_sydney@mcgraw-hill.com

CANADA
McGraw-Hill Ryerson Ltd.
TEL +905-430-5000
FAX +905-430-5020
http://www.mcgrawhill.ca

GREECE, MIDDLE EAST,
NORTHERN AFRICA
McGraw-Hill Hellas
TEL +30-1-656-0990-3-4
FAX +30-1-654-5525

MEXICO (Also serving Latin America)
McGraw-Hill Interamericana Editores S.A. de C.V.
TEL +525-117-1583
FAX +525-117-1589
http://www.mcgraw-hill.com.mx
fernando_castellanos@mcgraw-hill.com

SINGAPORE (Serving Asia)
McGraw-Hill Book Company
TEL +65-863-1580
FAX +65-862-3354
http://www.mcgraw-hill.com.sg
mghasia@mcgraw-hill.com

SOUTH AFRICA
McGraw-Hill South Africa
TEL +27-11-622-7512
FAX +27-11-622-9045
robyn_swanepoel@mcgraw-hill.com

UNITED KINGDOM & EUROPE
(Excluding Southern Europe)
McGraw-Hill Education Europe
TEL +44-1-628-502500
FAX +44-1-628-770224
http://www.mcgraw-hill.co.uk
computing_neurope@mcgraw-hill.com

ALL OTHER INQUIRIES Contact:
Osborne/McGraw-Hill
TEL +1-510-549-6600
FAX +1-510-883-7600
http://www.osborne.com
omg_international@mcgraw-hill.com